I0118690

Why Thirty-Three?
Searching for Masonic Origins

Why Thirty-Three?

SEARCHING FOR MASONIC ORIGINS

S. Brent Morris, PhD

Westphalia Press
An Imprint of the Policy Studies Organization
Washington, DC
2019

WHY THIRTY-THREE?: SEARCHING FOR MASONIC ORIGINS
All Rights Reserved © 2019 by Policy Studies Organization

Westphalia Press
An imprint of Policy Studies Organization
1527 New Hampshire Ave., NW
Washington, D.C. 20036
info@ipsonet.org

ISBN-10: 1-63391-819-X
ISBN-13: 978-1-63391-819-1

Cover and interior design by Jeffrey Barnes
jbarnesbook.design

Daniel Gutierrez-Sandoval, Executive Director
PSO and Westphalia Press

Updated material and comments on this edition
can be found at the Westphalia Press website:
www.westphaliapress.org

For Terry & Mary Pat, my two greatest accomplishments.
You have excelled in ways I never dreamed possible. I am proud.

Contents

Foreword: The Accomplishments of Brent Morris

O ver the past decades, the works of Brent Morris have helped to define the advances made in the study of social capital, fraternalism, and associations. Until the middle of the twentieth century, history was chiefly political, military, diplomatic, and constitutional. Social history consisted of multiple themes and topics without a central form of organization. Discussions and analysis of social structures and processes were minimal before the 1960s.

As the definition of social history was refined in the second half of the twentieth century, social science analytical processes were utilized more than the traditional interpretation of texts through hermeneutics. The scarcity of published research and analysis of Freemasonry and other fraternal organizations was not for lack of material, as the potential for archival research was certainly there. Nor was it entirely a case of obscurity, as every town and most villages had not one lodge hall but several, and if one's neighbor was not a Freemason, he might well be an Odd Fellow or Granger or Pythian. Lapels sported arcane symbols indicating little understood affiliations to the unaffiliated. With scarce published research, what this all meant was a mystery. It continues to be a hard to understand subject. Genealogists, for example, have only relatively recently found lodges to be a valuable source as the keepers of records as to the affiliations of great-great grandfathers.

The Masonic fraternity supported libraries rather early in the development of fraternalism. Albert Pike, the noted Masonic ritualist, gathered a large library in Washington, D.C., which continues to this day as part of the headquarters of the Southern Jurisdiction of the Scottish Rite. Many grand lodges in the United States that supervise a state's Masonic activities, notably Pennsylvania, New York, and Iowa, maintain extremely extensive collections.

Discussing all of this in today's context without reference to the work of Brent Morris would be nigh on impossible. For one thing, he is a legendary editor. Over the years he has applied his talents to enhancing the reputations of others, whose eye for error was less than his. Shelves of his editing accomplishments, including journals and books in an ever-growing army, testify to his ability to spot mistakes that would have embarrassed their authors. Those efforts alone qualify him as an unsung hero.

It is his original work, as this volume testifies, that earns him his prominence as a historian. He is a mathematician and scholar of math with a long career in government service of a confidential nature. Morris has applied this, as some articles herein testify, to the statistics of Masonry. This work will not date, contrary to what one might suppose, and that is one reason for presenting it. Woe to anyone who deals with the particular periods he documents without searching out what he says about that time period. His comments on the growth and decline of lodge rosters secure him a permanent position in fraternal historiography.

That however is not by any means the whole story. His uncurbed curiosity has driven him to investigate the origins and sources of Masonic degrees, and he has pursued them back into the mists of the seventeenth and eighteenth centuries. Very few people have his command of the reputedly thousand degrees that are part of this tradition. Referencing a thousand degrees is by no means a stretch of the imagination. Some are still worked today as part of the Scottish and York Rites as well as preserved by the Grand College of Rites.

For those of us who are limited in the time we can give to our memberships, the fact that Dr. and Brother Morris along with a few others have helped preserve and explore a centuries-old and somewhat neglected but important part of the Enlightenment and Western culture is a source of pride. For the general reader, who wonders about the Masonic references in Tolstoy or Kipling or Mozart, this is as good a place as any to get an idea of the variety of topics compassed.

Wallace E. Boston, Jr.
President, American Public University System

> *Dr. Wallace is a 32nd degree Scottish Rite Mason, and has taken a keen interest in the history of Charles Town in West Virginia, where the headquarters of the American Public University System is located and which has a number of associations with George Washington's Masonic membership.*

Author's Preface

B eing asked to assemble a collection of your papers for publication is both humbling and slightly unnerving. It's humbling that someone (Westphalia Press in this instance) thinks there are enough potential readers to make such a venture worthwhile. It's unsettling because it is so close to the sorts of tributes that come near the end of an artist's career. My mind was put at ease, however, when I read that a retrospective is just "an exhibition or compilation showing the development of the work of a particular artist over a period of time." Fair enough. My interests in Freemasonry (the subject of this compilation) have evolved over time and it could be useful to see that evolution.

My previous collection of papers (*A Radical in the East,* Iowa Research Lodge No. 2, 1993, 2009) showed my great interest in membership trends and comparative statistics, exemplified by "Boom to Bust in the Twentieth Century" and "Voting with their feet." Over time, my interests have evolved, and this collection reflects that.

When I created the Scottish Rite Research Society in 1991, I had a burning interest in the origins of the "high degrees," and especially the Scottish Rite. You can see this in "Why 33?," the first paper presented to the SRRS and the lead article in the first volume of *Heredom,* the transactions of the SRRS. There are other articles in the group that look at the "high degrees," the Order of the Royal Secret in the United States, and the *Francken Manuscripts.*

The next broad grouping is American Freemasonry in general, starting with the polite breakaway of U.S. grand lodges from England, to the spread of Masonic ritual, to the early representation of Prince Hall Freemasonry in newspapers. A study of the latter convinces me that white Masons quietly helped and supported their black brethren at the time of the chartering of African Lodge No. 459. This group of articles ends by showing the export of several Masonic organizations from the United States to the United Kingdom.

Is It True What They Say about Freemasonry? by Arturo de Hoyos and myself has been through four editions and is a response to anti-Masonry. Several papers in this collection look at the topic of anti-Masonry from an overview of its major themes specific to specific instances of misrepresentations. I end with a factual response to the tired claim that Albert Pike was a member of the Ku Klux Klan. There is at present no primary evidence of Pike's membership, and only unsubstantiated claims made well after his death. I lay out all the details of what is known and claimed in hope that future researchers will at least accurately cite their sources.

I wrap up with two final groups. One on Sherlock Holmes and Freemasonry, including a biography of Charles Warren, the Commissioner of Police (and thus Inspector Lestrade's boss), and the premier Master of Quatuor Coronati Lodge. The other group includes analyses of early Masonic documents: the 1688 *Tripos* at Trinity College, Dublin; *The Post-Boy* exposure of 1723; and the *Harlequin Grand Vol-Gi* of 1730, which gives us new insight to the Gormogons.

My review of these papers satisfies me that my interests have expanded. I think that each article tells an interesting story that leads to a better understanding of Freemasonry. I hope that you will agree.

—March 10, 2019, Laurel, Maryland

The High Degrees in the United States: 1730–1830

Freemasonry in the United States had an unusual early history. Imported from Europe—England, Scotland, Ireland, France, and Germany—it quickly became one of the most important colonial organizations. "In the generation of the [American] revolution, Masonry's ability to embody the period's diverse cultural demands gave it enormous power."[1] It remained an exclusive organization through the revolution, and then began expanding it membership base into the middle class. It is ironic that the Craft was attacked for its perceived elite influence as it began to open up its membership.

In 1826 in New York, William Morgan published an exposé of Masonic rituals.[2] He was later abducted by Masons in Canandaigua, New York, and subsequently disappeared. It was widely believed he had been murdered as part of a Masonic conspiracy. The public outcry led to the creation of the first major "third party" in American politics, the Anti-Masonic Party. By 1830, Freemasonry was dead or sleeping in most of the United States. Like Pompeii after Vesuvius, nearly everything Masonic was destroyed by the eruption of anti-Masonry. It was not until 1840 that the fraternity began to recover from this nearly fatal blow.

Thus, we can neatly frame the initial era of American Masonry between two events: the opening of the first lodge in about 1730 and the near destruction of the Craft by about 1830. Freemasonry grew and evolved in the United States during this period, primarily through importation of rites and degrees. The innovations that occurred were refinements, not wholesale manufacture of degrees. American Masons seemed well aware their fraternity was a European creation and looked to that continent as the source and origin of all that was "regular" in Masonry. There is little evidence of American ritual creativity at this time.

---

1 Steven C. Bullock, *Revolutionary Brotherhood* (Chapel Hill and London: University of North Carolina Press, 1996), 275.

2 William Morgan, *Illustrations of Masonry* (Batavia, NY: David Miller, 1826).

1730: The Beginnings of American Masonry

Like so many Masonic events, the first appearance of Freemasonry is not precisely known. Jonathan Belcher (1681–1757), a native of Cambridge, Massachusetts, and later Governor of the Colonies of Massachusetts and New Hampshire from 1730 to 1741 and the Colony of New Jersey from 1747 to 1757, was made a Mason in London ca. 1704. He is one of the very few Masons known to have joined the Craft before 1717.[3] It is possible he held private Lodges at his residence before time-immemorial or chartered Lodges appeared. On June 5, 1730, the premier Grand Lodge appointed Daniel Coxe (1673–1739) Provincial Grand Master for New York, New Jersey, and Pennsylvania, giving the first official Masonic recognition of the English colonies. Bro. Coxe does not seem to have exercised his authority, even though he lived in New Jersey from 1731 to 1739.[4] The Grand Lodge of Pennsylvania possesses a book marked "Liber B" which contains the records of the earliest known Pennsylvania and American Lodge. The first record is for June 24, 1731, and in that month Benjamin Franklin (1705–1790) is entered as paying dues five months back. Franklin's entry implies Lodge activity from at least December 1730 or January 1731.[5]

No earlier Lodge records exist in the United States, though there are suggestive comments in newspapers.[6] Thus, we are safe in setting 1730 as the date for the beginning of American Masonry.[7] Whatever Masonic meetings may have been held before 1730 were not recorded, and activity after 1730 rapidly increased and is documented.

As we move forward from 1730, we see an increasing Masonic presence in the English Colonies. The first lodge in Boston was constituted July 30, 1733, at the house of Edward Lutwych, an inn at the Sign of the Bunch of Grapes in King Street. In 1736, Solomon Lodge No. 1 of Charleston, South

---

3   David Crockett, *First American Born* (Bowie, MD: Heritage Books, Inc., 1992).

4   Henry W. Coil et al., *Coil's Masonic Encyclopedia* (New York: Macoy Masonic Publishing and Supply Co., Inc., 1961), s.v. "Coxe, Daniel."

5   Coil, s.v. "America, Introduction of Freemasonry into."

6   Melvin M. Johnson, *The Beginnings of Freemasonry in America* (Kingsport, TN: Southern Publishers, Inc., 1924).

7   It is worth noting that Massachusetts, Virginia, and some other states have traditions of Masonic meetings earlier than Pennsylvania. To declare dogmatically that Pennsylvania is the source and origin of American Freemasonry is to run the risk of friendly but intense disagreement from other grand lodges.

Carolina, held its first meeting. By 1738, there is evidence of Masonry in Savannah, Georgia, and New York City, and 1739 saw the meeting of the lodge at Portsmouth, New Hampshire. Additional Provincial Grand Masters were appointed after Daniel Coxe from 1733 through 1787: twenty-two by the moderns, six by the ancients, and four by Scotland.

Most American Lodges originated from one of the British Grand Lodges—England, Scotland, and Ireland, though Germany, France, and other Grand Lodges issued charters. Traveling British military Lodges spread Masonry through much of North America as they initiated civilians in the towns where they were stationed. Also imported from England was the rivalry between the Ancient and Modern Grand Lodges. Many states had competing Grand Lodges that eventually merged after the Union of 1813 in London, though South Carolina did not see Masonic unity until 1817. Modern Masons tended to be conservative in promoting the fraternity, prosperous, and loyalists, while Ancient Masons were aggressive in expanding Lodges, working-class, and revolutionaries. After the American Revolution, United States Masonry was strongly Ancient in its organization and practice.

Prince Hall and African Lodge No. 459

In 1775, John Batt initiated fifteen free African-Americans in Boston. Batt was Sergeant in the 38th Regiment of Foot, British Army and Master of Lodge No. 441, Irish Constitution. When the Regiment and Lodge departed in 1776, the fifteen new Masons were left with a permit to meet, to walk on St. John's Day, and to bury their dead, but not to make Masons. They in turn applied to the Grand Lodge of Moderns for a warrant and were chartered as African Lodge No. 459 on September 29, 1784, with Prince Hall as the first Master.[8]

In 1792, when the Grand Lodge of Massachusetts was formed, African Lodge did not join but remained attached to England. This could be due to loyalty to the premier Grand Lodge or to racism from the newly formed Grand Lodge. However, the Grand Lodge of Massachusetts also didn't recognize St. Andrews Lodge, which had a Scottish charter.[9] There is evidence that white Masons visited African Lodge and that England relied on Prince

---

8   Charles H. Wesley, *Prince Hall: Life and Legacy*, 2nd ed. (Washington: United Supreme Council, 33°, S.J., P.H.A., 1983), 34–35; Joseph A. Walkes, *Black Square and Compass*, 3rd printing (Ft. Leavenworth, KS: Walkes Book Co., 1980), 21.

9   Charles H. Wesley, 99–100.

Hall for information on Boston Lodges.[10] In any event, African Lodge continued its separate existence until 1813 when it and all other English-chartered American lodges were erased from the roles of the newly formed United Grand Lodge of England. Then in 1827, officers of African Lodge declared themselves independent and constituted themselves as a Grand Lodge. From these origins grew the large, parallel Masonic organization known today as "Prince Hall Masonry."

The Influence of Itinerant Masonic Lecturers

The early forms of Masonic ritual in the United States are even less known that those in England and France. We do not have the large number of eighteenth-century documents—Gothic constitutions, manuscript catechisms, memory aides—that can be found in Europe. Presumably, the first rituals were transmitted mouth-to-ear, and Lodges may have patterned their ceremonies after some of the exposés, either imported or printed domestically. The first American exposé was Benjamin Franklin's 1730 reprint of *The Mystery of Freemasonry*, but there do not seem to have been any exposés of American ritual practices until the anti-Masonic period, ca. 1826–1840.

With a diversity of ritual sources, the work in American Masonic Lodges must have been variegated during the 1700s. This began to change in 1797 when Thomas Smith Webb (1771–1819) published *The Freemason's Monitor or Illustrations of Masonry*. It acknowledged that "The observations upon the first three degrees are many of them taken from Preston's 'Illustrations of Masonry,' with some necessary alterations" to make them "agreeable to the mode of working in America."[11] For example in the cornerstone ceremony, Preston says, "No private member, or inferior officer of a private lodge, is permitted to join in the ceremony." Webb is much more democratic and allows the participation of "such officers and members of private lodges as can conveniently attend."[12]

Webb was the first and most prominent of several Masonic Lecturers who toured the country teaching a uniform of ritual to Lodges, Chapters, and any other body they could convince to pay their fees. These lecturers often

---

10 Charles H. Wesley, 91.

11 Thomas Smith Webb, *The Freemason's Monitor or Illustrations of Masonry*, new and improved ed. (Salem, MA: John D. Cushing, 1821), 1.

12 S. Brent Morris, *Cornerstones of Freedom* (Washington: Supreme Council, 33°, S.J., 1993), 140.

had "side degrees" available for sale or as gifts. Webb trained Jeremy Ladd Cross (1783–1861) who succeeded Webb as the generally recognized chief ritualist. Cross's great contribution was his 1819 *The True Masonic Chart or Hieroglyphic Monitor*. It was largely Webb's *Monitor* with a few small textual changes and one major visual addition: forty-two pages of engravings by Bro. Amos Doolittle.

Doolittle's engravings did more than illustrate Cross's text, they provided a memory map for students learning the ritual. Each image on a page was a milestone in the lectures. By associating an image with a portion of ritual, it was possible to mentally review an entire lecture by thumbing through a few pages of Cross's *Chart*. The book was very successful and has influenced the artwork in almost every subsequent American Masonic monitor.

Other Masonic lecturers trained by or with Webb and Cross include John Barney (1780–1847), James Cushman (1776–1829), David Vinton (d. 1833), and John Snow (1780–1852). They each seemed to concentrate on a different part of the country, much as salesmen have defined territories. There was some cooperation among the lecturers and not a small amount of competition. These teachers, with the aid of Cross's *Chart* and similar books, helped standardize ritual and spread ceremonies, such as the Royal and Select Master Degrees.

The Royal Arch

The first "high degree" to appear in America was the Royal Arch Degree. In fact, the first recorded conferral of this degree anywhere occurred in December 1753 at Fredericksburg Lodge in Virginia, where George Washington (1731–1799) was initiated an Entered Apprentice in 1752. The American Royal Arch ritual is based upon the story of Jeshua, Zerrubabel, and Haggai and the rebuilding of the second Temple in Jerusalem. The degree began to spread steadily throughout the colonies:

1758—organization of Jerusalem Chapter in Philadelphia;

1769—organization of St. Andrew's Chapter, Boston;

1790—organization of Cyrus Chapter Newburyport, Massachusetts;

1792—organization of a Chapter in Charleston, South Carolina;

1794—organization of Harmony Chapter, Philadelphia.

Other unrecorded or forgotten degrees and chapters doubtlessly occurred. In 1795, the First Grand Chapter was formed in Pennsylvania, and in 1797, the first national American organization was created—the General Grand Chapter of the New England States, which is today the General Grand Chapter of the United States. Additional Grand Chapters quickly followed in Massachusetts, Connecticut, New York, and Rhode Island in 1798. By 1830, there were twenty-one Grand Chapters in the United States.[13]

The early conferral of the Royal Arch Degree seemed to be based on the authority inherent in the charter of a Lodge. Not surprisingly, it was Ancient Lodges that were most likely to see this high degree authority inherent in their charters. Royal Arch Chapter in the United States, in contrast to their English counterparts, quickly organized themselves into state Grand Chapters and, with the exception of Pennsylvania and Virginia, quickly placed themselves under the authority of the General Grand Chapter. This federal form of Masonic government paralleled the federal government adopted with the U.S. Constitution in 1789.

One amusing quirk of American Royal Arch Masonry is worth noting: our presiding officer is not the King, representing Zerrubabel, but the High Priest, representing Jeshua. The generally accepted explanation is that American patriots couldn't stand to have a "King" rule over them, even in a Masonic context. Thus, Royal Arch Chapter officers were reorganized to give the governing position to the High Priest.

As Lodges had a "chair degree," the Past Master's Degree, it only made sense that the Royal Arch should have one too, and so the Order of High Priesthood came into being. It is not mentioned in Webb's 1796 *Monitor*, but it is in his 1802 edition as well as Cross's 1819 *Chart*. It is usually conferred on High Priests before they can assume the Oriental Chair of Solomon. The degree, still worked today, may have had European ancestors, but its genealogy is uncertain. It is also known as the Order of Melchizedek, and there is mention of such an Order conferred in Massachusetts in 1789. It is not certain the degrees are connected by anything other than name.

The Growth of the Chapter Degrees

As in England, the Royal Arch Degree in the United States can only be conferred on Past Masters. American practice soon required the conferral of the

---

13 Coil, s.v. "Royal Arch Masonry."

chair ceremony to qualify candidates as "virtual Past Masters." The Chapter degree seems to have contained the essential elements of the Lodge degree, but the candidate was given humorous trials and tribulations to endure. The earliest record of the Mark Degree is in 1783 at the Royal Arch Chapter in Middleton, Connecticut. Soon the Mark was adopted by Royal Arch Chapters as the first in their sequence of degrees. This is in contrast to most European jurisdictions where the Mark is independent and controlled by its own Grand Lodge.

The Most Excellent Master Degree, a uniquely American degree in origin, first appeared by name at the Middleton Chapter with the Mark Degree in 1783. Its legend revolves around the completion of the Temple of Solomon and the placement of the keystone in the Royal Arch. It may contain elements from older European degrees, but its current organization is unique to the United States. Thomas Smith Webb published a description of this degree in his 1797 monitor as the third of three degrees leading to the Royal Arch, and it has remained in that position until today. The sequence of degrees conferred in American Royal Arch Chapters since then (except for Virginia and West Virginia) is

1. Mark Master Mason,

2. Past Master,

3. Most Excellent Master,

4. Royal Arch Mason,

5. Order of High Priesthood for High Priests.

The Cryptic Degrees

The Degrees of Royal and Select Master seem to have originated as side degrees available from itinerant Masonic lecturers. They are known collectively as the "Cryptic Degrees" or the "Cryptic Rite" because their legend deals with the secret vault or crypt beneath King Solomon's Temple. The Select Master Degree was conferred at Charleston, SC, in 1783, and the Royal Master Degree in New York City in 1804. In 1810, the degrees became permanently associated together with the formation of Columbia Grand Council of Royal and Select Masters in New York City.[14] (Even

---

14 Coil, s.v. "Rites, Masonic, II, Cryptic Rite."

though the "Grand" is in the name, the body was local.)

Cross included these two degrees in his popular 1819 illustrated monitor, producing a nine-degree system extending from Entered Apprentice to Select Master. The degrees were some times conferred in Royal Arch Chapters, but slowly emerged as independent Masonic bodies, governed by state Grand Councils of Royal and Select Masters and a national General Grand Council. The earliest independent Councils were formed in

1810—New York City,

1815—New Hampshire,

1817—Massachusetts, Virginia, and Vermont,

1818—Rhode Island and Connecticut.

By 1830, there were Grand Councils in ten states. Under the influence of Cross's *Chart* and other monitors, the Select Master's Degree came to be viewed at the culmination of "Ancient Craft Masonry," even if Councils were found in only a few metropolitan areas and their degrees available to only a few. This is probably the beginning of the American "York Rite," consisting of the Chapter of Royal Arch Masons, Council of Royal and Select Masters, and Commandery of Knights Templar.

Knights Templars and the American York Rite

The first reference to a Masonic Templar degree is found in the minutes of St. Andrews Lodge, Boston, an Ancient Lodge, when on April 9, 1769, William Davis received the Excellent, Super Excellent, Royal Arch, and Knight Templar Degrees. South Carolina has a seal dated 1780, Maryland has a Templar diploma dated 1782, and New York records the degree in 1783. In 1796, the first Commandery (or Encampment or Priory) was established in Colchester, Connecticut, and eventually received a charter from England in 1803.[15]

Today in America, a Commandery of Knights Templar confers the Order of the Red Cross, the Order of Malta, and the Order of the Temple on Christian Masons. In 1816, the Order of Malta was placed as the last degree in the series until 1916 when it returned to second place. The Red Cross legend is similar to the Knight of the East and Prince of Jerusalem detailing the re-

---

15 Coil, s.v. "Knights Templar (Masonic)."

turn of Zerubbabel from Babylon to Jerusalem to rebuild the Temple. It tells an interesting story and provides important background in understanding Masonic Temple legends, but it is entirely out of place among Christian chivalric orders. Nonetheless, it remains and provides an important part of the York Rite legends.

Taken together, the Craft Lodge, Royal Arch Chapter, Royal and Select Council, and Knights Templar Commandery form the American "York Rite." The name is inexact as the degrees did not originate in York, England, but then again the Scottish Rite did not originate in Scotland. Lodges became widespread in the states, Chapters were found in larger towns, and Commanderies were less common. The broad base of the York Rite and its democratic government made it very popular in the United States. Reflecting the widespread belief that the York Rite was the purest and oldest form of Masonry, some American Grand Lodges originally styled themselves, "Ancient York Masons" (A.Y.M.).

The Ancient and Accepted Scottish Rite

The most notable high degree event in the United States occurred on May 31, 1801, when John Mitchell (ca. 1741–1816) elevated Frederick Dalcho (1770–1835) to the 33rd Degree, and they then elevated another seven until there was a constitutional number to open a Supreme Council. Their actions were announced to the world in a circular dated December 4, 1802. The opening of the first Supreme Council 33° was preceded by considerable "Scottish" activity.

Etienne Morin (1693?–1771) received authority in 1761 from Paris or Bordeaux to promote Masonry throughout the world. This included propagating a rite of twenty-five degrees, sometimes known as the Rite of Perfection. Morin moved to San Domingo and soon appointed six Inspectors General.[16] The most successful of these was Henry Andrew Francken (d. 1795), from whom fifty-two Inspectors descended, though he only appointed six himself. After Morin's arrival in America, bodies of his rite were soon established:

1764—Loge de Parfaits de Écosse, New Orleans, Louisiana;

---

16 Harold van Buren Voorhis, *The Story of the Scottish Rite of Freemasonry* (New York: Press of Henry Emmerson, 1965), 15.

1767—The Ineffable Lodge of Perfection, Albany, New York;

1781—Lodge of Perfection, Philadelphia, Pennsylvania;

1783—Lodge of Perfection, Charleston, South Carolina;

1788—Grand Council, Princes of Jerusalem, Charleston, South Carolina;

1791—King Solomon's Lodge of Perfection, Martha's Vineyard, Massachusetts;

1792—Lodge of Perfection, Baltimore, Maryland;

1797—Sublime Grand Council, Princes of the Royal Secret, Charleston, South Carolina;

1797—La Triple Union, Chapter of Rose Croix, New York.[17]

Inspectors propagated the degrees of this rite with little organization, often for the fees they could negotiate. The Supreme Council's motto, Ordo ab Chao, is indeed appropriate for the situation. Webb's *Monitor* had monitorial instructions for the ineffable degrees, which served to make American Masons aware there was more than the York Rite. Thus, when the Mother Supreme Council formed itself in 1801, it did not operate in a vacuum.

In August 1806, Antoine Bideaud, a member of the Supreme Council of the "French West India Islands," visited new York City and found an opportunity to make a little extra money. He conferred the Scottish Rite degrees on four Masons for $46 each and then created a "Sublime Grand Consistory, 30°, 31°, and 32°." Bideaud's authority was for the islands only and certainly did not extend into New York, which was under the jurisdiction of the Charleston Supreme Council.[18]

In New York City in October 1807, Joseph Cerneau (d. 1827?), a jeweler from Cuba, constituted a "Sovereign Grand Consistory of Sublime Princes of the Royal Secret." Cerneau was a "Deputy Grand Inspector, for the

---

17 Kent Walgren, "An Historical Sketch of Pre-1851 Louisiana Scottish Rite Masonry." *Heredom* 4 (1995): 190; Samuel H. Baynard, Jr., *History of the Supreme Council, 33°*, 2 vols. (Boston: Supreme Council, 33°, N.M.J., 1938), 97–100.

18 Baynard, 152.

Northern part of the Island of Cuba" under Morin's rite. His patent limited him to confer the 4° through 24° on Lodge officers, and the 25° once a year. Early records are sufficiently vague that it cannot be determined if the original members of Cerneau's Consistory thought they had the 25° or the 32°. With even less authority than Bideaud, Cerneau launched his foray into high degree Masonry in New York.[19]

The Bideaud organization was "healed" by Emmanuel de la Motta, Grand Treasurer of the Mother Supreme Council on December 24, 1813. This group assumed control of what is today known as the Northern Masonic Jurisdiction. The Cerneau Consistory ignored de la Motta's actions, but decided they had to expand their degrees to thirty-three to "keep up with the competition." They eventually claimed jurisdiction over the "United States, Their Territories, and Dependencies." Thus, in 1830, there were three competing Supreme Councils in the United States. All three became dormant during the anti-Masonic period.

Side Degrees

The last category of pre-1830 degrees is "side degrees," conferred under irregular circumstances with little formal authority. They sometimes were communicated by itinerant lecturers, sometimes by Masons who possessed the degree, sometimes for a fee, sometimes for free. Some of these degrees could have coalesced into a rite if anti-Masonry hadn't crushed them. There is scant information on them, sometimes little more than a title mentioned in passing. A search of all American Lodge minutes before 1830 might yield a few more names, but probably no more rituals.

Some of our information comes from two exposés from the anti-Masonic period, David Barnard's 1829 *Light on Masonry* and Avery Allyn's 1831 *A Ritual of Freemasonry*. Both authors seemed to have been originally motivated in "saving" the American public by exposing the "evils" of Freemasonry. However, general interest in Masonry was spurred on by the public conferral of the degrees by anti-Masonic troupes. This interest, in turn increased demand for exposés, especially those complete with passwords and grips. Bernard obliged this demand by adding the secret work from Delaunaye's *Thuileur*, without regard for whether it matched the American de-

---

19 Baynard, 155–56; Joseph Cerneau, Patent of Authority, July 15, 1806, Baracoa, Cuba, Manuscript in the hand of Mathieu Dupotet(?), Archives, Supreme Council, 33°, S.J., Washington, DC.

grees he described.[20] It is often difficult to know if the degrees described were widely worked, if at all. Of these many degrees, only the Heroines of Jericho seems to be an American original. It survived and is worked today by Prince Hall Masons.

Another source of pre-1830 side degrees is a series of newspaper articles, "Recollections of a Masonic Veteran," by Robert Benjamin Folger (1803–1892). Published in 1873–1874, these articles describe his fifty years in Masonry with a few comments about side degrees. Finally, there is tantalizing evidence that Zorobabel Lodge No. 498 in New York City worked the Rectified Scottish Rite and may have conferred the fourth degree, Scottish Master.[21]

Pre-1830 American Masonic Side Degrees

Knight of the Christian Mark, Bernard, Allyn

Knight of the Holy Sepulchre, Bernard, Allyn

Holy and Thrice Illustrious order of the Cross, Bernard, Allyn

Knight of the Three Kings, Allyn

Knight of Constantinople, Allyn, Folger

Secret Monitor, Allyn, Folger

Ark and Dove (RAMs only), Allyn

Mediterranean Pass, Folger

Knight of the Round Table (fun degree), Folger

Aaron's Band (similar to High Priesthood), Folger

Master Mason's Daughter (for women), Folger

True Kindred (for women), Folger

Heroine of Jericho (RAMs, wives, and widows), Allyn

---

20 Walgren, 98.

21 S. Brent Morris, *The Folger Manuscript* (Bloomington, IL: Masonic Book Club, 1993), 4, 26, 27, 31.

1830: The End of the First Era of American Masonry

As early as March 1826, a New York Mason named William Morgan began plans to publish the "secrets of Freemasonry." This created quite a stir in his small town of Batavia, New York. Neither Morgan, nor his potential readers, nor the local Lodge seemed aware that ritual exposés had been available in the United States since at least 1730 when Benjamin Franklin republished *The Mystery of Freemasonry*. Masons tried to purchase the manuscript from Morgan's publisher, David Miller, a former Entered Apprentice Mason. When this failed, Miller's printing company was set on fire twice, presumably by Masons, but others claim it was a publicity stunt by Miller.

Morgan, a ne'er-do-well in frequent debt, was jailed in Canandaigua, New York, for a debt of $2.00 assigned to Nicholas G. Chesbro, Master of the Lodge at Canandaigua. On the next day, September 12, 1826, Chesbro appeared at the jail with several other Masons and discharged his claim against Morgan. They escorted Morgan outside and into a waiting carriage. Before entering the carriage, Morgan was heard crying during a scuffle, "Help! Murder!" He was driven north to Niagara County and held in the old Powder Magazine at Ft. Niagara until September 19. Morgan was never seen thereafter.[22]

Morgan's abduction, disappearance, and presumed murder set off a social and political crisis in the United States. Many came to believe that Freemasonry was a secretive power behind the government, thwarting the will of the people, and murdering those who dared cross it. Religious leaders denounced the fraternity as anti-Christian. Soon the fear of Masonry manifested itself in the creation of the first major "third part" in American politics: the Anti-Masonic Party. The party attracted reformers, abolitionists, and idealists, but its primary purpose was the destruction of Freemasonry and other "secret societies." From about 1826 to 1840, the anti-Masonic movement swept across the country, destructive in some places, barely noticed in others. In 1826, New York had 480 Lodges and by 1835, only 75 remained. The Grand Lodge of Vermont dwindled to the point that only the Grand Master, the Grand Secretary, and the Grand Treasurer attended Grand Lodge, and the Supreme Councils of the Scottish Rite were dormant. The northeastern states, where the Craft was most prosperous, endured the worst destruction, but few parts of the country were spared.

---

22 Coil, s.v. "Morgan Affair."

By the time the Anti-Masonic Party collapsed as a political force in 1840, Freemasonry began to reemerge, but as a more conservative and religiously oriented organization.

References

Allyn, Avery. *A Ritual of Freemasonry.* Boston: John Marsh and Co., 1831.

Baynard, Samuel H., Jr. *History of the Supreme Council, 33°.* 2 vols. Boston: Supreme Council, 33°, N.M.J., 1938.

Bernard, David. *Light on Masonry.* Utica, NY: William Williams, 1829.

Bullock, Steven C. *Revolutionary Brotherhood.* Chapel Hill and London: University of North Carolina Press, 1996.

Coil, Henry W. et al. *Coil's Masonic Encyclopedia.* New York: Macoy Masonic Publishing and Supply Co., Inc., 1961.

Crockett, David. *First American Born.* Bowie, MD: Heritage Books, Inc., 1992.

Folger, Robert Benjamin, S. Brent Morris, ed. *Recollections of a Masonic Veteran.* Bloomington, IL: Masonic Book Club, 1995.

Johnson, Melvin M. *The Beginnings of Freemasonry in America.* Kingsport, TN: Southern Publishers, Inc., 1924.

Morgan, William. *Illustrations of Masonry.* Batavia, NY: David Miller, 1826.

Morris, S. Brent. *Cornerstones of Freedom.* Washington: Supreme Council, 33°, S.J., 1993.

————. *The Folger Manuscript.* Bloomington, IL: Masonic Book Club, 1993.

Voorhis, Harold van Buren. *The Story of the Scottish Rite of Freemasonry.* New York: Press of Henry Emmerson, 1965.

Walgren, Kent. "An Historical Sketch of Pre-1851 Louisiana Scottish Rite Masonry." *Heredom* 4 (1995): 189–206.

Walkes, Joseph A. *Black Square and Compass.* 3rd printing. Ft. Leavenworth, KS: Walkes Book Co., 1980.

Webb, Thomas Smith. *The Freemason's Monitor or Illustrations of Masonry.* New and improved ed. Salem, MA: John D. Cushing, 1821.

Wesley, Charles H. *Prince Hall: Life and Legacy,* 2nd ed. Washington: United Supreme Council, 33°, S.J., P.H.A., 1983.

First published: 1998 Blue Friar Lecture published in W. McLeod and S. B. Morris eds., *A Daily Advancement in Masonic Knowledge* (Bloomington, IL: Masonic Book Club, 2003).

The Royal Secret in America before 1801[1]

May 31, 1801, is the most significant date in the history of high-degree Masonry in the United States. On that day, the Mother Supreme Council of the World was opened by John Mitchell and Frederick Dalcho in Charleston, South Carolina, and in the course of the year, "the whole number of Grand Inspectors General was compleated agreeably to the Grand Constitutions."[2] By this act the Order of the Royal Secret of twenty-five degrees (often called the Rite of Perfection) was transformed into the Ancient and Accepted Scottish Rite of thirty-three degrees.[3]

Before the creation of the Mother Supreme Council, the high degrees were spread through an inconsistent system of Inspectors, each of whom could appoint an unrestricted number of Inspectors without limit to authority. Records are scarce, but two Inspectors seem to have been working in the Western hemisphere before 1761: "Lamolere de Feuillas, made a Deputy prior to 1750 in France, and Bertrand Berthomieu, made a Deputy by

---

1   Originally presented in Paris, August 31, 2004, and published in translation as "L'Ordre du Royal Secret en Amérique avant 1801," in *Le Rite Écossais Ancien et Accepté: Mise en Perspective Historique Deux Siècles Après, colloque international* (Paris: Sources, 2004), 5–19.

2   Supreme Council of the U.S.A., *Circular throughout the Two Hemispheres. Universi Terrarum Orbis Architectonis Gloria ab Ingentis. Deus Meumque Jus. Ordo ab Chao* (Charleston, SC: Thomas B. Bowen, 1802).

3   The twenty-five degree system that evolved into the Ancient and Accepted Scottish Rite is properly known as the "Order of the Royal Secret," though it has been misidentified for more than a century as the "Rite of Perfection." In a private communication with the author, Alain Bernheim points out that the first use of the correct name by twentieth-century authors appears to be by W. W. Covey-Crump and S. H. Perry in their unpublished paper, "Order of the Royal Secret: Its History and Mystery," referenced in the "April 1954 Minutes of the History Committee, Supreme Council, 33°, A.A.S.R., N.M.J.," 31. Bernheim went on to confirm the correct name of the Order by verifying the transcription of a patent from Etienne Morin to Antoine Charles Menessier de Boissy in the name of the "Sublime Commanders of the Order of the Royal Secret." Arturo de Hoyos points out that the *Circular throughout the Two Hemispheres* refers to Frederick the Great as "Grand Commander of the order of Prince of the Royal Secret."

Feuillas in 1753 in the West Indies."[4] It is not known if Feuillas or Berthomieu appointed further Inspectors.

In 1761, Etienne Morin received a patent at Paris that authorized him to
propagate the Rite throughout the world. He arrived in Jamaica in 1762 or
1763 and soon appointed six Inspectors General, including Henry Andrew
Francken as a Deputy Inspector General.[5] Francken, in turn, established
a Lodge of Perfection in Albany, New York, in 1767 and created six other
Deputy Inspectors General. He also prepared at least three books with the
rituals translated into English.[6] Eventually, fifty-two Inspectors descended
from Francken, and at least seventy-five75 Inspectors were appointed in
American before 1801.[7]

The Inspectors and Deputies did more than reproduce themselves; they
conferred the Ineffable (4°–14°) and Sublime (15° and above) Degrees
upon Master Masons and occasionally established bodies. Again records are
scarce, but at least the following eight bodies were established before 1801:

1. 1764—*Loge de Parfaits d'Écosse*, New Orleans, Louisiana;[8]

2. 1767—The Ineffable Lodge of Perfection, Albany, New York;

3. 1781—Lodge of Perfection, Philadelphia, Pennsylvania;

4. 1783—Lodge of Perfection, Charleston, South Carolina;

5. 1788—Grand Council, Princes of Jerusalem, Charleston, South
    Carolina;

---

4   Henry W. Coil et al., *Coil's Masonic Encyclopedia* (New York: Macoy Publishing and
    Masonic Supply Co., 1961), s.v. "Morin, Stephen."

5   Harold van Buren Voorhis, *The Story of the Scottish Rite of Freemasonry* (New York:
    Press of Henry Emerson, 1965), 15; Alain Bernheim, "Questions About Albany," *Here-
    dom* 4 (1995): 142.

6   The three known copies of the Francken Manuscript are owned by the Supreme Coun-
    cil, 33°, N.M.J., U.S.A., United Grand Lodge of England, and Supreme Council, 33°, for
    England and Wales.

7   Voorhis, 56–57.

8   *Loge de Parfaits d'Écosse* seems to have been part of the Bordeaux system from which
    emerged Etienne Morin and the Order of the Royal Secret. From the scanty records
    available, we cannot know for certain what degrees were worked during its brief exis-
    tence in New Orleans, but almost surely, it would have been a subset of those in a Lodge
    of Perfection. Alain Bernheim, private communication to the author.

6. 1791—King Solomon's Lodge of Perfection, Holmes Hole (now Tisbury), island of Martha's Vineyard, Massachusetts;

7. 1792—Lodge of Perfection, Baltimore, Maryland;

8. 1797—Sublime Grand Council, Princes of the Royal Secret, Charleston, South Carolina.[9]

These basic facts of high-degree activity before the creation of the Supreme Council are well known and have been repeated in many places. What they fail to do is to inform us how the high degrees appealed to American Masons, how the Inspectors spread the degrees, and how the bodies operated. The answers to these questions help us understand the acceptance of the Mother Supreme Council.

The Appeal of the High Degrees to American Masons

The Craft or Blue Degrees were being conferred by 1730 in America, and twenty-three years later in December 1753, Fredericksburg Lodge in

---

9   For New Orleans, see Kent Walgren, "An Historical Sketch of Pre-1851 Louisiana Scottish Rite Masonry." *Heredom* 4 (1995): 190; Alain Bernheim, "Notes on Early Freemasonry in Bordeaux (1732–1769)." *Ars Quatuor Coronatorum* 101 (1988): 90, 100. For the other bodies, see Samuel H. Baynard, Jr., *History of the Supreme Council, 33°,* 2 vols. (Boston: Supreme Council, 33°, N.M.J.), vol. 1, 97–100.

In an earlier paper, I mistakenly referred to *La Triple Union* Chapter of Rose Croix (1797) as a body of the Order of the Royal Secret. In fact, it was a chapter of the Royal Order of Scotland. "The High Degrees in the United States: 1730–1830," *The Philalethes,* 51, no. 2 (April 1998): 36.

There are suggestions of other bodies. For example, a certificate and two patents issued in 1768 by Francken to Jeremiah van Rennsselaer, Samuel Stringer, and Moses M. Hays hint at a Council of Princes of the Royal Secret. The documents were issued "under the Celestial Canopy of the Zenith which answers to 41 Deg[rees]: 30 M[inutes]: N[orthern]: L[atitude]:" which corresponds to Newport, Rhode Island, the 1774 residence of Hays. No other evidence for the council exists. Alain Bernheim, "Questions About Albany," pp. 157–61, 166.

"A 'Sovereign Chapter of Rose Croix [de Heroden]' was also constituted in Charleston prior to 1802.... But neither the Supreme Council's Manifesto nor Mackey's manuscript History, nor any other work which we have been able to find, discloses the former's date or source of authority." Charles S. Lobinger, *The Ancient and Accepted Scottish Rite of Freemasonry* (Louisville, KY: Standard Printing, 1932), 150. The existence of this chapter is confirmed by the *Annual Register of the Brethren Who Compose the Sublime Grand Lodge of Perfection of South-Carolina* (Charleston: T. B. Bowen, 1802), reproduced in Ray Baker Harris, *History of the Supreme Council, 33°, ... Southern Jurisdiction, U.S.A.: 1801–1861* (Washington: Supreme Council, 33°, S.J., 1964), 306–16.

Virginia recorded the first conferral anywhere of the Royal Arch Degree. American Master Masons soon realized that they had not received the entire account of the Master's Word and that the Royal Arch was required to complete the story. Royal Arch Masonry became popular as more Masons sought to complete their Masonic knowledge. The steady spread of the Royal Arch was aided by the growing dominance in America of Antient lodges that conferred the degree on the authority of their Craft warrants. At least five Chapters independent of lodges were created by 1794, the Grand Chapter of Pennsylvania was instituted in 1795, and the General Grand Chapter of New England States was formed in 1796. The first Knight Templar conferral was in 1769, and there is sporadic evidence of the order until 1796 when the first Encampment (now Commandery) was formed in Connecticut.[10] The ten degrees and orders of what has come to be known as the American "York Rite" were summarized and given wide publicity in Thomas Smith Webb's *Freemason's Monitor; or, Illustrations of Masonry* (1797).

American Masons enthusiastically pursued further light in Masonry, but because the Order of the Royal Secret was of French origin and had no tradition in English lodges, these high degrees were little known. These ceremonies must have seemed like alluring rumors only available from remote non-English lodges or from traveling Masonic lecturers. The fragmentary knowledge of Sublime Masonry was aided by occasional tantalizing mentions in Masonic books.

The first American book on Masonry was Benjamin Franklin's 1734 reprint of Anderson's *Constitutions of the Free-Masons*. A total of 626 volumes dealing with Freemasonry were published in America through 1800; ten of these dealt with precursors of the Scottish Rite.[11] For the interested student of Masonry, these ten books provided hints of knowledge beyond that found in lodges of English origin.

1787—*The Memorial of Lodge, No. 40, on the Registry of Pennsylvania, to the Right Worshipful Grand Lodge.* This ten-page pamphlet is a complaint that the Grand Lodge of Ancient York Masons of

---

10 Morris, "The High Degrees in the United States," 36.
11 Kent Walgren, *Freemasonry, Anti-Masonry and Illuminism in the United States, 1734–1850: A Bibliography*, 2 vols. (Worcester, MA: American Antiquarian Society, 2003), vol. 1, 3–134.

South Carolina (the Ancients' Grand Lodge) was formed irregularly. However, page 5 gives intriguing hints of a form of Freemasonry different from that in England. "Brother Joseph Myers, Junr. was then, and actually is (under the jurisdiction of the late Prussian Monarch) an Inspector General and Grand Master of and over the Ineffable Degrees of Masonry. The second, brother James Fallon, is and was a regular Past-Master ... made and installed in a ... Lodge of Ineffable Masons at Philadelphia, under a regular commission...."[12]

1797—[Charles Louis Cadet de Gassicourt], *The Tomb of James Molai.* This is a 22-page translation of the 1796 French original. Page 8 explains that Jacques de Molay established four chapters with twenty-seven members each who have special privileges in Masonic Lodges: "When they enter a Lodge they have the exclusive right of crossing in the middle of the carpet which is opposite the throne. All Freemasons of Lodges are ignorant who they are."

1797—Thomas Smith Webb, *The Freemason's Monitor; or, Illustrations of Masonry.* This was the first American "monitor" of Masonic degrees, giving prayers, charges, and non-secret portions of ritual. It was widely distributed, translated into Spanish, and went through several editions before Webb's death. Part II of this book has descriptions of the eleven degrees of a Lodge of Perfection on pages 227–66, including information about who replaced Hiram Abiff at King Solomon's temple, how the ruffians were dealt with, and how the lost word was recovered. Webb's *Monitor* was extremely influential in establishing and disseminating the "standard American" ritual. Its widespread popularity must have brought the Sublime Degrees to the curious attention of many American Masons.

1798—John Robison, *Proofs of a Conspiracy against All the Religions and Governments of Europe.* This is the first American edition of this influential book, which created hysteria at the idea that the Illuminati were secretly infiltrating the governments of the world and possibly America. On page 384, Robison comments on Abbé

---

12 All comments on these ten books are from Kent Walgren, "A Bibliography of Pre-1851 American Scottish Rite Imprints," *Heredom* 3 (1994): 61–67; spelling corrections have been made in this transcription.

Barruel's rituals of the Knight of the Sun and Knight Rose Croix. Here is another instance of tantalizing references to Masonic degrees unfamiliar to most American Masons.

1798—John Robison, *Proofs of a Conspiracy*. The second American edition.

1799—Augustin de Barruel, *Memoirs, Illustrating the History of Jacobinisn*, vols. I, II, III, and IV. Because there were three separate printers for the four volumes, Walgren assigns each a separate entry in his bibliography. There are more provoking hints of unseen forces in Freemasonry: "occult lodges" (which de Barruel termed "*arrieres loges*"). In volume II, the reader can find descriptions of the Degree of Elect (page 161), Knight of the Sun (page 163n), higher degrees of Scotch Masonry (pages 163–68), Degree of Rose Croix (pages 168–72), Mystical Masonry (pages 172–74), and Knight Kadosh (pages 174–75). Volume III deals specifically with Weishaupt's degrees of Illuminism, but to the general Masonic reader, it all points to even more continental degrees unknown to English lodges. Further mention of continental degrees is in volume IV: African Brethren, Knights of the Eagle, the Adept, the Sublime Philosopher (page 81); Knights of Palestine, Knights Kadosh, Scotch Directory (pages 97–100); Scotch Architect (page 328).

1800—Robert Griffith Wetmore, *A Feeble Attempt to Promote the Felicity of Campbell's Mark Master's Lodge in Duanesburgh[, New York]*. On page 6, Wetmore says, "When I first became your neighbor, I was in Possession of thirty degrees in Masonry (including those styled ineffable) and therefore considered myself as having arrived to the ne plus ultra. ..."

Webb's *Freemason's Monitor* was the first authoritative guide to working the ten degrees and orders of American York Rite: Craft (three degrees), Royal Arch (four degrees), and Knights Templar (three orders). It also gave exciting information about an exotic type of Masonry known to few American Masons and must have generated great curiosity among its readers. At that time, a typical American lodge room was rather simply decorated with pillars in the west, an altar in the center, and an illuminated "G" in the east. Compare this austerity with the lavish description Webb gives for just one of the Ineffable Degrees.

Observations on the Degree of Provost and Judge.

This lodge is adorned with red, and lighted by five great lights; one in each corner, and one in the center. The master is placed in the East, under a blue canopy, surrounded with stars, and is stiled [sic], Thrice Illustrious.[13]

The Worshipful Master of an American Craft or Blue Lodge wore his usual clothes with a ribbon around his neck from which hung a square. His apron was probably homemade and decorated by his wife, sister, or mother. There are many images of George Washington and Benjamin Franklin in such simple but dignified attire. Again compare the description Webb gives to the luxurious dress of the presiding officer of the "Degree of Knights of the Ninth Arch, or Royal Arch."

The most potent grand master, representing Solomon in the east, [is] seated in a chair of state, under a rich canopy, with a crown on his head, and a scepter in his hand. He is dressed in royal robes of yellow, and an ermined vestment of blue satin, reaching to the elbows; a broad purple ribbon from the right shoulder to the left hip, to which is hung a triangle of gold.[14]

After being enticed since the 1760s with allusions to, and hints of, mysterious Masonic degrees preserving the full story of the Craft, American Masons were given clear information in 1802. The Mother Supreme Council published its *Circular throughout the Two Hemispheres*, announcing itself and explaining the degrees under its control. The *Circular* can be viewed as a wonderfully written sales brochure, enticing candidates to join by explaining why the Ineffable and Sublime Degrees are necessary to fully understand Freemasonry. It gave many examples of why the High Degrees are both superior and essential.

- The Supreme Council alone is governed with historically correct documents.

  Much of the history of Masonry in the early ages is so mixed with fable and enveloped with the rust of time that little satisfaction can

---

13 Thomas Smith Webb, *Freemason's Monitor; or, Illustrations of Masonry*, 2nd ed. (New York: Southwick and Crooker, 1802), 233.

14 Webb, 244.

be obtained; but as we approach nearer to our own times we have authentic records for our government.[15]

- The first three degrees are only a preparation for the higher degrees.

   [The three first, or Blue Degrees,] were formed as the test of the character and capacity of the initiated, before they should be admitted to the knowledge of the more important mysteries.

- The true Master's Word was lost to the Blue Degrees with the death of Hiram Abiff, but the Ineffable and Sublime Degrees still possess it.

   It is well known to the Blue Master that King Solomon and his Royal visitor were in possession of the real and pristine word, but of which he must remain ignorant, unless initiated into the sublime degrees.

- The Ineffable and Sublime Degrees have preserved their ceremonies uncorrupted.

   Much variety and irregularity have unfortunately crept into the Blue degrees in consequence of ... those who are unacquainted with the Hebrew language, in which all the Words and Pass-Words are given ... Not so the superior degrees, they appear in that Sublime dress which their founders gave them....

- The Ineffable and Sublime Degrees continue the tradition of the crusaders and base their degrees on authentic records discovered in Palestine.

   While [27,000 Masons accompanying the Christian Princes in the Crusades were] in Palestine, they discovered several important Masonic manuscripts, among the descendants of the ancient Jews, which enriched our Archives with authentic written records, and on which, some of our degrees are founded.

From the introduction of the Royal Arch in 1753 to the *Circular throughout the Two Hemispheres* in 1802, American Masons had been advised directly and indirectly that the Craft degrees didn't tell the entire story of Masonry. Not every Mason was induced to pursue further light, but for those that

---

15 Supreme Council, *Circular throughout the Two Hemispheres*. All further quotes from this section are from the *Circular*.

were, it must have been challenging to know when to stop. Suggestions of yet one further revelation—perhaps the *ne plus ultra*—might come with the next visitor from overseas, in the latest publication, or at the hands of an itinerant Masonic lecturer.

The Spread of the High Degrees by Masonic Lecturers

Freemasonry came to the United States from many sources and in varied forms. The early lodges had little guidance for their rituals and ceremonies, probably relying on equal doses of oral tradition and printed exposures. Four ritual exposures were published in America before 1801, all reprints of English originals: *The Mystery of Free-Masonry* (1730); *Masonry Dissected* (1749/50); *Hiram: Or the Grand Master-Key* (1768); and *Jachin and Boaz* (1774–1801). "Prior to the publication of Morgan's work, [*Illustrations of Masonry by one of the fraternity* (1826)], [*Jachin and Boaz*] was the most important exposé published on American soil, and greatly aided ritual uniformity."[16] While there were doubtless other imported exposures available, it was exposure of the Antient working of *Jachin and Boaz* that most influenced American ritual. It went through ten American editions before 1801, while the other three American exposures were never reprinted.[17] We may infer from its popularity that *Jachin and Boaz* was used widely, if informally, by American lodges to guide their ritual.

Nature abhors a vacuum, and into the vacuum of American Masonic ritual appeared itinerant Masonic lecturers. These uniquely American entrepreneurs traveled the country teaching uniform workings of the three Craft Degrees, the four degrees of the American Royal Arch system (Mark Master Mason, Past Master, Most Excellent Master, and Royal Arch), and "side" degrees. The great unifier of American ritual was Thomas Smith Webb, who is known to have used *Jachin and Boaz* to teach his students.[18] Webb formalized the ceremonies in *Jachin and Boaz*, adjusted the language to American vernacular, and filled in the procedural gaps. He extended the language and

---

16 Arturo de Hoyos, "David Bernard's *Light on Masonry*: An 'Anti-Masonic Bible'," *Heredom* 12 (2004): 10, 12.

17 Walgren, *Freemasonry: A Bibliography*, vol. 2, 993.

18 "[Solomon Southwick] obtained possession of a printed copy of the very identical edition of JACHIN AND BOAZ, out of which he was himself taught the first three degrees of Masonry, by the late Thomas S. Webb.... Mr. Webb lectured them from it, as he did me...." *National Observer*, vol. II (Albany, May 23, 1828), no. 44, whole No. 122, [p. 4], quoted in de Hoyos.

forms of his Craft work to the Royal Arch and taught and certified other lecturers. In 1797, Webb published *The Freemason's Monitor*, which was a teaching tool that helped cement his ritual codification. As noted before, it also must have piqued interest in the high degrees.

Little is known about the business practices of Masonic lecturers, but we can make some reasonable inferences from the 1782–1808 register of Abraham Jacobs and the 1817–1820 diary of Jeremy Ladd Cross.[19] If we assume that each Inspector of the Order of the Royal Secret was an itinerant lecturer of some sort, then perhaps a total of 100–150 such peddlers offered their services to Masonic bodies and individual Masons. In addition to "lecturing" on the Craft and Royal Arch Degrees (which meant teaching the ritual and floor work from memory), these lecturers sold or gave side degrees to their customers and chartered various bodies under their authority.

Jeremy Cross's diary gives us a good idea about the business of a successful lecturer. While his diary entries are for 1817 to 1820, finances then could not have been too different from the period before 1801. His fee for lecturing for a day in 1817 seems to have been $4, about $55 in 2003, and he established Councils of Select Masters for $20, about $275 today.[20] He became a Masonic lecturer in 1814, but by 1818 was still in debt and hoping to settle down.[21] On August 17, 1817, he started out from Haverhill, New Hampshire, traveling by coach and boat, and arrived in Richmond, Virginia, on December 4, a trip of 635 miles. He often stayed with Masons and regularly dined with them even when he stayed in a hotel. During the seventeen-week trip to Richmond, he established at least six Councils of Select Masters ($120/$1,650) and spent some twenty-nine days lecturing

---

19 Abraham Jacobs' register is in the archives of the Supreme Council, 33°, N.M.J., Lexington, MA, and was excerpted from July 22, 1782, to November 26, 1808, in Robert B. Folger, *The Ancient and Accepted Scottish Rite, in Thirty-Three Degrees* (New York: By the author, 1862, 1881), Appendix, 71–110. Jeremy Ladd Cross's diary from August 17, 1817, to April 2, 1820, was published in Eugene E. Hinman, et al., *A History of the Cryptic Rite*, 2 vols. (NP: General Grand Council, 1931), vol. 2, 1223–98.

20 Samuel H. Williams, "What Is the Relative Value?" Economic History Services, April 2004, URL: http://www.eh.net/hmit/compare/. Any comparison of values over 200 years is tenuous. Nonetheless, the comparisons we give provide a passable approximation.

21 "About 4 years since [June 5, 1818,] I commenced the occupation of a Masonic Lecturer. ... I now think that if I were free from debt and had any other way of acquiring a livelihood I should become quite domesticated." Cross diary, June 5, 1818, and May 2, 1818, Hinman reprint, 1257 and 1266.

in Lodges and Chapters ($116/$1,595). His total income for the trip down to Richmond was about $236/$3,245.

To get a very rough estimate of his expenses, note that during his stay in Washington, DC, he paid $8.75 for 3 1/2 days room and meals at Thomas Crafford's Union Hotel, or $2.50 per day.[22] The cost for lodging in smaller towns must have been less, say about $1.50–2.00 per day. If he used hotels or taverns for one-half to two-thirds of his trip and stayed with brothers the rest of the time, then he spent about $90–160 on lodging, very nearly half of his income. By the time we add in his transportation and miscellaneous expenses, it's easy to see why after four years of lecturing he was still in debt.

His diary is imprecise on the number of Councils created, the days of paid lecturing, and his fees, but we can still get a feel for the economics of his 1817 trip from New Hampshire to Virginia by looking at his diary entries for October 9–16, 1817, a particularly busy eight days for him.

A $4 daily lecturing fee appears to have been the accepted rate. The Grand Lodge of Massachusetts on July 22, 1805, appointed Benjamin Gleason to be Grand Lecturer, and after one year lecturing the Massachusetts lodges he received $1,000 or about $15,600 in 2003.[23] If Gleason lectured about twenty-one days a month, then he received about the same compensation per lecture as Cross.

Cross's fortunes as a lecturer significantly improved in May 1818 when the Grand Lodge of Connecticut appointed him "Grand Lecturer, to visit the several Lodges in this jurisdiction, and instruct them in the correct mode of working and lecturing; and that each subordinate Lodge be required to pay into the Treasury of the Grand Lodge the sum of ten dollars, at or before the next Grand Communication, for the purpose of defraying the expense of such visitation." Further, "each Lodge shall pay Bro. Cross' expenses when actually employed by such Lodge in giving lectures and instructions; and no Lodge shall be bound to pay said sum of ten dollars, unless they first have had the benefit of said lectures at least two and a half days."[24] Cross

---

22 Cross diary, December 2, 1817, Hinman reprint, 1240.

23 *Proceedings of the Most Worshipful Grand Lodge of Ancient Free and Accepted Masons of the Commonwealth of Massachusetts: 1792–1815* (Cambridge, MA: Caustic-Claflin Co., 1905), 287, 288, 358.

24 E. G. Storer, *The Records of Freemasonry in the State of Connecticut with a Brief Account of Its Origin in New England and the Entire Proceedings of the Grand Lodge from Its first Organization, A.L. 5789* (New Haven: E. G. Storer, 1859), 293, 294.

J. L. Cross's Diary for October 9–16, 1817[25]	Comments
9th. At 4:00 A.M. I took my seat in the stage and by 8:00 I arrived at Lantwecks Bridge, a small village south of New Castle, [Delaware] stopped at a small Tavern.... I met the Brethren in the Eve and gave a Lecture.	• $4 for lecturing
10th. Spent the day with Maj. Moody in viewing the small but pleasant village. I spent the evening at his house … and returned [to the Tavern and] had some further chat with the Brethren & received my penny.	*The "further chat with the Brethren" might mean lecturing, and "received my penny" means he was paid.* • $4 for lecturing? RECEIVED: $8 for lecturing October 9 & 10
11th. After breakfast I started for Dover, [Delaware] … and arrived in Dover about 2:00 P.M. I soon became acquainted with the Hon. William Hall.… Lectured with the Companions in the Evening—	• $4 for lecturing
12th. Sunday. …	*Cross faithfully observed the Sabbath and did no work on the day.*
13th. Spent the day mostly with Br. Hall. In the Eve I met the Companions. Exhibited the work in the Chapter and established a Council of Select Masters.	*This could be private instructions for Br. Hall.* • $4 for lecturing • $20 for a Council of Select Masters
14th. Spent the day with Bro. Hall and the Eve with the Companions.	*This could be more private instructions for Br. Hall.* • $4 for lecturing?
15th. … gave some directions to lay out $20 in provisions &c &c.	*Ordering $20 in provisions indicates he probably stayed at a tavern.*
16th. Settled with the Companion and received my wages, took dinner with [Dr.] Naudim and at 2 P.M. took the stage and rode to Milford, [Delaware] where I [arrived] at sun down. Stopped at Mr. Godwin's Hotel.	RECEIVED: $32 for lecturing October 11, 13, & 14 and for establishing the Council of Select Masters on October 13

---

25 Cross diary, October 1817, Hinman reprint, 1231–34. Spelling and punctuation have been regularized to modern usage.

was now making the "standard" $4 per day *plus* expenses, and he had more-or-less guaranteed employment with each of the Connecticut lodges. In 1818, there were about fifty-eight lodges in Connecticut,[26] which would generate about $580/$9,048 in lecturing fees; he also instituted about a dozen Councils of Select Masters for another $240/$3,744. Another boost to his prosperity came in 1819 when he published *The True Masonic Chart; or, Hieroglyphic Monitor.* This popular book went through eight editions by 1850 and was followed by *The Templar's Chart or Hieroglyphic Monitor* in 1820 (two editions by 1850) and a business of selling engraved aprons and other Masonic supplies.

Abraham Jacobs does not appear to have lectured in the Craft degrees, nor does his register indicate what his fees were. However, we know that Cross and Gleason received $4 per day to instruct in the seven Craft and Royal Arch Degrees at about this same time and that Cross received $20 to establish a Council of Select Masters, conferring only one degree. Further, in 1806, Antoine Bideaud of the Southern Supreme Council conferred the 4° through 32° in New York City on J. J. J. Gourgas and four others for $46, or about $1.50 per degree.[27] Thus, it is not unreasonable to suppose that Jacobs received $10–20 per individual when he conferred the thirteen degrees of the Lodge of Perfection and the Council of Princes of Jerusalem, perhaps giving a discount for a larger class of candidates.

On November 9, 1790, Moses Cohen initiated Jacobs "a Knight of the Sun, with full power to initiate brethren and constitute Lodges," and this is what he did.[28] He conferred the Ineffable, Sublime, and other "side" degrees to supplement his income from teaching Hebrew. While his register gives no information about his income, it does give us insight as to how he conferred degrees, from which we can conjecture the methods of other Inspectors.

On nineteen days from June 10 to July 3, 1792, Jacobs conferred the thirteen degrees of Secret Master through Prince of Jerusalem on sixteen brothers in Augusta, Georgia. His register entry for June 14 was typical of how the degrees were conferred.

---

26 Joseph K. Wheeler, *The Centennial: One Hundredth Anniversary of the Most Worshipful Grand Lodge of Connecticut* (Hartford: Peck & Prouty, 1890), 109.

27 Baynard, Jr., *History of the Supreme Council*, vol. 1, 153.

28 Abraham Jacobs, *Register. Rules and Statutes of the Sublime Degrees, of Masonry*, Folger reprint, 77.

June 14th. This day conferred the degrees of *Provost and Judge* on Brother Zimmerman and Prescott, also the degrees of *Intendant of the Building*, or Grand Master in Israel. Brother James Gardner attended and received the degrees of *Secret Master* and *Perfect Master*, with every requisite instruction.[29]

Usually, one or two degrees were conferred each evening, but since not everyone could be present, degrees were repeated, as on June 14. Jacobs had no assistance in conferring the degrees, and so the ceremonies were anything but "full form." It is reasonable to ask: Why did it take so many evenings to confer the degrees? The explanation may be in the phrase from June 14 in Jacobs' register, "with every requisite instruction."

Arturo de Hoyos, Grand Archivist and Grand Historian of the Supreme Council, 33°, S.J., believes that Jacobs dictated the ceremonies to the candidates, and they transcribed the rituals for their personal use. In support of this contention, the Archives of the Supreme Council, 33°, S.J., have several small unbound books with individual degrees transcribed into them. Consider the title page of one undated book with the Knight of Kadosh rituals written on fifty-eight of sixty-four 12×16.5 cm pages.

Knight of Kadoch
or White & Black Eagle
Inspector of all lodges
Grand Elect
~~24th~~
29th degree
Gd elected Knt of
Kadosh[30]

What is significant is that "24th" is marked out and replaced by "29th." Prior to 1801, the Degree of Kadosh was the twenty-fourth in the Order of the Royal Secret, but the *Circular throughout the Two Hemispheres* lists the Kadosh as the twenty-ninth degree (and it later became the thirtieth). Thus, de Hoyos dates the manuscript to sometime before 1801. It was prepared under the aegis of the Order of the Royal Secret, but soon after its owner

---

29 Jacobs, *Register*, Folger reprint, 85.

30 The text "29th degree Gd elected Knt of Kadosh" is in a different hand from the original

must have transferred allegiance to the new Supreme Council and the ritual was renumbered and renamed in a different hand. Note that it was only necessary to renumber degrees above 22°, Prince Libanus, since the two systems agree through there, and it is only such renumbered degree books that can be confidently dated as being written before 1801. The Supreme Council invited all holders of patents from the Order of the Royal Secret to turn them in and receive a patent from the new body.

Few of these books are extant for probably several reasons. First, there were never very many recipients of these degrees, as witnessed by the few bodies established before 1801 and the paucity of comments in Grand Lodge proceedings. Next, during the American Anti-Masonic Period of 1826–1842, renouncing Masons were encouraged to destroy all of their Masonic paraphernalia. Finally, no less an authority than Albert Pike encouraged the destruction of earlier and unapproved versions of Scottish Rite degrees and recommended that "old and worthless cahiers of degrees, be committed to the flames."[31]

We can now assemble a model of how the Inspectors spread the high degrees. Armed with their patents, they gathered from one to several candidates, summarized the degree ceremonies, and taught the words and grips. After each abbreviated ceremony, the Inspectors dictated the rituals to the new members who transcribed them for their personal use. Some Inspec-

---

title, and beneath it is marked "C. W. Moore" in a third hand. 29° Mss., N.P., N.D., Early S.C., Archives, Supreme Council, 33°, S.J., U.S.A.

31   "It was ordered that all rituals of the 18th, 30th and 33d Degrees in this Jurisdiction, which have not been prepared under the supervision, or with the approval of the Supreme Council be destroyed wherever they can be obtained, and that all members of the Rite be requested to carry this resolution into effect, so far as it may be in their power to do so." *Transactions of the Supreme Council of Sovereign Grand Inspectors General of the Thirty-Third and Last Degree, Ancient and Accepted Scottish Rite, for the Southern Jurisdiction of the United States of America, at Four Several Sessions Holden ... 1861, ... 1862, ... 1865, ... 1866* (New York: Masonic Publishing and Manufacturing Co., 1866), 12.

"I [Pike] have made a thorough examination of the Registers, Letters, and other documents in our Archives,—some of which I found to be worthless, and many of great value. I have taken steps to have all that *are* of any value, bound, that they may be preserved.... I recommend that this course be adopted with all that is worthy of preservation; and that all with is *not*, and especially the old and worthless cahiers of degrees, be committed to the flames." *Transactions of the Supreme Council of Sovereign Grand Inspectors General of the Thirty-Third and Last Degree, Ancient and Accepted Rite, for the Southern Jurisdiction of the United States of America* (New York: Macoy and Sickels, October 1860), 18.

tors, like Abraham Jacobs, encouraged their candidates to apply for warrants from appropriate authority, though obviously few followed through.[32] Unfettered by Grand Lodge regulations, the Inspectors were free to peddle their wares wherever they found willing candidates. Their customers, either lured by sales pitches for exclusive degrees or drawn by the promise of further light in Masonry, eagerly paid for the information. The degrees were conferred as well as possible by the Inspector with perhaps a few brothers assisting. The new candidates were then permitted to transcribe the rituals for their later study and use, perhaps in organizing a high-degree body with a warrant.

The Operation of High-Degree Bodies in America before 1801

According to the first U.S. census in 1790, the total population was 3,893,635, and the five largest cities were New York City (33,131), Philadelphia (28,522), Boston (18,320), Charleston, S.C. (16,359), and Baltimore (13,503). Five high-degree bodies were located in three of the five largest American cities, with Charleston alone accounting for three bodies. Albany (3,498) was the nineteenth largest American city and had one body. The surprise location for a high-degree body is Holmes Hole on the island of Martha's Vineyard, Massachusetts. The 1790 census shows only about 350 people in the town, though the surrounding Dukes County had a population of 3,245, which if it were a city would have ranked it as the twentieth largest. Thus, the bodies of the Order of the Royal Secret were mostly located in the largest urban centers, which should have given them excellent exposure to Masons.[33]

---

32 "July 3d, [1792].... On condition that [Brothers Milton, McCall, Urquhart, Gardner, and Zimmerman] would apply to the Council [of Princes of Jerusalem] in Charleston for instructions requisite, that was not in my power to give them I advanced the above named brethren to the degree of Princes of Jerusalem...." Jacobs, *Register*, Folger reprint, 88.

33 It is important to note that the 1790 population numbers included slaves: U.S., 694,280 out of 3,893,635 or 18%; New York City, 2,369 out of 33,131 or 7%; Philadelphia, 210 out of 28,522 or 1%; Boston, 0 out of 18,320; Charleston, 7,684 out 16,359 or 47%; Baltimore, 1,255 out of 13,503 or 9%; Albany, 572 out of 3,498 or 16%; Martha's Vineyard, 0 out of 350. Freemasons would have come only from the free population. *Heads of Families at the First Census of the United States Taken in the Year 1790: New York* (Washington: Government Printing Office, 1908), 8, 9; *Heads of Families at the First Census of the United States Taken in the Year 1790: Pennsylvania* (Washington: Government Printing Office, 1908), 10; *Heads of Families at the First Census of the United States Taken in the Year 1790: Massachusetts* (Washington: Government Printing Office, 1908), 8,

We have very few extant records of any of these bodies.

- The first *hauts grades* body in the United States was established in New Orleans. *Loge de Parfaits d'Écosse* opened there on April 12, 1764, and worked the "Bordeaux system," but being first did not guarantee longevity.[34] Shortly after France ceded New Orleans to Spain through the 1763 Treaty of Paris, Freemasonry either went underground or died out completely in the city. Only one document remains of *Parfaits d'Écosse*, the minutes of two meetings; we know nothing about its operations or influence.[35] The *hauts grades* did not formally return to New Orleans until 1807.[36]

- The Ineffable Lodge of Perfection of Albany was chartered by Henry Andrew Francken in 1768. Its register is in the archives of the Supreme council, 33°, N.M.J., and records 123 meetings from 1768 to 1774, with no meetings held in 1772. The extant minutes are banal, and do not reflect the promise of the sublime perfection of Craft Masonry.[37]

- The Minute Book of the Lodge of Perfection in Philadelphia, established by Solomon Bush, has been preserved by the Grand Lodge of Pennsylvania and was reprinted in 1915. It records the meetings from the first in 1781 to the abrupt last one in 1789. While the members did write to Frederick the Great, the proceedings are otherwise unexceptional.[38]

- Isaac Da Costa organized the Sublime Grand Lodge of Perfection in

10; *Heads of Families at the First Census of the United States Taken in the Year 1790: South Carolina* (Washington: Government Printing Office, 1908), 9; *Heads of Families at the First Census of the United States Taken in the Year 1790: Maryland* (Washington: Government Printing Office, 1907), 9; Charles E. Banks, *The History of Martha's Vineyard, Dukes County, Massachusetts*, 3 vols. (originally published), vol. 1, 28–30.

34 The evolving "Bordeaux system" is discussed in Alain Bernheim, "Early Freemasonry in Bordeaux," 33–132. Bordeaux produced both Etienne Morin and the Order of the Royal Secret.

35 Herbert H. Stafford, trans., Sharp document No. 64, Sharp-Bordeaux Translations, Archives, Supreme Council, 33°, S.J., U.S.A.

36 Walgren, "An Historical Sketch," 190, 191; Bernheim, "Early Freemasonry in Bordeaux," 90, 100.

37 Bernheim, "Questions About Albany," 139–87.

38 Julius F. Sachse, *Ancient documents relating to the A. and A. Scottish Rite in the Archives of the R.W. Grand Lodge of Free and Accepted Masons of Pennsylvania* (Philadelphia: Grand Lodge of Pennsylvania, 1915).

Charleston in 1783. "On the 13th of June 5796 the Lodge room, re-cords, jewels and furniture of the Ineffable Lodge of Perfect and Sub-lime Masons were consumed by fire, which, added to other causes, suspended the meetings of the of the Sublime Lodge (except some occasional ones for special purposes)...."[39]

- Five years after Da Costa organized the Lodge of Perfection in Charleston, Barend M. Spitzer, Abraham Forst, and Joseph M. Myers opened a Grand Council of Princes of Jerusalem in 1788 in the city. Its jurisdiction over Lodges of Perfection and Councils of Princes of Jerusalem was recognized at least by Abraham Jacobs who instructed his initiates to apply to Charleston for a charter.[40]

- King Solomon's Lodge of Perfection at Holmes Hole (now Tisbury), on the island of Martha's Vineyard, was created by Moses Michael Hays, Deputy Inspector General, in 1791, when he was serving as Grand Master of the Grand Lodge of Massachusetts (Antients). In 1797, the body surrendered its charter to the Grand Lodge and re-ceived a new charter with the same name but solely as a Craft Lodge. King Solomon's Lodge of Perfection surrendered its jewels, charter, and records in 1822, and all were destroyed when the Grand Lodge in Boston burned.[41]

- Henry Wilmans, "Grand Inspector, General," established a Lodge of Perfection in Baltimore, but the only remaining document is the "Constitution and Laws of the Grand Elect, Perfect, and Sublime Masons" signed by seventy-seven members in 1792, four of whom

---

39 "Copy of the Bye-Laws of the Sublime Grand Lodge of South Carolina," *Official Bulletin of the Supreme Council of the 33d Degree for the Southern Jurisdiction of the United States*, 8, no. 2 (September 1888): 733. This document came from the collection identified by Albert Pike as "Documents copied from the Register of Bro∴ Moses Holbrook, 33°." Arturo de Hoyos, Grand Archivist and Grand Historian, Supreme Council, 33°, S.J. has correctly identified the documents as coming from Frederick Dalcho's register on the basis of handwriting comparison.

40 See note 29.

41 *Proceedings Grand Lodge of Massachusetts, 1792–1815*, 112; Baynard, *History of the Su-preme Council*, vol. 1, 98. *Proceedings of the Most Worshipful Grand Lodge of Ancient Free and Accepted Masons of the Commonwealth of Massachusetts for the Years 1815 to 1825 Inclusive* (Boston: Caustin-Claflin, n.d.), pp. 428, 624; Banks, *The History of Martha's Vineyard*, "Annals of Tisbury," vol. 2, 70–82, quoted at http://history.vineyard.net/banks2e.htm. The 1797 charter was granted to "King Solomon's Lodge *of* Perfection" though references after 1816 are to "King Solomon Lodge's *in* Perfection." The earlier name follows the terminology of high-degree bodies while the latter does not.

became Grand Master of Maryland. There is a reference in 1804 to Concordia Lodge No. 13 of Baltimore settling a rent account with "Sublime Lodge" for $150. This seems to indicate that the Lodge of Perfection survived at least twelve years. Nothing else is known about it.[42]

- Charleston became the center of American high-degree Masonry in 1797 when a Sublime Grand Council of Princes of the Royal Secret was opened there under authority from Hyman Isaac Long. This was the last high-degree body to be formed before 1801.

The only Ineffable or Sublime bodies still working in 1801 were probably in Baltimore and definitely in Charleston. While not many of these bodies survived more than a few years, those in Charleston provided the fertile ground from which emerged the Supreme Council of the United States. Most of these high-degree bodies operated near several blue lodges and other bodies. Their mere presence brought the Sublime Degrees to the attention of other Masons in their area, but attention was not enough to insure success or interest.

Bodies of the Royal Secret before 1801 operated without any central direction; there was no state or national leadership. In contrast, there were Grand Lodges in twelve of the original states by 1791, with Delaware forming its Grand Lodge in 1806. Some Grand Lodges permitted their lodges to work the Mark, Royal Arch, and other degrees by virtue of their warrants. By 1801, the York Rite was beginning to take off. There were Grand Chapters of Royal Arch Masons in at least seven states, Royal Arch Masonry was seen as the logical and natural extension of Craft Masonry, and the Knights Templar had a "Grand Encampment in the City of Philadelphia."[43]

A subtle but important distinction between operations of the York Rite and the Order of the Royal Secret may be that the Ineffable and Sublime degrees had an intellectual appeal, while the York Rite degrees—especially the Chapter degrees—had popular elements of boisterous fun. This difference can be seen by the willingness of initiates of the Order of the Royal

---

42 Edward T. Schultz, *History of Freemasonry in Maryland*, 4 vols. (Baltimore: J. H. Mediary, 1884), vol. 1, 327, 333–35.

43 Massachusetts, Rhode Island, Connecticut, New York, Pennsylvania, Maryland, and Virginia had Grand Chapters by 1801. Webb, *Freemason's Monitor*, pp. 288–93; Schultz, *Freemasonry in Maryland*, vol. 1, 313.

Secret to pay for the privilege of just transcribing rituals—certainly a scholarly approach to Masonry of greatest appeal to the literate. Few of the men elevated by Inspectors participated in meetings because there were hardly any bodies for them to attend, but they seemed to be satisfied to read and study the rituals.

We really don't know what happened during pre-1801 American Masonic meetings, but the exposures of the American Anti-Masonic Period (ca. 1826–1842) let us make tenuous inferences about that earlier era. David Bernard's *Light on Masonry* (1829) was the major exposure of the time, going through five increasingly detailed editions between April and December 1829, and Avery Allyn's *A Ritual of Freemasonry* (1831) was its chief competitor.[44] Both books sought to destroy the fraternity by exposing its rituals and portraying it in the worst possible light. Thus, any negative depiction must be considered in light of the authors' ultimate goal. Their descriptions reflected local ritual variants that may or may not have been more widely popular. Arturo de Hoyos points out that such variants are an expected consequence of the York Rite's tradition of mouth-to-ear ritual. The written tradition of the Ineffable and Sublime Degrees allows much less variation.

If Bernard's and Allyn's exposures can be believed, the degrees of a Royal Arch Chapter offered participants rowdy, mischievous initiation pranks. These degrees, especially the Royal Arch, provided a logical conclusion to the Master Mason Degree, while seemingly providing some innocent fun during the ceremonies—a popular combination much more successful than merely transcribing and studying rituals. Their descriptions of the Royal Arch Chapter Degrees, the most widely worked of the high degrees, tell of several opportunities to embarrass and surprise the candidates.[45] Allyn even provided comical drawings of the ceremonies, highlighting the discomfiture of the candidate.[46]

---

44 de Hoyos, "David Bernard's *Light on Masonry*," 71.

45 During the reception of a Mark Master Mason, the candidate was supposedly made to believe that he will be "marked" on his chest with a blow from a chisel and mallet. "This is supposed to be the most interesting part of the degree; and is made so, by the pains taken to frighten the candidate. If the floor, bowl, chisel, and mallet are bespattered with blood, or something which resembles it, and the 'executioner' acts his part well, the candidate must necessarily feel very uneasy during the ceremony:—This generally gives great satisfaction to the brotherhood, and is often the subject of their secret discourse for weeks afterwards." David Bernard, *Light on Masonry*, 1st ed., 3rd state (Utica, N.Y.: William Williams, 1829), 98.

46 Avery Allyn, *A Ritual of Freemasonry* (Boston: John Marsh, 1831), plates 5 (Master

In contrast with the Chapter degrees, their descriptions of "Eleven Ineffable Degrees," are austere and solemn, almost like historical plays.[47] Bernard had advanced to the 6°, Intimate Secretary, and Allyn had received none of the Ineffable and Sublime Degrees, so they had little firsthand evidence of what went on in a Lodge of Perfection.[48] However, neither author would have missed an opportunity to emphasize any negative aspect, even rumored. The simplicity of their descriptions supports the idea that the ceremonies were indeed serious without amusing features for observers. The Ineffable and Sublime Degrees may not have spread rapidly because they lacked the humorous initiation possibilities of the Royal Arch Chapter Degrees. We will likely never know.

Conclusion

The Supreme Council of the United States appeared at a time when American Masons were becoming aware there was Masonic knowledge beyond the Craft Lodge. This awareness was spread by itinerant lecturers, books, and bodies of the Order of the Royal Secret. The Order, with its largely uncontrolled Inspectors, lacked the organizational infrastructure to survive. Its daughter, the Ancient and Accepted Scottish Rite, had the characteristics that guarantee greatness. In 200 years, it has grown to become the largest and most widespread branch of the Masonic fraternity. Today, it has even greater possibilities of greatness than in 1801.

Acknowledgments

I am indebted to two of my fellow Mackey Scholars who have generously given me invaluable assistance. Ill. Bro. Arturo de Hoyos, 33°, Grand Archivist and Grand Historian, Supreme Council, 33°, S.J., provided me with support, inspiration, and guidance through many conversations about the Order of the Royal Secret. Ill. Bro. Alain Bernheim, 33°, refined my references and suggested important enhancements to the text.

Mason), 7 (Mark Master), 9 (Past Master), 11 (Most Excellent Master), and 15 (Royal Arch).

47 Bernard, *Light on Masonry*, 87–144, 183–211. Avery Allyn, *A Ritual of Freemasonry*, pp. 87–164, 278–95. Descriptions of other lesser-known degrees are also simple and austere.

48 Bernard apparently was not satisfied with attaining only the 6°, so he exaggerated his Masonic standing in later years and described himself as a "Grand Elect Perfect and Sublime Mason." (de Hoyos, "David Bernard's *Light on Masonry*," 24–25.)

First Published: In French, "L'Ordre du Royal Secred en Amérique avant 1801," trans. Yves Michaud, *Le Rite Écossais Ancient Accepté: Mise en perspective historirque deux siècles après* (Paris: 2004), 5–18; in English, *The Plumbline,* vol. 16, no. 2 (Summer 2009), and no. 3 (Fall 2009)

Henry Andrew Francken &
His Masonic Manuscripts

Welcome to the Report on the Special Committee on the Francken Documents. I am Brent Morris, managing editor of *The Scottish Rite Journal*. Before I begin our report, I would like to thank

- Jean-Loup Graton of the Bibliotheque Nationale for supporting and hosting the conference.

- Professor Paul Rich, the obsessive maniac who brought this conference to fruition in less than twelve months (and I describe him thus because only an obsessive maniac could do what he accomplished).

- Pierre Moliere of the Grand Orient Library who has handled so many arrangements, especially those of the Francken Manuscript study group. Pierre Moliere is also very generous. He told our committee that he had chilled a case of Dom Perignon champagne for our refreshments, but when he found out that food and drink could not be present in the same room with some of the manuscripts, he sent the champagne back to the Grand Orient supply room. Maybe next time!

I have been asked to chair this session because I am an amateur—in the basic sense of the word, I am a lover of the subject. For at least 25 years, I have been studying and tracking the manuscripts prepared by Henry Andrew Francken. It has been a dream of mine that all known copies of Francken's manuscripts could be brought together to be studied. Pierre Moliere, Librarian of the Grand Orient de France, has taken this dream a step farther by arranging with the Bibliothèque National de France to borrow the "Santo Domingo Manuscript" (Baylot FM⁴ 15). The Santo Domingo Manuscript is a French collection of rituals that is a near if not direct relative of Francken's manuscripts.

It is somewhat frightening to be thrust into this position. My formal background is in theoretical mathematics and computer algorithms, little connected to reality, and certainly nothing as real as paper, watermarks, ink, handwriting, and so on. Nonetheless, I volunteered and so here we are. (Perhaps more correctly, Paul Rich said to me, "Brent, you've been talking about the Francken Manuscripts for years. Here's your chance to do something other than talk. Put up or shut up!")

I'll begin by giving a brief overview of Francken and what was known about his manuscripts before the World Conference on Fraternalism, Freemasonry, and History. Then we'll talk about our study procedure and what we accomplished.

The largest and most widely dispersed system of high-degree Masonry is the Ancient and Accepted Scottish Rite of thirty-three degrees. It originated in 1801 in Charleston, South Carolina, based upon the Order of the Royal Secret of twenty-five degrees (often called the Rite of Perfection).[1] Unlike some high-degree systems, the Ancient and Accepted Rite has a definite date of birth and well-known founders. Its parent, however, has a more shadowy genealogy. The Order of the Royal Secret seems to have appeared with Estienne Morin when he arrived in Santo Domingo in 1763, but its rituals and ceremonies are well known.

Soon after his arrival, Morin set about establishing high-degree bodies and himself as the high-degree authority of the western hemisphere (or at least the Caribbean). Sometime between 1763 and 1767, Morin appointed Henry Andrew Francken, a naturalized British citizen and resident of Jamaica, "Deputy Inspector General of all the Superior Degrees of Free and Accepted Masons in the West Indies."[2] It was Francken who first brought the Order to the British colonies of North America and also appointed other Deputy Inspectors who propagated the rite. He thus prepared the way for the birth of the Scottish Rite.

At least as important as spreading the Royal Secret, Francken preserved its rituals by translating them from French into English and making at least four copies. The Scottish Rite thus has, in addition to a definite birthday and well-known founders, detailed rituals from its origins. There have been many subsequent changes and alterations to the rituals of the Scottish Rite by various Supreme Councils, but they all can be measured against those of

---

1   The system has most often been called the "Rite of Perfection." Alain Bernheim clearly showed that its proper name is "Order of the Royal Secret."

2   A. R. Hewitt, "Another Francken Manuscript Rediscovered," *Ars Quatuor Coronatorum* 89 (1976): 208.

the Order of the Royal Secret and the foundational work of Henry Andrew Francken.

Much more is known about the life of Francken than that of Morin. Francken was born in 1820 and arrived in Jamaica in February 1857. Just over a year later, on March 2, 1758, he became a naturalized British citizen. A 1762 petition to the Vice-Admiralty Court shows Francken had been an appraiser, a marshal, and sergeant-at-mace in the court.[3] In 1763, Estienne Morin passed through Jamaica on his way to Santo Domingo and had his first opportunity to meet Francken.[4] Francken's wife, Elizabeth, died in 1764, and in 1765, he was appointed an interpreter for Dutch and English for the Vice-Admiralty Court. From these linguistic skills, we can infer he was born in Holland[5] or a perhaps a Dutch colony. As a professional translator, it's easy to see how he came to translate and transcribe the rituals of the Order of the Royal Secret.

After being appointed court interpreter in 1765 and with the permission of Lt.-Gov. Moore, Francken traveled to Albany, New York, and New York City, both with Dutch-speaking populations. He married Johanna Low of Newark, New Jersey,[6] and on December 8, 1765, they became the godparents of Johanna Low, daughter of Nicholas and Sarah Low (Johanna's sister).[7] In 1768, he formed Ineffable Lodge of Perfection at Albany, New York, and it opened January 11. The records of the Ineffable Lodge of Perfection indicate that it ceased activity on December 5, 1774.[8] Also in 1768, he made Moses Michael Hays a Deputy Inspector and Knight Kadosh with the power to constitute Grand Chapters of Knights of the Sun and of Kadosh in the West Indies and North America.[9]

Francken was one of two deputies specifically named a founding member of a grand chapter of Princes of the Royal Secret by Stephen Morin in Kings-

---

3 Richardson Wright, "Freemasonry on the Island of Jamaica," *Transactions of the American Lodge of Research* 3, no. 1 (1938–39): 126–61.

4 A[lain] B[ernheim], "Francken, Henry Andrew," http://www.vrijmetselaarsgilde.eu/ Maconnieke%20Encyclopedie/Franc-M/fra-f-02.htm#fransF-14.

5 Wright, "Jamaica," 159.

6 Bernheim, "Francken."

7 According to the records of the Dutch Reformed Church, NYC, accessed May 20, 2015, http://www.wikitree.com/wiki/Francken-12.

8 "Scottish Rite," en.wikipedia.org accessed May 24, 2015.

9 Bernheim, "Francken."

ton, April 30, 1770.[10] In 1771, four to eight years after meeting Morin, he produced his earliest known dated book of constitutions and rituals for the 15°–25°. This manuscript was rediscovered in 1976 and is now in the possession of the Supreme Council for England and Wales. Its spine was marked "Manuscript Ritual of the late Col. Graham of Claverhouse," and a note says the manuscript once belonged to a Captain Graham of Drynie(?) and Claverhouse who, after a period in the West Indies, returned to Scotland.[11] It suffered the indignity of the 25° being cut out shortly after arriving in the Supreme Council, and it suffered near destruction when submerged in water for over six months when the bank vault in which it was stored flooded.

Francken's second wife, Johanna, died in 1777, and in 1782, he was appointed Master of the Revels. This was a largely ceremonial post that "gave him authority over all theatrical performances and the balls and entertainments given by the governor." It also had an annual stipend of 100 guineas.[12] As late as 1783, he was still the official Dutch interpreter for the island,[13] and in that year, he was appointed a customs inspector.[14]

Of greater Masonic interest in 1783, Francken prepared another manuscript with rituals 4°–25° for Deputy Inspector David Small.[15] It was forgotten until 1855 when according to a note in the London *Freemasons' Magazine*, it came into the possession of an unnamed English Brother. It was purchased the next year by Enoch Terry Carson of Ohio, a prominent American Mason, and subsequently purchased by Samuel Crocker Lawrence of Massachusetts, upon whose death in 1911, it went his library to the Grand Lodge of Massachusetts. This version was rediscovered in 1935 in the archives of the Grand Lodge of Massachusetts and given to the Supreme Council, 33°, NMJ.[16]

Francken prepared at least two other ritual manuscripts, but they do not contain details to let us date them. A third manuscript in Francken's hand with the rituals 4°–25° was found in the archives of the Provincial Grand

---

10 Bernheim, "Francken."
11 Hewitt, "Another Francken Manuscript," 208, 209.
12 Wright, "Jamaica," 160.
13 Wright, "Jamaica," 159.
14 Bernheim, "Francken."
15 Hewitt, "Another Francken Manuscript," 208.
16 Hewitt, "Another Francken Manuscript," 208.

Lodge of Lancashire in Liverpool around 1984 and is on loan to the UGLE library. "On the verso of the first unnumbered folio is the inscription, 'Received from John Caird, Edinburgh—Jas. Caird, Liverpool 30th August 1815'. This is surrounded by a lengthy note by one M. A. Gage recording that on the same date it was given to him by Jas. Caird…. He removed to Liverpool in 1811…. Reference to 1786 in the text provides evidence of an 'earliest possible date.'"[17]

A fourth undated manuscript by Francken with rituals 4°–24° was given by H. J. Whymper to the District Grand Lodge of the Punjab. It is now in the possession of Naveed Ahmed of Lahore, Pakistan. Little has been published about this version. The UGLE Library microfilmed it decades ago and catalogued it as "Rite of Twenty-Five Degrees" but without an author. Thus, it remained camouflaged from researchers using the search term "Francken," but it was rediscovered about 2010.

In 1790, Francken lost his post as customs inspector and requested financial aid from the government, having lost his job, been twice widowed, and having house twice destroyed by hurricanes. He was twice given £100.[18] In 1793, he was again appointed Master of the Revels, and in 1794, he was appointed an assistant judge of the Court of Common Please for Port Royal and prepared his will. His will contained these instructions: "It is my positive will that my funeral expenses shall not exceed the sum of £20 currency; my coffin to be made of plain deal without any lining on the inside and only blackened outside; to be put into my Coffin in the Cloaths I shall die in and my body not to be washed, and to be carried to the grave without being carried in the Church."[19]

Henry Andrew Francken died May 20, 1795, survived by his son Parker Bennett Francken of St. Kitts, his daughter, Mary Long Goutris, and his granddaughter, Elizabeth Goutris. He was buried May 24 in Kingston Parish Churchyard.[20]

This then is a brief summary of what we knew about Henry Andrew Francken and his manuscripts. What did we hope to discover over the two days we

17 John M. Hamill, "A Third *Francken MS* of the Rite of Perfection," *Ars Quatuor Coronatorum* 97 (1984): 200.

18 Bernheim, "Francken."

19 Wright, "Jamaica," 161.

20 Wright, "Jamaica," 161.

had to study these documents? Perhaps little or perhaps much—it depend-
ed on the gods of research. I think I can say that we made progress without
being overly effusive.

Let me give you an example of what we looked for when examining the
manuscripts. In 1997, while studying the 1783 manuscript at the Library of
the Supreme Council, Northern Masonic Jurisdiction, USA, I discovered
that several of the pages facing the start of a degree show unusual ghost
images from extra pages that were inserted between the pages. These extra
inserted pages had drawings of tracing boards and remained undisturbed
between the pages long enough for their images to transfer onto the facing
page. Alain Marchiset, an antique book dealer who joined in our studies,
estimates that it would take at least three to six months for the ink from the
tracing boards to burn into the facing pages. In some cases, the acid in the
paper of the extra pages has caused large rectangular stains. There are at
least nine such ghost images of tracing boards, and there may be more, but
some technology other than the naked eye and ordinary light are required.
As it turned out no ghost images were found in any other version. They are
unique to the 1783 Francken.

While I hoped we would find something as dramatic as ghost images, I decided we would be satisfied if we could leave with intelligent questions. It
was probably hoping for too much to think we could leave this conference
with exciting new discoveries. But sometimes exciting questions are almost
as good. Keep in mind that not all attendees agreed with every finding or
not as strongly as everyone else. Thus, what I will present are consensus
results.

1. The 1771 Francken is in a different hand from the other manuscripts.
   It is also not signed by Henry Andrew Francken. Most thought it was
   created by a different writer, but there was a strong dissent that it may
   indeed have been written by Francken but with altered writing, perhaps due to stress or trauma. If it is by a different hand, then it is like
   the "Jamaica Manuscript," a copy of a Francken by a different writer.
   (The Jamaica Manuscript is a contemporary ritual manuscript that
   was reprinted earlier this year by the Scottish Rite Research Society
   and is available on their page.)

2. The 1783, West Lancashire, and Ahmed manuscripts are the same size
   with the same number of pages. The 1783 and Ahmed manuscripts

have similar bindings. England & Wales was dis-bound as part of the conservation work after it was submerged, but Susan Snell will compare the preserved binding with that of West Lancashire.

3. The watermark on the paper of the Ahmed and West Lancashire manuscripts bear "G R" for "Georgius Rex." Susan Snell believes the watermark and common size and binding indicate these being common United Kingdom record books for use by courts and civil servants. Naveed Ahmed believes the paper and blank books were used by George III for his library. Susan will check the British and Jamaican government libraries for similar books with government records from the period.

4. There is at least one missing intermediate text. The Santo Domingo Manuscript is written in French. As one example, the ritual for the Knight of the Sun is written in the center of the page with dense additions in both margins. The Francken manuscripts have these two pieces of writing smoothly integrated together. There are many small variations in language in the Francken manuscripts that lead Alain Marchiset to conclude that Francken translated each copy from a French mother document that represents the merged texts of the Santo Domingo.

5. In the 22°, Prince of Libanus, each manuscript has a paragraph that begins "This celebrated nation…." However, the Ahmed manuscript, one of the oldest, was written without the word "celebrated," which was inserted later. This leads us to conclude it is not the English mother for the others, but reinforces out belief there is a French mother.

6. The United States had several lodges of perfection in east coast port cities: Charleston, South Carolina; Philadelphia, Pennsylvania; Newport, Rhode Island; Albany, New York; and others, yet none of them are known to have a copy of the Francken manuscript. It appears that Francken prepared and most likely sold these manuscripts to British Officers, as they all made their way back to Britain with most coming through Scotland; they were not given to the Lodges of Perfection. We know that Francken was in difficult financial straits when he petitioned the Jamaican government for relief in 1790. Perhaps, he supplemented his income with his skills as a professional scrivener, using blank books from the Jamaican court's supply cabinet, and selling the fruits of his labors to British officers. This would explain the absence,

thus far, in the archives of American Lodges of Perfection and the apparent travels to Great Britain via army officers.

7. All agreed there are most likely other undiscovered copies made by Francken or copies of Francken made by other writers in archives around the world. To support this contention, Paul Ninin wrote to me yesterday afternoon—24 hours ago—to say there are two Francken manuscripts in The Hague in the possession of the Latomia Foundation and the Supreme Council for the Netherlands.[21] Of course, we now must compare the handwriting, paper, binding, and text. There will indeed be more to report at the next World Conference!

First published: *Ritual, Secrecy, and Civil Society* (spring 2016)

----

21 Subsequent research indicates the Latomia images are those of the manuscript from the Supreme Council for England and Wales.

"Why Thirty-Three?"
—A Revisit

Co-authored with Arturo de Hoyos

The lead article in Heredom *volume 1, entitled "Why Thirty-three?", was a launching point for the new Scottish Rite Research Society, presenting several enigmas about the Rite which we hoped might be answered in future volumes. Now, twenty-five years later, we revisit those questions with some updated information. Several mysteries have been solved; others still remain to be explored and answered. In this revisited version, we have modified and updated the original article, and invite our readers to continue researching until all these mysteries have been resolved.*

In 1797, four years before the establishment of the Mother Supreme Council, Thomas Smith Webb published his landmark book, *Freemason's Monitor or Illustrations of Masonry*. His book was an abbreviation of William Preston's 1772 *Illustrations of Masonry*, arranged to suit the American Masonic environment. Webb's work formed the foundation for what is considered "standard" American Masonic ritual. His work with the ritual was expanded upon by Jeremy Ladd Cross, John Barney, and other itinerant Masonic lecturers of the eighteenth century.

In the first edition of the *Freemason's Monitor* (1797), there was a section "containing an account of the Ineffable Degrees of Masonry," those conferred in Lodges of Perfection. These bodies were established under Stephen Morin's "Order of the Royal Secret" (wrongly called the "Rite of Perfection" until corrected by Alain Bernheim). Webb's description of the Degree of Perfection, or Grand, Elect, Perfect, and Sublime Mason explains that "[t]he jewels appertaining to this degree [include] ... a gold ring with this motto, 'Virtue unites what Death cannot part.'" A quick check of some of the oldest manuscript rituals in the Archives of the Mother Supreme Council, including the *Jamaican Francken Manuscript,* one of the oldest English versions of what would become that Scottish Rite degree, shows that

47

a gold ring with this motto has always been given to those receiving the Degree of Perfection. Several questions immediately present themselves.

1. How long has a gold ring been associated with the 14°?

It appears that the golden ring has always been a part of the 14° ritual of the Supreme Council, 33°. Even the pre-1801 rituals of Grand Commander John Mitchell's (copied by James Rouse in 1822) include the ring, as does the 1803 manuscript used by Albert Mackey to communicate the Scottish Rite degrees to Albert Pike in 1853. Every other copy we examined, in both the Southern and Northern Masonic Jurisdictions, also includes the golden ring.

It's important to recall that the Scottish Rite was not the first Masonic order to have this degree. Rather, we inherited it from an earlier twenty-five-degree system known as the Order of the Royal Secret. Under that system, which was created by 1762 by Stephen Morin, the 14° retained its position as the Perfection degree. Even then, the degree included the golden ring. Looking back even further, we find the earliest reference in a degree known as the Perfect English Master Degree, which dates to 1740 (*Kloss Manuscript XXV*). In that degree, we find language remarkably similar to that which occurred in later rituals of the 14°:

> Receive also this ring as a sign of the covenant you have contracted with virtue and the virtuous ... Promise that it will leave your finger only at your death and that you will only leave it to your virtuous wife, your eldest son or to him who has merited your friendship.

And later, in the catechism:

Q. What did you contract upon receiving this Degree?

A. A double alliance with virtue and the virtuous.

Q. What is its mark?

A. This golden ring, which signifies purity.

This "double alliance" produced the 14° motto known today, "Virtus junxit mors non separabit" (which is inscribed inside the ring). The Perfect English Master also appeared as the 13° in the collection printed in the *Conversations Allegoriques* (1763). Hence, the golden ring of the Perfect English Master is clearly a precursor of the 14° of that in the Order of the Royal Secret, and later of the Scottish Rite ring.

Contemporary 14° and 33° rings. Museum. Supreme Council, 33°, SJ USA.

2. Where is the oldest example of a 14° ring?

The evidence just cited shows that 14° rings have been used for at least 217 years in the Scottish Rite in the United States alone, and for at least 278 years in Europe if we include the Perfect English Master. Since 14° rings have been given out for two centuries, then there must be an oldest ring lurking in some Masonic museum. But, where is that oldest one? Unfortunately, we just don't know yet. We can surmise, however, that the oldest 14° rings won't include the Latin motto, "Virtus junxit mors non separabit." Henry Andrew Francken's early rituals merely state that the inscription is "Virtue unites, what death cannot separate," and the Latin motto came later. Also, some Scottish Rite rituals and monitors of the mid-1800s use the motto "Mors non disjungat, quid virtus conjunxit."

3. When did a distinctive ring become associated with the 33° and where is the oldest example of a 33° ring?

The 33° ring is the only other official ring of the Scottish Rite, and it's mentioned in oldest copy of the 33° known to exists: Frederick Dalcho's manuscript copy (ca. 1801–1802). The language used in its reception suggests that it was modeled after that of the 14° ring.

> He then places upon the wedding finger of his left hand, a plain gold ring ... on the inside of which is engraved the following Motto viz. "Deus Meumque Jus"—and the name of the owner—and says to him, "With this ring I wed you to the order, your Country, & your God, & receive you & acknowledge you as a Sovereign Grand Inspector General. Let it put you in remembrance of the

solemn obligations you have taken to the order. Swear to me, never to part with it, but when near your death, and then to give it to your wife—oldest son daughter or dearest friend as a sacred deposit— under a solemn promise to part with it in the like manner."

4. Where was the 33° "jewel" first described and when did it come into general use?

Another distinctive item of regalia as- sociated with the Scottish Rite is the "Grand Decoration of the Order," some- times mistakenly called the jewel of the Thirty-third Degree (the double-headed eagle is actually the jewel of the degree). The Grand Decoration of the Order is not described in any of the early surviv- ing manuscripts of the Supreme Council of Charleston. Notably, it is lacking from Dalcho's ca. 1801–1802 copy of the *Con- stitution, Statutes, Regulations* (aka *Grand Constitutions of 1786*), and is curiously mentioned for the first time some thirty years later. We first find the Grand Dec- oration mentioned in a Latin version of the *Constitutions of 1786* transcribed in the "Golden Book" of Marie Anthonio Nicholo Alexandro de Jachim de San- ta Rosa de Roume, Marquis de Sainte Rose, Comte de Saint Laurent, who claimed to be the Grand Commander of a Supreme Council for New Spain, Mex-

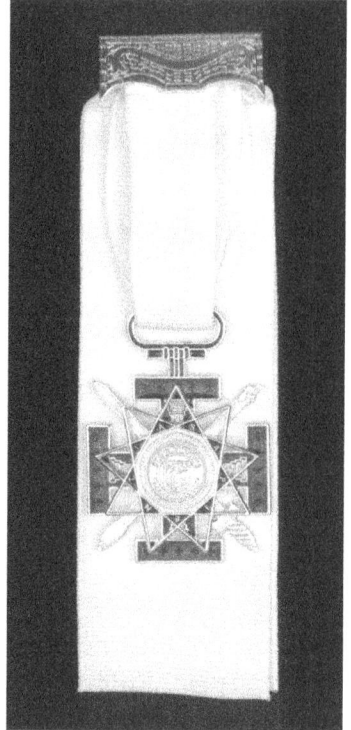

Contemporary 33° jewel. Museum. Supreme Council, 33°, SJ USA.

ico, Terra Firma, South America, the Canary Islands, etc. Saint Laurent, as he is commonly known today, appears to have been appointed Grand Commander of this mysterious body in 1816 by the Count de Grasse Tilly. The Grand Decoration is first described in Article 2 of an Appendix to the *Grand Constitutions of 1786* (Golden Book, folio 36 verso). The use of the Grand Decoration does not seem to have become common until the Grand Commandership of Albert Pike.

5. What is the history of caps in the Scottish Rite?

Anyone attending a Scottish Rite meeting for this first time, especially in the Southern Jurisdiction, is quickly struck by the distinctive caps worn by our members indicating their degree. While their use is now the norm, caps are a fairly recent addition to the Rite's regalia.

Although ritual manuscripts do not describe a particular cap, we know from photographs that some members, perhaps during the mid-1880s, occasionally wore a black cap without insignia. Caps also appear to have been used in a few degrees of the "Cerneau" Scottish Rite. They are seen in crude engravings in Jonathan Blanchard's exposé, *Scotch Rite Masonry Illustrated* (1887).

Two of the earliest known photographs of Scottish Rite degree caps.
William Cleburn, 33°, IGH (left), 1911 *Transactions.*
Marshall Atkinson Weir, 33°, IGH (right), 1919 *Transactions.*

Scottish Rite caps were certainly worn during the early 1900s, because in 1909, it was resolved "That from and after this session of the Supreme Council every Sov∴ Grand∴ Inspector-General shall wear the cap of his rank while attending the sessions of this Supreme Council" (1909 *Transactions*, 186). From the casual way in which they are mentioned here they seem to have been common knowledge. Just two years later, in the 1911 *Transactions*, we find an obituary with a photograph of William Cleburn,

33° IGH, wearing a black cap with a double-headed eagle on the front, which was likely an older photo in which he wore his 32° cap. And, just a few years later, in the 1918 *Transactions*, is a photo of Marshall Atkinson Weir, 33°, IGH, wearing a white cap with the patriarchal cross. These photos suggest that the caps were of the same style as those officially adopted at the Supreme Council's session of 1927, when they became official. Their depiction in the 1927 *Transactions* reveals that they are of the style worn today.

6. Where did Thomas Smith Webb get the information on the Ineffable Degrees for his 1797 *Freemason's Monitor*?

While we do not know where Webb received his information about the Ineffable Degrees, the very fact that the degrees are mentioned gives us insight to the precursors of the Scottish Rite. Were the Ineffable Degrees so popular that the descriptions in his *Monitor* were eagerly welcomed, or did Webb include the information to tease his readers and increase his sales?

The Lodge of Perfection, erected by Henry Andrew Francken in Albany in 1767, ceased to operate in 1774. In fact, most American Masons were unfamiliar with the Ineffable Degrees, even as late as 1830, in the middle of the Morgan episode, when the rituals were exposed in print. One Mason even wrote that the degrees "were never heard of, even by name, in the history of Masonry."

Webb was a more than friend of Masonry. He was the creator of the York Rite and served as Grand Master of the Grand Lodge of Rhode Island in 1813–1814. His descriptions of the Ineffable Degrees were at worst intended to draw greater sales, but he may have simply wanted to provide as much information as he could about Masonry as he knew it. But, where did he get his information? According to Herbert T. Leyland, Webb's biographer:

> It is not known where Webb obtained the material of these eleven degrees. Although a Lodge of Perfection had been established in Albany in 1767, it was dormant during the years Webb lived in that city, and it seems certain that he was not made a member of the Lodge. He may have received the monitorial data from some Albany Mason who had been a member of the Lodge and had possession of the rituals, or Webb may have gathered the data on one of his visits to Boston or Philadelphia.

7. What does Bérage's *Les Plus Secrets Mystères* (1766) tell us about the evolution of Scottish Rite degrees?

Not all authors are as benign as Webb. Exposés of Masonic rituals have been popular books for centuries, and they sometimes give the only insight we have into an aspect of the evolution of Masonic rituals and ceremonies. Erasme Pincemaille's *Conversations Allégoriques, Organisées par la Sagesse* [*Allegorical Conversations Arranged by Wisdom*] (1763) was the first printed description of rituals that evolved into Scottish Rite degrees. Containing the catechisms of thirteen degrees, it was originally intended as an *aide-mémoire* for Masons, and was not an exposé. This was followed by Monsieur Bérage, *Les Plus Secrets Mystères des Hauts Grades de la Maçonnerie Dévoilés* [The Most Secret Mysteries of the High Grades of Masonry Unveiled] (1766). This exposé was wildly successful with the public, not only because it unveiled the "most secret mysteries" but also because it was a book prohibited by the French government. Its study provides a similar understanding of some Scottish Rite rituals as *Three Distinct Knocks* (1760) and *Jachin and Boaz* (1762) provides for Craft ritual.

8. What is the source of the degrees in Bernard's anti-Masonic exposé, *Light on Masonry*?

As noted above, the Lodge of Perfection, erected by Henry Andrew Francken in 1767 demised in 1774. It was revived in 1820 by Giles Fonda Yates, who became an officer of the Supreme Council at Charleston (S.J.) and who would later transfer his membership and become Grand Commander of the N.M.J. in 1851. His friend and relative by marriage, the Rev. Nathan N. Whiting, was second-in-command in Schenectady's Delta Lodge of Perfection and the Albany Consistory of Sublime Princes of the Royal Secret. During the Morgan affair Whiting betrayed Masonry, and deceived Yates when he borrowed and loaned his ritual manuscripts to the Rev. David Bernard, who had himself once belonged to Delta Lodge of Perfection, but was only a 6°, Intimate Secretary. The rituals exposed in *Light on Masonry* were not only those of the Lodge of Perfection, and Council of Princes of Jerusalem, but also most of the "sublime degrees" (Scottish Rite rituals) of the Supreme Council at Charleston, which had been delivered to Yates in 1825 by John Barker, an agent of that Council. It also included several "detached degrees"—supposedly conferred in France and in America as honorary degrees—which were translated from the *Recueil Précieux de la Maçonnerie*

Adonhiramite (Paris, 1786). The entire story of this affair is told in detail by Arturo de Hoyos in *Light on Masonry: The History and Rituals of America's Most Important Masonic Exposé* (2008).

9. When and where did Scottish Rite reunions originate?

The notion of a Scottish Rite reunion is suggested by the Thirty-second Degree ritual, which includes a type of tracing board known as the symbolic camp; in one place, it brings together all the degrees of the Scottish Rite under a tent. According to early rituals of this Degree, one of the passwords meant "reunited to accomplish," while the symbolic camp represented a "reunion of Masons of all degrees." Hence, we use the word "reunion" to refer to a gathering of Scottish Rite Masons assembled to confer the Degrees.

The Scottish Rite in America has developed a distinct method of conferring the degrees in the periodic reunions of our Valleys. The *Constitutions of 1762* require the deliberate (and obviously symbolic) delay of eighty-one months between 1° and 25°. Thus, the rapid conferral of degrees at a reunion flies in face of at least symbolic delays if not actual practice of the Scottish Rite. Freemasonry as a society venerates tradition, even in the face of common sense. It is thus hard to imagine that such a radical concept as a reunion was easily adopted. It is not yet known where the first reunion occurred.

10. How quickly accepted was the idea of a Reunion?

Although we cannot say how quickly the idea of reunions were embraced, it appears that conferring the degrees on multiple people at once was almost a norm. Indeed, references to the conferrals suggest that two features commonly associate with the Scottish Rite degrees were common even in the 1800s: (1) conferring the degrees on more than one person at a time, and (2) somewhat of a rapid advancement. Albert Pike was not a fan of either practice. Rather, he preferred that the degrees be conferred slowly, only after the initiate had learned the meaning, symbolism, and philosophy of each degree.

11. When and where did elaborate staging come to be used for Scottish Rite degrees?

Another distinctive feature of American Scottish Rite degrees is their elaborate staging and costuming—elaborate beyond the dreams of our founders. Professor C. Lance Brockman of the University of Minnesota, Twin Cities, has made a study of stage sets belonging to various Scottish Rite Valleys. In many cases, our Valleys have unwittingly preserved wonderful examples of theatrical art previously thought lost.

Wendy Rae Waszut-Barrett determined that "Staged degree work became popular during the 1860s in Cincinnati, Ohio." She views "the incorporation of theatrical scenery as a phenomenon fueled by direct competition for membership throughout the Northern Masonic Jurisdiction." "The introduction of theatrical backdrops for Scottish Rite degree work was facilitated by the Northern Masonic Jurisdiction's unique governing statutes over the presentation of Scottish Rite degree work as well as their legislative independence from Albert Pike." Pike opposed the theatrical presentation of degrees. Lost to modern Scottish Rite tradition, though they may have been enjoyed by our earlier Brethren.

12. Is there any evidence that the festivals mentioned in the *Constitutions of 1762* were ever celebrated?

The *Constitutions of 1762* require Princes of Jerusalem to celebrate two feast days: November 20, when their ancestors made their entry into Jerusalem and February 23, to celebrate the rebuilding of the Temple. Knights of the East celebrate the rebuilding of the Temple and the equinoxes, March 22 and September 22. The Grand Elect Perfect Masons celebrate the dedication of the first Temple on July 5. The *Constitutions of 1786* require two festivals: "one on the first of October when our property was sequestrated and given to the Knights of Malta, and the other on the 27th of December, St. John the Evangelist's day." Were they celebrated? That's a question that could only be answered by checking the minutes of early Masonic bodies.

13. What is the history of Scottish Rite Maundy Thursday observance?

When did it come to replace the formerly mandated festivals? Did this change first occur in Europe or in America?

The Maundy Thursday ceremony of our Chapters of Rose Croix is the most widely celebrated of Scottish Rite, and was mandated by the Statutes and Regulations of the Sovereign Chapter Rose Croix of France, in 1786. The ceremony doesn't appear to have replaced the former feasts. Albert Pike first discussed how the Masonic Banquets were to be performed, by translating a part of Clavel's *Histoire pittoresque de la franc-maçonnerie* (1843) as part of his "Materials for the History of Freemasonry in France" (1876). He followed up with an article on "Feast Days of the Ancient and Accepted Scottish Rite" in 1884.

14. When was the first Maundy Thursday celebration held in the United States?

Unfortunately, we just don't yet have the records to answer this question.

15. When was the "Sign of the Good Shepherd" adopted in the Southern Jurisdiction as the "Scottish Rite attitude of prayer?"

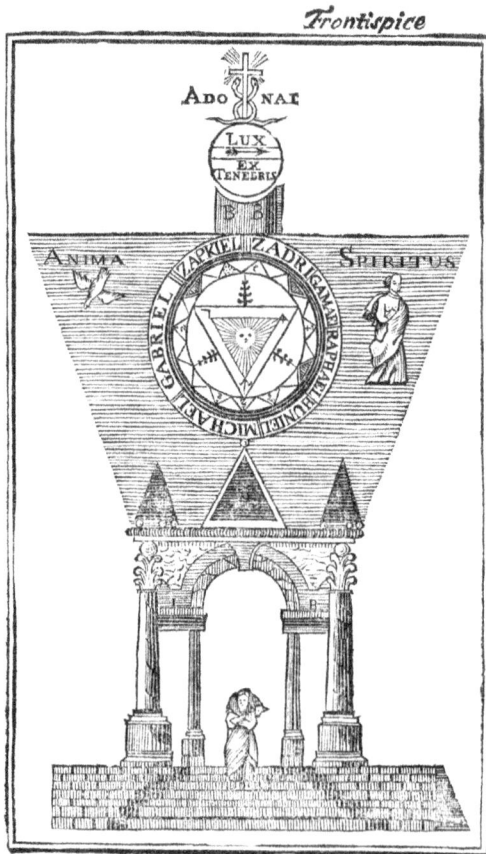

M. de Bérage, *Les Plus Secrets Mystères des Hauts Grades de la Franc Maçonnerie Dévoilés* (1766), frontispiece.

Closely associated with the Rose Croix Degree in the Southern Jurisdiction is the "Sign of the Good Shepherd," or the Scottish Rite attitude of prayer. The sign is first described in the "Chevalier de l'Aigle, du Pélican, de Rose-Croix de Saint André ou le Parfait Maçon" [Knight of the Eagle, or Pelican, of Rose Croix of Saint Andrew or the Perfect Mason] (Kloss Ms. XXVII-40), which is sometimes called the Strasburg Rose Croix ritual of 1760, being the oldest known Rose Croix ritual. After describing the posture, the ritual states, "The Token is called the Sign of the Good Shepherd." The frontispiece of *Les Plus Secrets Mystères* (1766) shows a temple with a robed shepherd on the steps holding a lamb in the Sign of the Good Shepherd. This could be the first time this sign was depicted. At what point it became the attitude of prayer remains a mystery, but it's easy to see how a reverent folding of the arms for prayer gave way to the Sign of the Good Shepherd.

16. What is the history of the Feast of Tishri?

In recent years, the Feast of Tishri has become a popular celebration in the Southern Jurisdiction, and it, like Maundy Thursday, is not mentioned in our founding documents, certainly not as an obligation of Perfect Elus. The Feast of Tishri is mentioned in an article on "Feast Days of the Ancient and Accepted Scottish Rite" in 1884.

17. When were distinctive crosses adopted to indicate a Scottish Rite Mason's degree?

Beginning with the ritual of 1861, Rose Croix members were informed that they were entitled to use a triangle, surmounted by a cross before their signature. The other degrees followed suit. The Patriarchal Cross was first introduced in Albert Pike's 1868 revision of the 33° ritual, which stated that the member was entitled to place it before his signature. Sovereign Grand Inspectors General use a Patriarchal Cross with crosslets, and the Sovereign Grand Commander uses a cross crosslet-crossed. After sharing this ritual with the Northern Masonic Jurisdiction, they were similarly adopted and the signatures styles of both jurisdictions were illustrated in the *Proceedings of the Supreme Council, Northern Masonic Jurisdiction* (1870), 48. Although already in use, a similar description was printed in the *Statutes* of the Southern Jurisdiction in October 1921. The various crosses of the 33° also appear on the official caps.

48 PROCEEDINGS OF THE

The Supreme Council for the Southern Jurisdiction of the United States, by its Great Seal and the Signatures of its Dignitaries.

ALBERT PIKE,
Sov∴ Gr∴ Com∴

Lieut∴ Gr∴ Com∴   *Gr∴ Prior, H∴ E∴*

HENRY BUIST   GILES M. HILLYER,
Gr∴ Chancellor, H∴ E∴   *Gr∴ Minister of State, H∴ E∴*

[SEAL.]   JOHN J. WORSHAM,
Treasurer Gen∴ H∴ E∴

ALBERT G. MACKEY,
Sec∴ Gen∴ H∴ E∴

The Supreme Council for the Northern Jurisdiction of the United States, by its Great Seal and the Signatures of its Dignitaries.

Sov∴ Gr∴ Com∴

Lieut∴ Gr∴ Com∴   *Gr∴ Min∴ of State.*

[SEAL.]

Gr∴ Treas∴ Gen∴ H∴ E∴   *Gr∴ Sec∴ Gen∴ H∴ E∴*

Gr∴ Keeper of the Archives.

Joint resolution by the Supreme Councils, 33°, SJ and NMJ, showing signature crosses of the officers. *Proceedings of the Supreme Council ... Ancient and Accepted Scottish Rite, for the Northern Masonic Jurisdiction ... 1870,* p. 45.

18. How many Supreme Councils have existed in the United States?

One of the principal goals of the founders of our Mother Supreme Council was to bring order out of chaos in the high degrees. While today all seems ordered and calm, the journey to our current state of prosperity was not easy. The road is littered with literally dozens of failed Supreme Councils. Some arose from schisms, some from illegitimate authority, some from greed, and some from spite. There were Supreme Councils that claimed jurisdiction over only a single state, for example, in New York, Connecticut, California, and Louisiana. The Ancient and Primitive Rite of Memphis originally controlled somewhere from ninety-one to ninety-seven degrees. Later they constricted their degrees to thirty-three and reformed themselves into a Supreme Council. Stories of this sort are almost endless. So, how many "Supreme Councils" have existed in the United States thus far? We don't yet know.

19. Why was "Cerneauism" so persistent?

The most persistent irregular Scottish Rite movement was that started by Joseph Cerneau in New York in 1807. Cerneau had legitimate authority to work Morin's twenty-five degree Order of the Royal Secret, but only for the northern part of Cuba. However, Cerneau overstepped his authority when he claimed control over thirty-three degrees, probably the better to enable him to compete with the Scottish Rite. His Supreme Council and its many descendants and off-shoots and revivals plagued legitimate Scottish Rite Masonry until the beginning of the twentieth century and spread throughout the Northeast and Midwest. In 1855, the Cerneau bodies in New Orleans transferred their allegiance to the Southern Jurisdiction, and in 1867, the Supreme Council merged into the Northern Supreme Council. Peace prevailed a few years, but in 1881, the Cerneau Supreme Council was revived and spread again with great energy.

20. Why was Albert Pike so adamant in his opposition to Cerneauism?

The Cerneau movement became a *bête noire* for Albert Pike. He had battled the "Cerneaus" during the early years of his tenure as Grand Commander and was responsible for the ultimate merger in 1867. Then in 1881, when the Cerneaus once again rose up, Pike opposed them with an amazing zeal and fury. His attacks on the Cerneau Supreme Council seemed to go well beyond what was required to unseat an upstart challenger. Pike seems to have been particularly upset because the Cerneau Masons claimed to be the only *regular* Scottish Rite Masons in the country. In response, Pike continued to emphasize that the Southern Jurisdiction was, in fact, the "Mother Supreme Council of the World."

21. What is the story of those "Perjurers, Apostates, and Renegades in the City of Baltimore?"

In the Archives of the Supreme Council, 33°, S.J., is a black leather-bound book prepared by Albert Pike and marked *Book of Infamy*. The book lists the names of almost seventy members of the Mother Supreme Council who went over to the Cerneau Supreme Council after 1881. The introduction to one section of names is particularly intriguing:

> Perjurers, Apostates, and Renegades in the City of Baltimore who, disloyal and rebellious because they were not permitted to confine the A∴ and A∴ Scott∴ Rite in Maryland to Knts. Templars, crowned themselves with dishonour and infamy by shameless recreancy and desertion to Cerneauism, April 1884.

The story of these "apostates" can only be understood considering the complicated history of the Scottish Rite in Maryland. The following account is necessarily abbreviated, but helps us to understand what happened. What follows is adapted from the account given by Masonic historian, Bro. Edward T. Schultz, who was himself an active participant.

The Scottish Rite was first established in Maryland in 1820 but "slept" during the Morgan affair from about 1826 until it was reestablished in 1861 with the creation of Grand Consistory under the authority of Albert Pike. The outbreak of the Civil War ceased activity and in 1870, the Grand Consistory of Maryland was reorganized. The members of the Scottish Rite enjoyed "the utmost harmony and good feeling," although the bodies were not growing. In an effort to increase membership, Albert Pike opened a new Lodge of Perfection. This was done without advance notice to the members of the then existing Lodge of Perfection, or even the Grand Consistory of Maryland. On August 25, 1881, the members of the old Lodge of Perfection simply received a circular informing them to be present *on that same day* at 6:00 p.m. to witness the creation of the new body, known as

Albert Pike Lodge of Perfection, No. 4. The new body became subordinate to the Grand Consistory of Maryland. Pike then accused the old members of certain offenses.

> The principal of the charges urged by the Grand Commander against the Brethren, were, that the Scottish Rite Masons of Maryland sought to prevent the creation of a Lodge of Perfection, from persons not Knight Templars. That they were bound by a bargain made with the Knight Templar that no Mason not a Templar, should be permitted to receive the Scottish Rite degrees, and that said agreement would require them to refuse to receive as visitors members of the Rite who were not Templars, also that their determination was to exclude Israelites from the benefits of the Rite.

Pike reiterated these charges in a circular to the members of the Supreme Council. The members of the Grand Consistory not only denied the charges, but felt that circulation of the charges was "wholly uncalled for, and that a due regard for their self-respect, both as men and Mason, required a surrender of the Charters of the bodies of which they were members," which occurred on September 24, 1881.

After this was done, the unaffiliated Scottish Rite Masons first sought to be charted by the Northern Masonic Jurisdiction, which was not done because of its close association with the Mother Supreme Council. They then learned that there were two Cerneau Supreme Councils, each claiming to be legitimate. After an investigation by Ferdinand J. S. Gorgas (committee chairman), Edward T. Schultz, and three others, it was concluded that none was regular or legitimate. The story continues below.

22. What is the story of Ferdinand James Samuel Gorgas?

The story of Ferdinand James Samuel Gorgas is a continuation of that just told above. His is the first name in *Book of Infamy*. He was a distinguished physician and dentist who had been coronetted a 33° jointly by the Grand Commanders of the Northern and Southern Jurisdictions in 1878. Today, the honor society of the University of Maryland Dental School is named after Dr. Gorgas. After he renounced the Southern Jurisdiction, he eventually became the Grand Commander of one of the two Cerneau Supreme Councils that existed at that time.

Prof. Ferdinand J. S. Gorgas, 33°, MD, DDS, Dean of the Dental School, University of Maryland, and Grand Commander of the "Cerneau" Supreme Council. Note double-headed eagle on his tie. From https://19thcenturybaltimore.wordpress.com, accessed March 21, 2018.

Gorgas was very much attached to the York Rite in Maryland. He served as Grand High Priest of the Grand Royal Arch Chapter in 1880, as Grand Thrice Illustrious Master of the Council of Royal and Select Masters in 1878, and as Grand Commander of Grand Encampment in 1880. He was also one of the most active Scottish Rite members of the older bodies in Maryland: he served as Thrice Puissant Master from 1874 until 1881, as Most Wise Master from 1878 to 1881, and as Eminent Preceptor of the Council of Kadosh in 1878 (declining advancement in 1879).

Following his withdrawal from the Southern Jurisdiction and his negative report on the two Cerneau Supreme Councils, at a meeting on February 13, 1884, it was first proposed to reactivate the Order of the Royal Secret of 25°, which excited enthusiasm, but was not done.

But on Maunday Thursday following, April 10th, 1884, Bro. Gorgas, the chairman of the committee who had reported adversely as to the claims to legitimacy of both of the so-called Cerneau Councils, without consultation with the other members of the committee, circulated an application among the Brethren while seated at the social board for affiliation with the Body known as the Peckham Supreme Council, to which application, then, and at later dates, the following Brethren subscribed their names, or have since affiliated with that Body...

Then follows a list of fifty-five names, headed by that of Ferdinand J. S. Gorgas, who was subsequently installed Sovereign Grand Commander of his Supreme Council. It may be added that Schultz, and twenty-one of the former members of the older bodies continued to assemble informally on Maunday Thursday, "feeling no small degree of pride in knowing that although unaffiliated they are entitled to be acknowledged and received as Scottish Rite Masons by all regular bodies throughout the world."

23. Who joined and was active in the early Lodges of Perfection?

The high degrees of early "Scots" or "Scottish Masonry" were first established in New Orleans by Louise-François Tiphaine in the *Loge de Parfaits d'Écosse*, which was founded April 12, 1764, nearly four years before Henry Andrew Franken established his Ineffable Lodge of Perfection in Albany, New York. The *hauts grades* also appeared early in Baltimore, Philadelphia, and Charleston. They almost certainly did not draw their membership from the "ordinary" Masons of those cities. Further, Masons with these exotic "high degrees," sometimes claimed extraordinary prerogatives for themselves, must have caused some stir among their brethren. Who were the first members of these exotic degrees? They appear to have been Brothers who traveled abroad (often to the Caribbean and/or France), were themselves foreigners, or who moved in social circles which included foreigners and/or influential persons in society.

24. How did the early Scottish Rite Masons interact with other Masons and with the grand lodge?

It appears that those interested in the "high degrees" were also interested in all aspects of Masonry. Frederick Dalcho, second Grand Commander of the Supreme Council at Charleston, was also the Grand Chaplain of the

Grand Lodge of South Carolina, and many of the early Scottish Rite members were active in the Grand Lodges, including people like DeWitt Clinton, who was both Grand Commander of the Cerneau Supreme Council and Grand Master of New York, and Thomas W. Bacot, an avid Cerneau Scottish Rite Mason from Charleston, who was the first Grand Master of the Grand Lodge of Ancient Free Masons of South Carolina. In brief, the Scottish Rite members appear to have simply been enthusiastic Craft Masons, who supported their Grand Lodges.

25. How did Grand Consistories function in the states and what led to their elimination?

During the first expansion of the Scottish Rite, some states had Grand Consistories that worked with the Sovereign Grand Inspectors General to control the Scottish Rite for that state. The last Grand Consistory was in the state of Kentucky, but it and all the others have been eliminated. Grand Consistories were most active when distance was an impediment to communication. The Grand Consistories exercised powers, such as issuing their own charters, which are now exclusively held by the Supreme Council. In the twentieth century, the Supreme Council consolidated its powers and absorbed the Grand Consistories, converting them into Orients, which placed all Scottish Rite bodies on an equal footing.

26. What caused the explosive growth of Scottish Rite Masonry at the turn of the twentieth century?

At the turn of the twentieth century, the Scottish Rite accounted for less than 4% of Master Masons in the United States, while today we account for nearly 33%. The moral lessons and degree pageantry of the York Rite is equal to that of the Scottish Rite, and yet the Scottish Rite grew in prominence and strength at a surprising rate that was much faster than that of the York Rite. Why was this? The evidence suggests that it was a combination of things.

In April 1860, Joseph Fletcher Brennan, editor of *The American Freemasons New Monthly Magazine*, published an article on "The Ancient and Accepted Rite." Although a member of the Scottish Rite, Brennan was a strong proponent of the York Rite who viewed the Scottish Rite's growing popularity with suspicion. He noted its growing prominence during Pike's tenure, when it was previously "scarcely heard of, save in Louisiana." Brennan considered the new growth and popularity "alarming." He outlined what he perceived to have been previous difficulties for the Rite, which he admits Pike was able to overcome with the able assistance of prominent men. He later complained that even the names of the Scottish Rite Degrees carried an appeal above those of the York Rite, and that it would eclipse the latter, reducing the latter to side-show.

> Thus has been inaugurated a movement which will divide closely, if not eventually claim entirely, the benefits heretofore enjoyed by the Chapters and Councils of the American Organization. Wherever that organization has its Grand Lodges, the Ancient Rite will have its Lodges of Perfection, Sovereign Chapters of Rose Croix, Councils of Kadosch Knights, and Consistories of Sublime Princes, before which the Chapters of Royal Arch and Councils of Royal and Select Masters will shrink into gradual decay. For who is going to be a simple Mark Master, when he can, for the same amount of money, be a *Secret Master?* Who is going to be a Chapter Past Master, when he can be a *Perfect Master?* Who is going to subject himself to the tame and watery procedure of taking the degree of Excellent Master, when he can run the spirited risk of having his wizen bifurcated by attempting the office of *Confidential Secretary?* Who will be exalted into the ridiculous position attributed to aspirants for the Royal Arch, when he can be advanced to the dignity of a *Provost and Judge,* and, clothed in the robes of state, grasp the hilt of the sword of justice without fearing its edge?

Were Brennan's comment and fears valid? Although it is not possible to answer for Masons of that time, we are not aware of any articles which suggest that members were induced to join the Scottish Rite for lofty titles. Rather, we suggest that a gradual awareness of its superior degrees, aided by a growing number of publications and the zealous promotion of its degrees helped. During the earlier days of Masonry, it was not uncommon for the leaders of some of the organizations to benefit financially for supporting a rite or system, and helping it grow. This was also done in the Scottish Rite. In the late nineteenth and early twentieth centuries, the Sovereign Grand Inspectors General could quite literally "take stock" in the Scottish Rite, and receive a portion of a new member's initiation fee. That sounds like quite an incentive to help the organization grow!

27. What led to the disestablishment of Councils of Princes of Jerusalem and the creation of Councils of Kadosh in the Southern Jurisdiction?

When the Scottish Rite was established in Charleston in 1801, Princes of Jerusalem held a position of special importance and prestige. In fact, there was no Council of Kadosh, 19°–30°, as now found in the Southern Jurisdiction but rather a Council of Princes of Jerusalem, 15°–16°, between the Lodge of Perfection, 4°–14°, and Chapters of Rose Croix, 17°–18°. Following the Morgan Affair of 1826–1842, and the revival of the Scottish Rite, the Supreme Council began to exercise its powers as "Sovereigns of Masonry." The semi-autonomous Lodges of Perfection and Councils of Princes of Jerusalem, which predominately held power under the Order of the Royal Secret, were taken over by the Scottish Rite. In the Southern Jurisdiction, Albert Pike restructured the main bodies as we have them now, while the Northern Masonic Jurisdiction retained the older structure.

28. Who did Stephen Morin appoint as Deputy Inspectors General and what were his reasons?

High ranking officers of several Masonic systems often kept a "register" or "golden book" in which they transcribed records, including the lines of descent through which they received their authority, as well as copies of the patents they issued to others. It is likely that Morin also kept one, although it has not been found. This means that we do not know the names of all the persons whom he empowered to act on his behalf. However, we do know the names of four of them: Henry Andrew Francken, Senior Deputy Inspector General (over two hemispheres), empowered sometime between 1762 and 1767 in Jamaica; Antoine Charles Mennessier de Boissy, Deputy Inspector General, June 1, 1770, Jacmel, San Domingo; William Winter, Provincial Grand Master in the Craft (Moderns), as President and Grand Commander of the Grand Chapter in Jamaica; William Adams, Deputy Inspector General, April 30, 1770, Kingston, Jamaica. The reasons why he selected them in particular are not known. It may be that political influence or fluency in another language was a factor, but until relevant correspondence is discovered, it's anyone's guess.

29. What were the accomplishments, if any, of these Deputy Inspectors General?

The Scottish Rite as we know it today is essentially the result of Stephen Morin's evangelizing efforts, although he would not have succeeded had it not been for his deputies. The most successful of his Deputy Inspectors General was Henry Andrew Francken, who himself appointed five other deputies. Governed by the *Constitutions of 1762*, they established numerous bodies along the eastern seaboard. Although the loose system of government of Morin's Order sometimes led to ineffective and occasionally unscrupulous leadership, the system was ultimately responsible for the establishment of Scottish Rite Masonry. The *Constitutions of 1762*, which governed the Order of the Royal Secret, were constrained and improved by the *Constitutions of 1786*, which govern the Scottish Rite. This superior system kept in check many of the weaknesses of the earlier system.

30. What is the full story and results of Albert Pike's western trip?

During the later years of his life, Albert Pike made a lengthy western journey in which he established many Valleys of the Scottish Rite. The trip was by steamboat, horse, and train across rugged, uncivilized wilderness. On one level, the trip was a monument of human endurance, and on another, it established the structure of Scottish Rite Masonry in the western United States.

31. What administrative changes did Albert Pike make in the government of the Southern Jurisdiction?

Albert Pike is best remembered as a ritualist and writer. There was more to his accomplishments, though. He took command of the Southern Jurisdiction when it was small, poorly organized, and nearly broke. At his death, the Southern Jurisdiction was efficiently governed and well on its way to becoming one of the most influential Masonic organizations in the world today.

Pike set his hands to labor in all aspects of the Scottish Rite. He rewrote and revised all of its rituals, numerous times; he printed its constitutions and statutes, improving and revising the latter; he printed its official bulletins and transactions; he wrote numerous books on its symbolism and philosophy; and he traveled extensively to promote its interests. In short, there is almost no aspect of the Scottish Rite which he didn't influence.

32. What happened to the "side" degrees of the Deputy Inspectors General?

Some of the early patents of Deputy Inspectors General of the Order of the Royal Secret mentioned their authority to confer "detached degrees." These were also mentioned in the *Circular throughout the two hemispheres* (1802), which was the first printed document of the Supreme Council at Charleston. Among these degrees were "Select Masons of 27 and the Royal Arch, as given under the Constitution of Dublin. Six degrees of Maconnerie D'Adoption, Compagnon Ecossois, Le Maitre Ecossois & Le Grand Maitre Ecossois." Most of these degrees were seldom conferred in the United States and disappeared in the early 1800s. Aware that the "Maçonnerie d'Adoption" was included in the 1802 *Circular*, Pike rewrote the rituals, and printed the first three as *The Masonry of Adoption* (1866), but they excited little interest. There is evidence that the Cryptic degrees of Royal Master and Select Master, which were originally conferred by the Scottish Rite, came from detached degrees through the Caribbean. In 1868, the Supreme Council "relinquish[ed] all control over the degrees of Royal and Select Master," leaving them to solely the York Rite.

33. Why are there thirty-three degrees in the Scottish Rite?

The "Order of the Royal Secret" of twenty-five degrees was reorganized into the Scottish Rite with the addition of eight degrees, some of which may have been originally "side" degrees. There have been many speculations as to why the new Rite chose to have thirty-three degrees.

Was it because there are thirty-three articles in the "Grand Secret Constitutions"? Or was there a religious reason? Some have suggested it was because Jesus lived thirty-three years. Yet others look to Jewish mysticism, noting that there are twenty-two paths and ten *sefirot* on the Kabbalistic "tree of life," and that the number thirty-three could be seen as presiding over this mystical union. Or was it simply because Charleston, South Carolina, lies at about 33° North Latitude? In the latter case it was, quite literally, the Supreme Council of the Thirty-third Degree. The speculations are virtually endless, but as yet no firm answer has been given to this basic question about Scottish Rite Masonry.

REFERENCES

Baynard, Samuel H. Jr. *History of the Supreme Council, 33°.* 2 vols. Boston: Supreme Council, 33°, N.M.J., 1938.

Bernard, David. *Light on Masonry.* Utica, NY: William Williams, Printer, 1829.

Carter, James D. *History of the Supreme Council, 33° (Mother Council of the World) Ancient and Accepted Scottish Rite of Freemasonry, Southern Jurisdiction, U.S.A., 1861–1891.* Washington, DC: Supreme Council, 33°, 1967.

————. *History of the Supreme Council, 33° (Mother Council of the World) Ancient and Accepted Scottish Rite of Freemasonry, Southern Jurisdiction, U.S.A., 1891–1901.* Washington, DC: Supreme Council, 33°, 1971.

Arturo de Hoyos. "David Bernard's *Light on Masonry*: An 'Anti-Masonic Bible.'" *Heredom* 12 (2004): 9–89.

———— and S. Brent Morris. *Allegorical Conversations Arranged by Wisdom.* Washington: Scottish Rite Research Society, 2012.

Francken, Henry A. Manuscript Rituals and Regulations. [1770]. Typescript. Archives, Supreme Council, 33°, S.J., Washington, DC.

Harris, Ray Baker. *History of the Supreme Council, 33°, (Mother Council of the World) Ancient and Accepted Scottish Rite of Freemasonry, Southern Jurisdiction, U.S.A., 1801–1861.* Washington, DC: Supreme Council, 33°, 1964.

Jackson, A. C. F. *Rose Croix: A History of the Ancient and Accepted Rite for England and Wales.* Revised and Enlarged Edition. Shepperton, England: Lewis Masonic, 1987.

Katz, Phillip M. "Freemasonry Under the Cloak: A Masonic Text of the Old Regime." *The Cryptic Scholar* (Winter/Spring 1991), 22–39.

Leyland, Herbert T. *Thomas Smith Webb: Freemason, Musician, Entrepreneur.* Dayton, OH: The Otterbein Press, 1965.

Lobinger, Charles Sumner. *The Ancient and Accepted Scottish Rite of Free-

masonry. Louisville, KY: Standard Printing Co., Inc., 1932.

[Pike, Albert.] *Book of Infamy.* 1883–1884. Archives, Supreme Council, 33°, S.J., Washington, DC.

————. *Grand Constitutions of Freemasonry, Ancient and Accepted Rite.* New Edition. N.p.: J. J. Little & Co., 1904.

Waszut-Barrett, Wendy Rae. "Theatrical Interpretations of the Indispensable Degrees." *Heredom* 12 (2004): 141–62.

Webb, Thomas Smith. *Freemason's Monitor or Illustrations of Masonry.* 1797. Reprint. NY: Masonic Historical Society of New York, 1896.

The Polite Revolution: The Formation of American Grand Lodges, 1777–1806

> If a Brother should be a Rebel against the State, he is not to be
> coutenanc'd in his Rebellion, however he may be pitied as an un-
> happy Man; and, if convicted of no other Crime, though the loyal
> Brotherhood must and ought to disown his Rebellion, and give no
> Umbrage or Ground of political Jealousy to the government for
> the time being; they cannot expel him from the *Lodge,* and his Re-
> lation to it remains indefeasible.
>
> —Charge II. *Of the* Civil Magistrate *supreme and subordinate*
> *The Constitutions of the Free-Masons,* 1723

"Conventional wisdom" can sometimes give you a broad understanding of difficult subjects. It can also simplify complex ideas beyond
recognition. In the case of Freemasonry and the American Revolution,
conventional wisdom tells us that loyalists belonged to lodges of the Moderns and patriots affiliated with the Ancients. After the success of the Revolution, the Moderns departed and left the field to the Ancients, who then
proceeded to reconstruct the established Masonic organization as they had
the political order. This broad-brush summary does not do justice to the
details nor to a Masonic revolution that was decidedly polite, as contrasted
to the parallel political revolution. The independence of American Freemasonry—as that of the American colonies—established a pattern that has
inspired many followers. In the absence of generally recognized procedures
for forming new Grand Lodges, American Masons created their own methods, though they often backed into independence.

Freemasonry in Colonial America

Like so many Masonic events, the first appearance of Freemasonry in
America is not precisely known. Jonathan Belcher, a native of Cambridge,
Massachusetts, and later Governor of the Colonies of Massachusetts and
New Hampshire from 1730 to 1741 and the Colony of New Jersey from

1747 to 1757, was made a Mason in London around 1704. He is one of the very few Masons known to have joined the Craft before 1717.[1] It is possible he held private Lodges at his residence before time-immemorial or chartered Lodges appeared. On June 5, 1730, the premier Grand Lodge appointed Daniel Coxe Provincial Grand Master for New York, New Jersey, and Pennsylvania, giving the first official Masonic recognition of the English colonies. Bro. Coxe does not seem to have exercised his authority, even though he lived in New Jersey from 1731 to 1739.[2] The Grand Lodge of Pennsylvania possesses a book marked "Liber B" which contains the records of the earliest known Pennsylvania and American Lodge. The first record is for June 24, 1731, and in that month, Benjamin Franklin is entered as paying dues five months back. Franklin's entry implies Lodge activity from at least December 1730 or January 1731.[3]

No earlier Lodge records exist in the United States, though there are suggestive comments in newspapers. Consider these words from the *Boston Gazette* for August 29, 1720, about the death of Mr. Benjamin Dowse in a hunting accident: "He was very much beloved and is universally lamented, being a Person of Exemplary Piety and Industry, and Good Temper, and a Widows Only Son." Mr. Dowse was predeceased by his father and brother, and he left a mother and three sisters. Suggestive though this account is, it is not definitive proof that Masons met in America in 1720.[4]

We are thus safe in setting 1730 as the date for the beginning of American Masonry.[5] Whatever Masonic meetings may have been held before 1730 were not recorded or the records have been lost, and activity after 1730 rapidly increased and is documented. In addition to Bro. Coxe, England established several other Provincial Grand Lodges and Grand Masters. Coxe's deputation was unique in granting the authority to Masons to elect the Coxe's successors. Specifically: Masons "in all of any of the said Prov-

---

1 David Crockett, *First American Born* (Bowie, MD: Heritage Books, Inc., 1992).

2 Henry W. Coil et al., *Coil's Masonic Encyclopedia* (New York: Macoy Masonic Publishing and Supply Co., Inc., 1961), s.v. "Coxe, Daniel."

3 Coil, s.v. "America, Introduction of Freemasonry into."

4 Melvin M. Johnson, *The Beginnings of Freemasonry in America* (Kingsport, TN: Southern Publishers, Inc., 1924).

5 It is worth noting that Massachusetts, Virginia, and some other states have traditions of Masonic meetings earlier than Pennsylvania. To declare dogmatically that Pennsylvania is the source and origin of American Freemasonry is to run the risk of friendly but intense disagreement from other Grand Lodges.

inces, Shall and they are hereby Impowered every other year on the feast of St. John the Baptist to elect a Provincial Grand Master. ..."[6]

The fortunes of these Provincial Grand Lodges waxed and waned during the following decades. Some were blessed with dynamic leaders who nurtured and expanded the Craft, while others had periods without effective administration. Two factors complicated matters for American Masonic leaders: the rivalry between the Ancients and Moderns in England and the growing political turmoil in America. The Masonic fraternity overcame these problems in a way that reflects well on the cement of brotherly love that bound their members together. They laid the foundation for an independent American Masonic system with millions of members, tens of thousands of lodges, and scores of retirement homes, orphanages, and national hospitals.

Polite Confusion

American revolutionary Masons fought and died for political independence but still cherished their ties to Great Britain. Their rebellion was political, not Masonic, and there was little bitterness or acrimony on either side as mortal combatants engaged in Masonic matters. This seeming contradiction was wonderfully illustrated by a meeting on February 7, 1780, of American Union Lodge, a military lodge chartered by the Modern (and mostly loyalist) St. John's Grand Lodge of Massachusetts and attached to the Connecticut Line of the Continental Army. The war had been fought for five years, and the American forces could not foresee their decisive victory a year away at Yorktown, Virginia. The Americans had done the unthinkable in separating from king and country. They had endured the bitter winter of 1777 in Valley Forge and the onslaughts of the world's greatest military machine. And yet, they assumed a deferential posture in most things Masonic. The rebel soldiers, led by General Mordecai Gist, petitioned the Grand Lodges if the United States to create a General Grand Lodge, but only after obtaining "approbation and confirmation" from their "Grand Mother Lodge."

To the RIGHT WORSHIPFUL, the Grand Masters of the several Lodges in the Respective United States of America.

---

6   Huss, 19.

UNION—FORCE—LOVE

...

We beg leave to recommend the adopting and pursuing the most necessary measures for establishing one Grand Lodge in America, to preside over and govern all other lodges of whatsoever degree or denomination. ...

To accomplish this beneficial and essential work, permit us to propose that you, the Right Worshipful Grand Masters of a majority of your number, may nominate as Most Worshipful Grand Master of said lodge, a brother whose merit and capacity may be adequate to a station so important and elevated, and transmitting the name and nomination of such brother, together with the name of the lodge to be established, to our Grand Mother Lodge in Europe for approbation and confirmation. ...[7]

During the war, control of the Provincial Grand Lodge of Pennsylvania (Ancients) went from loyalists to patriots, depending on which forces were present. "Lodge No. 3 [of Philadelphia] held the warrant of the Grand Lodge, whose [mostly patriot] members had fled the city. Under that authority, it formed itself into a Grand Lodge—an irregular proceeding—and [in 1778] warranted a military lodge" in the British Army's Seventeenth Regiment of Foot.[8] The regiment's original Irish charter was replaced by a Scottish one, subsequently lost at the battle of Princeton, New Jersey. The lost Scottish charter was replaced by the Pennsylvania warrant for Unity Lodge No. 18 and the new charter was itself lost a year later at the battle of Stony Point, New York. This time, however, the charter and regalia fell into the hands of American General Samuel H. Parsons, a member of American Union Lodge. The captured Masonic material was returned to the British lodge with the following letter.

West Jersey Highlands, July 23, 1779

Brethren: When the ambition of monarchs or jarring interest of contending states, call forth their subjects to war, as Masons we are

---

7   J. Hugo Tatsch, *Freemasonry in the Thirteen Colonies* (New York: Macoy Publishing and Masonic Supply Co., 1933), 208–9.

8   Wayne A. Huss, *The Master Builders: A History of the Grand Lodge of Free and Accepted Masons of Pennsylvania* (Philadelphia, Grand Lodge F. & A.M. of Pennsylvania, 1986), 40.

disarmed of that resentment which stimulates to undistinguished desolation; and however our political sentiments may impel us in the public dispute, we are still Brethren, and (our professional duty apart) ought to promote the happiness and advance the weal of each other. Accept therefore, at the hands of a Brother, the Constitution of the Lodge Unity No. 18, to be held in the 17th British Regiment which your late misfortunes have put in my power to restore to you.

Samuel H. Parsons[9]

As touching as this fraternal story is, the epilogue says even more about the character of the Masons involved.

In March 1786, Three years after American independence had been achieved, the officers of [Unity Lodge No. 18] wrote to the Grand Lodge of Pennsylvania to inquire as to the status of its warrant, which they feared had been canceled. They expressed their wish to continue Masonic affiliation with the Grand Lodge and offered to pay all back dues. The Grand Lodge replied that it wished the same result, allowed the regiment to determine its own dues as all records pertaining to it had been misplaced or lost, and promised to search for the missing warrant. It extended its best wishes for the welfare and prosperity of the military lodge. These communications were curiously devoid of any of the bitterness or hostile feeling that one might expect to find between former enemies.[10]

This difficulty in carrying hostilities from the battlefield into the lodge room was mirrored by American Masons' difficulty in embracing the Ancients–Moderns dispute with the enthusiasm of the English. There were indeed Ancient and Modern American lodges and Grand Lodges, and they often denied recognition to each other. However, except in South Carolina, this denial was seldom vigorous and often honored in the breach. It was as if the American Ancients and Moderns knew they weren't supposed to like each other, but they weren't really sure why. This polite confusion is illustrated by the By-Laws of the lodge at Joppa, Maryland.

---

9   Tatsch, 212–13.
10 Huss, 40.

Joppa [, Maryland,] November 21st diem A.D. 1765, A.L. 1765 A.M. 5768.

…

Therefore by and with Consent of the Right Worshipfull Worshipfull Master and the Right Worshipfull Wardens and other Worshipfull Officers and Brethren of this Lodge be It Enacted and it is hereby Enacted that the following Articles be Laws fundamental for the use of this Lodge only subject as by our Warrant Specified.

…

14th [of 24]. That none who hath been admitted in any Modern Lodge shall be Admitted as a Member of this Lodge without taking the respective Obligations Peculiar to ancient Masons.—[11]

Joppa Lodge certainly did not want any Ancients joining them, but they seem to have made an oversight when they obtained their charter: they were Number 346 on the Grand Lodge of Moderns, not the Ancients! The lodge eventually obtained an Ancient charted from the Grand Lodge of Pennsylvania, but their confusion is typical of how the Ancients–Moderns dispute muddled along in America.

In 1761, the Moderns' Provincial Grand Lodge of Massachusetts voted to prohibit its members from attending the Ancient Lodge of St. Andrew (which eventually received its charter from Scotland), even though a list of St. Andrew's members shows fifteen were made Masons in the Moderns Grand Lodge. A dozen years later in 1773, St. John's Grand Lodge voted to allow visitors from St. Andrew's Lodge and their Provincial Grand Lodge. This legislative fiat effectively ended the Ancients–Moderns dispute in Massachusetts, and is typical of how the dispute was settled throughout the states.

Backing into Independence

The shooting started in 1775, and on July 4, 1776, the thirteen united States of America issued their Declaration of Independence from Great Britain. After five years of warfare, the combined American and French forces defeated General Lord Cornwallis at Yorktown, Virginia, on October 19,

---

11 Edward T. Schultz, *History of Freemasonry in Maryland of All the Rites introduced into Maryland, from the Earliest Time to the Present,* 4 vols. (Baltimore: J.H. Mediary & Co., 1884), vol. 1, 38–39, 51.

1781, which effectively ended the Revolutionary War. The formal end came with the signing of the Treaty of Paris on September 3, 1783. During this unsettled period, American Masonry had a precarious existence. Some lodges were virtually unaffected by the war, while others dissolved. Control of some grand lodges swung from patriots to loyalists and back to patriots. The fieriest political revolutionaries could at the same time maintain a firm attachment to their mother grand lodge.

Masonic independence began as necessary actions to insure a stable government of the fraternity; there was often no plan or real desire to permanently sever Masonic ties. Contact with Great Britain was limited and erratic during the war, if not dangerously near to treason, so some Provincial Grand Lodges felt they had little choice but to elect their own Grand Masters. Some of these first steps at self-government were realized only later to be acts of independence. As more states took over their own Masonic governance, and as the revolution moved toward a successful conclusion for the former colonies, the remaining states came to view independent state Grand Lodges as the natural evolution from Provincial Grand Lodges. Dissent to Masonic separation from England became almost nonexistent, and the later votes for independence became unanimous endorsements of the new nation.

In the lists that follow, I have ranked the states by the year I believe a Grand Lodge considered itself independent. It is not intended to challenge which state has the first or oldest Grand Lodge, but to provide yet another way of studying our gentle craft.

1777—South Carolina

"Benjamin Franklin's private journal for 15 August 1734 contains a charge for 25 Books of Constitutions sent to Carolina,"[12] which is strongly suggestive of Masonic activity in the colony. In 1735, Lord Weymouth, Grand Master of England, granted a warrant to Solomon's Lodge in Charleston. The *South Carolina Gazette* in its issue of October 29, 1736, reported that "Last night lodge of the Ancient and Honorable Society of Free and Accepted Masons was held, for the first time...."[13] John Hammerton was elected Master and had been appointed Provincial Grand Master of South Carolina in 1736 by the Earl of Loudoun.[14]

---

12 Coil, s.v. "South Carolina."

13 Tatsch, 83.

14 Tatsch, 84.

The departure of the loyalist Provincial Grand Master, Sir Egerton Leigh, for England in 1774 because of political tensions had the unintentional effect of launching South Carolina Masons into independence. Leigh's absence left a void of Masonic leadership in South Carolina that had to be filled. In 1777, after the Declaration of Independence and armed conflict made requests to England impolitic if not impossible, South Carolina Modern Masons elected Barnard Elliot as "Grand Master of Masons," and an independently functioning Grand Lodge was born.[15] In 1780, British troops retook Charleston, and loyalist Masons revived the Provincial Grand Lodge, electing John Deas *Provincial* Grand Master in 1781.[16] The next meeting of the Grand Lodge was 1783, from which time on it acted like an independent body.

The Ancients were not idle in South Carolina. In 1760, the Grand Lodge of Scotland warranted one lodge, with others coming from the Ancient Grand Lodge of England and the Provincial Grand Lodge of Pennsylvania. Five of these Ancient lodges organized the Grand Lodge of Ancient York Masons of South Carolina on February 5, 1787.[17] Thus began the only really bitter Ancients–Moderns rivalry in the United States. There was an attempt at a merger in 1808, but it was not until December 28, 1817—four years after the union in England—that unity was achieved in South Carolina when the quarreling grand lodges merged.

1778—Virginia

The history of lodges in the Commonwealth of Virginia illustrates well the difficulties of tracing the origins of early American lodges. There were many sources of warrants: the Grand Lodge of Moderns chartered four lodges; Scotland four, Mother Kilwinning Lodge two, the Provincial Grand Lodge of Pennsylvania 3; the Provincial Grand Lodge of North Carolina one, and the Grand Orient de France one. The complexities are actually greater than indicated in this brief list. The Lodge of Fredericksburg apparently operated as a time-memorial lodge without charter as early as 1752, then received a charter from the Grand Lodge of Scotland in 1758. In 1757, Fredericksburg chartered Botentourt Lodge in Gloucester, and Botentourt in turn received a charter from the Moderns.[18]

---

15 Tatsch, 91.
16 Tatsch, 92.
17 Coil, s.v. "South Carolina."
18 Coil, s.v. "Virginia."

Williamsburg Lodge called a convention in 1777 attended by five lodges that voted unanimously to elect a Grand Master. Four more conventions met, and at the fourth meeting in 1778, John Blair was elected Grand Master of Virginia. The idea of Masonic independence for Virginia seems to have followed naturally from the earlier act of political independence. This is not a surprising sentiment from a state that produced revolutionary leaders such as George Washington, Thomas Jefferson, Patrick Henry, and James Madison. Further, there were doubts about the authority of Cornelius Harnett, Deputy Provincial Grand Master of North America. Harnett had been appointed Deputy to Joseph Montfort of North Carolina whom the Moderns in 1771 appointed Provincial Grand Master of and for America. Montfort's appointment seems to have been intended originally for North Carolina.

Following the pattern of other states, not all lodges affiliated with the new Grand Lodge. Alexandria Lodge No. 39 of Pennsylvania remained loyal to its Provincial Grand Lodge and later voiced dissent when Pennsylvania debated declaring independence from the Grand Lodge of Ancients. The Ancients–Moderns dispute briefly reared its head on December 12, 1798, when the Grand Lodge, "*Resolved,* That if any member of a Lodge under the jurisdiction of this Grand Lodge, shall *visit* or *work* in any Lodge of Masons, commonly called Modern Masons, or any Lodge of Masons not working agreeably to the ancient usages of York Masons, he shall be reprimanded by the Lodge to which he belongs, and if he should afterwards be guilty of a similar offence, he shall be expelled from the Lodge, and be excluded from the benefits of Masonry."[19]

1782—Massachusetts

On July 30, 1733, the premier Grand Lodge of England appointed Henry Price of Boston Provincial Grand Master of Free and Accepted Masons in New England. From this appointment grew St. John's Provincial Grand Lodge. Some twenty years later, the Grand Lodge of Scotland received a petition from brethren in Boston who requested a charter, which was granted to St. Andrew's Lodge and dated November 30, 1756, signed in 1759, and delivered in 1760. The Lodge of St. Andrew had an initial tense relation-

---

19 John Dove, *Proceedings of the M.W. Grand Lodge of Ancient York Masons of the State of Virginia from Its Organization, in 1778, to 1822* (Richmond, VA: James E. Goode, 1874), 193

ship with the older St. John's Grand Lodge which on April 8, 1761 "Voted That it be, and it is hereby recommended & Ordered by the Grand Master that no Member of a Regular constituted Lodge in Boston do appear at the Meeting (or Lodge so Call'd) of Scotts Masons in Boston not being regularly constituted in the Opinion of this Lodge." By 1773, St. John's Grand Lodge dropped the restrictions when they voted to allow Ancient masons to visit, and thus effectively ended the Ancients–Moderns dispute in Massachusetts.

Eight years later, the Lodge of St. Andrew was joined by three military lodges stationed in Boston—Duke of York Lodge No. 106 Scotland, Lodge 58 of England (Ancients), and Lodge 322 of Ireland—in requesting that the Grand Lodge of Scotland appoint Joseph Warren as Provincial Grand Master. This request was granted, and in 1769, Massachusetts saw two rival Grand Lodges competing as in England. It is ironic that the Master of the Lodge of St. Andrew, Joseph Warren, was one of the leading American revolutionaries, and yet he had happily joined with British military lodges in petitioning the Grand Lodge of Scotland for a warrant. This behavior was typical of the day: mortal opposition on the field of battle and fraternal cooperation in the Lodge.

Tensions between the colonists and England continued to grow, especially in Massachusetts, and on March 5, 1770, an angry but unarmed mob confronted a squad of English soldiers in Boston. After enduring taunts, rocks, and clubs, the soldiers fired on the mob, killing five. Revolutionaries quickly dubbed the event "The Boston Massacre," and the English soldiers were forced to evacuated Boston. On December 16, 1773, St. Andrew's Lodge had only five its meeting at the Green Dragon Tavern because, as the Secretary wrote, "Consignees of tea took up the brethren's time."[20] That same evening a group of "Mohawk Indians" left the Green Dragon Tavern and threw consignments of tea from three English ships into Boston Harbor. By April 19, 1775, events reached the point of no return at Lexington, Massachusetts. British troops faced American citizen-soldiers—the legendary "Minute Men"—across Lexington Green and soon thereafter was fired "the shot heard around the world." The American Revolution had begun.

---

20 Steven C. Bullock, *Revolutionary Brotherhood: Freemasonry and the Transformation of the American Social Order, 1730–1840* (Chapel Hill, NC: University of North Carolina Press, 1996), 113.

Provincial Grand Master Joseph Warren embodied the revolutionary sentiments of the Lodge of St. Andrew. On June 12, 1775, he joined hundreds of other patriots at the Battle of Bunker Hill in Boston. The superior British troops eventually won the fight, but had 1,054 casualties, nearly 40% of their ranks. The Americans lost 441, including Joseph Warren, and this incidentally led to the first step toward eventual separation of Massachusetts Masons from their mother Grand Lodges. On July 4, 1776, the colonies took the definitive step toward political separation when they declared their independence from England.

The death of Warren created a quandary for St. Andrews Provincial Grand Lodge: Did they have an existence independent of their Provincial Grand Master? Since the colonies were now at war with Great Britain, could they petition Scotland for another Grand Master? The Provincial Grand Lodge met on three times up to March 7, 1777, with Joseph Webb, Deputy Grand Master, presiding each time. Then on March 8, 1777, they elected Webb Grand Master—not *Provincial* Grand Master—and generally began acting like an independent Grand Lodge.[21] It's not entirely clear, however, if they thought of themselves as truly independent, because on June 10, 1782, to make things unambiguous, they "Resolved That this Grand Lodge be forever hereafter known and Called by the Name of the Massachusetts Grand Lodge of Ancient Masons, and, that it is free and Independent in its Government and Official Authority of any other Grand Lodge, or Grand Master in the Universe."

This resolution followed the surrender of General Cornwallis at Yorktown, Virginia, on October 19, 1781, which effectively ended the Revolutionary War. The formal end of the war came with the signing of the Treaty of Paris on September 3, 1783. The declaration by the Massachusetts Grand Lodge has no fiery rhetoric or list of grievances; it is a formal and polite statement of fact. The four-year delay between assuming *de facto* sovereignty and formally declaring independence is surprising since the leaders of St. Andrew's Lodge, and thus those of Massachusetts Grand Lodge, included revolutionary firebrands such as Paul Revere, whose midnight ride warned the citizens of Lexington, John Hancock, whose signature is the first and largest on the Declaration of Independence, and Major General Joseph Warren, whose heroic death at Bunker Hill inspired wavering patriots. What

---

21 *Proceedings in Masonry: St. John's Grand Lodge 1733–1972, Massachusetts Grand Lodge 1769–1792* (Boston: Grand Lodge of Massachusetts, 1895), 259.

is nothing short of astonishing is that in response to the Grand Lodge's declaration of independence, St. Andrew's Lodge voted 30 to 19 that "The Lodge cou'd not consent to the declaration, supposing it to be inconsistent with the principles of Masonry, necessary to be observ'd for the good of the Craft, amidst all the Variety of circumstances incident to the human affairs."[22] The lodge of political radicals could not bring itself to separate from its Masonic mother. A rump group, including Paul Revere, withdrew and formed a new lodge, Rising States, while St. Andrews remained loyal to the Grand Lodge of Scotland for 27 years until 1809 when it returned its charter to Scotland and united with the Grand Lodge of Massachusetts.

The older St. John's Grand Lodge seems to have fallen on hard times. There are no records of it meeting between 1775 and 1787, though newspaper, diary, and other accounts indicate continued if somewhat diminished activity. For example, on February 15, 1776, St. John's chartered American Union Lodge, the first military lodge in the Continental Army.[23] Provincial Grand Master John Rowe has been described as "a merchant and shipper and, while not openly Tory, was, to say the least, not an enthusiastic patriot."[24] He died on February 17, 1787, but there is no record that St. John's Grand Lodge elected a successor. First and Second Lodges of Boston had merged as St. John's Lodge in 1783, and Third and Fourth Lodges of Boston had dissolved. When the British pulled out of Boston, many loyalist members of St. John's left with them for Canada, as did the Grand Secretary, who carried lodge records and the grand lodge jewels.[25]

After several years of on-and-off discussions of union, Massachusetts Grand Lodge on December 5, 1791, voted "to Confer with the Officers of St John's Grand Lodge upon the Subject of a compleat Masonic Union throughout this Commonwealth and that said Committee report as soon as may be convenient."[26] The committee included Paul Revere and John Warren, brother of Joseph Warren. On March 5, 1792, the two grand lodges united, with the younger Massachusetts Grand Lodge dissolving and merging into the senior St. John's Grand Lodge.

---

22 *Proceedings*, 459.

23 Thomas S. Roy, *Stalwart Builders: A History of the Grand Lodge of Masons in Massachusetts, 1733–1978* (Boston, Grand Lodge of Massachusetts, 1980), 52.

24 Coil, s.v. "Massachusetts."

25 Bullock, 113.

26 *Proceedings*, 380.

1786—Pennsylvania

Daniel Coxe's jurisdiction as Provincial Grand Master included New York, New Jersey, and Pennsylvania.

Evidence indicates that the Grand Lodge of Pennsylvania was meeting in Philadelphia as early as 24 June 1731.... No one is certain, however, how this body was established. If Coxe authorized it, it should more properly be referred to as a "Provincial" Grand Lodge, but if organized without the specific approval of the representative of the Grand Lodge of England, which is also possible, it should be termed an "Independent" Grand Lodge.[27]

Incomplete records show that Benjamin Franklin served as Grand Master of this Grand Lodge for at least one year and as Deputy Grand Master for at least three years.[28] The Pennsylvania Moderns chartered four lodges in Philadelphia, and then withered with the advent of the Ancient masonry. "Although apparently inactive after the establishment of the 'Ancient' Grand Lodge in 1761, remnants of the 'Moderns'; Masons persisted until the early 1780s."[29] Thus, there was little opportunity for Ancients–Moderns disputes in Pennsylvania.

Ancient Masonry began in Pennsylvania with Lodge No. 4 chartered in 1757 by the Modern Provincial Grand Lodge. Most of the original members of the lodge had been made Masons in the Ancient manner, and they soon adopted Ancient working in their lodge. The Moderns revoked their charter after only six months, and in 1758, the lodge received a warrant as No. 69 from the Ancients in London.[30] This lodge then petitioned London for a Deputy Grand Master in Pennsylvania, elected their own Grand Master while awaiting a response, and were granted a Provincial Grand Warrant on July 15, 1761.

When the British occupied Philadelphia, the loyalist Masons ran the Grand Lodge. Among their actions was the earlier mentioned chartering of a military lodge in the British Seventeenth Regiment of Foot. When the British departed Philadelphia in 1778, the patriot Masons resumed control. They

---

27 Huss, 18.

28 Huss, 281.

29 Huss, 27.

30 Huss, 32.

did not revoke the actions of their loyalist predecessors, but by 1782, they had issued seven military warrants to American units. Thus, it was possible for Masons from different Pennsylvania lodges to face each on opposite sides of a battlefield.

The first Pennsylvania *Ahiman Rezon* was published in 1783, the year of the signing of the Treaty of Paris. Perhaps anticipating eventual Masonic autonomy from England, it said that a Grand Lodge was an "absolute and independent body, with legislative authority" to govern the craft within its jurisdiction.[31] In 1786, the Grand Lodge invited its subordinate lodges to debate independence at the September quarterly communication. The representatives of the twelve lodges in attendance, about one-third of Pennsylvanian lodges, unanimously adopted the following resolution.

> That this Grand Lodge is, and ought to be, a Grand Lodge, Independent of Great Britain or any other Authority whatever, and that they are not under any ties to any other Grand Lodge except those of Brotherly Love and Affection, which they will always be happy to cultivate and preserve with all Lodges throughout the Globe.[32]

The Provincial Grand Lodge of Pennsylvania closed *sine die*, and the next day "The Grand Lodge of Pennsylvania, and Masonic Jurisdiction thereunto belonging," with the same officers and regulations, began functioning. Yet another revolution through a polite but firm announcement.

1786—Georgia

James E. Oglethorpe organized the Colony of Georgia as a refuge for debtors, and by tradition opened the first lodge on February 10, 1733/1734, in Savannah. This time immemorial lodge was chartered as No. 139 sometime before March 1, 1735/1736, and came to be known as Solomon's Lodge. Two other Modern lodges were chartered in Georgia in 1774 and 1775, but these soon disappeared. In 1784, Pennsylvania chartered an Ancient Lodge, and the next year Solomon's decided to become Ancient itself. Yet again, Modern masonry yielded to Ancients. On December 16, 1786, these two lodges organized the Grand Lodge of the Most Ancient and Honorable

---

31 Huss, 46.
32 Huss, 56.

Fraternity of Free and Accepted Masons according to the Old Institutions in the State of Georgia.[33]

1786—New Jersey

While Daniel Coxe's 1730 deputation included the Provinces of New York, New Jersey, and Pennsylvania, New Jersey's first lodge was not established until 1761 by the Provincial Grand Lodge of New York, successor to Coxe. This first lodge, called St. John's, survived the revolution as did two lodges chartered by the Ancients in Pennsylvania. The formation of the Grand Lodge of New Jersey was unique in that a convention of all New Jersey masons—not lodges—was called for December 18, 1786, for the purpose of creating a Grand Lodge. Then with no hesitation, the delegates formed the Grand Lodge of New Jersey and elected officers.[34]

1787—Maryland

At the end of the Revolutionary War, there were eight Ancient lodges in Maryland, all chartered from Pennsylvania. In 1783, representatives of five met to establish an independent Grand Lodge and to receive a charter from Pennsylvania. They elected Dr. John Coats, Past Deputy Grand Master of Pennsylvania, as their new Grand Master. At this time, Pennsylvania had not yet declared itself independent and doubted if it had the authority to charter another Grand Lodge. After four years of correspondence, delegates of Maryland lodges voted on April 19, 1787, to form a Grand Lodge regardless of approval from Pennsylvania and reelected Dr. Coats as Grand Master.

1787—New York

The first Provincial Grand Master in America was Daniel Coxe, appointed on June 5, 1730, by the premier Grand Lodge with a jurisdiction of New York, New Jersey, and Pennsylvania. Coxe exercised little if any of his authority, but his successors from Richard Riggs, 1737, to John Johnson, 1771, created more than a score of Modern lodges in New York by 1776. The fortunes of the Moderns took a downturn with the outbreak of the revolution. Provincial Grand Master John Johnson fled to Canada and lat-

33 Coil, s.v. "Georgia."
34 Coil, s.v. "New Jersey."

er returned to command the King's troops in western New York throughout the war.[35] As the war turned in favor of the colonists, Johnson could not return to the state, His Deputy, Dr. Middleton died, and the Moderns appointed no new Provincial Grand Master. Adding to the misfortunes of the Moderns, many of their lodges started accepting charters from the Ancients. The Modern Provincial Grand Lodge was effectively wiped out.[36]

In 1781, the Articles of Confederation were ratified on March 1 giving the colonies a new form of government with the formal name of the "United States of America." Seven months later, the combined American and French forces defeated Cornwallis's army at Yorktown, Virginia, and marked the beginning of the end of the war. In January of the same year, representatives of six Ancient lodges, including three British military lodges, met in New York City and determined "that for the good of the Antient Craft, it would be highly necessary to appoint a Grand Master for this Province."[37] The Ancient Grand Lodge complied with the request and issued a warrant on September 5, 1781, appointing Rev. William Walter Provincial Grand Master of New York. The Provincial Grand Lodge was organized fourteen months later on December 5, 1782, but the New York body, unlike most other Ancient Provincial Grand Lodges, was strongly loyalist. This inclination to the crown was probably due to the body's organization in New York City, which was occupied by British troops; New York country lodges were decidedly more patriotic.

The American Revolution formally ended on April 15, 1783, with the signing of the Treaty of Paris. The remaining British troops along with many loyalists made plans to evacuate New York City. On September 19, 1783, the Provincial Grand Lodge met and adopted the following resolution.

The Propriety of leaving the Grand Warrant, by which this Lodge is established in the Province of New York being fully discussed, it was resolved, that the same should be left and remain in the case of such Brethren as may hereafter be appointed to succeed the present Grand Officers, the most of whom being under the

---

35 Coil, s.v. "New York."

36 Tatsch, 70.

37 H. P. Nash, "Origins of the Grand Lodge of New York," *Transactions of the American Lodge of Research* 3(2): 278–402.

necessity of leaving New York upon the removal of His Majesty's Troops.[38]

The Provincial Grand Lodge elected its own officers, and began to function as an independent body. Once again Masonic actions were governed by fraternal courtesy, this time from the departing British troops and loyalists who chose to leave the warrant and Grand Lodge organization intact for the military victors. The Grand Lodge was weakened by the departure of so many of its loyalist members, but in a shrewd move, they elected as Grand Master Robert R. Livingston, Chancellor (now Governor) of New York.[39]

While the Grand Lodge of New York acted like an independent body, a few details remained unsettled. Lodge No. 2 in 1786 asked for consideration of "the propriety of Holding a Grand Lodge under the *Present Warrant*, and the *Authority* from which it is derived."[40] On June 6, 1787, the Grand Lodge of New York definitively settled the question with a self-confirming statement of its independence.

The Grand Lodge of this State is established according to the antient & universal usages of masonry, upon a Constitution formed by the representatives of the regular Lodges, convened under a legal Warrant from the Grand Lodge of England.... And your Committee further beg leave to report, that in their opinion, nothing is necessary or essential in the future proceedings of the Grand Lodge upon the subject matter referred to them but that a committee be appointed to prepare a Draft of the Style of Warrants to be hereafter granted by the Grand Lodge, conformable to the said Constitution....[41]

The last detail was settled in 1788 when the Grand Secretary had a new Grand Lodge seal cut with the word *Provincial* removed from the inscription.

1787—North Carolina

By 1786, the Articles of Confederation were proving to be impractical for governing the new nation, and a convention was held in Philadelphia

---

38 Nash, 291.
39 Tatsch, 70.
40 Nash, 291.
41 Nash, 292.

in 1787 to consider revisions. What emerged was not a mere revision of the Articles, but an entirely new government created by the Constitution. At this time, the logic of independent grand lodges in each independent state was overwhelming. There was little remaining debate, and the action in each state was virtually automatic and unanimous. Joseph Montfort of North Carolina, appointed Provincial Grand Master of and for America in 1771, died in 1776. It is debatable whether his warrant was actually intended for all of America, but his death did leave the craft in North Carolina leaderless. Nearly every lodge then went dark during the war, and only revived as soldiers returned home. A convention was held on 24 June 1787, but without a majority of the lodges in the state. Unlike other states, North Carolina masons waited until a majority of their lodges could be present. A convention of eight lodges created the Grand Lodge of North Carolina on December 12, 1787.

1789—New Hampshire

Henry Price of Boston chartered St. John's Lodge at Portsmouth, New Hampshire, on June 24, 1736. Forty-four years later on March 17, 1780, St. Patrick's Lodge was established at Portsmouth with a charter from Massachusetts, but this time from the Ancient grand lodge.[42] The Ancient and now independent Grand Lodge of Massachusetts then chartered three more lodges in New Hampshire from 1784 to 1788. On July 8, 1789, five brethren from two lodges met and resolved, "That there be a Grand Lodge established in the State of New Hampshire, upon principles consistent with and subordinate to the General Regulations and Ancient Constitutions of Free Masonry."[43] The Grand Master and other grand officers were installed on April 8, 1790.

1789—Connecticut

Freemasonry got its start in Connecticut when St. John's Grand Lodge of Massachusetts chartered Hiram Lodge at New Haven on August 12, 1750. By the end of the Revolution, there were sixteen Lodges: six from the Moderns in Massachusetts, four from the Moderns in New York, three from the Ancients in Massachusetts, and three of unknown origin. Thirteen of the

---

42 Tatsch, 196.

43 H. L. Stillson and W. J. Hughan, eds., *History of the Ancient and Honorable Fraternity of Free and Accepted Masons and Concordant Orders* (Boston & New York, Fraternity Publishing Co., 1891), 231.

lodges met in convention March 13, 1783, to organize a Grand Lodge, but with no results. There was a second convention in 1783, a Grand Master was elected in 1784, a third convention was held in May 1789, and then finally on July 8, 1789, a constitution was adopted, the Grand Master re-elected, officers installed, and the present Grand Lodge was formed.[44]

1791—Rhode Island

Rhode Island masonry is descended from the Modern St. John's Provincial Grand Lodge of Boston which chartered St. John's Lodge at Newport in 1749 and another St. John's lodge at Providence in 1757. It is curious that the first St. John's Lodge originally was limited to conferring only the first two degrees, but the members convinced Provincial Grand Master to expand their authority to all three degrees. The two St. John's Lodges formed the Grand Lodge of Rhode Island on June 27, 1791, which may be the most Modern of American Grand Lodges.[45] The coat of arms of the Grand Lodge of Rhode Island is a duplicate of the premier Grand Lodge.

1806—Delaware

Ancient lodges were the only kind known in Delaware. The Provincial Grand Lodge of Pennsylvania warranted the first Delaware lodge on December 27, 1769, and five more through 1802. The Grand Lodge of Maryland, itself originating from Pennsylvania, chartered two lodges in 1792 and 1806. Representatives of three of these lodges met on June 6, 1806, to form the Grand Lodge of Pennsylvania. Pennsylvania objected to the formation of the new Grand Lodge because Wilmington Lodge owed it dues, the installation and opening of the grand lodge were irregular, and less than five lodges formed the new grand lodge. Pennsylvania did not similarly object when other Grand Lodges were formed with fewer than five lodges. Maryland also objected to the new Grand Lodge. Delaware ignored both objections and stayed the course, eventually gaining recognition as a regular grand lodge.

---

44 Stillson & Hughan, 253, Tatsch, 184, Coil, s.v. "Connecticut."

45 Tatsch, 168–70, 173.

REFERENCES

Bullock, Steven C. *Revolutionary Brotherhood: Freemasonry and the Transformation of the American Social Order, 1730–1840.* Chapel Hill, NC: University of North Carolina Press, 1996.

Cheney, Harry M. *Symbolic Freemasonry in New Hampshire.* New Hampshire: Grand Lodge of New Hampshire, 1934.

Coil, Henry W. et al., *Coil's Masonic Encyclopedia.* New York: Macoy Masonic Publishing and Supply Co., Inc., 1961.

Crockett, David. *First American Born.* Bowie, MD: Heritage Books, Inc., 1992.

Dove, John. *Proceedings of the M.W. Grand Lodge of Ancient York Masons of the State of Virginia from Its Organization, in 1778, to 1822.* Richmond, VA: James E. Goode, 1874.

Green, Charles E. *History of the M∴ W∴ Grand Lodge of Ancient, Free and Accepted Masons of Delaware.* Wilmington, DE: Grand Lodge A.F.&A.M. of Delaware, 1956.

Huss, Wayne A. *The Master Builders: A History of the Grand Lodge of Free and Accepted Masons of Pennsylvania.* Philadelphia, Grand Lodge F.&A.M. of Pennsylvania., 1986.

Johnson, Melvin M. *The Beginnings of Freemasonry in America.* Kingsport, TN: Southern Publishers, Inc., 1924.

Nash, H. P. "Origins of the Grand Lodge of New York," *Transactions of the American Lodge of Research* 3, no. 2 (1939–1940): 278–402.

Parramore, Thomas C. *Launching the Craft: The First Half Century of Freemasonry in North Carolina.* Raleigh, NC: Grand Lodge of North Carolina, A.F.&A.M., 1975.

Proceedings in Masonry: St. John's Grand Lodge 1733–1972, Massachusetts Grand Lodge 1769–1792. Boston: Grand Lodge of Massachusetts, 1895.

Roy, Thomas S. *Stalwart Builders: A History of the Grand Lodge of Masons in Massachusetts, 1733–1978.* Boston: Grand Lodge of Massachusetts, 1980.

Rugg, Henry W. *History of Freemasonry in Rhode Island.* Providence, RI: Grand Lodge of Rhode Island, 1895.

Rutyna, Richard A. and Peter S. Stewart. *The History of Freemasonry in Virginia.* Lanham, MD: University Press of America, 1998.

Schultz, Edward T. *History of Freemasonry in Maryland of All the Rites Introduced into Maryland, from the Earliest Time to the Present.* 4 vols. Baltimore: J.H. Mediary & Co., 1884.

Stillson, H. L. and W. J. Hughan, eds., *History of the Ancient and Honorable Fraternity of Free and Accepted Masons and Concordant Orders.* Boston & New York, Fraternity Publishing Co., 1891.

Tatsch, J. Hugo. *Freemasonry in the Thirteen Colonies.* New York: Macoy Publishing and Masonic Supply Co., 1933.

First Published: *Ars Quatuor Coronatorum,* 116(2003)

Itinerant American Masonic Lecturers

SUMMARY

The spread of Freemasonry in the United States was supported by itinerant Masonic lecturers, sometimes appointed by Grand Lodges but often operating as independent entrepreneurs. They taught Craft ritual based on William Preston's lectures as rearranged and edited by Thomas Smith Webb of Massachusetts, which is the basis of the ritual in nearly all American Grand Lodges. They also taught the Royal Arch and Knights Templar rituals, sold ritual monitors and regalia, and peddled other degrees and orders.

The Grand Lecturer of New York informs us, notwithstanding all this discussion, that he found, during the last year, no less than five different systems of work and lectures existing in that State, and that four of them prevailed in a single lodge—so that, until the labor began, the brethren did not know which particular system was to be the order of the evening.

Philip C. Tucker, G.M. of Vermont
Address of the Grand Master, 1859

Freemasons are fascinated with ritual and ceremony. After lodge meetings, especially when brothers of different jurisdictions are together for degree work, there are predictable and fascinating discussions about language, floor work, and local ritual variations. When trying to track down the origins of these differences, however, one of the most common explanations is, "We've always done it that way." Another, possibly better explanation is the way Masonic ritual was spread in the late 1700s and early 1800s through itinerant lecturers who relied on their memories to preserve the ceremonies. These entrepreneurs were often self-appointed and tried to make a dollar where they could. This paper outlines origins and growth of American Masonic ritual and gives vignettes of several of these brothers who had such a great influence on Freemasonry in America.

Pre-1826 American Masonic Ritual Exposés

Masonic ritual came to the United States from many sources: principally England, Scotland, and Ireland, but also France and Germany, to name but a few. There was no ritual guidance for American lodges from their mother grand lodges and certainly none in the colonies. Lodges had little choice but to rely on oral tradition and printed exposés before the appearance of William Preston's *Illustrations of Masonry* in 1772. Even then, there wasn't much help with the details of conferring the degrees or opening and closing a lodge, only lots of lectures. The first American editions of Preston didn't appear until 1804.[1]

The best idea of the ritual used in American lodges before 1826 comes from ritual exposés. English, French, and other such volumes were surely imported as soon as they were printed, but American imprints would have been less expensive, and the relative popularity of different exposés is probably a good indication of their acceptance and use by American lodges. During the ninety-six years from Benjamin Franklin's publication of "The Mystery of Free-Masonry" in 1730 to William Morgan's abduction and disappearance in 1826, only eight Masonic ritual exposés were published in America.[2]

1730—"The Mystery of Free-Masonry" (Benjamin Franklin's reprint of the London *Daily Journal* exposé)[3]

1749/50—Prichard, Samuel, *Masonry Dissected*

1768—*Hiram: Or the Grand Master-Key*

1774—*Jachin and Boaz* (twenty-eight editions between 1774 and 1826, including one in Spanish)

1812—[Guillemain de Saint Victor, Louis], *Recueil Précieux de la Maçonnerie Adonhiramite*

1812—*4ème Grade sous le Titre de Maître-Parfait*

1 Kent Walgren, *Freemasonry, Anti-Masonry and Illuminism in the United States, 1734–1850: A Bibliography*, 2 vols. (Worcester, MA: American Antiquarian Society, 2003), vol. 1, 175.

2 Walgren, vol. 2, 1046; for commentary on each of these volumes, especially Parker's *The Masonic Tablet*, see Arturo de Hoyos, "David Bernard's *Light on Masonry*: An 'Anti-Masonic Bible,'" *Heredom* 12 (2004): 10–18.

3 Henry W. Coil, et al., *Coil's Masonic Encyclopedia* (New York: Macoy Publishing and Masonic Supply Co., 1961), "Rituals," 567.

1812—Rohr, John [and Smith Allison], *The Free Mason's Instructor*

1822—Parker, Daniel, *The Masonic Tablet* (four editions in 1822)

Jachin and Boaz, representing the ritual practices of both the Moderns and Ancients, was the most popular, going through twenty-eight American editions from 1774 to 1826.[4] Parker's 1822 *The Masonic Tablet*, alone among the pre-1826 exposés, even had a second edition. The American popularity of *Jachin and Boaz* paralleled its success in England, where it went through thirty-four edition up to 1800.[5] Arturo de Hoyos, noted ritual scholar, explained its importance to American Masonic ritual.

> Prior to the publication of Morgan's work, [*Jachin and Boaz*] was the most important exposé published on American soil, and greatly aided ritual uniformity. In May 1828, ex-Mason Solomon Southwick (editor of the anti-Masonic newspaper *The National Observer*) stated that Thomas Smith Webb, the "father" of American Craft ritual, held a copy of *Jachin and Boaz* in his hands while teaching him and other young Masons their work (this would account for the strong similarities between it and the "model Webb work").[6]

The Masonic Tablet by Daniel Parker, written in a simple cipher to protect its contents from non-Masons, was the first exposé of uniquely American ritual.[7] The fact that it had four editions in its year of publication indicates its popularity among its intended audience of Masons. It might have eclipsed *Jachin and Boaz* in popularity, but no further editions were published before William Morgan's abduction and disappearance in 1826 brought a halt to nearly all things Masonic in the United States.

Morgan's abduction, an unauthorized act by renegade Masons, led to the approximately fifteen-year "Anti-Masonic Period" from 1826 to 1841, the near destruction of Freemasonry in the northeastern states, and the publication of some sixteen new ritual exposés (in fifty-one editions) during that time. *The Masonic Tablet* had just one more edition in 1845, after Masonry began to revive, and *Jachin and Boaz* had only three more American edi-

---

4 Harry Carr, ed., *Three Distinct Knocks and Jachin and Boaz* (Bloomington, IL: Masonic Book Club, 1981), 181–84; Walgren. vol. 2, 993–94.

5 Carr, *Three Distinct Knocks and Jachin and Boaz*, 78.

6 De Hoyos, "David Bernard," 10–12.

7 De Hoyos, "David Bernard," 13.

tions in 1826 and 1827, before going out of print, its popularity presumably eclipsed by more detailed and contemporary exposés.

The Rise of Itinerant Masonic Lecturers

Not all American ritual instruction was self-taught from unauthorized books. A class of fraternal entrepreneurs rose to meet the needs of lodges and brothers interested in advancing in Masonic knowledge. Perhaps, the first traveling instructor in Masonic ritual was a well-read brother with experience in military drill, or possibly he was an eager student of the fraternity who had collected many different ritual manuscripts and exposés. This new capitalist could have started as an altruistic helper, received an honorarium for his efforts, and then realized there was money to be made in the business. The first itinerant Masonic lecturer was unknown, but soon they were traveling the country peddling their wares. Some, no doubt, were like the "leg of mutton Masons" who conferred so-called degrees in exchange for a mutton dinner. Others skated closer to the edge of respectability. Three representative self-appointed lecturers are discussed below.

Abraham Jacobs. Abraham Jacobs is typical of the more respectable self-appointed lecturers. We are fortunate that his "Register" is preserved in the library of the Supreme Council, 33°, Northern Masonic Jurisdiction of the United States.[8] It gives us an important glimpse into his operations from 1792 to 1808.

Jacobs recorded that he received the Second Degree on July 22, 1782, in Boston's famous St. Andrew's Lodge, and the Master Mason Degree in Solomon's Lodge No. 1, Charleston, South Carolina, at an unspecified date.[9] On May 1, 1788, he received the "Grand and Sublime degree of Perfection," 14° of Etienne Morin's Order of the Royal Secret, in the Sublime Lodge of Perfection in Charleston, South Carolina.[10] In the spring of 1790,

---

8 Abraham Jacobs' register is in the archives of the Supreme Council, 33°, N.M.J., Lexington, MA, and was excerpted from July 22, 1782, to November 26, 1808, in Robert B. Folger, *The Ancient and Accepted Scottish Rite, in Thirty-Three Degrees* (New York: By the author, 1862, 1881), Appendix, 71–110.

9 Jacobs in Folger, 73.

10 The twenty-five degree system that evolved into the Ancient and Accepted Scottish Rite is properly known as the "Order of the Royal Secret," though it has been misidentified for more than a century as the "Rite of Perfection." In a private communication with the author, Alain Bernheim points out that the first use of the correct name by twentieth-century authors appears to be by W. W. Covey-Crump and S. H. Perry in

Jacobs was living in Kingston, Jamaica, and became a "Patriarch Noachite and Sovereign Knight of the Sun, with full power to initiate brethren and constitute Lodges."[11] "The November following Brother Abraham Jacobs left the island, when he received his certificate, with every necessary requisite for promoting the Craft in the City of Savannah and State of Georgia."[12] Thus began his career as a Masonic degree peddler.

Jacobs' first entry in his Register for conferring degrees was dated 1792 in Augusta, Georgia, about two years after he left Jamaica. We don't know how he advertised his services or created interest in the "high degrees," but presumably it was by word of mouth, perhaps by talking up his "wares" at lodge meetings in the area. The first American publication to explicitly give "An Account of the Ineffable Degrees of Masonry," 4°–14° of the Order of the Royal Secret, was Thomas Smith Webb's *The Freemason's Monitor; or, Illustrations of Masonry*, and that wouldn't be published for another five years.

The economics of conferring high degrees can be deduced from his diary entries for the summer 1792. Bro. Godfrey Zimmerman of Augusta, Georgia, wrote to Jacobs on May 27, 1792, and said "there will be at least ten or twelve who will join and freely comply with your demand, namely, that of bearing your expenses until your return to Savannah.... My house and table you will please accept of during your stay amongst us, and your time will be made as agreeable as lays in our power...."[13] Eventually, sixteen Augusta brothers received the Fourth through Sixteenth Degrees from Jacobs. For twenty evenings, from June 10 through July 3, 1792, Jacobs conferred degrees on his candidates. Usually, one or two degrees were conferred each evening, but since not everyone could be present, degrees were repeated. "Arturo de Hoyos, Grand Archivist and Grand Historian of the Supreme

---

their unpublished paper, "Order of the Royal Secret: Its History and Mystery," referenced in the "April 1954 Minutes of the History Committee, Supreme Council, 33°, A.A.S.R., N.M.J.," 31. Bernheim went on to confirm the correct name of the Order by verifying the transcription of a patent from Etienne Morin to Antoine Charles Menessier de Boissy in the name of the "Sublime Commanders of the Order of the Royal Secret." Arturo de Hoyos points out that the *Circular throughout the two Hemispheres* refers to Frederick the Great as "Grand Commander of the order of Prince of the Royal Secret."

11 Jacobs in Folger, 74–77.
12 Jacobs in Folger, 76.
13 Jacobs in Folger, 83.

Council, 33°, S.J., believes that Jacobs dictated the ceremonies to the candidates, and they transcribed the rituals for their personal use. In support of
this contention, the Archives of the Supreme Council, 33°, S.J., have several
small unbound books with individual degrees transcribed into them."[14]

Jacobs never logged his fees for conferring degrees, but he did record in
1802 that another group of eleven candidates in Savannah paid $50 to the
Sublime Council of Princes of Jerusalem in Charleston, South Carolina, for
a warrant, Constitution, and By-Laws for a Lodge of Perfection, 4°–14°.[15]
The going rate for degree peddling around 1800 seemed to be about $0.50
to $1.50 per degree, so it's reasonable to assume that if the fee for a war-
rant was $50, then Jacobs received about $10 to $20 per candidate for the
Ineffable Degrees plus room, board, and full expenses.[16] All of this *and* his
time was "made as agreeable as lays in [the candidates'] power...." Prof.
Steven Bullock of Worcester Polytechnic Institute estimates that skilled la-
borers of that era made about $1 per day, or about $260 per year.[17] Thus,
each candidate represented somewhere between two and four weeks' wag-
es for a skilled laborer. By contrast, George Washington made $25,000 a
year as president from 1789 to 1797, or about $100 a day. By either of these
measures, Jacobs was well compensated and had a nice supplement to his
income as a Hebrew teacher. His Register records four classes of candidates: sixteen in 1792; eighteen in 1796; twelve in 1801–1801; and eleven
in 1802.[18]

By September 1804, Jacobs had moved to New York City and was again
teaching Hebrew and supplementing his income by conferring high degrees. Neither activity provided enough income, and Oliver M. Lowndes,
33°, Sheriff of New York, "made him the offer of a position [as a clerk] in the
Sheriff's office provided he made a written agreement to cease conferring
the degrees in the State of New York, nor within forty miles of its line."[19] In
late winter 1826, Jacobs conferred the high degrees on a group of twenty-

14 Morris, "Royal Secret," 14.

15 Jacobs in Folger, 99–100.

16 Morris, "Royal Secret," 13.

17 Prof. Steven Bullock, Wooster Polytechnic Institute, Wooster, Massachusetts, email to
the author, October 24, 2007.

18 Jacobs in Folger, 1792, 84–88; 1796, 89–91; 1801–1802, 92–93; 1802, 95–96.

19 Robert B. Folger, "Recollections of a Masonic Veteran," part 6, *New York Dispatch,* June
27, 1873.

nine New York City Masons in Trenton, New Jersey, for the last time that such work of his has been recorded. He couldn't pass up the opportunity to make a little extra money, but he kept his word and conferred the degrees outside of the forty-mile limit.[20]

Jacobs died "several years" before 1874 and just before his death gave his Masonic manuscripts, books, records, etc. to Henry C. Atwood, a member of the 1826 Trenton high-degree class.[21] Atwood was Grand Master of two schismatic Grand Lodges in New York and Grand Commander of several clandestine Supreme Councils.[22]

James H. C. Miller. A more shadowy and much less respectable lecturer is James H. C. Miller, whose career was detailed by Arturo de Hoyos.[23] His birth and death are unknown as is his receipt of the Master Mason Degree, but he was peddling degrees during the 1820s.

Miller was the driving force behind an unattached Masonic order that conferred chivalric grades, usually in connection with
encampments of Knights Templar and Knights of Malta. Ritual
manuscripts and exposures reveal that the system, known as the
order of the Holy Cross, was conferred under authority of a body
calling itself the "Ancient Council of the Trinity," the three degrees
it conferred were:

(1) Knights of the Christian Mark, and Guards of the Conclave;

(2) Knights of the Holy Sepulchre;

(3) The Holy and Thrice Illustrious Order of the Holy Cross,
called a Council.[24]

Arturo de Hoyos estimates that by 1829, there were about forty Councils and almost five hundred members.[25] Miller no doubt had seen the

20 Folger, "Recollections,"

21 Robert B. Folger, "Recollections of a Masonic Veteran," part 30, *New York Dispatch*, May 24, 1824.

22 S. Brent Morris, *The Folger Manuscript* (Bloomington, IL: Masonic Book Club, 1993), 55–82.

23 Arturo de Hoyos, "The Posthumous Success of James H. C. Miller, Degree Peddler," *Heredom* 8 (1999–2000): 169–217.

24 De Hoyos, "James H. C. Miller," 171.

25 De Hoyos, "James H. C. Miller," 172.

rise of other American high-degree Masonic bodies, such as the General Grand Chapter of Royal Arch Masons (1798), the Supreme Councils of the Ancient and Accepted Scottish Rite (1801 and 1813), and the Grand Encampment of Knights Templar (1814). If he had produced an equally popular and widely accepted Masonic order, then Miller could have had a paying position, such as lecturer or secretary. Such was not to be the case.

Miller first met with an emphatic condemnation in 1828 from the Grand Encampment of Knights Templar of New York: "This Grand Encampment altogether denies the power and authority of any man or body of men, to make innovations in or upon, the regular established orders of Masonry, by the introduction of clandestine degrees...."[26] New York Knights Templar were required to withdraw from the Order of the Holy Cross, and local Encampments could not have members or visitors who continued to belong to the order nor accept as candidates members of the Holy Cross who had not renounced their membership.[27]

His next Masonic condemnation came in 1829 when Moses Holbrook, Grand Commander of the Supreme Council at Charleston wrote to J. J. J. Gourgas, Secretary General of the Supreme Council at New York City, about Miller. "A Br calling himself Doctor J. H. C. Miller has been here—he first applied to me to get him Charity, and after obtaining from the Grand R[oyal] A[rch] Chapter—$10. He turned to giving (rather pedling [sic]) a degree called by him Holy Cross.... The moment that he was found taking money for his degree—that moment his career was stopped."[28]

It's hard to understand the fervency of the denunciations of Miller's new Masonic order. Perhaps the Grand Encampment and the Supreme Councils feared competition from another high-degree system, especially the Grand Encampment since membership in the Order of the Holy Cross required one to be a Knight Templar and thus could be viewed as "higher" or a "step beyond." It's entirely possible that Miller's personality clashed that those of the existing officers of the older orders. Regardless of the motives for these denunciations, the anti-Masonic movement, which had been brewing in New York since 1826, erupted and Miller's creation was swept away with nearly everything else Masonic.

---

26 De Hoyos, "James H. C. Miller," 179.

27 De Hoyos, "James H. C. Miller," 179–80.

28 De Hoyos, "James H. C. Miller," 178.

Whether caused by Masonic condemnations or the general anti-Masonic sentiment, Miller's Order of the Holy Cross ceased to exist shortly after 1829. Miller, however, just moved his Masonic activities to greener pastures. On December 9, 1835, the General Grand Chapter of Royal Arch Masons issued a charter for San Filipe de Austin Royal Arch Chapter No. 1 of Texas, then a state in Mexico, with Samuel M. Williams as High Priest or First Principal and James H. C. Miller as King or Second Principal.[29] The next day the Grand Encampment of Knights Templar issued a charter to San Felipe de Austin Encampment of Knights Templar No. 1 with Williams as Grand Commander and Miller as Generalissimo.[30] It is not known if Miller peddled any degrees while in Texas, but apparently, he soon wore out his welcome and reportedly north to Nebraska and Ohio where he established more Masonic bodies.[31] It is not known how or where his career ended. Miller's most enduring legacy, however, is that his Order of the Holy Cross and Knight of the Holy Sepulcher—condemned by New York Knights Templar—were used by Robert Wentworth Little when he created the Order of the Red Cross of Constantine about 1865.[32]

Antoine Bideaud. Not all degree peddlers had long careers like Jacobs or Miller; some careers were shorter and more opportunistic. Antoine Bideaud, a member of the Supreme Council of the Windward and Leeward Islands, had full authority to confer the Ineffable and Sublime Degrees in his country—but not in the United States.[33] In 1806, in New York City on his way to France, he met J. J. J. Gourgas and four other Frenchmen who were interested in the Scottish Rite. Seeing a business opportunity and ignoring the limitations of his authority, Bideaud conferred the 4° through 32° on the five brothers and pocketed some quick money. After creating a Consistory of Sublime Princes of the Royal Secret in New York, Bideaud sailed off to France and left his protégés to fend for themselves. J. J. J. Gourgas later realized and commented on the irregularity of the proceedings: "This act

---

29 *Compendium of the Proceedings of the General Grand Chapter of Royal Arch Masons of the United States, from the 24ᵗʰ Day of October, 1797, to the 2ⁿᵈ Tuesday of September 1856* (Baltimore: Joseph Robinson, 1859), 99–100.

30 *Proceedings of the General Grand Encampment of the United States, 1835,* 40.

31 Arturo de Hoyos, Grand Archivist and Grand Historian, Supreme Council, 33°, S.J., private communication to the author.

32 De Hoyos, "James H. C. Miller," 184.

33 Charles S. Lobingier, *The Supreme Council, 33°, Mother Council of the World* (Louisville, KY: Standard Printing Co., 1931), 816–17.

of Bideaud's was completely irregular, unconstitutional. He had no right or power within any part of these United States of America, but then he was tempted and did succumb at the rate of five times $46 or $230."[34]

Although their degrees had been conferred irregularly, Emanuel de la Motta, Grand Treasurer General of the Mother Supreme Council, healed the five brothers in 1813. Their organization became the Supreme Council for the Northern Masonic Jurisdiction and thirty-two years later chartered the Supreme Council for England and Wales. It is ironic that de la Motta and Jacobs, both of the Jewish faith, were instrumental in forming the Northern Masonic Jurisdiction which later excluded Jews until the 1950s.

While the eventual dividends of Antoine Bideaud's entrepreneurial activity proved beneficial to the fraternity, the American Masonic "establishment" was not sanguine in its opinion of itinerant lecturers. The Grand Lodge of Maine foreshadowed the Grand Encampment of New York's 1828 condemnation of James H. C. Miller's activities. In 1823, Maine's Committee on the Subject of a General Grand Lodge of the United States reported on the pros and cons of such an organization. Among the points in favor, "The erection of a national Grand Lodge will … abolish the degrading and ruinous practices of unlicensed lectures [and] interdict the mercenary introduction of false degrees...."[35] The "degrading and ruinous practices of unlicensed lectures" are not detailed, but the strong language makes it appear to be a problem. The dilemma was solved as unlicensed lecturers were put out of business by the anti-Masonic movement. When Freemasonry reemerged in the early 1840s, grand lodges endorsed and approved their own lecturers, and the fraternity was too weakened to support any additional high degrees.

Thomas Smith Webb and the "Standard American Work"

Thomas Smith Webb was born in Boston in October 1771 and died in Cleveland, Ohio, in 1819. He apprenticed as a printer and bookbinder and received the degrees of Entered Apprentice on December 24, 1790, and Fellowcraft and Master Mason on December 24, 1790, in Rising Sun Lodge No. 5 of Keene, New Hampshire. There is no indication of why he

---

34 J. J. J. Gourgas in Samuel H. Baynard, Jr., *History of the Supreme Council, 33°*, 2 vols. (Boston: Supreme Council, 33°, N.M.J., 1938), vol. 1, 153.

35 *Proceedings of the Grand Lodge of Maine*, 1823, 89.

was allowed to join some eleven months before he attained his majority. Two years later his father died, he returned to Boston, and then in 1793 moved to Albany, New York, where he established a printing business and became friends with an English Mason, John Hanmer, who taught him the lectures of William Preston.[36] Hanmer is said to have been a member of the Lodge of Antiquity in London and, if so, surely was familiar with Preston and his lectures.[37]

Some English edition of William Preston's *Illustrations of Masonry* was advertised for sale in the Barber & Southwick bookstore in Albany in July 1796.[38] Between this book and Hanmer's instructions, it is easy to see how Webb became familiar with Preston's work and published in 1797 *The Freemason's Monitor; or, Illustrations of Masonry: In Two Parts.*

Harry Carr put the work of Web and Preston in context with English ritual at that time.

Webb, was then barely twenty-two years old and [Hanmer's and his] mutual interests drew them together. This was the period when the English Masonic ritual was at its highest stage of development. Hutchinson and Calcott had published their works; Preston was in his prime, and the 1792 edition of his *Illustrations of Masonry* had just appeared. This was the 8th edition, as popular and successful as its predecessors, and it was almost a bible to the English Craft. Webb took the book, retained sixty-four pages of Preston's work intact, word for word, cut out a few minor items, and rearranged others, and published it in 1797, under the title *Freemasons' Monitor or Illustrations of Freemasonry*.[39]

---

36 Coil, "Webb, Thomas Smith," 680.

37 Everett R. Turnbull and Ray V. Denslow, eds., *A History of Royal Arch Masonry*, 3 vols. (Trenton, Mo.?: General Grand Chapter Royal Arch Masons, 1956), vol. 1, 249. However, "John Hanmer, with whom Webb was to be closely associated during the remainder of his stay in Albany, is said to have been an Englishman and a member of the London Lodge of Antiquity. Both statements lack verification." Herbert T. Leyland, *Thomas Smith Webb: Freemason, Musician, Entrepreneur* (Dayton, OH: Otterbein Press, 1965), 57.

38 Allen E. Roberts, foreword to *The Freemason's Monitor or Illustrations of Masonry in Two Parts*, by Thomas Smith Webb (Albany, NY: Spencer and Webb, 1797; reprint, Bloomington, IL.: Masonic Book Club, 1996), xiii.

39 Harry Carr, "As Others See Us (Freemasonry in the U.S.A.)." accessed October 21, 2007, http://www.masonicworld.com/education/files/artnov02/as_others_see_us.htm.

The concepts of intellectual property and plagiarism were not well developed in 1797, but Webb remarkably acknowledged his debt to Preston in his preface. "The observations upon the first three degrees, are principally taken from Preston's 'Illustrations of Masonry,' with some necessary alterations."[40] Webb's *Monitor* contained the "remarks" and "observations" on the degrees conferred in American Royal Arch Chapters: Master Mark Mason [*sic*]; Past Master (only obliquely referred to in the 1797 edition); Most Excellent Master; Royal Arch Mason. There were also remarks on the Knights Templar, Knights of Malta, and the Ineffable Degrees, 4° through 14°, plus a "Sketch of the History of Masonry in America." All together it was a remarkable volume and went through eighteen editions (four in Spanish) from 1797 to 1826.[41]

More remarkable than his *Monitor*, however, was Webb's private and unpublished accomplishment: he organized, regularized, and systematized American Masonic ritual. Using *Jachin and Boaz*, Preston's *Illustrations of Masonry*, and John Hanmer's guidance, so everyone assumes, Webb produced what could be called the "American Standard Work." American Grand Lodges at that time persistently sought uniformity of work in their ritual—if only they could discover what the "true original" was. By adapting Preston's lectures to the widely used template of *Jachin and Boaz*, Webb produced impressive, consistent ceremonies that became immensely popular. He may not have found the true original rituals of Masonry, but his work was so much better than anything else available that all American grand lodges (except Pennsylvania) adopted it and stopped searching.

Grand Lodge Approved Lecturers

Today, American grand lodge have a Grand Lecturer or similar officer whose responsibility is to preserve and teach the approved ritual and ceremonies. This is accomplished by various means, including Deputy Grand Lecturers assigned to areas, regional ritual schools, and formal testing and certification of ritualists. The preservation of the ritual is particularly important in those grand lodges that have no written ceremonies and rely entirely on mouth-to-ear instruction. The first Grand Lecturers were expected to travel around the state, to teach a uniform working, and to avoid what

---

40 Webb, [v].

41 Walgreen, vol. 2, 1,022.

the Grand Lodge of Maine termed the "degrading and ruinous practices of unlicensed lectures."

"Degrading and ruinous" is strong language to describe itinerant lecturers. However, the following observation on one of the lecturers' side degrees— if true—shows how these traveling brothers might be considered hustlers and just a step above snake oil salesmen.

> Degree of Knights of the Three Kings, the obligation includes the clause:
>
> "I furthermore promise and swear, that I will not confer this degree upon any person without the *hope of fee or reward*."*
>
>> *It is believed that this degree was invented by some of our grand lecturers, who make it their business to travel from lodge to lodge and instruct men in the mysteries of ancient Freemasonry.
>> They have incorporated in the oath a clause which prohibits them from conferring the degree without pay, and by this means they often replenish the small change.
>> After they have conferred the degree, they gravely say: "You see, sir, that I must receive some *trifling* compensation, just to *save the oath*." (!!)
>> "How much is customary?" inquires the brother.
>> "Oh, any trifling sum, 25 or 50 cents, just to save the oath, *merely a matter of form*."[42]

Benjamin Gleason (1777–1837). In 1805, Isaiah Thomas, Grand Master of the Grand Lodge of Massachusetts appointed Benjamin Gleason as "Grand Lecturer and Instructor." Gleason summarized his qualifications and traced his Masonic lineage to Thomas Smith Webb in a letter of November 26, 1843, to Charles W. Moore.

> It was my privilege, while at Brown University, Providence, R.I., (1802–2,) to acquire a complete knowledge of the lectures in the *three* first degrees of Masonry, *directly* from our much esteemed Brother T. S. Webb, author of the Free Masons' Monitor; and in

---

42 Avery Alyn, 1831. *A Ritual of Freemasonry* (Boston: John Marsh & Co., 1831), 202–3.

consequence was appointed and commissioned by the Grand Lodge of Massachusetts and Maine, Grand Lecturer, devoting the whole time to the instruction of the lodges under the jurisdiction....[43]

In a printed address sent to all lodges explaining the appointment of Gleason, Grand Master Thomas said "great and serious inconveniences have arisen, and continue to arise, to our Most Ancient and Honorable Fraternity from the rude, imperfect, and in many instances, erroneous Lectures and modes of work in many of our Lodges...."[44] The subsequent instructions of Grand Master Thomas give a good indication how the Grand Lecturer and Instructor was to operate.

> Our M. Worshipful Grand Master has commissioned and directed our [said] Bro. Gleason to visit all the Masonic Districts in this Commonwealth, and carefully and seasonable to notify the several R. W'l Masters and W'l Wardens of the Lodges in said Districts, to meet at such times and at such places or Lodge-rooms, in each District, as may be convenient....

> And the said Grand Lecturer and Instructor is enjoined to continue his lessons and instructions at each meeting in a District, or parts of Districts, as the case may be, for six days successively, Sundays excepted, or longer if needful to accomplish the necessary instruction; but not to exceed twelve days in any one place....

> It is expected the Grand Lecturer and Instructor by strict punctuality and attention will complete his visits in one year from the 1st of August 5805; he will be entitled to a reasonable compensation for his services,—the part, to each Lodge, of that compensation will be but small.... His compensation will average about 15 dollars from each Lodge. [Massachusetts had eighty-six lodges in 1807.][45]

---

43 *Proceedings of the Most Worshipful Grand Lodge of the State of Vermont* (Burlington, VT: Danforth & Smalley, 1860), 25.

44 *Proceedings of the Most Worshipful Grand Lodge of Ancient Free and Accepted Masons of the Commonwealth of Massachusetts, 1792–1815* (Cambridge, MA: Caustic-Claflin Co., 1905), 283.

45 *Massachusetts*, 285, 286, 350–51.

Gleason's compensation, set in documents by Grand Master Thomas, seemed substantial. "Bro. Benj. Gleason bearing all his own expenses during said year, shall receive a compensation of one thousand dollars if any part of that sum is paid by the Grand Loge aforesaid, and not more than twelve hundred dollars if the whole of said sum of 1200 dollars is paid by the several lodges."[46] At the quarterly communication of June 8, 1807, Gleason is listed as Grand Lecturer, and a committee reported that he received $930 from the lodges he visited and was due $70 from the grand lodge to make the guaranteed $1,000.[47] Six months later, he was listed as Past Grand Lecturer at the annual communication of December 14, 1807. [48] Either Gleason was not satisfied with lecturing or more likely the grand lodge didn't consider his position a permanent one.

Grand Lodge of Vermont. Two years later in 1809, the Grand Lodge of Vermont followed the lead of Massachusetts, its neighbor to the south. The American interest in—or perhaps obsession with—a uniform mode of work was a driving force behind creating a "Grand Visitor" as was teaching morality and ethics. Vermont proposed more modest remuneration: $50 per year from the Grand Lodge and $2 per day plus expenses from the lodges visited. It is interesting to note that Bro. Jonathan Nye presented the report of the committee recommending creation of the position was elected as Vermont's first Grand Visitor.

[October 9, 1809]

Resolved, That there shall be a Grand Visitor, appointed by ballot in the Grand Lodge, whose duty it shall be to visit the several Lodges throughout this State, to teach them Masonic Lectures to inculcate and enforce a particular regard to the moral precepts of the Institution, and to recommend that harmony and love which is the glory of this institution. That said visitor shall be authorized and empowered to preside in all Lodges he may visit, call on all the members of the several Lodges, to give regular and punctual attendance on their respective communications, and use his utmost exertion to render the Masonic Family in the State an united band of brothers.

---

46 *Massachusetts,* 291.

47 *Massachusetts,* 358.

48 *Massachusetts,* 355, 367.

Your committee would further recommend that the said visitor enter on the duties of his office on the 1st day of December next, that he tarry with each Lodge at least two days, and longer if necessary, and impress on the minds of the members the value and importance of the institution, and continue his visits regularly throughout the State, agreeably to his own appointments, of which he shall give the several Lodges he may so visit due notice; and that said visitor shall be paid for his services the sum of two dollars per day, and all necessary expenses from the several Lodges he may visit.

All of which is humbly submitted.

JONATHAN NYE,
For Committee

Read and adopted.

...

Resolved, That as the person who may be appointed to the office and duty of Grand Visitor will necessarily be obliged to spend considerable time, which will not come regularly within the time occupied in the actual visitation of the Lodges, this Grand Lodge will give to such person as shall be appointed and perform the duties to its acceptance, the sum of fifty dollars.

On motion, the ballots were taken for a Grand Visitor, by which Brother Jonathan Nye was elected to that office.[49]

Grand Lodge of Maine. The Grand Lodge of Maine had some difficulties in getting its traveling Grand Lecturer started. It gave a certificate on October 25, 1825, to Samuel Kidder appointing him Grand Lecturer, and then only fifteen months later on January 12, 1827, it was "*Ordered,* That the subordinate Lodges under this jurisdiction be directed to receive no further instructions from any Grand Lecturer, but to look for information from the District Deputy Grand Masters, until the further order of this Grand Lodge."[50] At the 1828 communication, it was decided to divide the state's

---

49 *Early Records of the Grand Lodge of the State of Vermont F.&.A.M. from 1704 to 1846 Inclusive* (Burlington, VT: Free Press Association, 1879), 130, 131.

50 *Grand Lodge of the Most Ancient and Honourable Fraternity of Free and Accepted Masons of the State of Maine* (Portland, ME: Shirley & Edwards, 1826), 18; *Maine* (Portland, ME: Arthur Shirley, 1827), 28.

fifty-six lodges into three districts with one appointed lecturer per district, and "the lecturers thus employed, shall receive each $1.50 per day, and have their traveling and incidental expenses paid."[51] One year later, the Grand Treasurer's account showed four line items related to lecturing:

Expenses of committee on the subject of a uniform mode of lecturing	18.00
Bro. Darling's bill for lecturing	166.47
Bro. Wadsworth's bill for lecturing	171.11
Bro. J. Miller's bill for lecturing	7.36
Total Lecturing Expenses	$442.94[52]

This total was 21% of the Grand Lodge's 1828 expenditures and was less than one-half of what Benjamin Gleason made in 1805 in the adjacent state of Massachusetts.

Jeremy Ladd Cross (1783–1860). One of the most successful itinerant lecturers was Jeremy Ladd Cross who made the transition from independent degree peddler to officially appointed Grand Lecturer. He kept a diary for 1817–1820, and it gives great tremendous insights to the business of Masonic lecturing.[53] He started his career in 1814 and four years later had misgivings about his chosen vocation. "About 4 years since [5 June 1818,] I commenced the occupation of a Masonic Lecturer. … I now think that if I were free from debt and had any other way of acquiring a livelihood I should become quite domesticated."[54]

His diary is the best available reference to understand the economics of traveling lecturers, even through some entries are vague as to whether he reimbursement. On August 17, 1817, he started out from Haverhill, New Hampshire, traveling by coach and boat, and arrived in Richmond, Virginia, on December 4, a trip of 635 miles over 109 days. He often stayed with Masons and regularly dined with them even when he stayed in a hotel. He received $4 per day for "lecturing"—instructing lodges and chapters in

51 *Maine.* (Portland, ME: Shirley & Hyde, 1828), 16.

52 *Maine.* (Portland, ME: Shirley & Hyde, 1829), 10–11.

53 Jeremy Ladd Cross's diary from August 17, 1817, to April 2, 1820, was published in Eugene E. Hinman, et al., *A History of the Cryptic Rite*, 2 vols. (NP: General Grand Council, 1931), vol. 2, 1,223–98.

54 Cross diary, June 5, 1818, and May 2, 1818, Hinman reprint, 1,257 and 1,266.

the ritual and floor work of the degrees, the installation of officers, funeral ceremonies, and so on. As a side business, he chartered Councils of Select Masters for $20. (At that time, the Royal Masters Degree had not been combined with the Select Masters to create the order known today.)

During his sixteen-week trip to Richmond, he established at least six Councils of Select Masters for $120 and spent some days lecturing for $116. Thus, his total income for the trip was about $236. To get a very rough estimate of his expenses, note that during his stay in Washington, DC, he paid $8.75 for 3½ days room and meals at Thomas Crafford's Union Hotel, or $2.50 per day.[55] The cost for lodging in smaller towns must have been less, say about $1.50–2.00 per day. If he used hotels or taverns for one-half to two-thirds of his trip and stayed with brothers the rest of the time, then he spent about $90–160 on lodging—very nearly half of his income of $236. When his transportation and miscellaneous expenses are added in, Cross barely cleared a few dollars a week, less than a skilled laborer would have made. It's easy to see why after four years of lecturing, he was still in debt.

Cross's fortunes took a turn for the better in 1818, shortly after his trip to Richmond. Although in 1809, the Grand Lodge of Connecticut had declined to appoint inspectors for its lodges, at its May 1818 session, it reversed itself and appointed Cross Grand Lecturer with the reasonable assurance of a steady income.[56] His vocational choice was beginning to pay off! The Grand Lodge of Connecticut

> *Resolved,* that Bro. Jeremy L. Cross be and he is hereby authorized, as Grand Lecturer, to visit the several Lodges in this jurisdiction, and instruct them in the correct mode of working and lecturing; and that each subordinate Lodge be required to pay into the Trea-

---

55 Cross diary, December 2, 1817, Hinman reprint, 1,240.

56 "[May 17, 1809] A proposition in writing, without signatures, said to come from Union Lodge, No. 31, New London, for dividing the Lodges within this jurisdiction into Masonic districts, and to appoint inspectors for the purpose of visiting the several Lodges and introducing uniformity in the mode of working, together with sundry other things therein particularly mentioned, was introduced and read. After some discussion the question was put, whether at this time it would be expedient or necessary to do anything on the subject, and resolved in the negative." E. G. Storer, *The Records of Freemasonry in the State of Connecticut … and the Entire Proceedings of the Grand Lodge from its First Organization, A.L. 5789* (New Haven, CT: E. G. Storer, 1859), 217.

sury of the Grand Lodge the sum of ten dollars, at or before the next Grand communication, for the purpose of defraying the expense of such visitation.

Resolved, That it shall be the duty of the Master of each Lodge to give the Grand Lecturer a certificate of the number of days spent with them in lecturing, and each sum, not exceeding four dollars per day, as each Lodge may pay said Grand Lecturer, taking his receipt therefore, shall be considered as part of said sum of ten dollars.

Resolved, That each Lodge shall pay Bro. Cross' expenses, when actually employed by such Lodge in giving lectures and instructions; and no Lodge shall be bound to pay said sum of ten dollars, unless they first have had the benefit of said lectures at least two and a half days.

Resolved, That it be recommended to the several Lodges in the State, not to employ any person to lecture with them, but such as shall be approved and appointed by this Grand Lodge.[57]

Cross was now receiving his $4 per day *plus* expenses, and he had a captive audience of fifty-six lodges, each of which had paid in $10 advance for 2½ days of lecturing.[58] With the exclusive "Grand Lodge franchise" for Connecticut, Cross would have no official competitors and could expect an annual income of $560 plus expenses. As a bonus, his traveling would be confined to small region of about 90 by 55 miles. (As a point of comparison, in 1821, the Grand Lodge of Connecticut "resolved, that in future the expenses of the Grand Chaplain, in traveling to and from, and attending on Grand Lodge, be paid after the rate of nine cents a mile for travel, and one dollar fifty cents per diem."[59])

The comments by Dayspring Lodge No. 30 of Connecticut indicate that Cross's efforts were well received and appreciated by the lodges he visited. "In October, 1818, Bro. Jeremy Cross, Grand Lecturer, visited the Lodge and delivered the Lectures of each degree to the Brethren in such a manner that they 'voted to subscribe for three copies of the emblematic monitor by

---

57 *Records of Freemasonry in the State of Connecticut,* 293–94.

58 Joseph K. Wheeler, *The Centennial: One Hundredth Anniversary of the Most Worshipful Grand Lodge of Connecticut* (Hartford, CT: Peck & Prouty, 1890), 109.

59 *Records of Freemasonry in the State of Connecticut,* 316.

the Grand Lecturer, Bro. Cross, and also to employ him two days more.'"[60]

The "emblematic monitor" referred to in the report of Dayspring Lodge was Cross's 1819 *The True Masonic Chart or Hieroglyphic Monitor*. It built upon Webb's *Freemasons' Monitor* by including additional emblems, explanations, and ceremonies. Cross's great innovation, however, was having Bro. Amos Doolittle engrave thirty-eight full-page plates illustrating the emblems of the nine degrees of American Craft Lodges, Royal Arch Chapters, and Royal and Select Councils. More than that, the emblems were arranged in the order in which they occurred in the lectures, so a student thumbing through the plates was reminded of both the words of the ritual and the correct sequence. The book was an invaluable memory aid to Cross's students and must have provided a nice supplement to his income wherever he lectured. (Note that Dayspring Lodge purchased three copies after his visit.) Nearly, all subsequent American Masonic monitors by any author have illustrations that politely can be said to be "inspired" by *The True Masonic Chart*. (Less charitable commentators might use the word *plagiarized*.)

Sales of *The True Masonic Chart* must have been given a boost by the official endorsement at the 1820 session of the Grand Lodge of Connecticut. "*Resolved*, That this Grand Lodge approve of the 'Masonic Chart, or Hieroglyphic Monitor,' published by Bro. Jeremy L. Cross, and recommend it for use as a text book in all the Lodges working under this jurisdiction."[61]

With all of Cross's apparent success as Grand Lecturer, it appears odd that the 1819 Grand Lodge session, two brothers "were appointed a committee to liquidate the accounts of Bro. Jeremy L. Cross, as Grand Lecturer, with power to draw on the Grand Treasurer for such balance as they find due to him for his services."[62] In 1820, "The Grand Secretary reported that several Lodges had failed to pay the expenses incurred by the visits of the Grand Lecturer; which report was continued, and the Grand Secretary directed to write to the Masters of these Lodges, and urge them to make payment."[63]

---

60 *History of Dayspring Lodge No. 30* in Douglas A. Gray, "Who Was Jeremy Ladd Cross?," Thomas Smith Webb Chapter of Research No. 1798, Transactions and Papers, accessed November 1, 2007, http://www.thomaswebb.org/Papers/Who_Was_Jeremy_Ladd_Cross.pdf.

61 *Records of Freemasonry in the State of Connecticut*, 310.

62 *Records of Freemasonry in the State of Connecticut*, 304.

63 *Records of Freemasonry in the State of Connecticut*, 308.

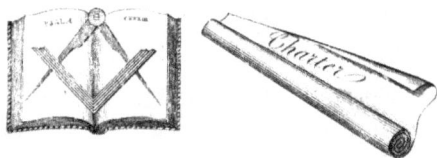

Plate 4, Entered Apprentice Degree, Third Section, Jeremy L. Cross,
The True Masonic Chart, or Hieroglyphic Monitor
(New Haven, CT: Flag & Gay, 1819).

While this sounds like the end of Bro. Cross's service to the Grand Lodge of Connecticut, he was present at the 1820 session as Junior Grand Deacon, pro tem., and at the sessions of 1821, 1822, 1823, and 1824 as Grand Lecturer.[64]

At the 1821, 1822, and 1823 sessions, he was elected Grand Lecturer, but in 1824, no Grand Lecturer was elected, and in 1825, the new constitution does not list the Grand Lecturer as an officer.[65] After this, Jeremy Cross's

---

64 *Records of Freemasonry in the State of Connecticut*, 305, 311, 323, 325, 351.
65 *Records of Freemasonry in the State of Connecticut*, 313–14, 326, 337, 353, 372.

name is absent from lists of grand officers. We do not know if perhaps the Grand Lodge of Connecticut was dissatisfied with his performance, or if he was offended by something, possibly having the Grand Lecturer no longer an elected office. He just seems to disappear. He did not drop out of Masonry, however.

In 1821, Cross brought out *The Templar's Chart, or Hieroglyphic Monitor* which gave the emblems, explanations, and ceremonies for the Order of the Red Cross, the Knights of Malta, and the Knights Templar, the orders conferred by American Knights Templar. He expanded his Masonic business to include printed aprons. Then in 1851, he became Sovereign Grand Commander of the clandestine "Cerneau" Supreme Council and required that candidates for the 14° be Royal Arch Masons and that candidates for the 15° be Knights Templar. These requirements lasted for a year, after which Cross resigned. He eventually retired to New Hampshire and laid down his working tools in 1860.

The Legacy of Itinerant Lecturers

If one were to concentrate on the foibles and failings of American itinerant lecturers, then it would be hard to find much to recommend them. They were opportunistic merchants who sought what the market would bear for their wares, much like William Finch, who sold manuscript lectures, tracing boards, aprons, and more, and the esteemed William Preston, who gave a money-back guarantee "to any subscriber who is not '*Master of either the first or second degree*' within twelve lessons."[66] On the other hand, how would any of us look if others only focused on our foibles and failings?

It took a certain admirable audacity to go on the road and make a living selling memorized ceremonies. Their only bona fides were a few pompously worded certificates with impressive seals. And yet the fraternity is richer for their efforts, however self-aggrandizing their activities may appear in retrospect. Without them there would be no Order of the Red Cross of Constantine or Select Masters. The Ancient and Accepted Rite would not have spread as widely before the Morgan Period, and it might not have survived at all. American Grand Lodges adopted the lecturers' style of traveling schools of instruction when they appointed their official Grand Lecturers. Itinerant American Masonic Lecturers were colorful and sometimes

---

66 Yasha Beresiner, "Aspects of Masonic Ephemera … Before 1813," *Ars Quatuor Coronatorum* 111 (1998): 1–23.

scorned, but through their efforts, American Freemasonry spread and assumed the successful form it has today.

It is fun to have horse thieves in your family tree—if they are not too closely related!

———————————————

First Published: *Ars Quatuor Coronatorum*, 121 (2008)

Early Newspaper Accounts of Prince Hall Freemasonry

Co-authored with Paul Rich

Part 1: Open Territory

In 1871, an exasperated Lewis Hayden[1] wrote to J. G. Findel[2] about the uncertain and complicated origins of grand lodges in the United States and the inconsistent attitudes displayed toward the chartering in Boston of African Lodge No. 459 by the Grand Lodge of England: "The territory was open territory. The idea of exclusive State jurisdiction by Grand Lodges had not then been as much as dreamed of."[3] The general theme of Hayden's correspondence with Findel was that African-American lodges certainly had at least as much—and possibly more—claim to legitimate Masonic origins as the white lodges did, and they had been denied recognition because of racism.[4]

The origins of African-American Freemasonry in the United States have generated a large literature and much dispute. Freemasonry was part of a new social landscape that took shape during and after the American Revolution[5] and included African-Americans from the earliest days of the nation, and it has had a continuing and considerable impact on African-Americans, where a robust fraternal life over two centuries has been most influenced by the Prince Hall tradition.[6] Freemasonry was a "tool kit" of ideas for black

---

1   Hayden was a former slave who was elected to the Massachusetts legislature and raised money to finance John Brown's anti-slavery raid on Harper's Ferry. His early life is described by Harriet Beecher Stowe in her book, *The Key to Uncle Tom's Cabin*.

2   Findel was a member of *Lodge Eleusis zur Verschwiegenheit* at Baireuth in 1856 and editor of the *Bauhütte* as well as a founder of the *Verein Deutscher Freimaurer* (Union of German Freemasons) and author in 1874 of *Geist unit Form der Freimaurerei* (Genius and Form of Freemasonry).

3   Lewis Hayden, *Masonry Among Colored Men in Massachusetts* (Boston: Lewis Hayden, 1871), 41.

4   Hayden, *passim*.

5   Robert A, Gross, *The Minutemen and Their World* (New York: Hill and Wang, 1976), 173.

6   Ron Kelley, "Brotherly influence: Prince Hall Freemasonry's Lasting Impression on

community formation just as it was for the white majority and provided a moral vision to replace the sense of limitation born of slavery,[7] constituting "resources for development and a defense against white racism."[8] The issue of the legitimacy of the origins of African-American Freemasonry is of more than passing importance to the history of race in America. A contentious subject, focus of much of the debate has been over the alleged regularity of African-American lodges and whether they had authentic charters from older recognized grand lodges. The suspicion has been that racially discriminatory attitudes "relied on abstruse procedural arguments and the historical record, all ingeniously manipulated."[9]

Inevitably discussion of African-American Freemasonry recalls an extraordinary individual, Prince Hall, who was not only an important Mason of African origins but also one of the most important Freemasons to come out of the formative days of the Republic. His early life is sometimes unclear but, as the ensuing pages illustrate, his Masonic membership paralleled a later career as an adroit and articulate proponent of natural rights.[10] The common claim is that he was initiated on March 6, 1775, with fourteen other African-Americans, by Sergeant John Batt of Irish Lodge No. 441 of the 38th Regiment of Foot, then stationed in Boston.[11] Initially granted a "permet" to march on St. John's Day and to

African-American Fraternal Orders," *Phylaxis*, 39:1 (1st quarter 2012), 20. See Theda Skocpol, Ariane Liazos, and Marshall Ganz, *What a Mighty Power We Can Be: African American Fraternal Groups and the Struggle for Racial Equality* (Princeton and Oxford: Princeton University Press, 2006), 6.

7 David Hackett, "The Prince Hall Masons and the African American Church," in *All Men Free and Brethren: Essays on the History of African-American Freemasonry*, eds., Peter P. Hinks and Stephen Kantrowitz (Ithaca and London: Cornell University Press, 2013), 138–39.

8 Hackett, 141.

9 Martin Summers, "Arguing for Our Race," in Hinks and Kantrowitz, 158.

10 Samuel K. Roberts, *In the Path of Virtue: The African American Moral Tradition*, (Cleveland: Pilgrim Press, 1999), 23.

11 The 38th left Athlone, Ireland in 1774 for Boston where during 1775 it fought in the Battle of Breeds Hill (Bunker Hill). In 1776 it was posted to New York, and stayed in the area until 1783. Formed in 1705 and originally Lillington's Foot, in 1751, it was numbered the 38th Regiment of Foot, and in 1782 as the 38th (1st Staffordshire) Regiment of Foot. Later, the regiment became part of the South Staffordshire Regiment and then, in 1959, the Staffordshire Regiment. In 2007, The Staffordshire Regiment became 3rd Battalion The Mercian Regiment. See "A brief history of the Staffordshire Regiment," accessed July 5, 2013, http://staffordshireregimentmuseum.com/history.html

bury their dead, Bro. Hall applied on behalf of the lodge to the premier Grand Lodge, the "Moderns," in London for a charter that was granted in 1784 and finally, after much delay was physically delivered to Boston in 1787. Out of these events was born African Lodge No. 459 that eventually transformed itself into "African Grand Lodge No. 1," from which Prince Hall Masons descend.

There are alternative accounts of the first initiations. Peter Hinks and Stephen Kanrowitz point out that it could have occurred in 1778 or that Prince Hall could have been initiated in 1775 and the other men in 1778.[12] Like Prince Hall's early life, there have been a number of alternative scenarios advanced that call for more examination of regimental histories and personal memoirs. Considerable scholarly work remains to be done, and the study of this fascinating if controversial period of Freemasonry is helped by bringing together, facilitated by their appearance online, the transcripts of early newspaper references to "African Lodge" and "Prince Hall." We are surprised given their significance that this has not been done more exhaustively. To accomplish this, we have relied primarily on electronic databases, and particularly on "America's Historical Newspapers" published by Readex, a division of NewsBank, and Genealogy Bank. The optical character recognition of these digitized scans varies in quality, and the databases we have usedon't include every newspaper of the period nor every issue of those papers they have reproduced. Thus, it is more than likely that there are other articles our searches didn't find.

One of our important discoveries is neglected evidence of white Masons helping Prince Hall and African Lodge and expressing an affinity. For example, Bro. Nathan Willis's *Independent Chronicle*[13] published Prince Hall's dignified response to a sarcastic story about African Lodge's 1782 celebration of St. John's Day, and Bro. Benjamin Russell's *Massachusetts Centinel*[14]

---

12 Peter P. Hinks and Stephen Kantrowitz, "Introduction: The Revolution in Freemasonry," in Hinks and Kantrowitz, 3.

13 Willis was a journeyman on the paper's staff who went on to be editor of the Portland *Eastern Argus*. Jeffrey L. Pasley, *The Tyranny of Printers: Newspaper Politics in the Early American Republic* (Charlottesville and London: University of Virginia Press, 2001), 223.

14 Russell was an apprentice of Isaiah Thomas, publisher of the famous *Masachusets Spy* and Grand Master of Massachusetts, 1802–1805 and 1809–1810. Russell founded the *Centinel* in 1784 and was one of the printers, "more forthright in their opinions than their colonial predecessors had been, but they settled into the role of reliable auxiliaries

published a series of positive stories about African Lodge, including a touchingly hopeful poem for racial harmony in the Craft (reprinted here in entirety for the first time) celebrating the receipt of African Lodge's charter. This brotherhood contrasts with other, later white Masons publically ignoring or denouncing or defaming Black Masons and then privately providing support.

Albert Pike displayed a notable example of this ambient behavior toward Black Masonry. In 1875, he wrote to the white Grand Lodge of Ohio, "Prince Hall Lodge was as regular a lodge as any lodge created by competent authority, and had a perfect right (as other lodge in Europe did) to establish other lodges, making itself a mother Lodge." And yet in the same letter, he said, "I took my obligations to white men, not to negroes. When I have to accept negroes as brothers or leave Masonry, I shall leave it."[15] Palliatively, Pike later gave a copy of his Scottish Rite rituals to Thornton A. Jackson, Prince Hall Grand Commander, S.J., sometime after 1887, when Jackson assumed office, and before 1891, when Pike died.[16]

The apparently earliest newspaper reference is for December 30, 1782, only seven years after Prince Hall was initiated, and our account arbitrarily stops in 1827, the year of the "Declaration of Independence of African Lodge." During this forty-five year period, we found thirty unique articles (some of which are now reprinted here), each giving an insight to the earliest days of Prince Hall Masonry.

The first example is in December 30, 1782, *The Independent Ledger,* and the *American Advertiser,* Boston, vol. 5, no. 243, published by Edward Draper and John West Folsom:

---

to the victorious Whig establishment, which was growing steadily more disenchanted with the democratic, localistic political fervour the Revolution had unleashed." Pasley, *The Tyranny of Printers,* 40. "Unlike most Federalist printers, Russell pursued a political career in his own right, becoming a prominent local officeholder beginning in 1805. Besides positions on the Boston School Committee, Board of Health, and as a city alderman, he represented Boston in the state legislature from 1805 to 1805 continuously, capping his career with a term on the Executive Council." Pasley, 233.

15 *Proceedings of the Grand Lodge of the Ancient and Honorable Fraternity of Free & Accepted Masons of the State of Ohio at is Sixty-eighth Annual Grand Communication begun and held at Columbus, October A.L. 5875* (Cincinnati: Western Methodist Book Concern Press, 1875), 49–50.

16 Arturo de Hoyos, "On the Origins of the Prince Hall Scottish Rite Rituals," *Heredom* 5 (1996): 52.

B O S T O N,   D e c .   3 0.
...

On Friday laſt (27th inſt) the feaſt of St. John the
Evangeliſt was celebrated by SAINT BLACK's Lodge
of *Free* and Acc-pt-d M-ſ-ns, who went in procef-
ſion, preceded by a band of muſick, dreſſed in their
aprons and jewels, from *Brother* Gl-pions, up State-
Street, and thro' Corn hill to the houſe of the *Right
Worſhipful* GRAND MASTER, in Water ſtreet,
where an elegant and ſplendid entertainment was given upon the occaſion.

This brief notice seems to be mocking African Lodge with a sarcastic reference to "Saint Black's Lodge," though the rest of the article is neutral and
presumably accurate. "Brother Gl-pions" refers to Louis Glapion (d. 1813),
a hairdresser and member of African Lodge, who with George Middleton
(1735–1815) built a home 1786–1787 at what is now 5–7 Pinckney Street
on Beacon Hill in Boston, which still stands today.[17] Col. Middleton was
commander of the famous Black regiment, the Bucks of America, and third
Master of African Lodge.[18] "Water Street" refers to the residence and leather workshop of Prince Hall that was also used by African Lodge as a meeting place.[19]

There then appeared in reply to this jibe a gentle and sensible rebuttal by
Prince Hall himself. On January 9, 1783, in *The Independent Chronicle and
Universal Advertiser*, Boston, vol. 15, no. 530, published by Bro. Nathan
Willis:

17 "Louis Glapion, George Middleton, owners and occupiers. Wooden dwelling; East on
Clapboard Street; South on Jona Mason & Garrison G. Otis, Land 1,925 square feet;
house, 345 square feet, 1 story, 4 windows; value $600." *A Report of the Record Com-
missioners of the City of Boston*. 1798. Boston, 1890, 482, in Charles H. Wesley, *Prince
Hall Life and Legacy*, 2nd ed. (Washington, DC: United Supreme Council, SJ, 1983), 83.
The house is designated by the National Park Service as a Boston African-American
National Historic Site.

18 Wesley, *Prince Hall*, 50; Gregory S. Kearse, "The Bucks of America and Prince Hall
Freemasonry during the American Revolution," *Prince Hall Masonic Digest* (Washington, D.C.: Prince Hall Grand Lodge of DC, 2012), 40, no. 1 (April 2012): 8.

19 Wesley, *Prince Hall*, 84. A letter from Hall to William White, Secretary of the Grand
Lodge, London, May 17, 1787, is signed "Living in Wourter Street at the sine of the
Golden Fleece in Boston where our Lodge is now held." William Upton, "Prince Hall's
Letter Book," (13) [Wesley gives the citation as letter 13 from Upton's *AQC* paper, but
the full quote is not there. Perhaps it refers to Upton's *Light on a Dark Subject* (1899)
or his *Negro Masonry* (1902)]; Prince Hall to William Moody, August 12, 1785, signed
"Master of the African Lodge, at the Golden Fleece in Water Street, Boston." Upton, 58.

Mr. WILLIS,

OBSERVING a fketch in Monday's paper, printed by Meff's Draper and Folfom, relative to the celebration of the feaft of St. John, the Evangelift, by the African Lodg — the Mafter of the faid Lodge being Poffeffed of a charitable difpofition towards mankind, we therefore hope the publifher of the faid fketch meant nothing elfe but a candid defcription of our proceffion, &c. — therefore, with due fubmiffion to the public our title is not *St. Black's Lodge*, neither do we afpire after high titles, but our only defire is, that the Grand Architect of the Univerfe would Diffufe in the hearts the true fpirit of Mafonry which is love to God, and univerfal love to all mankind: Thefe I humbly conceive to be the two grand pillars of Mafonry. Inftead of a fplendid entertainment, we had an agreeable one, in brotherly love. With humble fubmiffion to the above publifher and the public, I beg leave to fubfcribe myfelf your humble fervant,

PRINCE HALL,

Mafter of the African Lodge No. 1. dedicated to the St. John.

N. B. Neither do we dedicate our Lodge to St. John, but by being Chriftians, and made under that denomination, chufe to do fo; but were we to dedicate for anciency, or for honour, we could trace it from the creation.

This is Prince Hall's dignified response to the anonymous carp at "St. Black's Lodge" published eleven days earlier, albeit in a competing paper, and is characteristic of his reserve in responding to critics. It is worth nothing that

Nathaniel Willis was a member of St. Andrews Lodge No. 235, and perhaps provided a sympathetic venue for Bro. Hall's rejoinder.[20] This is not as we shall see the only instance of a brother white Mason publishing positive material about African Lodge and its members.

Then, more than a year later, on October 20, 1784, the Massachusetts *Centinel*, Boston, vol. 2, no. 9, published by Bro. Benjamin Russell, carried the following surprising notice:

SIX SHILLINGS Reward.

LOST, the CHARTER of a certain GRAND LODGE: Any person that has found the same, and will leave it with the Printers hereof shall be intitled to the above reward.

P. H—LL, Grand Secretary.

The advertisement was another sarcastic dig apparently written by someone familiar with the status of African Lodge's charter. On March 2, 1784, Prince Hall had written to William Moody in London and asked that he present African Lodge's request for a warrant before the Grand Master of England. The charter for African Lodge No. 459 was issued on September 20, 1784, but not sent to Boston because the fee had not been paid. The fee paid was over £6 0s. 8d., so the reward of six shillings was a trifling, less than 1/20th of the charter fee.[21]

Benjamin Russell (1761–1845) was a member of Rising States and St. John's Lodges of Boston, Jr. Grand Warden of the Grand Lodge of Massachusetts, 1811–1812, Sr. Grand Warden, 1813, and Grand Master, 1814–1816.[22] After this one mocking notice, Russell's *Centinel* thereafter turned to publishing sympathetic notices of African Lodge and Prince Hall. Evidence of this are a series of articles about the death of Luke Belcher. A notice appears on August 18, 1786, *The American Recorder and Charlestown*

---

20 *Lodge of St. Andrew, and the Massachusetts Grand Lodge* (Boston: Lodge of St. Andrew, 1870), 235.

21 Upton, 56–57.

22 William R. Denslow, *10,000 Famous Freemasons* (Richmond, VA: Macoy Pub., 1957), vol. 4 (Q–Z), s.v. Benjamin Russell.

Advertiser, Charlestown, vol. 1, no. 708, published by John W. Allen and Thomas C. Cushing:

> Died, his excellency Luke Belcher, late governour of the Africans in this town. He was universally refpected by every rank of citizens.

Luke Belcher was apparently enslaved by Jonathan Belcher (1681/1682–1757), Governor of New Hampshire (1729–1741), Massachusetts (1730–1741), and New Jersey (1747–1757), founder of Princeton University, and the first American-born Freemason. One could think that calling Luke Belcher "his excellency" and "governour of the Africans" was sarcasm, but that seems grossly out of place in an obituary notice, especially since the publishers could have simply ignored Belcher's death. It seems significant that the death of an African American received any notice at all. The informal titles probably reflected both Luke's status among African Americans and his relationship with the Belcher family. This death notice is expanded August 19, 1786, *Massachusetts Centinel,* Boston, vol. 5, no. 44, published by Bro. Benjamin Russell, and reprinted August 24, 1786, *The New York Morning Post and Daily Advertiser,* New York City, no. 760, published by William Morton:

> *On Monday laft was fummoned by the all-fubduing Monarch, from this fublunary abode, Luke Belcher, aged 42, by birth an African, formerly of the family of his late Excellency Governour Belcher; and on Thurfday laft his remains were refpectfully depofited in the Dreary manfion of the filent, attended by a lengthy proceffion of friends and refpectable characters, preceded by a band of brothers, in union, denominated the African Lodge of Free and Accepted Mafons, in the garb and ornaments of the craft, led by the Tyler and Stewards of the order, bearing the infignias of their refpective offices, preferving that due decorum and becoming refpect requifite on fo ferious an occafion, and characteriftick of the honourable fraternity.—The corps being carried into church, where the funeral fervice was performed, the body*

of their friend and brother they left with its parent earth, the tenement appointed for all living—contemplating that it was in reſerve for them to do as he had done—that they muſt all follow his example, for

"The ſcepter'd King—the burden'd ſlave;
"The humble and the haughty die;
"The rich—the poor—the baſe—the brave;
"In duſt without diſtinction lie."

Though our departed friend could not boaſt of any very elevated diſtinctions in life, he has left behind the "pearl of great price"—a character many of his apparent ſuperiors need not be aſhamed to imitate, but without which even the ſons of affluence are poor indeed. His ſalutary inſtructions to thoſe of his own kindred, to "lead lives void of offence,"—to live within compaſs, and act upon the ſquare, cannot be injurious to the lives of others, if carried into practice, not even to thoſe ſuperficially diſtinguiſhed by nature, unfortunately having, perhaps, little elſe to boaſt of than a different complexion. But will the moſt circumſpect— the moſt harmleſs walks of life—the mind being the dwelling place of every good and generous principle —of every maſonick virtue, ſecure from the arreſt of the ghaſtly Conqueror? Ah, no! Cæſar and Scipio, Pompey and Cato have ſubmitted, tacitly confeſſing their inability to laſt to ſecure a retreat.

Compared to many obituaries of the time, this is an unusually long notice. Bro. Benjamin Russell published this fulsome obituary, and it is in marked contrast to the sham reward notice for the missing African Lodge charter he published two years earlier on October 20, 1784. Luke Belcher's notice was more than a half column, when most death notices were only a few lines. It not only praised his character, but also gave a dignified description of African Lodge's participation in the funeral. Further, the notice squarely chastises those who may feel superior but who have "little else to boast of than a different complexion." It seems significant that this lengthy obituary of an African American was repeated by at least four newspapers from Middletown, Massachusetts, to Philadelphia.[23] (The four lines of poetry, "The scepter'd king …," is from the drinking song "Plato's Advice.")[24] Prince Hall and his brethren had overcome the fact that, "The black subculture was considered by white New Englanders to be at or near the bottom of the social scale."[25]

Given the toing and froing of public view of African-American Freemasonry, it would have been an appreciative Prince Hall when he opened the pages of his paper on May 2, 1787, *The Massachusetts Centinel*, Boston, vol. 7, no. 13, published by no less than Bro. Benjamin Russell:

AFRICAN LODGE.

BY Captain SCOTT, from London, came the CHARTER, &c. which his Royal Highnefs the Duke of CUMBERLAND, and the Grand Lodge of Great Britain, have been gracioufly pleafed to grant to the African Lodge, in Bofton. Af the Brethren have a defire to acknowledge all favours fhewn them, then in this publick manner return particular thanks to a certain Member of the fraternity, who offered the fo generous reward in this paper fome time fince, for the Charter fuppofed

---

23 Reprinted—
  August 26, 1786, *The Daily Advertiser*, New York, vol. 2, no. 4, published by Francis Childs;
  August 26, 1786, *The New York Morning Post, and Daily Advertiser*, New York, no. 762, published by William Morton;
  August 29, 1786, *The Pennsylvania Packet, and Daily Advertiser*, Philadelphia, no. 2,351, published by Bro. John Dunlap (1747–1912), Lodge No. 2, Philadelphia, and David C. Claypoole;
  September 11, 1786, *The Middlesex Gazette*, Middletown, Massachusetts, 1, no. 45, published by Moses H. Woodward and Thomas Green.

24 It was published at least as early 1771 in George Alexander Stevens, comp., *The Choice Spirit's Chaplet: or, A Poesy from Parnassus* (Whitehaven, England: John Dunn, 1771), 267–68.

25 William D. Piersen, *Black Yankees: The Development of the Afro-American Subculture in Eighteenth-Century New England* (Amherst: University of Massachusetts Press, 1988), 60.

to be loft; and to affure him, though they doubt of his real friendfhip, that he has made them many good friends.   P R I N C E   H A L L

Bofton, April 30. 1787.

This announcement from Prince Hall is his great triumph: the premier Grand Lodge of England recognized the legitimacy of African Lodge and granted it a charter. Russell makes an about-face, generously putting aside his earlier sarcasm. Prince Hall's response is restrained like that he made to the earlier notice about "St. Black's Lodge," and yet he deftly buries his detractor with kindness when he refers to his "so generous reward." He goes on to say that the detractor, presumably a white Mason, has made African Lodge "many good friends." It's possible that one of those new friends was Bro. Benjamin Russell, the publisher of the *Centinel*. After the hoax notice of the "so generous reward" for the missing charter, the coverage of African Lodge in the *Centinel* over the years was uniformly positive. We would like to think that Bro. Russell had second thoughts about mocking fellow Freemasons, perhaps after meeting with Prince Hall and becoming his friend. The article was reprinted: May 18, 1787, *The Pennsylvania Packet, and Daily Advertiser*, Philadelphia, no. 2584, published by Bro. John Dunlap and David C. Claypoole.

The news appeared elsewhere as well. May 5, 1787, *The Salem Mercury: Political, Commercial, and Moral*, Salem, no. 30, published by Bro. John Dabney and Thomas C. Cushing:

> In Capt. Scott, lately arrived from London, the African Lodge, in Bofton, received a Charter, which his Royal Highnefs, the Duke of Cumberland, and the Grand Lodge of Great-Britain, have been pleafed to grant.

The notice summarizes Prince Hall's announcement and is similar to shipping announcements of the day. John Dabney (1752–1819) was a member of Essex Lodge, Salem, Massachusetts.

Hardly routine was what appeared on May 5, 1787, *The Massachusetts Centinel*, Boston, vol. 7, no. 14, published by Bro. Russell. The paper carried this remarkable poem:[26]

---

26 The poem "Masonry," *Massachusetts Centinel*, May 5, 1787, seems to have been only

M A S O N R Y.

THRO'OUT the globe's extenfive round,
  The fire of love extends,
Which glows in true mafonick hearts—
That family of friends!

Ev'n AFRIC's SONS—ill-fated race!
  Now feel its genial heat;
With charter'd rights, from England's Duke
  THE SABLE LODGES MEET.

No more shall COLOURS difagree;
  but hearts with hands unite;
For in the wond'rous myftery,
  There's neither BLACK nor WHITE.

And lest a BLEACHED BROTHER shou'd,
  in fcorn turn up his nose—
Know that a PRINCE* may favours take,
  From Dukes, nor honour lofe.

────────

A PRINCE – Mafter of the African Lodge – H-ll
is only an American addition to his name.

This poem wonderfully expresses the ideals of Freemasonry and is remarkable for transcending the racism of the period with idealistic optimism, especially in the third stanza. It gave highly positive publicity to African Lodge and included the clever wordplay of a duke giving favors to a prince. The poem is unsigned, and with only three days between the notice of receipt of the charter and the poem, the anonymous poet must have been quickly commissioned by Russell or was Russell himself.

Russell published on December 5, 1807, the obituary notice of Prince Hall in the *Columbian Centinel* (successor of the Massachusetts *Centinel*)

────────

cited three times, and then only recently: Adam Potkay and Sandra Burr, eds., *Black Atlantic Writers of the Eighteenth Century: Living the New Exodus in England and the Americas* (New York: St. Martin's Press, 1995), 16; Laurie F. Maffly-Kipp, *Setting Down the Sacred Past: African-American Race Histories* (Cambridge, MA: Harvard University Press, 2010) 31; Peter P. Hinks and Stephen Kantrowitz. "Introduction: The Revolution in Freemasonry," in *All Men Free and Brethren*, eds., Hinks and Kantrowitz, 6.

announcing his death "yesterday morning." This notice was repeated in at least six other newspapers. It is significant that Russell who was the first to publish the notice about the arrival of the charter followed by the positive and supportive poem was also the first to publish Hall's obituary. Was Russell in the end a Masonic friend of Prince Hall and African Lodge, or even a general supporter of African-Americans?

Part 2: A Man Betoken to None

That Prince Hall was made a Freemason by British soldiers during a period of confrontation between the British and the colonists something about his independence of character and the contradictions of his time, and more attention needs to be paid to his position in colonial Boston in addition to his role as founder of a lodge. His life is an argument that individuals make history rather than are its creation: newspapers of the eighteenth century give us an idea of the leadership accounting for the success of African-American Freemasonry and place the movement in context. Prince Hall was an extraordinary man of many parts.[27]

On this point, Professor Alan Gilbert of the University of Denver has asserted that the American Revolution should be regarded as two revolutions in process. In a recent book, *Black Patriots and Loyalists*, he writes that, "Those who fought for independence sometimes did so to oppose emancipation. Conversely, in which may at first seem like a paradox, some of those who fought to crush the incipient rebellion for American 'freedom' did so to further their own freedom from slavery, embracing British offers of emancipation in return for their service in the imperial cause."[28]

So, the British soldiers who initiated Prince Hall may have been sympathetic to the indignities suffered by blacks in the colonies. It does seem there was a paradoxical element to the revolutionary era in which Prince Hall

---

27 The numerous newspaper accounts we quote in this series sustain our feeling and the view that Davis took in his early (1946) account: "easily the most distinguished American Negro of his day." Harry E. Davis, *A History of Freemasonry Among Negroes in America* (Philadelphia: United Supreme Council, Ancient & Accepted Scottish Rite of Freemasonry, Northern Jurisdiction, U.S.A. (Prince Hall Affiliation), 1946), 14. Compare in a contentious account of the Prince Hall movement, Henry Wilson Coil Sr., John MacDuffie Sherman, with assistance of Harold Van Buren Voorhis, *A Documentary Account of Prince Hall and Other Black Fraternal Orders* (NP: Missouri Lodge of Research, 1982), 18.

28 Alan Gilbert, *Black Patriots and Loyalists: Fighting for Emancipation in the War for Independence* (Chicago and London: University of Chicago Press, 2012), viii.

lived, as the monarchical British were in respects ahead of the revolutionary new Americans in their negative view of slavery. Indeed, Harry Davis
suggests that because of long service in the West Indies, British regiments
may have had black members who were Masons.[29] (Many members of the
first Masonic lodge in Boston, St. John's, were Loyalists and more than
twenty of them fled when the British evacuated Boston.[30])

No incident in his life better illustrates the complexity of a situation in
which Hall found himself than what transpired just shortly after he had
handled the drawn out business of acquiring a proper charter from the
English grand lodge.[31] At the center of the episode is the recognition of a
Masonic secret sign. Masonic recognition stories are a genre of their own,
usually turning on an incident when someone in distress gives a Masonic
sign and is rescued. And it is true that a word or sign has brought relief not
only to the destitute but to soldiers on the battlefield and frontier scouts
about to be scalped. However, there is no more dramatic rescue than that
recorded in early 1788 (February 18, 1788, *The American Herald*, Boston,
vol. 7, no. 332, published by Edward Eveleth Powars):

> Aſ infamous an action has been perpetrated with-
> in a few days paſt as ever blotted the annals of
> humam nature. The Captain of a veſſel, in the
> employ of a foreigner, engaged a number of ne-
> groes, to go down to one of the iſlands in the vici-
> nity of this town, to work: having got them on
> board his boat, he directly proceeded to the veſſel
> and confined them : this being done he immediately
> ſet ſail, and having arrived off Salem, he ſent on
> ſhore and inveigled a number more of unfortunate
> black on board. Having thus far succeeded in his

---

29 Davis, 31–32, "by 1790, fifty Antients regimental warrants had been granted within the
    British army, the majority of which were granted to regiments posted to North Ameri-
    ca." Ric Berman (Brighton, Chicago, Toronto: Sussex Academic Press, 2013), 64. Nor
    have historians responded to the challenge of Harold Van Buren Voorhis to investigate
    white members of Prince Hall lodges. See Voorhis, *White Brethren in Prince Hall Ma-
    sonic Lodges*, (Whitefish, MT, Kessinger Legacy Reprints, 2008, reprinted from Harold
    Van Buren Voorhis, *Negro Masonry in the United States* (New York: Henry Emmerson,
    1940). No date or other bibliographical information is offered, which is often the case
    with Kessinger Masonic reprints.

30 Henry May, *History of St. John's Lodge of Boston* (Boston: Saint John's Lodge, 1917), 57.

31 For a brief but useful outline of the event, Davis, 181–82.

deteftable purpofe, he purfued his voyage, either to fome of the fouthern ftates, or to the Weft-Indies, where, in all probability, he will difpofe of them to linger out a wretched exiftence in the worft of Slavery. Blufh humanity ! And recoil civilizations, at the conduct of men who profefs to be guided by thy principles.

This is the first report we have found so far of the infamous kidnapping which inspired Prince Hall to petition the Massachusetts legislature to abolish the slave trade. It really improves in its dramatics on any Dan Brown story or Walt Disney movie about the Craft. It also is important in documenting intercession for a black brother by a white merchant who took brotherhood seriously, which in the future history of Prince Hall lodges in contact with white Freemasonry was, to put it mildly, not always to be the case.[32]

In reviewing the circumstances of the kidnapping, it is useful to remember that by the 1770s, there were over a half million slaves in North America, so free blacks like Hall were in a minority and constantly in danger of being snatched by slave merchants.[33] Slavery had been abolished in Massachusetts in 1783 but fugitive slaves from jurisdictions where it was legal were subject to repatriation. (February 26, 1788, *The New York Packet*, New York City, no. 779, published by Samuel and John Loudon):

Meffieurs Printers,

TEARING the unhappy African from his native country, and from all that is dear to man, into a land of ftrangers and perpetual fervitude, is an evil upon which the ableft pens have been exercifed in the moft pathetic addreffes to the feelings of the benevolent : But the more execrable practice of man-ftealing, where the devoted victim has obtain-

---

32 "Freemasonry was therefore compromised by antiblack, antifemale, anti-Catholic, anti-Jewish, antiradical, and anti-immigrant sentiments, such that the Ku Klux Klan was 'quite successful in recruiting Masons to its ranks.'" Michael A. Gomez, *Black Crescent: The Experience and Legacy of African Muslims in the Americas*, quoting Dumeil [*sic.* Lynn Dumenil, *Freemasonry and American Culture, 1880–1930*, Princeton: Princeton University Press, 1964), 122] (New York: Cambridge University Press, 2005), 11–12.

33 Carole Boston Weatherford, *The African-American Struggle for Legal Equality in American History* (Aldershot, England: Enselow Publishers, 2000), 23. Slavery was abolished in Massachusetts in 1783, but not the slave trade until the Prince Hall intervention.

ed his manumiffion, in reward for many years faithful fervice, is fo truly diabolical, that we may rely
upon the concurrent cenfure of all, who are not def-
titute of generous fentiments, and their united efforts
to relieve diftrefs, and bring the perpetrators of fuch
nefarious crimes to condign punifhment. To this
purpofe the Printers are generally requefted to in-
fert the following extract of a letter dated
-Charlefton, Maffachufetts, Feb. 13, 1788.

'Solomon Babfon, mafter of the floop Ruby, under pretence of employing them to labor, decoyed
three free Negro men, belonging to Bofton, and
has carried them off. The floop cleared out for
Martinico, but I fufpect fhe is either gone to Charlef-
ton, S.C. or to Georgia. The Negroes were quiet, induftrious men, and have left wives and children in diftrefs, as well as a burden to the community. Every lover of Juftice muft feel refentment
againft fuch an outrage upon human nature. One
of the unfortunate men was a faithful fervant of
mine, made free in reward of his fidelity; and if
you can difcover the author, or gain any intelligence of thefe unfortunate fellows, you will oblige
a number of refpectable citizens, and fubferve the
caufe of humanity. The names of thefe injured
men were Wendham, Cato, and Luck.'

The newspaper account is based on an anonymous letter that is quoting
still another anonymous letter, one from Charleston. In sum, it refers to the
scandal of the kidnapping of the three free Blacks in Boston Harbor for sale
as slaves in Martinique. The "letter from Charleston" sounds as if it had been
published earlier in another newspaper, probably from Massachusetts. The
villain was Solomon Babson, who was the owner, bonder, and commander
of the Massachusetts brig *Ruby* and received a letter of marque to act as a
privateer against the British.[34] His kidnapping of Americans was not only

---

34 "Bonds of the Letters of Marque ... September 16, 1782: Ruby. Massachusetts brig.
Guns: 6. Crew: 21. Bond: $20,000. Master: Solomon Babson. Bonders: Solomon Bab-
son, Newburyport. John Babson, Newburyport. Joseph Tyler, Newburyport. Owner:
John Babson, Newburyport." Charles Henry Lincoln, *Naval Records of the American
Revolution: 1775–1788* (Washington: Government Printing Office, 1906), 449.

immoral but illegal, and it went far beyond his marque charter. One of his three victims, "Luck," was a member of Prince Hall's African Lodge.[35]

This incident inspired Prince Hall and other free Blacks in Boston to petition the Massachusetts legislature to abolish the slave trade, which is described in the next newspaper story, which was reprinted from, the March 19, 1788, issue of *The Independent Gazetteer; or, the Chronicle of Freedom* (Philadelphia, vol. 7, no. 707, published by Bro. Eleazer Oswald (1755?–1795), Lodge No. 2, Philadelphia). It appears in the April 8, 1788, issue of *The New York Morning Post and Advertiser* (New York City, no. 1268, published by William Morton):

> The following is a copy of a petition pre-fented to the General Court of Maffachufetts; which is taken from the original in the hand writing of the figner, who is a free Negro in the town of Bofton:
>
> *To the Honorable the Senate and Houfe of Repre-fentatives of the Commonwealth of Maffachu-fetts Bay, in General Court affembled, on the 27th of February 1788.*
>
> The Petition of the great number of BLACKS, Freemen of this Commonwealth.
>
> *Humbly fheweth,*
>
> THAT your petitioners are juftly alarmed at the inhuman and cruel treatment that three of our brethren, free citizens of the town of Bofton lately received. The Captain under pretence that his veffel was in diftrefs on an ifland below in this harbour, having got them on board, but them in irons, and carried them off from their wives and children, to be fold for flaves; this being the unhappy ftate of thefe poor men, what can your petitioners expect

---

35 *Collections of the Massachusetts Historical Society* (Boston: Massachusetts Historical Society, 1877), vol. 3, 5th series, 54–55. Hazard wrote to Belknap on April 5 and discussed Hall's petition and the kidnapping case, 28–29. Belknap also wrote to Hazard on April 18, 1788, and reviewed the kidnapping and Governor John Hancock's intervention with the Governor of Martinique, 32.

but to be treated in the fame manner by the fame fort of men?—What then are our lives and liberties worth, if they may be taken away in fuch a cruel and unjuft manner as this? May it pleafe your Honor's, we are not infenfible, that the good laws of this ftate, forbid all fuch bad actions; notwithftanding we can affure your Honors, that many of our Free Blacks, that have entered on board of veffels, as feamen, have been fold for flaves; and fome of them we have heard from, but know not who carried them away. Hence it is that many of us, who are good feamen, are obliged to ftay at home through fear, and the one half our time loiter through the ftreets, for want of employ; whereas if thy were protected in that lawful calling, they might get a livelihood for themfelves and theirs, which in the fituation they are not in, they cannot. One thing more we would beg leave to hint, that is, that your petitioners have for fome time paft beheld with grief, fhips cleared out from this harbour for Africa, and there they either fteal, or caufe others to fteal, our brothers and fifters, fill their fhips holds full of unhappy men and women, crouded together, then fet out to fiind the beft market, to fell them there like fheep for the flaughter, and then return here like honeft men, after having fported with the lives and liberty of their fellow men, and at the fame time call themfelves Chriftians. Blufh, O Heavens! At this, thefe our weighty grievances! We cheerfully fubmit to your Honors, without dictating in the leaft, knowing by experience that your Honors have, and we truft ever will in your wifdom do us that juftice that our prefent condition requires, as God and the good laws of this commonwealth fhall dictate you.

And as in duty bound, your petitioners fhall ever pray.

PRINCE HALL.

This letter substantiates that Prince Hall was not only a Masonic founding father but a well-known leader of the African-American community in Boston and indeed in America. His petition was reinforcing one brought by the Quakers, and he inspired the Boston clergy to submit one of their own. All this agitation bore fruit. The results of the changes that he demanded were an act passed on March 26, 1788, one month after his petition, "to prevent the Slave Trade, and for granting Relief to the Families of such unhappy Persons as may be Kidnapped or decoyed away from this Commonwealth."[36]

News of this was widely reprinted—

April 8, 1788, *The New York Packet*, New York City, no. 791, published by Samuel and John Loudon

April 11, 1788, *The Pennsylvania Packet, and Daily Advertiser*, Philadelphia, no. 2,867, published by Bro. John Dunlap

April 12, 1788, *The Independent Gazetteer; or, the Chronicle of Freedom*, Philadelphia, vol. 7, no. 728, published by Bro. Eleazer Oswald

April 16, 1788, *Connecticut Journal*, New Haven, no. 1,068, published by Thomas and Samuel Green

April 24, 1788, *Thomas's Massachusetts Spy: Or, the Worcester Gazette*, Worcester, vol. 17, no. 786, published by Bro. Isaiah Thomas

April 24, 1788, *The Cumberland Gazette*, Portland, Maine, published by Thomas B. Wait

Then, on August 23, 1788, readers of *The Pennsylvania Mercury, and Universal Advertiser* (Philadelphia, no. 278, published by Daniel Humphreys) were further updated:

Extract of a letter from Boſton.

...

An Extract of another letter from the ſame place.[37]

I have one piece of good news to tell you. The negroes who were kidnapped from hence laſt win-

---

36 See and compare as published by Thomas and Samuel Green. April 24, 1788, *Thomas's Massachusetts Spy: Or, the Worcester Gazette*, Worcester, vol. 17, no. 786, published by Bro. Isaiah Thomas and April 24, 1788, *The Cumberland Gazette*, Portland, Maine, published by Thomas B. Wait. Also Kaplan, *The Black Presence*, 210.

37 The immediately preceding article is an "Extract of a letter from Boston." Thus we can assume this story of Prince Hall is from the same letter.

ter are returned. They were carried to St. Bartho-
mew's and offered for fale. One of them was a
fenfible fellow, and a Free mafon. The merchant
to whom they were offered was of this fraternity;
they were foon acquainted; the negro told his ftory; they were carried before the governor, with the
fhip mafter and fupercargo. The ftory of the negroes was, that they were decoyed on board, under
pretence of working; the ftory of the others was,
that they were purchafed out of gaol; wherein they
had been confined for robbery. The Governor de-
tained them; the veffel put off immediately from
the ifland. They were kept within certain limits,
and a gentleman of the ifland, was bondfman for
them for fix months; in which time they fent here
for proofs, which arriving, they were liberated.

'The morning after their arrival here, they made
me a vifit, being introduced by Prince Hall, who
is one of the head men among the blacks in this
town. The interview was Affecting—There, faid
Prince, this is the gentleman who was fo much your
friend, and petitioned the Court for us—alluding to
the fhare which I had in the petition againft the flave
trade. They joined in thanking me; and really,
my dear fir, I felt, and do ftill feel, from this cir-
cumftance, a pleafure which is a rich compenfation
for all the curfes of the whole tribe of African tra-
ders, aided by the diftillers, which have been libe-
rally beftowed upon the clergy of this town for
their agency in the above petition.'

This "letter from Boston" was an excerpt of a letter of August 2, 1788, from
Rev. Jeremy Belknap, Boston, to Ebenezer Hazard, New York, apparently
published elsewhere (where we have not yet discovered).[38] (Belknap is the
gentleman whom Hall said "petitioned the court for us.") An account was
also reprinted—

August 29, 1788, *The New York Packet,* New York, no. 832, published by
Samuel and John Loudon

---

38 *Collections of the Massachusetts Historical Society* (Boston: Massachusetts Historical Society, 1877), vol. 3, 5th series, 54–55, 28–29, 32.

Surely, this is one of the most dramatic results of a Masonic sign by a distressed Mason ever recorded, and suggests by what it precipitated that Prince Hall was very much his own man, capable of charting a course that was betoken neither to British hierarchy or American "squirearchy." The repatriation of the three kidnapped men preceded by 200 years the celebrated legal battles that would enforce on a larger scale, the rights that Prince Hall demanded.

The event underlines that he was a Mason true to the Craft, but moreover a man true to his humanity. And his story gets—to borrow a Lewis Carroll phrase and to contradict the use of the word in respect to Prince Hall by Henry Wilson Coil[39]—curiouser and curiouser.

The Dog that Didn't Bark

In 1892, Bro. Arthur Conan Doyle published "Silver Blaze," a Sherlock Holmes short story. Inspector Gregory of Scotland Yard says to Holmes, "Is there any other point to which you would wish to draw my attention." Holmes replies, "To the curious incident of the dog in the night-time." The detective is puzzled: "The dog did nothing in the night-time." And Holmes replies, "That was the curious incident."

A negative fact is still a fact, and in this series about the origins of Prince Hall Freemasonry, there are a number of newspaper articles that were published about African-American Masons without any remark that they were untoward, extraordinary, or exceptional. They were ordinary reports of ordinary lodge business in all respects, but it was their ordinariness that was extraordinary.

- The June 22, 1789, *The Boston Gazette and the Country Journal* (Boston, no. 1811, published by Benjamin Edes and Son) reads:

  > *It is curious, fays a Correfpondent, to obferve the peculiar Strains of our late Advertifements*——DONE-GANI *tumbles in the Papers without* any permiffion *from the Selectmen, or any other Body whatever.*—— *While the poor African Lodge informs the Public, that a SERMON will be delivered,* by permiffion—— *When Tumblers, Strollers, &c. can impofe on the Town,*

---

39 Coil et al., ix.

*without Leave or License, and a worthy Man is oblig'd
to aſk "permiſſion" to preach a Sermon, we may
juſtly exclaim, O'Boſton ! How art thou fallen!*———•

• Reprinted—

June 30, 1789, *The New-York Daily Gazette*, New York, no. 153, published by John and Archibald M'Lean

There is no response or rebuttal by subscribers to this. The indignation that
a sermon needs permission but a carnival act does not is accepted without
any question by the readers. Nor is there any attention to the fact that the
lodge is an African-American one. The articles in the post-revolutionary
press seem to illustrate that for the papers and public, Masons are Masons.
Indeed, more regularity attached to the activities of Prince Hall and African
Lodge than of many other Masons and lodges of the period.

An example is the sermon referred to in the newspaper, probably the St.
John's Day sermon of June 14, 1789, preached by Rev. John Marrant, chaplain of African.[40] Marrant was called America's first black preacher and became chaplain of African Lodge in that same year that he delivered the address. Joseph A. Walkes considered that "It may very well have been the first
published speech by a Black American."[41] (There are several advertisements
that year for Donegani's circus acts, and for Marrant's published sermon.)

A few weeks later, there appeared a summary of Masons' celebrating St.
John's Day. Prince Hall activities are recorded in the same article as those
of other Masons:

• June 27, 1789, *The Massachusetts Centinel*, Boston, vol. 11, no. 30,
published by Bro. Benjamin Russell

The FESTIVAL of ST. JOHN,
In true maſonick ſtyle, was celebrated on Wedneſday, by the Ancient and Honourable Fraternity
of MASONS, at the Bunch-of-Grapes—on which

40 [John] Marrant, *A Sermon Preached on 24ᵗʰ Day of June 1789, Being the Festival of St.
John the Baptist, at the Request of the Right Worshipful the Grand Master Prince Hall, and
the Rest of the Brethren of the African Lodge of the Honorable Society of Free and Accepted
Masons in Boston* (Boston: Bible and Heart, 1789).

41 Joseph A. Walkes Jr., *Black Square & Compass: 200 Years of Prince Hall Freemasonry*, rev.

occafion the following Great Officers were in-
ftalled—The Right Worfhipful M. M. HAYS,
Grand Mafter;—AARON DEXTER, Efq. Grand
Steward.—SAMUEL BRADFORD, Efq. Grand
Sword-Bearer.—SIMON ELIOT, Efq. Grand Mar-
fhal—and Mr. NORTON BRAILSFORD, Grand
Deacon.

The African Lodge, No. 459, alfo celebrated
this feftival. At 11 o'clock, they proceeded in
their profeffional infignia to the South-School,
where their Chaplain delivered to them a fermon.
They afterwards dined together at their Hall.

• Reprinted—

July 4, 1789, *The New-York Daily Gazette,* New York City, no. 162, published by John and Archibald M'Lean

Then in the early autumn of the same year, the newspapers minuted the
death of Bro. Robert Livingston, Past Grand Master of New York, and of
Bro. Thomas Saunderson, Secretary of African Lodge and one of the fifteen
original initiates of the African Lodge.

• September 7, 1789, *The Boston Gazette, and the Country Journal,* Boston, no. 1822, Benjamin Edes:

DIED]—At New-York, Robert G. Livingfton, Efq.
——— At Kittery, Samuel Hirft Sparhawk, Efq
——— At Braintree, Deacon Jonathon Webb.
——— In this town, Mrs. Abigail Homer, aged 74.
Mrs. Mary Dixon, aged 101, fchool-mistrefs. Mrs.
Agnes Bradlee, aged 53. Mr. Thomas Saunderfon,
Secretary of the African Lodge, No. 1.

• Reprinted—

September 8, 1789, *The Salem Mercury,* Salem, vol. 3, no. 152, published by John Dabney and Thomas Cushing

September 10, 1789, *The American Herald; and the Worcester Recorder,*
Worcester, vol. 8, no. 420, published by Edward Eveleth Powars

---

ed. (Richmond, VA: Macoy Publishing & Masonic Supply Co., 1981), 24.

The sermon preached by Reverend Marrant in June had soon made its way into print

- September 14, 1789, *The Boston Gazette, and the Country Journal,* Boston, no. 1,823, published by Benjamin Edes and Son:

J u ſ t   P U B L I S H E D ,
And to be ſold at the *Bible* and *Heart*, in BOSTON.
A SERMON Preached by the Rev Brother
MARRANT, at the requeſt of the AFRICAN
Lodge of free and accepted MASONS, in Boſton, at
the Feſtival of St. John the Baptiſt, June 24, 1789.
SEPT. 13, 1789.

- Reprinted—

  September 26, 1789, *The Massachusetts Centinel,* vol. 12, no. 4, published by Bro. Benjamin Russell

  September 28, 1789, *The Boston Gazette, and Country Journal,* Boston, no. 1,825, published by Benjamin Edes and son

  October 7, 1789, *The Massachusetts Centinel,* vol. 12, no. 7, published by Bro. Benjamin Russell

An example of the continued good standing of Prince Hall is the letter to him of August 20, 1792, from the Grand Secretary of the English Grand Lodge, W.M. White, addressing him as Right Worshipful and asking for his help in getting information about a number of lodges as "we have never heard from them, since the commencement of the last war in America." Bro. White adds that he wishes African Lodge success for the year and is "happy to have it in my power to contribute thereto."[42]

There is lots of room for research about this decade. For example, there is a small mystery about a funeral notice of November 29, 1796. The departed brother's name is unknown, although a search can possibly produce it. We do know that the January 14, 1779, regulations of African Lodge list James Hawkins as an Entered Apprentice.[43]

---

42 William H. Grimshaw, *Official History of Freemasonry Among the Colored People in North America* (Montreal: Broadway Publishing, 1903), 88–89. Would that all of Grimshaw was based on archives!

43 Manuscript, A. J. Worsham, November 17, 1949, quoted in Wesley, *Prince Hall,* 155.

- November 29, 1796, *Polar-Star and Boston Daily Advertiser*, Boston, no. 47, published by Alexander Martin

African Lodge,
☞ The brethren of the African
Lodge are requefted to meet at brother JAMES
HAWKINS's, Devonfhire-ftreet, this afternoon at
3 o'clock; there to form a proceffion, and attend
the funeral of a deceafed brother   Nov 29

Prince Hall was well informed about the Craft and an articulate spokesperson, as shown in an advertisement of August 28, 1797.

- August 28, 1797, *The Boston Gazette, and Weekly Republican Journal,* Boston, no. 2337, published by Bro. Benjamin Edes

Just publifhed, and to be fold at Prince Hall's Shop, oppofite the Quaker Meeting Houfe, Quaker Lane

A CHARGE delivered to the African Lodge, June 24, 1797.
By the Right Worfhipful PRINCE HALL.

This is an advertisement for the second of two published charges by Prince Hall delivered to African Lodge. The first was in 1792, and this one is a small 18-page pamphlet "published by desire of the members of said Lodge" and delivered at Menotomy (now the town of Arlington, Massachusetts). [44]

A portion of the Charge reads:

> Live and aĉt as Mafons, that you may die as
> Mafons ; let thofe defpifers fee, altho' many of
> us cannot read, yet by our fearches and refearch-
> es into men and things, we have fupplied that
> defeĉt, and if they will let us we fhall call our-
> felves a charter'd lodge, of juft and lawful
> Mafons ; be always ready to give an anfwer to
> thofe that afk you a queftion; give the right

---

44 For a detailed analysis of Hall's 1792 charge, see Gregory S. Kearse, "Prince Hall's 1792 Charge: An Assertion of African Heritage," *Heredom* 20 (2012): 273–309.

hand of affection and fellowſhip to whom it
juſtly belongs let their colour and complexion
be what it will : let their nation be what it may,
for they are our brethren, and it is your indis-
penſible duty ſo to do ; let them as Maſons deny
this, and we & the world know what to think of
them be they ever ſo grand; for we know this was
Solomon's creed. Solomon's creed did I ſay, it
is the decree of the Almighty, and all Maſons
have learnt it : tis plain market language and
plain and true facts need no apologies.[45]

Now, admittedly not every press mention of African Lodge was laudatory
nor apparently were some members of the lodge itself free of the hubris
which sometimes marks even Masons.

- February 24, 1800, *Farmers' Museum Literary Gazette*, Walpole, N.H.,
  vol. 7, no. 360, published by Bro. Isaiah and Alexander Thomas

N U T S.

[ORIGINAL]

IN the metropolis of a ſiſter ſtate, there is a
reſpectable lodge of Free Masons, compoſed
of free people of colour. We learn that on the
ſame day that General Waſhington died, the
maſter of this African Lodge, "died alſo."
His name was Hawkins, and he died very
much regretted. His place was immediately
filled by Mr. Prince Hall, who ſucceeded in
the honours of his late friend and fellow
craftſman, Hawkins. On this occaſion a
member of the ſociety was appointed to write
and deliver an eulogy. We have not ſeen this
work, but we learn that the orator "acquitted
himſelf like a man." As his exordium is an

45 Prince Hall, *A Charge Delivered to the Africa Lodge June 24, 1797, at Menotomy* (Boston: Benjamin Edes, 1797), p. 18. Early American Imprints, Series 1, no. 32218
(filmed).

example of the fublimely ludicrous, we give it, as handed to use by a gentleman lately from B——, "Friends and fellow citizens, we have this day loft a Hawkins and a Washington! but thanks be to God, we have ftill left a Pickering, a Wolcott, and a Hall!"

- Reprinted—

March 8, 1800, *New Hampshire Sentinel,* Keene, vol. 1, no. 51, published by John Prentiss

March 12, 1800, *Massachusetts Spy, or Worcester Gazette,* Worcester, vol. 29, no. 1,405, published by Bro. Isaiah Thomas and son

March 26, 1800, *The Farmer's Monitor, Litchfield,* Connecticut, vol. 16, no. 763, published by Thomas Collier

This is an example of sardonic if perhaps deserved humor from *Farmers' Museum Literary Gazette.* The last page of this paper has the headline "The Dessert," and has sections marked "The Muses," with poetry, "Miscellany," with an article on errors of the press, and a section marked "Nuts," with two humorous stories. The story is obviously fictitious as there was no Master of African Lodge named Hawkins, and Prince Hall remained Master until his death in 1807. It likely refers to the James Hawkins mentioned in the November 29, 1796, funeral announcement. The joke seems to be that the speaker was so foolish that he equates lesser worthies like Pickering, Wolcott, Hall, and Hawkins with George Washington. Pickering and Walcott were probably Timothy Pickering (1745–1829) of Massachusetts, Secretary of State, and Oliver Wolcott, Jr. (1760–1830) of Connecticut, Secretary of the Treasury.

The publisher, Bro. Isaiah Thomas (1749–1831), Grand Master of Massachusetts in 1809, perhaps was not as sympathetic to Prince Hall or African Lodge as Masonic publishers Nathan Willis and Benjamin Russell had been. Or perhaps we should accept the piece as a deserved poke at all fraternal pomposity, no matter what the lodge.

In contrast, while Prince Hall was not George Washington, Adelaide M. Cromwell in her study of Black leadership in early Boston considers that four African-Americans stand out: the poetess Phillis Wheatley; the victim of the Boston Massacre, Crispus Attucks; the fifer of Revolutionary War folklore, Brazillai Lew; and Prince Hall. If they and other Black Americans of historical significance are less known, one might ponder why.[46]

Prince Hall is especially important because of the role that his Boston played in creating the American mythology: "The Pilgrims and the Puritans, the Boston Tea Party and Paul Revere, that very specific City on a Hill, had by the Civil War become part of the personal heritage of every individual who could claim a history of freedom.... New England had become the nation and, in the process, the nation had become New England."[47] His increased prominence in the story of America is overdue.

We conclude that this is a situation where Brother Sir Arthur Conan Doyle's remarks about the dog that did not bark is an apt way to describe how the press in the late 1790s treated Prince Hall and African Lodge in about the same fashion as it did other Masonic lodges. One cannot say the same for all Masonic commentators during the ensuing two centuries. Harold Van Buren Voorhis writes, "Over a period of many years I have read hundreds of discussions and opinions in Grand Lodge proceedings on this subject—among which are some of the most vitriolic attacks on Negroes and Negro Freemasonry. Yet, during the times when these attacks were in especially full bloom, as well as during periods of quiescence, there is only the evidence of our Negro brethren facing the issue very calmly as gentleman."[48] Prince Hall Masonry had as solid and honest a beginning as any of America's other Masonic lodges.

The Modern Clam-Eaters—Prince Hall Freemasonry at the End of the Eighteenth Century

One can be fairly sure when examining the newspaper references to Prince Hall in this series of articles that he too read them, and that many of the events recounted were common knowledge.[49] After all, the population of Boston in 1790 was only 18,320.[50] Furthermore, Hall was

46 Adelaide M. Cromwell, *The Other Brahmins: Boston's Black Upper Class, 1750–1950* (University of Arkansas Press, Fayetteville, 1994), 27–32.

47 Joanne Pope Melish, *Disowning Slavery: Gradual Emancipation and "Race" in New England, 1780–1860* (Ithaca and London: Cornell University Press, 1998), 236.

48 Harold Van Buren Voorhis *Negro Masonry in the United States* (New York: Henry Emmerson Publishers, 1945), 5.

49 Gregory S. Kearse, "Prince Hall's 1792 Charge: An Assertion of African Heritage," *Heredom* 20 (2012): 275.

50 Population History of Boston, acc.

proud of his lodge and was not inclined to accept anything resembling unjust criticism in the press.[51] Characteristically, as early as 1782 when an article appeared in *The Independent Ledger, and the American Advertiser* of Boston about a St. Black's Lodge having a procession on St. John's day to the house of its "Right Worshipful Grand Master," Hall. He immediately wrote to the paper that, "our title is not St Black's Lodge; neither do we aspire after high titles."[52]

The newspaper accounts testify to a well-ordered and active lodge that from 15 members in 1776, grew to 34 in 1787.[53] The letter in August 1792 to Hall from William White, the grand secretary of the grand lodge in London, asking for information about other lodges in Boston, is an indication that Hall and the lodge were considered in good standing.[54]

As the newspapers confirm the regularity of African-American Masonic activity, albeit subsequently blurred by so much misinformation propounded over the years, it is curious that more study has not been made of the actual reporting. Perhaps that is symptomatic of an unfortunate larger problem. Clemson University professors LaGarret J. King and Patrick Womac have written strongly about the way American history "ignores Black Americans who were also instrumental in developing and fighting for the philosophies of U.S. democracy. They deplore the omission of blacks "as persons involved in the national-building efforts of the United States."[55]

Given Masonry's emphasis on equality, the lack of scholarly attention to the upstanding role of African-American Freemasonry in early Boston is singular.[56] In their study of black fraternalism, Harvard professors Theda

---

http://physics.bu.edu/~redner/projects/population/cities/boston.html

51 But in our survey, we have come across only a few instances that were less than favorable.

52 David L. Gray, *Inside Prince Hall* (Lancaster, VA: Anchor Communications, 1904), 43.

53 Gray, 19.

54 Gray, 22.

55 La Garrett J. King and Patrick Womac, "A Bundle of Silences: Examining the Racial Representation of Black Founding Fathers of the United States Through Glenn Beck's Founders' Fridays." *Theory and Research in Social Education* 142, no. 1 (January–March 2014): 37.

56 "Over a period of many years I have read hundreds of discussions and opinions in Grand Lodge proceedings on this subject—among which are some of the most vitriolic attacks on Negroes and Negro Freemasonry. Yet, during the times when these attacks were in especially full bloom, as well as during periods of quiescence, there is

Skocpol, Ariane Liazos, and Marshall Ganz remark that the refusal of white Masons to acknowledge Prince Hall Masons was a hypocrisy that repudiated their claim to "apparently universal principles of brotherhood."[57] The fraternalism demonstrated by Prince Hall and his friends was in the face of obstacles that would have overwhelmed less hardy souls: "The only way we can understand this remarkably persistent commitment on inclusion and equality by the leaders of black fraternal institutions forged during decades of forced racial domination and segregation is to recognize that African American lodge members were, in an important sense, even more committed to core fraternal values than were whiter fraternalists."[58]

European customs would not serve the new United States, and so along with their fellow new citizens the members of the Prince Hall lodge sought to define themselves as Americans, embraced the development of traditions that gave the new country legitimatizing myths. An 1803 article in Boston's *Independent Chronicle* about the lodge observing the feast of shells demonstrates this.[59] The "Feast of Shells" is another name for Forefather's Day, established formally in 1769 at Plymouth, Massachusetts, to commemorate the landing of the Pilgrims. The name derives from clams and other seafood served at the celebration. The use of shells as dishes for food complimented the incorporation of scallop shells into architectural designs and made a reference to the scallop shell badges of pilgrims in medieval Europe, affirming the designation of the Plymouth settlers as Pilgrims. (Not to mention its use in Templar art and that the New England clambake became a firmly rooted gastronomic ritual.)[60]

---

only the evidence of our Negro brethren facing the issue very calmly as gentlemen.... The mountains builded out of mole-hills have not withstood the elements of careful scrutiny and are being leveled by the plumb of reason and the square of honest judgment." Harold Van Buren Voorhis, *Negro Masonry in the United States* (Bensenville, IL: Lushena Books, 2003), 5.

57 Theda Skocpol, Ariane Liazos, and Marshall Ganz, *What a Mighty Power We Can Be: African-American Fraternal Groups and the Struggle for Racial Equality* (Princeton and Oxford: Princeton University Press, 2006), 11.

58 Skocpol, 226.

59 *The Independent* was strongly Republican and anti-Masonic; the eighteen-year old son of Benjamin Austin Jr., the owner of the paper and a Republican with anti-Masonic views, was killed in a scuffle with Thomas O. Selfridge, a Federalist attorney. Controversially, Selfridge was freed by a jury of which Bro. Paul Revere was a member. Jayne E. Triber, *A Free Republican: The Life of Paul Revere* (Amherst, MA: University of Massachusetts Press, 1998), 189 ff.

60 Kathy Neustad, *Clambake: A History and Celebration of an American Tradition* (Am-

In Boston's *Independent Chronicle* for January 9, 1804:

The modern Clam-Eaters.
THE *Pilgrim's Sons* who dwell on earth,
God knows from whom they claim their birth,
On some pretence, as rumour tells,
Each year renew their *feast of shells*[61]

1. January 17, 1803, *The Independent Chronicle*, Boston, vol. 35, no. 2276, published by Abijah Adams and Ebenezer Rhoades

A TOAST at the *Feaſt of Shells*, parodized at a late meeting of the *African Lodge:*—

May that *Congreſs* which ſtood the friend of *poor Negro*, when *poor Negro* had no other friend in the world, be refitted and confirmed as the JACHIN, when *Africa*, (poor Negro's country) ſhalt stand the BOAZ of true political and ſocial Liberty, until ſun, moon and ſtars ſhall never ſhine again.

More research about the individual members of the early black lodges will be of outstanding value to Masonic historiography. Even small scraps of additional knowledge would help toward understanding what was the beginning of black associational life in America, [62] or in the convincing phrase of Gregory Kearse, "black cultural nationalism."[63]

But within African-American Freemasonry, there were a number of strands. The membership of the early Prince Hall lodges was diverse, as an obituary of an early member reminds us from the *New England Palladium*,—a

---

herst, MA: University of Massachusetts Press, 1992), 32–34.

61 "The Modern Clam-Eaters," *Independent Chronicle*, Boston, 36, no. 2378 (January 9, 1804).

62 The sermons, minutes, and correspondence should be pursued for suggestions of how the early Prince Hall Masons felt about their past, and see if there is anything to be said for Keith Moore's claim that Prince Hall "could be deemed the father of Afrocentrism. He was the first to acknowledge in America a history for African people." Keith Moore, *Freemasonry, Greek Philosophy, The Prince Hall Fraternity and the Egyptian (African) World Connection* (Bloomington, IN: Author House, 2008), 14.

63 Gregory S. Kearse, "Prince Hall's 1792 Charge: An Assertion of African Heritage," *Heredom* 20 (2012): 278–79.

reminder that Freemasonry was well established in the West Indies prior to the African Lodge Masonic activities in Boston. (For example, in Guadeloupe there were lodges established in 1766, 1768, and 1770.)[64]

2. August 2, 1803, *New-England Palladium,* Boston, vol. 22, no. 16, published by Alexander Young and Thomas Minns

DIED;

In this town, on the 23d inst. Mr. Joseph Dumass, a native of Guadaloupe, a coloured man. He has resided in this town for many years past; during which, he conducted himself with great propriety and decorum. He was a member of the African Lodge.

His brethren like Dumass were passing and Prince Hall himself died in 1807. Gregory Kearse makes much of the significance of his life span as set against the eventful days of the American Revolution and nation-making, and that he was in his forties when called upon to assert his Masonic role—a case of the right age at the right time: "This maturity of age advances the idea that Hall had access to and a grasp of the colonial political, social, and cultural pulse of his day."[65]

The passing of Prince Hall himself occasioned substantial press notice. If indeed Benjamin Russell became a supporter of African Lodge, as supported by the sympathetic articles he published in the *Columbian Centinel,* it is a sad coincidence that it fell to him to publish the first obituary of Prince Hall. This obituary, published on Saturday, December 5, indicated Hall died on Friday, December 4, not December 7 as marked on his tombstone.

64 See Lionel Augustine Seemungal, "The Beginnings of Freemasonry in Trinidad," Grand Lodge of Scotland site, accessed June 17, 2014, http://www.grandlodgescotland.com/masonic-subjects/masonic-articles/371-the-beginnings-of-freemasonry-in-trinidad. "The impressive global and temporal range of European Freemasonry and its connections to Africans and their descendants throughout the Diaspora comes into clearer focus in the Caribbean. The uniqueness of the Caribbean—its continuities of 'ruptures and discontinuities' constitute the markings of diasporas—position this area as a quintessential arena where we can begin to situate the diaspora consciousness at the heart of African American Freemasonry." Corey D. B. Walker, *A Noble Fight: African American Freemasonry and the Struggle for Democracy in America* (Urbana and Chicago: University of Illinois Press, 2008), 57.

65 Kearse, 284.

3. December 5, 1807, *Columbian Centinel,* Boston, no. 2471, published by Bro. Benjamin Russell

Yesterday morning, Mr. *Prince Hall*, Æt. 72, Master of African Lodge. Funeral on Monday afternoon at 3 o'clock, from his late dwelling house in Lendell's-Lane; which his friends and relations are requested to attend without a more formal invitation.

• Reprinted—

December 7, 1807, *Boston Gazette,* Boston, vol. 23, no. 28, whole no. 1156, published by John Russell and James Cutler

December 7, 1807, *Independent Chronicle,* Boston, vol. 39, no. 2,777, published by Abijah Adams and Ebenezer Rhoades

4. December 8, 1807, *Newburyport Herald,* Newburyport, Massachusetts, vol. 11, no. 70, published by Ephraim Williams Allen

OBITUARY.

...

In Boston, Mr. *Wm. Carlton*, Æt. 47—Mrs. *Abigail Averill*, Æt. 44—Mrs. *Elizabeth Pulsifer*, Æt. 61—Miss *Harriot Cushing*, Æt. 28—Mrs. *Elizabeth Pratt*, Æt. 31—Mr. *Prince Hall*, Æt. 72, Master of the African Lodge.

(The publisher, Bro. Ephraim Williams Allen (1779–1846) joined St. John's Lodge, Boston, in 1815, eight years after this notice, but renounced Freemasonry during the Morgan Affair and remained an anti-Mason until his death.)

• Reprinted—

December 8, 1807, *New-England Palladium,* Boston, vol. 30, no. 46, published by Alexander Young and Thomas Minns

December 12, 1807, *The Providence Gazette,* Providence, Rhode Island, vol. 43, no. 2293, published by John Carter

December 14, 1807, *Portland Gazette and Maine Advertiser,* vol. 10, no. 35, whole no. 503, published by Isaac Adams and Williams Jenks, Jr.

5. December 9, 1807, *The Democrat,* Boston, vol. 4, no. 99, published by Benjamin Parks

Died,

…

Mr. Prince Hall, aged 72—His remains were interred on Monday, in complete Masonic order, by the African Lodge, of which he was Master—A very large procession of blacks followed him to the grave.

• Reprinted—

December 10, 1807, *Boston Courier,* Boston, vol. 3, no. 27, published by Benjamin Parks

Certainly, his life was viewed as successful and significant:

Prince Hall used the structure and idealism of Freemasonry to gain a serious political public voice, to overcome slavery and racism, and to cross class barriers. He authored petitions to the Massachusetts Assembly urging full citizenship for blacks and an allowance for their participation in the young American Republic. He petitioned for schools and equal treatment under the laws governing the country. In 1797, he delivered the earliest publicly recorded antislavery address by a black person. What is significant about Hall's actions is the extent to which they reflect his early use of the "master's tools."[66]

However, now that he was gone, and as we shall see in our concluding article, the work of Prince Hall would have the square and compass applied to see if it was enduringly worthy, for without the leader, how would the enterprise fair? Writes Brent Morris about post-revolutionary Boston, "Given the loose situation in Massachusetts [which the authors plan to illustrate by reissuing an old history of St. John's, the first Massachusetts lodge] with an Ancient Grand Lodge, a weak Provincial Grand Lodge, and the Scottish St. Andrew's Lodge, African Lodge may have preferred to remain loyal to

---

66 Tamara L. Brown, Gregory S. Parks, Clarenda M. Phillips, eds., Anne S. Butler, "Black Fraternal and Benevolent Societies in Nineteenth Century America." in *African American Fraternities and Sororities: The Legacy and the Vision,* eds., Brown, Tamara L., Gregory S. Parks, and Clarenda M. Phillips (Lexington: University Press of Kentucky, 2005), 77.

the Modern Grand Lodge in London."[67] But that was no longer possible. The English grand lodges were about to merge as the United Grand Lodge of England and the American state grand lodges were leaving their British past and growing on their own terms. African Lodge faced the future without its founder and in an increasingly hostile environment.

The Manipulation of History

Power creates and manipulates history, which was the case with the narrative of African-American Freemasonry after the death of Prince Hall. The Haitian anthropologist Michel-Rolph Trouillot (1949–2012) emphasized the ways in which the past is silenced, as was in the case of African-American Freemasonry. He felt that one must be ever wary of the ways in which dominant cultures manipulate the master narrative. Control over the narrative is achieved by a process that Trouillot described as fact creation, fact assembly, fact retrieval, and retrospective significance. That is a fair description of what happened to the recounting of the role of Prince Hall and the story of the early days of African-American Freemasonry during the ensuing nineteenth and twentieth centuries.[68]

This suppression cannot be entirely blamed on the bowdlerizing efforts of white Freemasons bent on expurgating the evidence of early African-American lodges. For example, we do not know enough about the attitudes of African-American religious leaders toward the Craft.[69] One would expect that early African-American Roman Catholic leaders like Augustus Tolton and Daniel Rudd would have supported the Catholic view of Masonry, while of course there is ample countervailing evidence that Protestant African-American leaders were often involved in lodges. A thorough examination of who in the African-American religious community supported Freemasonry and who opposed it is overdue. Still, the denials of the legitimacy of Prince Hall Masonry came in great volume from white Freemasons and are an example of "*argumentum ad populum,* in which a thesis is asserted,

---

67 S. Brent Morris, *The Complete Idiot's Guide to Freemasonry* (New York: Alpha Books (Penguin), 2006), 59.

68 See Sarah Brooks, "Connecting the Past to the Present," *Theory & Research in Social Education* 42, no. 1, January–March 2014.

69 Cf. Roger Sansi, "Sorcery and Fetishism in the Modern Atlantic." in *Sorcery in the Black Atlantic,* eds., Luis Nicolau Pares and Roger Sansi (Chicago and London: University of Chicago Press, 2011), 33–34.

even acclaimed, because it resonates with the moral schemata and expectations of its audience, but at the cost of a dangerous suspension of analytic and political judgment."[70]

Despite this, what Prince Hall created before his death in 1807 lived after him. There is a certain appropriateness in the first publication of his death notice being in the *Columbian Centinel* as apparently the Boston publisher Bro. Benjamin Russell had become a supporter of African Lodge. This is suggested by the sympathetic articles we have referenced in this series, including the one that was published in the December 5, 1807, *Columbian Centinel* about the death of Bro. Hall, which appears to be his first obituary. (But this obituary indicated Hall died on Friday, December 4, not December 7 as marked on his tombstone.) The burial was on a Monday:

> Yesterday morning, Mr. *Prince Hall,* Æt. 72, Master of African Lodge. Funeral on Monday afternoon at 3 o'clock, from his late dwelling house in Lendell's-Lane; which his friends and relations are requested to attend without a more formal invitation.

• Reprinted—
December 7, 1807, *Boston Gazette,* Boston, vol. 23, no. 28, whole no. 1156, published by John Russell and James Cutler
December 7, 1807, *Independent Chronicle,* Boston, vol. 39, no. 2,777, published by Abijah Adams and Ebenezer Rhoades

The next obituary for Prince Hall was on December 9, 1807, *The Democrat,* Boston, vol. 4, no. 99, published by Benjamin Parks

Died,
...

Mr. Prince Hall, aged 72—His remains were interred on Monday, in complete Masonic order, by the African Lodge, of which he was Master—A very large procession of blacks followed him to the grave.

---

70 Corey D. B. Walker, *A Noble Fight: African American Freemasonry and the Struggle for Democracy in America,* (Urbana and Chicago: University of Illinois Press, 2008), 16.

- Reprinted—

  December 10, 1807, *Boston Courier,* Boston, vol. 3, no. 27, published by Benjamin Parks

Hall's demise did not mean an end to African-American Masonry. Fledgling lodges in other cities took root. This is seen by the notice in the December 24, 1811, *Poulson's American Daily Advertiser,* Philadelphia, vol. 40, no. 10,945, published by Zachariah Poulson:

NOTICE.

THE Brethren of the AFRICAN LODGE No 459, are hereby notified, that they are to meet at their Lodge room in Spruce street, on Friday, the 27th Instant, at nine o'clock in the morning, being the ANNIVERSARY OF ST JOHN *THE EVANGELIST*, in order to join the Procession which will move precisely at 11 o'clock, and proceed from thence to the African Episcopal Church of St. Thomas, where a Charity Sermon will be delivered on the occasion and a collection made for the benefit of the said Lodge

N. B. The Brethren are desired to be punctual in their attendance at the time specified.

By order of the W. M

James Johnson, *Sec.*

dec 20   20 24 17

- Reprinted—

  December 26, 1811, *Poulson's American Daily Advertiser,* vol. 40, no. 1

This Philadelphia lodge was, of course, chartered on the basis of the charter of the Boston lodge. The evidence indicates that the now several African-American lodges sought to interact with the white lodges. Take for example the October 3, 1818, *New York Daily Advertiser,* New York, vol. 11, no. 462, published by Theodore Dwight, William B. Townsend, and John W. Walker:

MASONIC NOTICE.

☞ The members belonging to the African
Lodge of free and accepted Masons, are requested to attend an extra meeting of said lodge, on
the 6th inst. Precisely at 6 o'clock P. M. for
the express purpose of receiving additional instructions in the sublime and exalted science
and mysteries of masonry, and at the same time
a general lecture thereon, and an inquiry into
the proficiency which each member of P. Lodge
has made since favours has been conferred upon
them; as, also, an exhibition and full explanation of the working or operating tools of each
speculative mason, with the various badges em-
blematical of their respective orders, on the degrees which have been by merit conferred upon
them, after which a jubilee will be performed
by the members of said lodge. Punctual at-
tendence is solicited. Masonic brethren belonging to other Lodges are respectfully invited
to attend, and will be most graciously received.
By order of   SANDY LATTION,
oct 2-31   R. W. Master.

• Reprinted—

October 5, 1818, *Mercantile Advertiser*, New York, no. 3559, published
by John Crookes

This is an explicit invitation in which the African Lodges invite white Masons (who would have been the only in the vicinity "belonging to other
lodges") to a meeting. Perhaps, there had been informal oral invitations;
perhaps the New York African Lodge had decided to begin an outreach
program; perhaps the New York African Lodge was trying to shame the
White lodges into welcoming African Lodge members.

The obituary notices continue as the original brothers of 1775 and others
pass on and they suggest that more research is needed into the genealogi-
cal background of individual lodge members. In the March 8, 1819, *Boston
Commercial Gazette*, Boston, vol. 51, no. 24, no. 2335, published by John
Russell and Simon Gardner:

DEATHS.

...

Yesterday, Mr. Robert Warr, A respectable man of colour, aged 39–funeral tomorrow afternoon, at 3 o'clock from his late home, in Nassau-street. Friends and relations are requested to attend.– ☞ The members of the African Lodge, are requested to attend the funeral of their late brother Warr.

Another appears on February 15, 1822, *The Salem Gazette,* Salem, Massachusetts, vol. 36, no. 14, published by Caleb Cushing and Ferdinand Andrew:[71]

DEATHS.

...

At Cambridgeport, Scipio Dalton, 72, deacon of the African Baptist Church in Boston, V. P. of the African Humane Society, and a respectable member of the African Lodge, of which he was senior warden.

The January 14, 1779, regulations of African Lodge list Scipio Dalton as a Fellowcraft.[72] He was a founder of Boston's African Society in 1796 and First African Baptist Church in 1805.

Still another passing is in the April 24, 1824, *Columbian Centinel,* Boston, no. 4,178, published by Bro. Benjamin Russell:

DIED,

...

Yesterday morning, Mr. John Jonah, aged 53. Funeral to-morrow afternoon, immediately after divine service, from his late dwelling house, in Warren-street—friends

---

71 "In 1822, Thomas Cushing left the paper due to poor health to Caleb Cushing and Ferdinand Andrews...." "*Salem Gazette.*" accessed April 12, 2013. http://www.wikipedia.org

72 Manuscript, Worsham, A. J. November 17, 1949, quoted in Charles H. Wesley, *Prince Hall: Life and Legacy,* 2nd ed. (Washington: United Supreme Council, S.J., P.H.A., 1983), 155.

and relations are requested to attend. ☞ The members of the African Lodge are invited to attend.

Then in terms of the future what is perhaps the most important newspaper notice about Prince Hall Masonry was published June 18, 1827, *Boston Daily Advertiser,* Boston, vol. 18, no. 40, published by Nathan Hale.

AFRICAN LODGE—No. 459.
GREETING :
BE it known to all whom it may concern,— That we, the Master, Wardens, and Members of the African Lodge, No. 459, city of Boston, (Mass.) U. S. of America, hold in our possession a certain unlimited Charter, granted Sept. 29, A. L. 5784, A.D. 1784, by Thomas Howard, Earl of Effingham, Acting Grand Master, under the authority of his Royal Highness Henry Frederick, Duke of Cumberland, &c. &c. &c. Grand Master of the most ancient and honourable Society of free and accepted Masons. Be it further known, that the Charter alluded to bears the seal of the Most Worshipful Grand Lodge at London, England, and was presented to our much esteemed and worthy brethren and predecessors, Prince Hall, Boston Smith, Thomas Sanderson, and several others, agreeably to a humble petition of their, sent in form to the above Grand Lodge.— Be it remembered, that according to correct information as regards this instrument, and the manner in which it was given, it appears to have been confined exclusively to the Africans, and to certain conditions. Whether these conditions have been complied with by our ancestors, we are unable to say; but we can add, that, in consequence of the decease of the above named brothers, the institution was, for years, unable to proceed, for the want of one to conduct its affairs, agreeably to what is required in every regular and well conducted Lodge of Masons. It is now, however, with great pleasure, we state, that the present age

has arrived to that degree of proficiency in the art, that we can, at any time, select from among as many, whose capacity to govern, enables them to preside, with as much good order, dignity and propriety, as any other Lodge within our knowledge. This fact can be proved by gentlemen of respectability, whose knowledge of masonry would not be questioned by any one well acquainted with the art. Since the rise of the Lodge to this degree of proficiency, we concluded it was best and proper to make it known to the Most Worshipful Grand Lodge from whence we derive our Charter, by sending written documents and monies, to fulfill the agreements of our ancestors, giving information of the low state to which it had fallen, its cause, &c. with its rise and progress; and also, soliciting further favours, whereby we might be placed on a different and better standing than we had heretofore. And notwithstanding this has been long since done, and more than sufficient time has elapsed for returns, yet we have never received a single line or reply from that Hon. Society. In consequence of this neglect we have been at a stand what course to pursue. Our remote situation prevents us from making any verbal communication whatever.— Taking all these things into consideration, we have come to the conclusion that, with what knowledge we possess of masonry, and as people of colour by ourselves, we are and ought by rights to be, free and independent of other Lodges.— We do, therefore, with this belief, publicly declare ourselves free and independent of any Lodge from this day—and that we will not be tributary, or governed by any Lodge than that of our own.— We agree solemnly to abide by all proper rules and regulations which govern the like fraternities —discountenancing all imposition to injure the Order—and to use all fair and honourable means to promote its prosperity; resting in full hope,

that this will enable us to transmit it in its purity
to our posterity, for their enjoyment.
Done at the Lodge, this, the 19th June, A. L.
5827, A.D. 1827. In full testimony of what has
been written, we here affix our names.
JOHN T. HILTON, R. W. M.
THOMAS DALTON, Sen. Warden.
LEWIS YORK, Jun. Warden.
J. H. PURROW, Secretary
June 26

This is the celebrated "Declaration of Independence by African Lodge."
It marks the end of the first phase of Prince Hall Masonry when African
Lodge worked as an English lodge. It also marks the beginning of a long
struggle for its history to be recognized by the white brethren. In 1874,
when the Grand Lodge of Ohio was considering the recognition of the
Ohio Prince Hall Grand Lodge, the Prince Hall Grand Master William
Parham was not in a very conciliatory mood when quoted in the *Masonic
Monthly*: "I do not propose to occupy the negro pew in the lodge-room, nor
wait until my white companions are served before my turn comes round.
We have had enough of that in the American Church to last through all
time.... The world listens with scorn and contempt to the loud-mouthed
professions of white American Masons, to which their lives and practices
are so constantly giving the lie."[73]

In sum, as the newspapers show, the documentary evidence as to Prince
Hall and his achievements far exceeds that of many individuals of his time,
black or white, and completely justifies the conclusion of Prof. Adelaide
Cromwell of Boston University and others that he deserves his place as
one of Boston's most prominent citizens, "with few peers there or elsewhere."[74] There was a robust African-American middle class in Boston in
the last decades of the eighteenth century and Hall was one of its prominent leaders.[75]

---

73 "Colored Masonry," *Masonic Monthly* 1, no.1 (April 1878): 7–8.
74 Adelaide M. Cromwell, *The Other Brahmins: Boston's Black Upper Class, 1750–1950*
(Fayetteville, AR: University of Arkansas Press, 1994), 32,
75 Joanne Pope Melish, *Disowning Slavery: Gradual Emancipation and "Race" in New England, 1780–1860* (Ithaca and London: Cornell University Press, 1998), 170.

Not much is known about the fourteen brothers initiated with Prince Hall in 1775, and for that reason, a final obituary will serve for the time being as an epilogue. While there is no indication in the obituary that this Peter Freeman was the Freeman who was a Freemason, he is a "colored man" and would have been thirty-four years old in 1775 and thus eighty-nine in 1830. This makes him a good candidate to be one of the fourteen initiated with Hall and perhaps the last of that immortal group of brethren to die.

March 3, 1830, *Norwich Courier*, Norwich, Conn., vol. 32, no. 1,650, new series, vol. 8, no. 49, published by John Dunham:

Died,

In this city, on the 21st ult. PETER FREEMAN, a colored man and a Revolutionary pensioner, aged 89.

• Reprinted—

March 9, 1830, *Rhode Island American, Statesman and Providence Gazette*, Providence, R.I., new series, vol. 1, no. 68, published by D. Mowry, B. F. Hallett, Editor, J. C. Parmenter, printer

With his passing, an era was over. The newspaper accounts bearing on Prince Hall discussed here have been available for over 200 years, if not as readily before the advent of the computer, but they have been the victims of cultural amnesia on the part of historians and the lack of critical memory of Masons. In contrast, Joseph A. Walkes Jr. made good use of some of them in his *Black Square & Compass* in 1979.[76] (He is conspicuous in his criticisms of William H. Grimshaw, whose work possibly misused the known documents. Of more value are the articles and monographs of Harold Van Buren Voorhis, culminating in his 1938 work *Negro Masonry in the United States,* now available in a Lushena Books edition.)

The issue was not regularity. Indeed, the universalism of Freemasonry is such a part of its identity over the centuries that irregularity rests with those lodges who continue to use spurious claims of irregularity to deny admission on the grounds of race; ironically, still today in the United States of all places, some so-called regular grand lodges are radically irregular in this respect, defying the central teachings of Masonry and embarrassing the

---

76 Joseph A. Walkes Jr., *Black Square & Compass: 200 Years of Prince Hall Freemasonry,* rev ed. (Richmond, VA: Macoy Publishing & Masonic Supply, 1981), 3–14.

Masonic bodies who still recognize them. One observer noted this with wisdom and sadness:

If African American men were deemed as Masonic equals, an ave-nue would be opened for other forms of social and political equality, ones that hitherto had been denied African Americans and served as the foundation for the existing social and political hierarchy. Thus the ideological underpinnings of Freemasonry contained the very real possibility of undermining the material conditions of the social, political, and economic arrangements of the a society that viewed African Americans as unworthy heirs to freedom and equal-ity, not to mention fraternity with European Americans—even in a brotherhood that espoused love for all humankind.[77]

First Published: *The Phylaxis,* vol. 60, no. 3 (2nd quarter 2013)—vol. 61, no. 3 (3rd quarter 2014)

---

77 Walker, *A Noble Fight,* 129–30.

The Structure of
American Freemasonry

I n the year 2000, the Masonic fraternity in the United States had about
1,700,000 members in about 10,000 lodges. Even though it has declined
from a peak membership of 4,200,000 in 1960, the Craft is still the largest and most widespread American fraternal organization, albeit without
a centralized, national headquarters. Any attempt to describe American
Freemasonry must of necessity focus on the broad structure as the differing
details of fifty-one independent mainstream grand lodges (plus forty-two
Prince Hall Grand lodges!) quickly become a hopeless maze of exceptions.

A Quick History of American Masonry

The first Mason in America appears to be John Skene, who is listed on the
rolls of Aberdeen Lodge in 1682 and came to the United States the same
year. The first American-born Mason seems to be Jonathan Belcher, born in
Cambridge, Massachusetts, 1681, and died in Elizabethtown, New Jersey,
1757. He became a Mason in England in 1704.

The premier Grand Lodge appointed Daniel Coxe Provincial Grand
Master for New York, New Jersey, and Pennsylvania on June 5, 1730.
The Grand Lodge of Pennsylvania has the records of the earliest known
American Lodge, which indicate activity back to at least 1730. Unrecorded lodges may have met earlier, but 1730 is a safe year to declare as the
beginning of American Freemasonry. By 1806, each of the thirteen original colonies had formed an independent grand lodge that had supreme
control of Freemasonry within its borders. This pattern continued until
there were fifty-one independent grand lodges, one for each state and the
District of Columbia.

The dispute between Moderns and Antients traveled across the Atlantic
with Freemasonry, though it was never quite as intense as in England. A
few colonies and states, South Carolina in particular, had both Antient
and Modern Grand Lodges. During the American Revolution, Modern
Masons tended to be conservative, wealthy, and loyal to England; Antient

Masons tended to active, working class, and revolutionary. Thus, after the Treaty of Paris ended the war in 1783 and established the independence of the former colonies, American Freemasonry was decidedly Antient in its practices.

George Washington became a Master Mason in 1753 in the Lodge of Fredericksburg, Virginia. He was proposed during the Revolutionary War as Grand Master of a Grand Lodge for the United States in 1780, but he declined the position (no doubt having other matters on his mind!). In 1793, George Washington laid the cornerstone of the United States Capitol with Masonic ceremonies. The apron, trowel, gavel, and other tools he used that day are still carefully preserved and cherished by Alexandria-Washington Lodge No. 22 of Virginia and by Potomac Lodge No. 5 of the District of Columbia.

Prince Hall, a free African-American living in Boston, was made a Mason in 1775 by a traveling Irish military lodge in Boston. In 1784, the premier Grand Lodge granted a charter to African Lodge No. 459 in Boston. At this time, Massachusetts had lodges loyal to at least three grand lodges: the Grand Lodge of Massachusetts, the Grand Lodge of Scotland (St. Andrews Lodge, Paul Revere's Lodge), and the premier Grand Lodge of England (African Lodge No. 459). African Lodge declared itself independent by at least 1827 and transformed itself into the Prince Hall Grand Lodge. From it has descended an independent Masonic tradition with forty-two grand lodges today and a parallel structure of collateral organizations.

William Preston's 1772 *Illustrations of Masonry* inspired Thomas Smith Webb to slightly revise the text for American use and publish it in 1797 as *The Freemason's Monitor or, Illustrations of Masonry*. Webb was a superb ritualist who took Antient workings, expanded them with Preston's lectures, and systematized the language and floor work. Webb traveled the country at the invitation and employ of Grand Lodges teaching his brand ritual and selling his *Monitor* as a supplement. He trained other itinerant lecturers, most prominently Jeremy Ladd Cross, each of whom had a territory in which they taught, much like traveling salesmen today. This form of ritual came to be called Preston-Webb or sometimes Webb-Cross and spread rapidly into every grand lodge except Pennsylvania. Today, the ritual in all American grand lodges is similar in its major points. Pennsylvania did not adopt Webb's alterations and thus has perhaps the oldest continuously used Masonic Craft ritual in the world.

The Operation of American Lodges

Most lodges today in the United States meet twice a month, some monthly, and a few weekly. It is rare for a regular lodge to meet less often than once a month, with research lodges a notable exception. The average American lodge has 170 members, with few larger than 300. A very active lodge in or near a major city could have 5-10 candidates a year, though most have many fewer. The most active lodges conduct regular business at their normal or "stated" meetings, and confer degrees at special or "emergent" or "called" meetings. Most lodges work degrees into their regular schedule, which would include speakers on nights when degree work is not on the agenda.

An applicant to an American lodge usually must be recommended by two members of the lodge. His petition must be received at a regular meeting at which time an investigating committee is appointed. He cannot be voted on for at least 30 days and only after the grand lodge has checked him against a register of rejected candidates, the committee has turned in their report, and, less universally, his name has been made known to the members and neighboring lodges. The ballot must be unanimous in most grand lodges, though some require two or three negative votes to reject a candidate.

After each degree, the new brother must memorize a "catechism" of 20–60 questions about the degree and pass an examination in open lodge. The questions and answers are usually taught "mouth to ear" by an instructor appointed by the lodge, though some grand lodges have printed aides or have substituted open-book tests on Masonic history, symbolism, and practices. Approval of the examination can vary from a ballot by all members present to consent by the Worshipful Master. The Master Mason catechism is not always required but is often necessary before a new member can join any collateral body. Only Master Masons are voting members of a lodge and business is normally conducted in that degree. Thus, there is some incentive to advance through the degrees without delay. The time from petitioning to becoming a Master Mason would normally take four to six months, unless the summer intervenes, during which time most American lodges are dark.

An American Lodge normally has the following officers in the progressive line: Jr. and Sr. Stewards, Jr. and Sr. Deacons, Jr. and Sr. Wardens, and Worshipful Master. A member would be appointed Jr. Steward and after six years serve a term as Master of the lodge—a total of seven years. The line is often shorter because of officers dropping out. The requirements for being Worshipful Master vary from grand lodge to grand lodge: from minimally serving as a Warden to passing an examination in the entire unwritten ritual.

The York Rite

As all Gaul is divided into three parts, most American Masons are convinced that Masonry is divided into two parts: the York and Scottish Rites. There is a generally blissful ignorance of the Rectified Scottish Rite, the French Rite, Emulation ritual, and so on. The York Rite consists of the Chapter of Royal Arch Masons (about 12% of American Masons), the Council of Cryptic Masons, and the Commandery of Knights Templar (about 10%). The organizational structure can be traced back to Thomas Smith Webb who also rewrote the rituals for these organizations. An American Royal Arch Chapter confers the degrees of Mark Master, Past Master (maintaining the tradition that only Past Masters could be advanced to the Royal Arch), Most Excellent Master (an American invention that celebrates the completion of Solomon's Temple), and Royal Arch Mason. The Cryptic Council, which is required in some states to become a Knight Templar, confers the degrees of Royal and Select Master. The Templar Commandery confers the Order of the Red Cross (an "embassy" degree involving Zerubabbel's return to Jerusalem from Babylon), the Order of Malta, and the Order of the Temple.

Each state has a Grand Chapter, a Grand Council, and a Grand Commandery that coordinate their activities to some extent. There is a national General Grand Chapter to which most Grand Chapters belong, though the real power and governance is wielded by the state Grand Chapters. The General Grand Council functions very much like its Royal Arch counterpart. The Grand Encampment of Knights Templar is the strongest national body of the York Rite, though each state independently elects its own Grand Commander.

The Scottish Rite

The Ancient and Accepted Scottish Rite had a very early start in the United States. New Orleans boasts the first Lodge of Perfection in 1764 followed by Albany, New York, in 1767. These bodies were part of the 25-degree system (called the "Rite of Perfection" or "Order of the Royal Secret") that was the immediate ancestor of the Scottish Rite. In 1801, this old rite was transformed by the addition of eight additional degrees and the creation of the first supreme council, the Mother Council of the World. Twelve years later, the Supreme Council for the Northern Masonic Jurisdiction was created by the Southern Jurisdiction, and the two supreme councils have shared governance of the rite in the United States ever since. About 38% of all American Masons belong to the Scottish Rite today.

Unlike the York Rite, which follows the Craft model of relatively small community lodges, the Scottish Rite has large, urban or regional bodies. Each major city will have only one Scottish Rite Valley with many hundreds of members, and larger Valleys could have thousands of members. The Scottish Rite degrees in the United States have evolved over the last century into theatrical productions involving elaborate sets, intricate costumes, and large casts. The basic level of membership is the 32°, though advancement to the 33° is only a little over 1%. Intermediate recognitions exist between the 32° and the 33°: the Knight Commander of the Court of Honour in the Southern Jurisdiction, and the Meritorious Service Award in the Northern Masonic Jurisdiction.

Androgynous Orders

The idea of a Masonic organization for men and women did not originate in America, but it seems to have blossomed here. Rob Morris of Kentucky created the Order of the Eastern Star in 1850 for female relatives of Masons and the order quickly spread. The Eastern Star has about 60% the size of Freemasonry and has a General Grand Chapter to which most states belong. There are other androgynous groups associated with lodges, such as the Order of the Amaranth and the White Shrine of Jerusalem, and groups for female relatives of members of other Masonic bodies, such as the Social Order of Beauseant associated with the Knights Templar relatives and Daughters of the Nile associated with the Shrine. The Eastern Star is by far the largest organization for ladies.

Social Organizations

After the success of the Eastern Star, the next expansion of American Masonry was into the realm of purely social or "fun" groups. In 1872, the Ancient Arabic Order Nobles of the Mystic Shrine was created in New York City for 32° Masons or Knights Templar. The Shrine was created during the heyday of American fraternal organizations, and it limited its membership to the most exclusive and expensive branches of the oldest and most exclusive fraternity. It quickly became a wild success. By the end of the nineteenth century, American Freemasonry was a conservative, moralizing organization, somewhat puritanical in its practices. (For example, abstinence at lodge functions was enforced by statute in most grand lodges.) The Shrine, in contrast, was created as the "playground of Masonry." Their initiation ceremonies were full of hijinks, their parades were famous, their conventions notorious, and their social events were lavish—and wet. About 29% of American Masons belong to the Shrine.

On the heels of the Shriners' success came the Mystic Order, Veiled Prophets of the Enchanted Realm in 1899 and the Tall Cedars of Lebanon in 1902. These groups soon adopted outstanding charities and evolved into a fun-loving social clubs. The Shriners have a national network of twenty-two hospitals treating at no charge children with orthopedic problems and burns. For 2003, the budget for the Shrine hospitals was $605 million!

Youth Organizations

Masonic development in the United States followed several waves: the Craft in the early- to mid-1700s; the York and Scottish Rites in the late-1700s to early-1800s; ladies organizations in the mid-1800s; and social organizations in the late-1800s. The last major expansion of American Masonry occurred in the early-1900s with the development of Masonic youth organizations—about the same time as the Boy Scouts and Girl Scouts were getting started. The three largest surviving organizations are the Order of DeMolay, 1919, the Job's Daughters, 1920, and the Order of Rainbow for Girls, 1922. Local chapters are sponsored by Masonic-related organizations with advisors usually from the sponsoring group. The membership age has changed over the years, and today is 11 or 13 through 21. Membership is open to any youth, except the Job's Daughters limit themselves to Masonic relations.

All the Rest

The United States is a large country with a large and complex Masonic structure. This paper has just touched on the major branches. There are Masonic stamp clubs, motorcycle clubs, and magicians clubs. There are invitational organizations, such as the Red Cross of Constantine, the Societas Rosicruciana in Civitatis Foederatis, the Allied Masonic Degrees, and many, many more. They add color, texture, and intricate detail to the Masonic landscape. However, their story must wait till another time.

BIBLIOGRAPHY

Coil, Henry W., et al. *Coil's Masonic Encyclopedia*. New York: Macoy Publishing and Masonic Supply Co., 1961.

Denslow, William R. *10,000 Famous Freemasons*, 4 vols. Transactions of the Missouri Lodge of Research, vol. 17, 1960.

Morris, S. Brent. "The Polite Revolution: The Formation of American Grand Lodges, 1777–1806," presented to Quatuor Coronati Lodge No. 2076, London, May 8, 2003.

The Impact of English Freemasonry on America and Vice-Versa

The contributions to America by British Freemasonry in general and English Freemasonry in particular have been immense. They laid the foundation for our fraternity that today encompasses over 1,100,000 members in more than fifty grand lodges and scores of appendant bodies.

There are many American Masonic firsts worth noting. Jonathan Belcher, colonial governor of New Hampshire, Massachusetts, and New Jersey, was made a Mason while traveling in Europe from 1704 to 1705; he returned as the first known American-born Mason and also one of the few known pre-1717 Masons. The first duly constituted lodge in America was First Lodge of Boston (later St. John's Lodge) chartered in 1733. While the Royal Arch originated in England, American is proud to have the first minuted conferral on December 22, 1753, at Fredericksburg Lodge No. 4 of Virginia, where only eight months earlier a young George Washington had become a Master Mason. In addition to the first minuted Royal Arch conferral in Virginia, St. Andrews Royal Arch Lodge (later chapter) of Boston has the first minuted conferral of the Knight Templar Degree on August 28, 1769.

While England and Scotland and Ireland generously shared the ancient and honorable fraternity of free and accepted Masonry with the British Colonies, the flow of fraternalism has not always been one-way from east to west. The contributions have also flowed from west to east as America has made contributions to the fabric of the British Craft. Inspired by the originators and by their unique local situations, Americans built upon and expanded the fraternal system they received. Five creations in particular merit notice: (1) the Ancient and Accepted Rite; (2) the Red Cross of Constantine; (3) the Order of the Eastern Star; (4) the Order of Royal and Select Masters; and (5) the Ancient Arabic Order of the Nobles of the Mystic Shrine.

Ancient and Accepted Rite or Rose Croix, 1826

The most successful American Masonic export may be the Ancient and Accepted Rite or Rose Croix. It is known as the "Ancient and Accepted Scottish Rite" in its country of origin, but it lost an adjective during the Atlantic journey. The rite had a long history before arriving in Britain in 1845 and may have in fact originated in England.

In 1733, Rawlinson's list of lodges has this entry, "115, Devil Tavern, Temple Bar, a Scotch Masons' Lodge," and Pine's 1734 engraved list of lodges has, "Scott's Masons' Lodge, Devil, Temple Bar."[1] No one quite knows what was going on in the Scotch Masons' Lodge, but it was sufficiently different from a Master Masons' Lodge that there was a notation in the list, presumably to keep non-Scotch Masons from showing up inadvertently. In 1735, the Lodge held at the Bear in Bath has this entry in their minutes: "On Oct. 28th 1735 ... On the same date Lodge of Masters met Extraordinary and our following Worthy Broths were made and admitted Scots Mastr. Masons."[2] Something seems to have been going on, and it was spreading.

The Grand Lodge of London and Westminster had been formed in 1717 with but two degrees, and eight years later on May 12, 1725, we have the first recorded conferral of the Master Mason Degree (arguably the first "high degree") in the Philo Musicæ et Architecturæ Societas.[3] And eight years thereafter brings evidence of yet another "high degree," the Scotch Mason or Master. Then in 1742, in Berlin, the movement spread, a Scottish lodge under the name of *de l'Union* was established "to let its younger Brethren aspire after the higher or so-called Scottish Masonry."[4]

Degrees increased rapidly after that, if *Le Parfait Maçon* of 1744 is to be believed.

It is said among the Masons, that there are still several degrees above that of the masters, of which I have just spoke; some say there are six in all, & others go up to seven ...

Instead of weeping over the ruins of the Temple of Solomon as their brethren do, the Ecossais are concerned with rebuilding it.

---

1   From Rawlinson's engraved list of Lodges of 1733 and Pine's engraved list of 1734. J. Lane, "Masters' Lodges," *AQC* 1 (1888): 167.

2   Edward Armitage, In the discussion of "The Origin of Additional Degrees," *AQC* 32 (1919): 40–41.

3   R. F. Gould, "Philo Musicæ et Architecturæ Societas Apollini [A Review]," *AQC* 16 (1903): 114.

4   Alain Bernheim, "Did Early 'High' or Écossais Degrees Originate in France?," *Heredom* 5 (1996): 100.

. . .

When the question arose of rebuilding the Temple of the Lord, Zerubbabel chose from the three grades of Masonry the most capable workmen; but as the Israelites had to suffer many obstacles & reverses during the course of their labors, at the hands of the Samaritans & of other neighboring nations, the work would never have been completed, had not this Prince taken the precaution of creating a fourth grade of Masons whose number he limited to 753, chosen from among the most excellent artists ...

Their work being much more arduous than that of the other Masons, they were also awarded a more favorable rate of pay: & to be able to recognize them, Zerubbabel gave them a sign & particular words.[5]

Allegorical Conversations was published in installments from 1763 to 1766 and gave the catechisms of a high-degree rite of ten degrees beyond Master Mason. Three years later M. de Bérage's *The Most Secret Mysteries of the High Degrees of Masonry Unveiled* showed the full rituals of a rite of seven degrees after Master Mason.[6] "Bérage's degrees were not necessarily the most popular or the most important of those being worked, but they were the first to be published, and thus set the standard for future high degrees."[7] The degrees in these books are recognizable as precursors of those in the Ancient and Accepted Rite.

At the same time as the various *hauts grades* were coalescing into rites, that is, a sequential arrangements of degrees telling a coherent story, Etienne (Stephen) Morin entered the field, destined to become one of the most successful propagators of high-degree Masonry.

On August 27, 1761, the French Grand Lodge (the Grand and Sovereign Lodge of St. John of Jerusalem) at Paris granted Morin

---

5   Harry Carr, ed., *The Early French Exposures* (London: Quatuor Coronati Lodge No. 2076, 1971), 197–98.

6   [Erasme Pincemaille], *Conversations Allégoriques Organisées par la Sagesse* (London [Berlin?], 1763–6); M. de Bérage, *Les Plus Secrets Mystères des Hauts Grades de la Maçonnerie Dévoilés* (Jerusalem [Holland?], 1766).

7   Arturo de Hoyos and S. Brent Morris, trans. and ed., *The Most Secret Mysteries of the High Degrees of Masonry Unveiled* (Washington: Scottish Rite Research Society, 2011), vii.

a patent as a Grand Inspector, "authorizing and empowering him to establish perfect and sublime Masonry in all parts of the world."

Morin, who wasted no time, promulgated a Masonic system or rite with twenty-five degrees which he called the "Order of the Royal Secret" (sometimes mistakenly called the "Rite of Perfection"). This Order included many of the most popular degrees worked at the time. Morin's Order was destined to become the parent of the Scottish Rite. Recent research suggests that Morin was personally responsible for combining the degrees he needed to create the Order of the Royal Secret.[8]

In 1763, Morin brought the Order of the Royal Secret with him to Jamaica, and from there, it spread throughout the Caribbean and to New Orleans and to the British colonies. Inspectors general and deputies acted as independent agents conferring the degrees for a fee (and for a higher fee creating inspectors and deputies). By 1809, there were at least seventy-nine of these entrepreneurs peddling their wares, and at least forty-two operated on the east cost of the United States.[9] Without a central authority the situation was chaotic. But then on May 31, 1801, in Charleston, South Carolina, the Order of the Royal Secret was transformed by the addition of eight degrees into the Ancient and Accepted Rite of thirty-three degrees. Thus, Ecossais or Scottish Masonry, apparently originating in London as a single degree moved to the continent, from there to the Caribbean, and from there to America. It was now ready to complete the circle.

Le Comte Alexandre Francois Auguste de Grasse-Tilly was one of the eleven founders of the first Supreme Council in Charleston in 1801. In 1804, he returned to France and established the Supreme Council of France. In 1819, the French Supreme Council offered "a patent to the Duke of Sussex of the 33° so that he could form a Supreme Council in Britain."[10] However, "since the Union of 1813, he had been trying to play down the high degrees

---

8   Arturo de Hoyos, *The Scottish Rite Ritual Monitor and Guide* (Washington: Supreme Council, 33°, SJ, 2007), 74.

9   Harold V. B. Voorhis, *The Story of the Scottish Rite of Freemasonry* (New York: Press of Henry Emmerson, 1965), 56–57.

10 A. C. F. Jackson, *Rose Croix: A History of the Ancient and Accepted Rite for England and Wales* (London: Lewis Masonic, 1980), 143.

to avoid dissension in the United Grand Lodge."[11] Thus, this first attempt to form an English Supreme Council died aborning. There were no such need to maintain harmony in Ireland, so in 1826, the Duke of Leinster became the first Sovereign Grand Commander of the Supreme Council of Ireland, chartered by the Southern Jurisdiction, USA.

The Duke of Sussex died in 1843, and in 1845, twenty-six years after the first failed attempt, a Supreme Council for England and Wales was finally chartered. Dr. Robert Thomas Crucefix, concerned that France might charter a Supreme Council, wrote to the Northern Masonic Jurisdiction, USA, urgently requesting a charter, which was quickly granted with Crucefix as Sovereign Grand Commander and Dr. George Oliver as Lieutenant Grand Commander. A. C. F. Jackson speculated that Crucefix wrote to the Northern Masonic Jurisdiction because they "only admitted Christians to the Rose Croix 18° and above, while the Southern Jurisdiction had been theist from its start."[12] "Dr [Charles] Morison, the first Sovereign Grand Commander in Scotland, had a patent of the 33° from Spain and then had it endorsed by the Supreme Council for France and the Grand Orient."[13] And thus, in 1846, the Supreme Council for Scotland was established, bringing the Ancient and Accepted Rite to all of Great Britain.

The Red Cross of Constantine, 1865

One of the most interesting Masonic exports from American to Britain arrived through the back door, so to speak. This order is the Red Cross of Constantine, formally known as the Masonic and Military Order of the Red Cross of Constantine and the Orders of the Holy Sepulchre and St John the Evangelist. It was "revived" by Robert Wentworth Little, second clerk and cashier in the Grand Secretary's office in 1865 when he found a record book in the archives of the United Grand Lodge of England.[14] On the basis of this book and mention of other "Red Cross" degrees worked in Britain, he created a new organization, claimed it was the continuation of a civil order of knighthood, and convinced the Masonic public to accept his fabrication as genuine. The claim of a "revival" may have been intended allow operation as an "Order of Chivalry" under article II of the 1813

---

11 Jackson, *Rose Croix*, 146, 148.

12 Jackson, *Rose Croix*, 162.

13 Jackson, *Rose Croix*, 177.

14 Ellic Howe, "Fringe Masonry in England 1870–85," *AQC* 85 (1972): 246.

Articles of Union, "But this article is not intended to prevent any Lodge or Chapter from holding a meeting in any of the degrees of the Orders of Chivalry, according to the constitutions of the said Orders."[15]

The American connection to this bold invention begins some fifty years previous, in the eighteen-teens or -twenties. This was the time of itinerant American Masonic lecturers, entrepreneurs active in the late-eighteenth and early-nineteenth centuries. They travelled from town to town and gave instruction in the "standard" American Webb–Preston work (which was strongly influenced by the 1762 exposure *Jachin and Boaz*), sold Masonic monitors, and peddled side degrees. While looked at with some scorn today, these lecturers created the foundation of nearly uniform American Masonic ritual and helped spread the Cryptic Rite among other degrees.[16]

James H. C. Miller, one of the itinerant lecturers, created an unattached chivalric order known as the Order of the Holy Cross that usually worked in connection with an encampment of Knights Templar. The Order of the Holy Cross conferred three-degrees: (1) Knights of the Christian Mark, and Guards of the Conclave; (2) Knights of the Holy Sepulchre; (3) The Holy and Thrice Illustrious Order of the Holy Cross, called a Council. Arturo de Hoyos estimates that by 1829, Miller had chartered about forty conclaves and had about 500 members. Indeed, Council No. 39 in Beaufort, South Carolina, was chartered on October 5, 1829.[17] The Order of the Holy Cross had the potential to growing into a national force, but the American Anti-Masonic Period intervened.

In 1826, William Morgan, a disaffected Mason in Batavia, New York, announced plans to publish the secrets of the Freemasons, including those of the Royal Arch. He was abducted by renegade Masons in September, and his disappearance and probable murder led to the creation by 1828 of the first successful third party in American politics, the Anti-Masonic Party. The Grand Lodge of New York lost ninety percent of their members, the Grand Lodge of Vermont closed, the Grand Lodge of Maryland lost one-half of their lodges, and other disruptions to Masonry occurred throughout the country. The Order of the Holy Cross disappeared, and their rituals

---

15 *Articles of Union between the Two Grand Lodge of Freemasons of England* (London: W. P. Norris, 1813), 2.

16 S. Brent Morris, "Itinerant American Masonic Lecturers," *AQC* 121 (2008): 1–19.

17 Arturo de Hoyos, "The Posthumous Success of James H. C. Miller, Degree Peddler," *Heredom* 8 (1999–2000): 169–218.

were published in David Bernard's *Light on Masonry* (1829) and Avery Allyn's *A Ritual of Freemasonry* (1831), the two most successful exposures of Masonic ritual of the era. Other authors plagiarized Bernard and Allyn, so it's hard to tell from whom subsequent plagiarists copied.[18] The other ingredients for Little's new recipe can be found in Richard Carlile's "An Exposure of Freemasonry!" published in *The Republican*.[19]

Arturo de Hoyos carefully studied the ca. 1865 rituals of (1) The Red Cross of Rome and Constantine, (2) Novice and Knight of St. John the Evangelist, and (3) Knights of the Holy Sepulchre, presumably written by Robert W. Little.[20] The Red Cross is based on the rituals published by Carlile with the addition of Bernard's sword presentation from his Knight Templar and Knight of Malta.[21] Large portions of the Novice and Knight of St John are copied from Bernard's Prince of the Royal Secret and Perfect Master Degrees; the Knight of the Holy Sepulchre is largely copied from Miller's Knight of the Holy Sepulchre in Bernard.[22] Thus without Miller and Bernard (or those who plagiarized Bernard), there would have had no basis for the rituals of the Red Cross of Constantine.

The epilogue to this tale of creative invention is a fitting response to Little's "discoveries." Between the 1865 and 1872, Order of the Red Cross of Constantine became remarkably popular, with sixty-two Conclaves chartered, including fourteen in Canada, eighteen in the United States, and eight in India.[23] In 1870, Demetrius Rhodocanakis commenced styling himself "Prince" and "Imperial Highness," and represented himself as Grand Master of the Order to the press. He published a book entitled: *The Imperial Constantinian Order of St. George. A Review of Modern Impostures and a Sketch of Its True History.* The "imposture" to which he referred was the

---

18 "Subsequent exposures, including George R. Crafts's *The Mysteries of Free Masonry* (1852), and Jabez Richardson [Benjamin Henry Day], *Richardson's Monitor of Freemasonry* (1860), were simply copied from the first two," de Hoyos, "Miller," 176.

19 Richard Carlile, "An Exposure of Freemasonry!," *The Republican* 12, no. (1): July 8, 1825; July 2, 15, 1825; July 3, 22, 1825; July 4, 29, 1825; August 6, 5, 1825; August 7, 19, 1825; August 8, 26, 1825; September 9, 2, 1825; September 10, 9, 1825; September 12, 23, 1825; September 13, 30, 1825; October 14, 7, 1825; October 15, 16, 21, 1825.

20 These ritual "extracts are from nineteenth-century documents and do not reflect subsequent revisions in the rituals of the Red Cross of Constantine." de Hoyos, "Miller," 210.

21 L. E. C. Peckover, "The Red Cross of Constantine," *AQC* 76 (1963): 79.

22 de Hoyos, "Miller," 210–17.

23 Ellic Howe, "Fringe Masonry in England 1870–85," *AQC* 85 (1972): 249n2.

"Red Cross of Constantine ...[24] The result was that Little effectively ceded the public order to "Prince" Rhodocanakis and limited his influence to the Masonic order.

None of the foregoing is intended to detract from the prominence and effectiveness today of the Red Cross of Constantine. It is a cautionary tale that not all family (or fraternal) traditions stand up under close scrutiny.

Order of the Eastern Star, 1868

The androgynous Order of the Eastern Star has only been moderately successful in Britain; nonetheless, it has endured for some 150 years. Androgynous or adoptive Masonic groups date back at least to the Order of the Mopses of *ca.* 1742, if that Catholic Order can be considered Masonic.[25] Certainly, the idea was full born by 1775 with the publication of *L'Adoption ou la Maçonnerie des Femmes en Trois Grades.* In the United States, the records are scant, but before the 1826 Morgan Affair, there appear to have been detached degrees for men and women, such as Mason's Daughter, Mason's Wife, True Kindred, and others. It's not clear if these early degrees are the same as later degrees with similar names. One of the earliest androgynous groups was the Heroines of Jericho, an adoptive degree for Royal Arch Masons and their wives and widows. It appeared in Allyn's 1831 *A Ritual of Freemasonry* and continues today in Prince Hall Royal Arch Masonry and is one of the three degrees of the Order of True Kindred, a mainstream androgynous body (its degrees being True Kindred and Good Samaritan). None of these early groups had any central organization; apparently any Mason who had received the degree could convene a meeting to confer it on others. It would not be until after the Anti-Masonic Period that a successful and robust androgynous order would appear.

The American Anti-Masonic Period started winding down in 1838 with the absorption of the Anti-Masonic Party into the Whig Party. By 1840, Freemasonry reemerged into the public and started growing again. In 1847, the Masons of Holmes County, Mississippi, established the Richland Literary

---

24 Andreas C. Rizopoulos, "The Three Mancunians: Yarker—Lawrence Archer—Rhodocanakis," *AQC* 113 (2000): 168; [Demetrius] Rhodocanakis, *The Imperial Constantinian Order of St. George: A Review of Modern Impostures and a Sketch of its True History,* (London: Longmans, Green, and Co., 1870).

25 Gabriel-Louis Pérau, *L'Ordre des Francs-Maçons Trahi et le Secret des Mopses Révélé* (Amsterdam, 1742)

Institute and in 1848, renamed it Eureka Masonic College. Rob Morris was hired to teach at the college. He had become a Mason in 1846 and believed that the advantages of Freemasonry needed to be shared with the female relatives of Masons. In 1850, while at Eureka Masonic College, he organized the degrees for the Order of the Eastern Star.[26]

The degrees or lessons are based upon women in the Bible: Adah, Jephthah's daughter from the Book of Judges; Ruth, the widow from the Book of Ruth; Esther, the wife from the Book of Esther; Martha, the sister from the Gospels of Luke and John; Electa, the "elect lady" from the Book of 2 John. A woman's eligibility is based upon her relationship with a Mason—wife, widow, mother, sister, and so on. While this requirement may seem quaint today, the Eastern Star was in fact a feminist step forward in 1850. Morris's invention had a rocky start, with an overly complicated organization, widespread opposition to "Ladies" Masonry', and the intervention of the American Civil War (1861–1865).[27] Finally, in 1868, Morris turned over the Eastern Star to Robert Macoy of New York who produced a successful system that included today's local chapters, state grand chapters, and a national general grand chapter. By 1884, the Eastern Star had expanded to "more than four hundred chapters, extending to thirty-three [out of thirty-eight] states and territories."[28]

We do not know when after 1850, the Eastern Star was introduced to Britain, but there was intriguing evidence in 1863. "At Troon, on the 9th, the Navigation Lodge, No. 86, in the most spirited manner, held a ball in the Portland Arms Assembly Room ... the brethren being in full Masonic regalia, and many of the ladies wearing the badge of the 'Eastern Star.'"[29] Were these ladies initiated in America or perhaps somewhere closer to home? Moving east, "The Order was introduced into Scotland in 1868 by Bro Robert Morris when he visited Edinburgh. The first recorded Chapter in Scotland is "VICTORIA" Chapter No 1, and the date of their Charter was 30th September 1874 ... The Order as we know it today was consecrated in

---

26 Harold Van Buren Voorhis, *The Eastern Star: The Evolution from a Rite to an Order* (New York: Macoy Publishing and Masonic Supply Co., 1954), 24.

27 Jean M'Kee Kenaston, *History of the Order of the Eastern Star* (Cedar Rapids, IA: Torch Press, 1917), 22–23; R. A. Gilbert, "'The Monstrous Regiment': Women and Freemasonry in the Nineteenth Century," *AQC* 115 (2002): 165–66.

28 Kenaston, *History,* 23.

29 *Freemasons Magazine and Masonic Mirror,* March 21, 1863, 236.

1903 and reconstituted by the Most Worthy Grand Matron of the General Grand Chapter in 1904."[30]

Things did not go as smoothly in England. The Eastern Star was not received well in the English Masonic Press. In 1870, the *Freemasons Magazine and Masonic Mirror* said: "We wish them no evil, but we must say that these very objections—"superfluous and useless"—applied by the friends of the Eastern Star to the other female degrees, we would apply to them."[31] The Order was denigrated in *The Freemason* of October 28, 1871, because "Divorce was perfectly free [in the central and other parts of America], and women had sometimes children by several husbands. ... The Eastern Star Order is calculated to lesson [*sic*] the evils known to exist in American territory, but its presence in Great Britain is not essential to the present social condition of the people."[32] If this wasn't enough, the United Grand Lodge of England forbade its members from joining Eastern Star chapters.

According to George Draffen of Newington, "The governing body of the Eastern Star in Scotland has removed all references to any Masonic connection from its Statutes and from its Laws and Constitutions and the Grand Lodge of Scotland, therefore, does not regard it as a Masonic Order."[33] In 2016, the Supreme Grand Chapter of Scotland, OES, operates ten chapters in England and one in Northern Ireland.[34] Thus, this Masonic import has a presence throughout Britain, though strongest in Scotland.

Royal and Select Masters, 1873

The youngest member of the American York Rite is the Council of Royal and Select Masters, coming in sequence between the Royal Chapter and the Knights Templar Commandery. Full membership requires receiving the two degrees of Royal Master and Select Master; there is an additional,

---

30 Supreme Grand Chapter of Scotland, Order of the Eastern Star, http://www.supremegrandchapterofscotland.co.uk, downloaded August 22, 2016.

31 *Freemasons Magazine and Masonic Mirror,* April 9, 1870, 287

32 C. S., "The Fair Sex and Adoptive Masonry," Part 9, *The Freemason,* October 28, 1871, 667.

33 George Draffen of Newington, comment on Harry Mendoza, "The Articles of Union and the Orders of Chivalry," *AQC* 93 (1980): 73.

34 Supreme Grand Chapter of Scotland, Order of the Eastern Star, http://www.supremegrandchapterofscotland.co.uk, downloaded August 22, 2016.

optional degree of Super Excellent Master. The origins of the principal degrees, like so many Masonic degrees, are murky.

It had been "believed that Thomas Lowndes first conferred the Royal Master Degree around 1805, in New York,[35] and the earliest known records are those of his Columbian Council No. 1, New York, which date from 1810."[36,37] Recent research by Arturo de Hoyos points to a 1795 date based on a ritual manuscript of Achille Huet de Lachelle and confirmed by a manuscript of Pierre Joseph Duhulquod.[38]

The Select Master Degree is thought to be the same as a detached degree mentioned in the "Manifesto of 1802" of the first Supreme Council of the Ancient and Accepted Rite

> Besides these degrees, which are in regular succession, most of the Inspectors are in possession of a number of detached degrees, given in different parts of the world, and which they generally communicate, free of expence [sic], to those Brethren who are high enough to understand them. Such as the Select Masons of 27...[39]

Certainly the title, "Select Masons of 27," conforms to the ceremony of the Select Master Degree. Philip Eckel is said to have established a Grand Council of Select Masters in 1792 in Baltimore, Maryland. Jeremy Ladd Cross, an itinerant American lecturer, in a four-month 1817 trip from Haverhill, New Hampshire, to Richmond, Virginia, chartered councils of Select Masters for $20 and taught the Craft degrees for $4 per day. He chartered at least six councils on this trip.[40] Cross combined the two degrees

---

35 *Proceedings of the Grand Council, Royal and Select Masters of the State of Vermont at the 45th Annual Assembly In the City of Burlington, Tuesday, June 9th, A.D. 1903, A:.Dep:. 2903.* vol. 5 (Windsor, Vermont: Journal Company, Book and Job Printers, 1903) No. 8, Appendix: "Report on the Committee on Correspondence 1903," 15.

36 *The Hudson River Trestle Board*, vol. 5 (Newburgh, New York, April 15, 1906), 68:577. See also Eugene E. Hinman, Ray V. Denslow, and Charles C. Hunt, *A History of the Cryptic Rite*, 2 vols. (Tacoma, WA: General Grand Council R. & S.M., U.S.A., 1931), 1:606–7.

37 Arturo de Hoyos, *Albert Pike's Reprints of Rituals of Old Degrees* (Washington: Scottish Rite Research Society, 2015), xxiii.

38 de Hoyos. *Old Degrees,* xxiii–xxiv.

39 *Circular throughout the Two Hemispheres* (Charleston, SC: Supreme Council of the 33d Degree fo the United States of America, December 4, 1802).

40 S. Brent Morris, "Itinerant American Masonic Lecturers," *AQC* 121 (2008): 15.

into a single system in 1818, but the General Grand Council of Cryptic Masons International was founded much later in 1880.

The Grand Council of New York chartered four London Councils in 1871, and two years later in 1873, they formed the Grand Council of Royal and Select Masters of England and Wales and its and the Colonies and Dependencies of the British Crown with G. R. Portal as grand master.[41] It is today headquartered at Mark Masons' Hall and is a successful part of the family of English Masonry.

Ancient Arabic Order, Nobles of the Mystic Shrine, 2006

The most distinctive American Masonic creation is doubtless the Shriners—the Ancient Arabic Order of the Nobles of the Mystic Shrine (AAONMS, which anagrams into "A MASON"). It started in 1870 at the Knickerbocker Cottage in Manhattan where actor William J. Florence, physician Walter M. Fleming, and other Masons often lunched. As happens in history, no single event but rather a confluence of events created the conditions for this innovation.

During the approximately fifteen-year American Anti-Masonic Period (ca. 1826–1841), Freemasons were accused of murder and subversion of the government as well as lesser offenses including irreligion and intemperance. The 1828 Convention of Seceding Masons Held at Le Roy, New York, specifically charged of Freemasonry, "It promotes habits of idleness and intemperance, by its members neglecting their businesses to attend its meetings and drink its libations."[42]

When Freemasonry returned to the public eye, about 1841, it was as a much more conservative and cautious organization. In 1826, the year William Morgan had been abducted, The American Temperance Society was formed and by 1833 had 1,250,000 members.[43] Thus, it was doubly prudent that Freemasonry be restrained and temperate, to both negate earlier charges and to conform to a growing societal movement. This almost-puri-

---

41 Eugene E. Hinman et al., *A History of the Cryptic Rite* (Tacoma, WA: General Grand Council, R.&S.M., 1931), 1:370–71.

42 "Declaration," Convention of Seceding Masons Held at Le Roy, [New York], July 4, 1828, in David Bernard, *Light on Masonry* (Utica, NY: William Williams, 1829), 454

43 Ernest H. Cherrington, *The Evolution of Prohibition in the United States of America* (Westerville, OH: American Issue Press, 1920), 93.

tanical conservatism led Rob Morris to complain, "The Order with us has too much of the pulpit, and too little of the table. A due intermixture of both was what the Craft in olden time regarded."[44]

During the American Civil War (1861–1865), the Northeast had benefitted financially as its factories produced military materiel. As a result, the post-war time was one of prosperity for the region. The end of the Civil War started a fifty-year period known as "The Golden Age of Fraternalism," during which time over 300 fraternal organizations were created. Many of these groups were mutual insurance companies, some were military-inspired marching and drilling societies, and others simply sought the pleasures of fraternalism less-exclusive than that of Freemasonry and Odd Fellowship, the two oldest and largest American fraternal groups. Thus, in 1870 Manhattan, the time was truly ripe for a flamboyant, exclusive fraternal order: enter Florence, Fleming, and the Shriners.

At this time in the United States, there were two paths of "high degree" Masonry: the "York Rite" and the "Scottish Rite." The York Rite, the older and more popular system of local bodies, was a three-step progression from the Royal Arch Chapter to the Royal and Select Council culminating in the Knights Templar Commandery. The Scottish Rite's regional bodies advanced members from the 4° to the 32° (the functional equivalent of the 18° in Britain). Thus, when the Shrine limited its members to Knights Templars or 32° Masons, it was requiring its initiates to first belong to the oldest and most exclusive American fraternal organization and then complete one of its two high-degree systems. In preparing to join the Shrine, candidates had to pay for multiple initiation fees and spend a year or more taking the preparatory degrees. It was a classic marketing example of exclusivity driving demand.

The Shrine rituals were the creation of Florence, despite elaborate origin myths to the contrary. Florence was inspired by a musical comedy he saw in Marseille, France, which was staged by an Arabian diplomat. Shriners became famous for their elaborate costumes and marching bands and units in civic parades. Because they did not claim to be a Masonic organization per se (they only drew their members from the Craft), they mostly avoided the straight-laced restrictions of grand lodge. Then in 1920, the Imperial Council voted to establish a Shriners Hospital for Crippled Children. This

---

44 Rob Morris, *The Poetry of Freemasonry* (Chicago: Werner, 1895), 253.

was when polio was epidemic and there was a pressing need for orthopedic care for its victims. The first hospital opened in 1922 in Shreveport, Louisiana, and today, there are twenty-two hospitals in the United States, Canada, and Mexico, providing orthopedic care, burn treatment, cleft lip and palate care, and spinal cord injury rehabilitation.[45] In 2000, the Shrine dropped the York and Scottish Rite requirements, and now any Master Mason can join.

For many years, UGLE would not allow a Shrine Temple or Club to operate on English soil; the only path of initiation was to be initiated in America or at an American military base. The rules changed, and starting in 2006 three Shrine Clubs operating under the Aahmes Shrines of Livermore, California, were established Anglian, Dartford, and London. In January 2016, Steven J. Turner, Dartford Shrine Club president, reported "London has not met for several Years and Anglian may cease to operate this year, Dartford however is struggling on and we now have several waiting to join."[46] It may be that the Shriners, who evolved to fill an ecological niche in a uniquely American environment, do not thrive outside of their native habitat.

First published: *Reflections on 300 Years of Freemasonry*, ed. John S. Wade (London: Lewis Masonic, 2017)

45 *Wikipedia: The Free Encyclopedia*, s.v. "Shriners", accessed August 28, 2016. https://en.wikipedia.org/wiki/Shriners#Shriners_Hospitals_for_Children.

46 "Introductions: New from the UK," *The Shriners Discussion Forum*, accessed August 28, 2016, http://theshriners.proboards.com/thread/313/new-uk?page=1.

American Freemasons and the Spirit of Freedom

E very Grand Lodge takes pride in the accomplishments of its famous members: The names of brothers Rudyard Kipling, Wolfgang A. Mozart, Johann W. von Goethe, Simón Bolívar, Henry Ford, and George Washington are just a few that immediately come to mind. American Freemasons, however, take particular pride in some of their early members, like Washington, because of their dedication to the spirit of freedom. It is an infectious spirit that has infused all of the craft and has spread around the world, making freemasonry feared by tyrants, dictators, and those who would deny people their basic rights.

America was colonized by men of widely different backgrounds and motives. Generally speaking, the northern colonies were founded by those in search of religious freedom, while the southern colonies attracted entrepreneurs seeking their fortunes in agriculture. There were few institutions that transcended colonial borders, and Freemasonry was one of those. In 1776, the American colonies declared their independence from England. Many—but certainly not all—of the prominent revolutionary leaders were Freemasons, and their lodge memberships provided a useful point of commonality.

Any list of prominent American revolutionaries must begin with George Washington, "The Father of His Country." He served as Commander-in-Chief of the Continental Army for eight years, ultimately defeating the English, and was elected the first President of the United States, the first modern democracy in the world. He declined becoming king of the new nation, and by the example of his personal conduct, political restraint, and modest ambitions, he established the principles of a civilian-controlled military and of a peaceful transfer of political power. His integrity set the standards for future American presidents and the leaders of all democracies.

Washington became a Master Mason in 1753 in Fredericksburg, Virginia. The Grand Lodge of Pennsylvania nominated him as "Grand Master General for the Thirteen United American States," which he declined. He did serve as the charter master of Alexandria Lodge No. 39, Alexandria, Virginia, 1788 and was reelected in 1789. There is no record of Washington presiding as master. The high point of his Masonic career came on September 18, 1793, when he laid the cornerstone of the U.S. Capitol with full Masonic ceremonies.

Americans' love for freedom began when they left the known world and traveled across the ocean to establish a new country. Whether they came to escape religious or economic or political restrictions, they came for freedom. As relations steadily worsened with England, the colonial leaders decided the time had come for action. The Declaration of Independence was signed by fifty-six freedom-lovers, nine of whom were Freemasons. The first and most prominent signature of this document is that of Brother John Hancock who used large, bold writing "so that King George III may read it without putting on his glasses."

After five years of bitter war, General Washington defeated Lord Cornwallis at Yorktown, Virginia, in 1781 and independence was secured. In that same year, an interim form of government for the new country was established when the thirteenth and last colony ratified the Articles of Confederation. Nine signers of this weak document were brothers. Despite the best intentions of the drafters, the Articles did not provide enough authority to the central government. By 1786, there was general agreement in the Congress that repairs were needed, and a Constitutional Convention was called for the next year. The delegates assembled in Philadelphia, and after spirited debate produced the Constitution of the United States. Of the fifty-five delegates, nine signers were Freemasons, including George Washington and Benjamin Franklin. Five other Masons were delegates but did not sign the Constitution, and six signers later joined the fraternity.

In addition to the signers of the Declaration of Independence, the Articles of Confederation, and the Constitution, thirty-three general officers of the Continental Army were Freemasons. Benjamin Franklin, Ambassador to France during the American Revolution, had been Deputy Provincial Grand Master of Pennsylvania. Paul Revere, whose "midnight ride" has been immortalized, went on to become grand master of Massachusetts. The Americans' cause of freedom attracted supporters for other countries, including two of Washington's general officers: the Marquis de Lafayette and Friedrich W. A. von Steuben. The "father of the American Navy," Admiral John Paul Jones, was a Craftsman, as was, alas, General Benedict Arnold, the traitor. It is often claimed that Thomas Jefferson was a Freemason, but no credible evidence exists to support this.

With men of this prominence supporting the revolution, it was no won-der that Americans came to accept Freemasonry at the exemplification of ideals of freedom. The capitol of the new nation, the city of Washington, had the support of Freemasons at its birth. The first boundary stone of the ten-mile square city was laid at the southern corner by Alexandria Lodge of Virginia in 1791. A year later, the brethren of Lodge No. 9 of Georgetown, Maryland (now Potomac Lodge No. 5 of the District of Columbia), laid the cornerstone of the "President House," which is now known as the White House. (It was later painted white to cover up the smoke stains left when the British burned it during the War of 1812.) The most famous Masonic cornerstone laying occurred in 1793 when George Washington, assisted by Alexandria Lodge of Virginia and Maryland's Lodge No. 9 of and Lodge No. 15 (now Federal Lodge No. 1 of the District of Columbia), laid the cornerstone of the United States Capitol.

America's Masonic revolutionary leaders are well known, but national service by Masons does not stop there. Fourteen presidents of the United States have been Master Masons: George Washington, James Monroe, An-drew Jackson, James K. Polk, James A. Buchanan, Andrew Johnson, James A. Garfield, William McKinley, Theodore Roosevelt, William H. Taft, War-ren G. Harding, Franklin D. Roosevelt, Harry S. Truman, and Gerald R. Ford. (Lyndon B. Johnson became an Entered Apprentice in 1937, but did not advance further.) These men served their country and Fraternity with pride. Two presided as grand master of their grand lodge: Andrew Jackson, Tennessee, and Harry S. Truman, Missouri.

One of the essentials principles built into the American form of govern-ment is the "separation of powers": executive, legislative, and judicial. There have been over one hundred Justices of the United States Supreme Court, at least thirty-four of whom were Masons. (The exact number is imprecise because eighteenth-century records are scanty and incomplete.) These jurists are the final "line of defense" against those who would chal-lenge freedom. Their sworn duty is to preserve the Constitution against all enemies, domestic and foreign. It takes a special bravery to make unpopular decisions to protect liberty. The first Chief Justice, John Jay, was a Mason, as were six others to hold that position. John Blair, Jr. and John Marshall were Grand Master of Virginia, and Earl Warren was

Grand Master of California. (During the Anti-Masonic Period, Marshall was not proud or enthusiastic about being a Mason.)

In addition to Washington's general officers, some of America's famous military leaders, who risked their lives for freedom at home and abroad, have also been Masons. Generals Douglas MacArthur, James H. Doolittle, Omar Bradley, John J. Pershing, George C. Marshall, Admiral Arleigh A. Burke. Freedom is not maintained only through military might. It is preserved also in the spirit of adventure, as exemplified by Astronauts Edwin E. "Buzz" Aldrin, Jr., Virgil Grissom, John H. Glenn, and Walter S. Schirra, Jr., among many, and aviator Charles A. Lindbergh.

Love of freedom may be inborn, but it requires careful nurturing to blossom. The American public schools are vast in their offerings of universal educational opportunities. Freemasons were among the organizers and planners of this amazing system, and they still staunchly support it. It is part of the heritage of freedom that is preserved for and transmitted to the nation's children.

Perhaps the spirit was best described by Brother Hubert H. Humphrey, Vice-President of the United States: "Freedom is the most contagious virus known to man." When citizens can meet freely and talk freely, when religious expression and economic endeavor are unfettered, when all can share in life, liberty and the pursuit of happiness, there can be no turning back. American Freemasons have fought for these rights for themselves and others, and are proud of their accomplishments.

BIBLIOGRAPHY

Bessel, Paul M. http://www.bessel.org

Coil, Henry W. et al. *Coil's Masonic Encyclopedia.* New York: Macoy Publishing and Masonic Supply Co., 1961.

Heaton, Ronald E. *Masonic Membership of the Founding Fathers.* Silver Spring, MD: Masonic Service Association, 1974.

Morris, S. Brent. *Cornerstones of Freedom: A Masonic Tradition.* Washington: Supreme Council, 33°, 1993.

First Published: "American Freemasons' Spirit of Freedom," *The Freemason's Raiment of Light: Spirit and Matter* (Tours, France: Association 5997, 2002), 171–75.

Voting With Their Feet

I love humanity. It's people I can't stand.

Linus van Pelt
Peanuts, *Charles Schulz*

A low rumble of thunder is an early warning sign of a rain storm. Anyone working in a well-run building should be familiar with the clanging of the fire alarms. Few have heard but nearly everyone knows about the distinctive warning sound of a rattlesnake. These are all obvious warnings of impending danger, warnings which we have been trained to heed or face grave consequences. Other warning signs are more subtle. Radon and carbon monoxide are colorless, odorless, fatal gasses that endanger—one killing quickly and the other over decades. And deformed frogs are being found by the thousands in Minnesota and Wisconsin.[1] The cause of their birth defects is not well understood, but scientists are taking their appearance as an urgent warning that something is seriously amiss in the environment.

For years, I have been interested in the ebb and flow of fraternal memberships in the United States.[2] I can state without fear of contradiction that fraternal membership is not now the social norm. All fraternal organizations have suffered during the last half of the twentieth century; some have declined to the point of virtual disintegration. It was while studying fraternal statistics in Maryland that I became aware of what may be a subtle warning sign for Freemasonry, perhaps a harbinger like the deformed frogs of Minnesota and Wisconsin.

I have been interested in explaining the different fortunes of the York and Scottish Rites in this century. In 1900, there were 839,000 Freemasons in the United States; Royal Arch Masons accounted for 27% and only 5%

---

1   William Souder, "Hundreds of Deformed Frogs Pose Environmental Warning." *Washington Post*, September 30, 1996, A1.

2   S. Brent Morris, "Trends Affecting American Freemasonry." *The Philalethes* 35, no. 2 (April 1982): 16–17; "The Public Image of Freemasonry." *The Royal Arch Mason Magazine* 14, no. 4 (winter 1982): 105–111; "The Siren Song of Solicitation." *The Royal Arch Mason Magazine* 14, no. 6 (summer 1982): 163–168; "Boom to Bust in the Twentieth Century." *Transactions of the Texas Lodge of Research* 23 (1987–88): 142–63.

were in the Scottish Rite. By 1995, there were 2,153,000 Freemasons, but by then 37% were in the Scottish Rite and only 15% were in the Royal Arch. The relative strength of the York Rite has declined from 27% to 15% while that of the Scottish Rite has risen from 5% to 37%. This is a significant realignment of American Masonic activity!

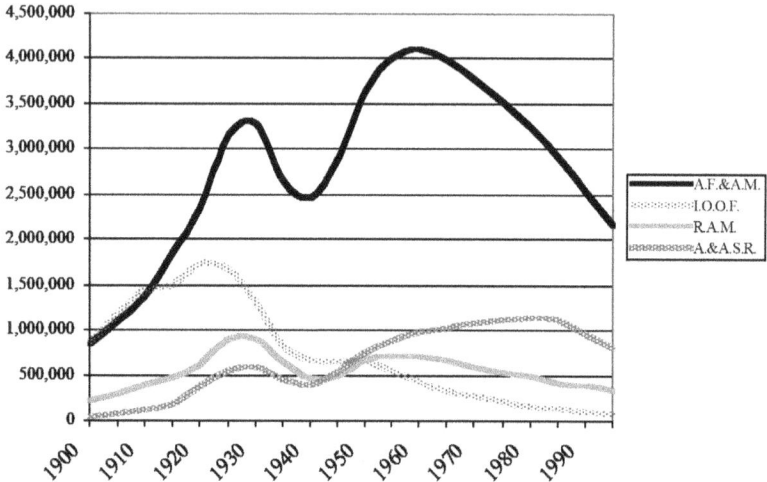

This relative decline in fortunes between the York and Scottish Rites has tried to be explained in various ways. The Scottish Rite is largely found in urban areas, and their dramatic increase in membership coincides with the rural to urban migration of the American population. The York Rite offers only one route to significant recognition: presiding over a local body. While no Masonic body could serve as a model of organizational efficiency, the Scottish Rite has a more stable governing structure with its long-serving state leaders who can institute and support consistent policies and goals. It has recently been suggested that the theatrical staging of Scottish Rite degrees so appealed to turn-of-the-century Masons, that it "eliminated the competition."[3]

As interesting as these speculations are, they are not as intriguing as another discovery I made as I studied fraternal membership in Maryland for the twenty-five year period from 1970 to 1995. In 1970, Maryland had 46,000 Masons, and by 1995, they had declined 42% to 26,900. By comparison,

---

3 C. Lance Brockman, "Catalyst for Change: Intersection of the Theater and the Scottish Rite." *Heredom* 3 (1994): 121–46.

Maryland Odd Fellows declined 63% from 2,610 to 971. Royal Arch membership declined 49% to 3,600 and the Scottish Rite declined only 5% to 8,794. These figures tell an interesting story about fraternalism in Maryland, but are part of a larger national trend of declining memberships in the United States. Odd Fellowship has been declining since about 1920, the York Rite since 1957, Freemasonry since 1959, and the Scottish Rite since 1978.

As I was doing my analysis, I decided to tally the new Masonic groups started in Maryland during the period from 1970 to 1995. My informal research, which probably overlooked several bodies, turned up the following new Masonic organizations in the state, and I doubt that Maryland is significantly different from other states.

Ancient, Free & Accepted Masons
Bayside Lodge
John R. Coats Memorial Lodge
Daylight Lodge
David Kerr Memorial Lodge

Philalethes Society
Southern Maryland Chapter

Maryland Masonic Research Society

Ancient & Accepted Scottish Rite
Southern Maryland Valley

Scottish Rite Clubs
Chesapeake Club
Conowingo Club
Carrol Club

Societas Rosicruciana In Civitatibus Foederatis
Maryland College

Royal & Select Masters
Acacia No. 24

Allied Masonic Degrees
Old Line Council No. 234
Southern Cross Council No. 268
Chesapeake Bay Council No. 278
Freestate Council No. 308
Eastern Shore Council No. 301
Tide Water Council No. 334

Royal Ark Mariners
Pride of Baltimore Lodge

Knight Masons of America
Baltimore Council

York Rite College of North America
Maryland College

New City Square Club

At least twenty-one new Masonic organizations were started during the twenty-five year period of 1970–1995. One of these groups was a regular Lodge, one was a Council of Cryptic Masons, and one was a Scottish Rite Valley. The other seventeen that I counted were associated Masonic groups at the fringe of Masonry. While the general adult male population in Maryland has little interest in the Craft, as witnessed by our declining membership, Maryland Masons themselves are enthusiastic. Almost once a year, they form a new Masonic body in the state. Maryland Masons are so zealous about Masonry that they seem to be constantly looking for more ways to enjoy the mystic bonds of fraternal fellowship, even as our Grand Lodge membership continues its slow, sad decline.

But Maryland Masons have no apparent interest in forming new Lodges or York Rite bodies. The list of new Maryland Masonic bodies speaks clearly to that. They love Masonic fellowship, but have no use for new lodges, the fundamental unit, the heart and soul of Masonry. And this is the interesting warning sign I alluded to earlier. Our most enthusiastic supporters—our active Masters Masons—are voting with their feet and quietly moving their Masonic activities to almost anything other than the basic Lodge.

In 1891 a young man moved to Chicago from Philadelphia. He began work as a soap salesman offering merchants baking powder as a premium for buying his soap. He noted that the merchants were more interested in the soap than the baking powder, so in 1892 he started selling soap and offered two packs of chewing gum as a premium. Once again his customers were more interested in his premium than his product, so in 1893 William Wrigley, Jr., a successful businessman who gave his customers what they wanted, went into the chewing gum business. The rest is history.

The thoughtful Mason must wonder why so much Masonic energy is being expended away from the Lodge. York Rite Masons in particular must wonder why we can't find candidates or officers, and yet these new Maryland groups, most of which draw their memberships exclusively from active York Rite Masons, are growing. It could be that these growing bodies require a simpler "infrastructure"—regalia, annual returns, and ritual proficiency—and are thus easier to start up and maintain. It could be that they are perceived as more prestigious and exclusive than Lodges or Chapters or Commanderies. Most of these groups formed in Maryland are "invitation" bodies that recognize some service to Masonry. Who doesn't like to be recognized for hard work? Who doesn't like to belong to an exclusive group, membership in which is recognized and admired? And yet why can't we generate that sense of exclusivity and recognition in a Lodge?

If I were smart enough to know the answers to the questions I have raised, I would sell the solution to each fraternal lodge in the country and become fabulously wealthy. In fact, we may be the wrong people to be asking the questions: we enjoy the status quo, and we revel in the current structure, otherwise we wouldn't be participating so enthusiastically (or reading essays like this one).

I would like to propose a possible answer: traditional Masonic bodies are overburdened with constricting rules and nitpicking regulations. We suffer from short-tenured leaders who are given almost limitless power and no time to use it effectively. Grand Lodges and Grand York Rite Bodies have little managerial continuity. Most Grand Lodges elect a new Grand Master each year, who barely has time to pick a motto and a flower before he's running around the state on the grand visitation circuit. He may start a new program or institute a new policy, but it will fade as fast as his flower without the wholehearted support of his successors, and they may have their own hobbyhorses to ride. Only the Scottish Rite, with its long-serving state leaders, has created a managerial structure in Masonry that allows organizational continuity of significant programs and policies, rather than the mindless maintenance of the status quo.

Most Masonic bodies have massively centralized authority, greater than that found in almost any other voluntary associations. Masonic presiding officers, both by tradition and by regulation, have extreme discretion in administering their enormous powers. Grand Lodges have this centralized authority, an executive officer who can rule by decree, and a network of District Deputy Grand Officers to enforce their rules and regulations. None of this makes it fun for local bodies. By contrast, the allied Masonic bodies that are showing growth lack a network to enforce the central authority. Their local groups are largely autonomous and have wide discretion in conducting their affairs. This freedom from central interference may be what is more appealing about an A.M.D. Council than a symbolic Lodge. These allied Masonic bodies are "lean and mean"—small organizations that can be flexible and can quickly respond to their members' needs.

Grand Lodges today are multi-million dollar operations, but they lack the managerial and organizational continuity they need to thrive. The foremost management theory today holds that decision making and authority should be delegated to the lowest possible level where local managers best understand the immediate needs of the organization. What if we elected Grand Masters to five year or longer terms? What if a Grand Master could start a program, nurture it, and see it to established and accepted in his jurisdiction? What if Lodges were given the flexibility and responsibility to make decisions for themselves? And what if Masons were encouraged and rewarded to form and participate in new Lodges?

Masonry is declining in membership as are nearly all other voluntary associations. Our members continue to be enthusiastic about the Masonic experience, just not in Lodges. There is hope for the Craft if we can focus our members' enthusiasm back at the main body of Masonry, but this will require difficult changes. Some of the most urgent changes are administrative, but they strike at the heart of our Masonic culture as it has evolved over centuries. Our basic rewards structure is predicated upon presiding, and no one wants to reduce rewards. There is no reason why accepted management techniques cannot be used in Masonry nor any reason why control cannot be returned to local Lodges. If we are not willing to put changes to a vote in our Grand Lodges, then our members will continue to vote with their feet and to move their Masonic energies to more rewarding activities. And if we could conduct post-election polls, we'd probably find a lot of these voters saying, "I love Masonry. It's Grand Lodges I can't stand."

———————————————

First published: *Transactions Texas Lodge of Research*, 33(2000)

Themes of Anti-Masonry[1]

Co-authored with Arturo de Hoyos

Anti-Masonry and anti-Mason have straightforward definitions—"opposition to Freemasonry" and "one opposed to Freemasonry,"[2] but like anti-Semitism, much more is involved than simple opposition to a group. Freemasonry has become a favorite whipping boy for those looking for a convenient "other" to blame for the world's problems, or at least those problems they believe are bedeviling the globe. The Masonic fraternity has been accused of supporting western capitalism,[3] Soviet communism,[4] world Jewry,[5] Satanism,[6] and secret underground extraterrestrial bases.[7] Where there is smoke, there is fire, so perhaps there are facts behind these charges that deserve further study.

John Wycliffe (1330–1384), the reformer and translator of the Bible into English, is said to have made perhaps the first published attack against Freemasons in 1383, some ten to twenty years before the *Regius Manuscript*, the earliest known document of the Freemasons. In his essay, "The Great

---

1   This essay is largely informed by S. Brent Morris, *The Complete Idiot's Guide to Freemasonry* (New York: Alpha (Penguin Group), 2006), "Religious Concerns about Freemasonry." chap. 16, 201–14, and "Albert Pike: Sovereign Pontiff of Masonic Mythology." chap. 13, 163–78.

2   Dictionary.com. Webster's Revised Unabridged Dictionary. MICRA, Inc., accessed February 28, 2009, http://dictionary.reference.com/browse/antimasonry and http://dictionary.reference.com/browse/antimason.

3   Lolly Zamoisky, *Behind the Façade of the Masonic Temple* (Moscow: Progress Publishers, 1989).

4   Gary H. Kah, *En Route to Global Occupation* (Lafayette, LA: Huntington House Publishers, 1992).

5   Léon de Poncins, *Freemasonry and Judaism: The Secret Powers behind Revolution* (Abbeville, France: F. Paillart, 1929); Adolf Hitler, *Mein Kampf* (Germany: Secker and Warburg, 1925); "The Covenant of the Islamic Resistance Movement," accessed March 6, 2009, http://avalon.law.yale.edu/20th_century/hamas.asp.

6   William T. Sill, *New World Order: The Ancient Plan of Secret Societies* (Lafayette, LA: Huntington House Publishers, 1990); Jack Harris, *Freemasonry: The Invisible Cult in Our Midst* (Towson, MD: Jack Harris, 1983); William Schnoebelen, *Masonry: Beyond the Light* (Chino, CA: Chick Publications, 1991).

7   Dan Sale, posted March 4, 1997, on www.reptilianagenda.com/research/r020500a.html.

Curs Expouned," Wycliffe attacked the "fre masons" on economic—not religious—grounds, for behaving like a trade union. "For they conspire together that no man of their craft shall take less on a day than they set. ... And that none of them shall do ought but only hew stone, though he might profit his master ... by laying on a wall. ..."[8] In other words, Freemasons would not work for less than the set wage and as hewers of stone would not take on work of another craft, the layers. Wycliffe, however, had no religious concerns with Freemasonry.

The first published religious attack in English appeared some 300 years later in 1698, nineteen years before the Premier Grand Lodge was formed in London in 1717. The leaflet contains two basic charges against the fraternity. First, the members swear oaths "against all without their following," presumably to support each other. Second, Freemasons are "meters in secret," which is the way of "Evil-doers."

TO ALL GODLY PEOPLE,

In the Citie of

LONDON.

Having thought it needful to warn you of the Mischiefs and Evils practiced on the Sight of GOD by those called Freed Masons, I say take Care lest their Ceremonies and secret Swearings take hold of you; and be wary that none cause you to err from Godliness. For this devllish Sect of Men are Meeters in secret which swear against all without their Following. They are the Anti Christ which was to come leading Men from Fear of GOD. For how should men meet in secret

---

8   "Also men of sutel craft, as fre masons and oþere, semen openly cursed bi þis sentence. For þei conspiren togidere þat no man of here craft schal take lesse on a day þat þei setten, þouȝ he schulde bi good conscience take moche lesse, and þat noon of hem schal make sade trewe werk to lette oþere mennus wynnyng of þe craft, and þat non of hem schal do ouȝt but only hewe stone, þouȝ he myȝt profit his maistir twenti pound bi o daies werk bi leggyng on a wal, wiþouten harm or penyng himself. See hou þis wickid peple conspireþ aȝenst treuþe and charite, and comyn profit of þe lond and ponyschiþ hem þat helpen frely here neiȝeboris." John Wyclif, "The Grete Sentence of Curs Expouned," in *Select English Works of John Wyclif*, ed. Thomas Arnold (Oxford: Clarenden Press, 1849), vol. 3, 333–34.

Places and with secret Signs taking Care that none observe them to do the Work of GOD; are not these the Ways of Evil-doers?

Knowing how that GOD observeth privily them that sit in Darkness they shall be smitten and the Secrets of their Hearts layed bare. Mingle not among this corrupt People lest you be found so at the World's Conflagration.

Set forth as a Warning to this Christian Generation by
M. Winter, and Printed by *R. Sare* at Gray's
Inn-gate, in *Holbourn.*
1698.[9]

It is curious how such a reputation developed for an organization that from its earliest days was faithful to church and crown. The "Standard Original" of the Gothic Constitutions of the freemasons, as reconstructed by Prof. Wallace McLeod begins with a clearly Christian invocation: "The might of the Father of Heaven, with the wisdom of the glorious Son, through the grace and goodness of the Holy Ghost, that be three persons in one Godhead, be with us at our beginning, and give us grace so to govern us here in our living that we may come to His bliss that never shall have ending. Amen." After the invocation and traditional history of Freemasonry, the Gothic Constitutions then give "charges" or instructions for the guidance of their members. The first two are that Freemasons be faithful to church and king. "The first charge is that ye shall be true men to God and the Holy Church; and that ye use no error nor heresy, by your understanding or by discreet or wise men's teaching. And also that ye shall be true liege men to the King without treason or falsehood; and that ye know no treason or treachery, but that ye amend it if ye may, or else warn the King or his council thereof."[10]

Perhaps private meetings (certainly not "secret" since Winter knew they were gathering together) and oath swearing were indeed causes for alarm. It is more likely that the Freemasons' spirit of toleration caused disquiet

---

9   John Hamill and R. A. Gilbert, *World Freemasonry: An Illustrated History* (Hammersmith, London: Aquarian press, 1991), 172.

10 Wallace McLeod, "The Old Charges," *Heredom* 14 (2006): 105–44.

among nonmembers. The premier Grand Lodge was formed in London in 1717, just twenty-nine years after the Glorious Revolution of 1688 had deposed the Catholic James II in favor of the Protestant William and Mary. Tensions were still high between Catholics and Protestants, and it was a radical religious and political idea to suggest any friendship could exist between the two sides, and yet this seems to be what London Masons promoted.

In 1723, Rev. James Anderson published the *Constitutions of the Free-Masons* for the Grand Lodge. He summarized the existing regulations and introduced religious toleration in "Charge I. Concerning God and Religion."

> A *Mason* is oblig'd by his Tenure, to obey the moral Law; and if he rightly understands the Art, he will never be a stupid *Atheist*, nor an irreligious *Libertine*. But though in ancient Times Masons were charg'd in every Country to be of the Religion of that Country or Nation, whatever it was, yet 'tis now thought more expedient only to oblige them to that Religion in which all Men agree, leaving their particular Opinions to themselves; that is, to be *good Men and true*, or Men or Honour and Honesty; by whatever Denominations or Persuasions they may [be] distinguish'd; whereby Masonry becomes the *Center* of *Union*, and the Means of conciliating true Friendship among Persons that must else have remain'd at a perpetual Distance.[11]

The puzzlement with Anderson's summary charge is what exactly did he mean by "that Religion in which all Men agree." While there has never been a formal pronouncement from the Grand Lodge of England, Charge I has generally been interpreted to mean that a beneficent God created the world and that He is the creator-father of all humankind, and that this is "that Religion in which all Men agree." By stopping religious discussions after this simple agreement, the Premier Grand Lodge apparently believed it could conciliate "true Friendship among Persons that must else have remain'd at a perpetual Distance." Such an idea is anathema to those who believe that individuals cannot decide for themselves what constitutes religious truth.

Pope Clement XII took notice of Freemasonry and in 1738 issued the first encyclical against the fraternity, "In Eminenti." The encyclical is too long to quote in full, but excerpts give a flavor for the condemnation.

---

11 James Anderson, *The Constitutions of the Free-Masons* (London: 1723), 50.

Men of any Religion or sect, satisfied with the appearance of natural probity, are joined together ... by a strict and unbreakable bond which obliges them, both by an oath upon the Holy Bible and by a host of grievous punishment, to an inviolable silence about all that they do in secret together. ... All prudent and upright men have passed the same judgment on them as being depraved and perverted. For if they were not doing evil they would not have so great a hared of the light. ... Therefore, bearing in mind the great harm which is often caused by such Societies ... and realizing that they do not hold by either civil or canonical sanctions and for the other just and reasonable motives known to us ... these same societies ... are to be condemned and prohibited.... under pain of excommunication ... from which no one can obtain the benefit of absolution, other than at the hour of death, except through Ourselves or the Roman Pontiff of the time. ... Moreover, We desire and command that ... inquisitors for heresy ... are to pursue and punish them with condign penalties as being the most suspect of heresy.[12]

It appears Clement XII followed the same logic of the 1698 London leaflet: Freemasons bind themselves together by a solemn obligation and they meet in private. (Lodge meetings were hardly secret since Masons met in public taverns, wore distinctive regalia, and were well known for drinking and singing after their meetings.) The tenets of Freemasonry were a threat not only to the true teaching of the Roman Catholic church, but also to the stability of governments and society.[13] There has been some suggestion that Clement was trying to influence the Hanoverian–Jacobite struggle in England and the restoration of the exiled Catholic James II. There has also been much fruitless speculation over what were "the other just and reasonable motives known to" Clement. A more practical motive for the condemnation could be the concern that the Masonic obligation might prevent a penitent from making a full confession.

The charges against Freemasonry became more specific in 1797 with the publication by Augustin Barruel, S.J. (1741–1820) of volumes one and two of *Mémoires pour servir à l'Histoire du Jacobinisme* and by John Robison (1739–1805) of *Proofs of a Conspiracy against all the Religions and*

---

12 accessed October 7, 2005. http://www.papalencyclicals.net.

13 Ronny Jenkins, "The Evolution of the Church's Prohibition Against Catholic Membership in Freemasonry," *The Jurist* 56 (1997): 736–37.

Governments of Europe, Carried on in the Secret Meetings of Free Masons, Illuminati, and Reading Societies, Collected from Good Authorities (Edinburgh: William Creech, 1797). Volumes three and four of *Mémoires* were published in 1798. These two conspiracists advanced the theory that Freemasonry was behind the excesses of the French Revolution. According to their theories, the overthrow of the French monarchy was planned by the Illuminati, a group created by Adam Weishaupt (1748–1830) in Bavaria. The Illuminati were recruited from Bavarian Freemasons with the goal of infiltrating governments and implementing Weishaupt's ideas of a benign government free of monarchs and religions. His "fraternity within a fraternity" lasted until 1784 when of Karl Theodor, Elector of Bavaria, discovered and suppressed the Illuminati. Weishaupt fled Bavaria and went into exile in Gotha.

Now, there were charges of some substance against Freemasons. Rather than mere secret meetings, sworn oaths, and "other just and reasonable motives," Freemasons were infiltrating the governments of Europe and were behind the Reign of Terror. Proof was not necessary as Robison was a Mason himself, Barruel was a Jesuit, and the Pope had personally condemned the fraternity. The worry of the Illuminati and the Terror was such that George Washington was asked if he believed the Illuminati or Jacobins had infiltrated American Masonic lodges. He replied to Rev. G. W. Snyder on October 24, 1798, that he "did not believe that the Lodges of Free Masons in this Country had, as Societies, endeavoured to propagate the diabolical tenets of the first, or pernicious principles of the latter (if they are susceptible of separation)."

Papal condemnations continued after "In Eminenti," and the most sweeping was in Leo XIII's 1884 "Humanum Genus." He said mankind is "separated into two diverse and opposite parts, of which the one steadfastly contends for truth and virtue, the other of those things which are contrary to virtue and to truth. The one is the kingdom of God on earth, namely, the true Church of Jesus Christ.... The other is the kingdom of Satan...." Leo said that Freemasonry belongs to the kingdom of Satan. He went on and condemned Freemasonry for supporting various unacceptable principles including that "power is held by the command or permission of the people, so that, when the popular will changes, rulers may lawfully be deposed" and that "each [youth] must be left at liberty to follow, when he comes of age, whatever [religion] he may prefer." Leo XIII also seemed to blame the demise of Papal civil authority on a Masonic conspiracy led by Freemason Giuseppe Garibaldi, the liberator and unifier of Italy. (From www.papalen-cyclicals.net, accessed October 7, 2005.)

The most malicious charge against the fraternity was the hoax created by Gabriel Antoine Jogànd-Pages (1854–1907) that Freemasons secretly worship Lucifer in the higher degrees. Jogànd-Pages is better known by his *nom de plume* of Léo Taxil. He was a French freethinker notorious for his irreligious and pornographic writings. In 1881, he published *The Secret Loves of Pius IX* and received the First Degree of Masonry. By 1882, he had worn out his welcome in his lodge and was expelled without advancing beyond 1° Entered Apprentice. Sometime after this, he concocted his grand scheme, apparently to embarrass the Roman Catholic Church and wreak a twisted vengeance on his former Masonic brothers.

Much to the shock of his freethinking friends and to the surprise of French Catholics, Taxil "converted" to Catholicism in 1885, a year after "Humanum Genus." He convinced a priest he was a murderer and did penance in a monastery. He then dropped the bombshell: shortly before joining the church, he had been a Freemason and could reveal their inner workings. Taxil knew his admission would get special attention, because Freemasonry was a particular concern of Pope Leo XIII.

Taxil began writing a series of books, about which he said, "My first books on Freemasonry consisted in a mixture of rituals, with short innocent parts inserted, apparently harmlessly interpreted. Each time an obscure passage occurred, I explained it in a way agreeable to Catholics who see Master Lucifer as the supreme grand master of Freemasons."[14]

After writing on Freemasonry for two years, he obtained an audience with Leo XIII in 1887. Following this, he revealed (actually invented) the innermost secret of Freemasonry: the New and Reformed Palladian Rite, a Lucifer-worshipping inner circle of men and women who ran Masonry. He created an evil Grand Mistress of Palladism, Sophia Walder, and her virtuous adversary, Diana Vaughan. Diana escaped from the evils of Palladism, converted to Catholicism, but now had to remain in hiding to avoid assassination by vengeful Masons. These stories captivated the Catholic hierarchy and the French public, much like a contemporary news story of a missing person.

---

14 Alain Bernheim, et al., "The Confession of Léo Taxil," *Heredom* 5 (1996): 151.

Palladism is a monstrous deception that never existed except in Taxil's mind. Credulous anti-Masons, fueled by "Humanum Genus" and other anti-Masonic encyclicals, started writing their own books, interpreting Masonic symbols in light of the newly revealed Palladism. Taxil incorporated and cross-referenced these books in the growing web of his hoax.

Three years after the death of Albert Pike (1809–1891), Taxil convinced Abel Clarin de la Rive that Pike had been the "Sovereign Pontiff of Universal Freemasonry" (a nonexistent position). De la Rive subsequently published in *La Femme et L'Enfant dans la Franc-Maçonnerie Universelle* that Diana Vaughan had carried Pike's "announcement" to the "Supreme Confederated councils of the World" (a nonexistent organization) that the inner circle of High Degree Freemasonry, 30°–33°, worshipped Lucifer. "That which we must say to the crowd is:—We worship a God, but it is the God that one adores with superstition. To you, Sovereign Grand Inspectors General [i.e., 33° Masons], we say this, that you may repeat it to the Brethren of the 32nd, 31st and 30th degrees—the Masonic religion should be, by all of us initiates of the high degrees, maintained in the purity of the Luciferian doctrine."[15]

Taxil's interconnected and self-referential books and quotes began collapsing on itself as more discerning readers demanded verification and proof. Finally, on April 19, 1897, in the hall of the Geographic Society in Paris, Léo Taxil confessed all to a stunned audience, after which a riot nearly broke out. A transcription of his confession was published six days later in the Paris weekly *Le Frondeur*.[16] De la Rive expressed his disgust and recanted his writing about Diana Vaughan in the April 1897 issue of *Freemasonry Unmasked*, a magazine devoted to the destruction of Freemasonry. "We have always been careful to publish special articles concerning Palladism and Diana Vaughan. We are now giving in this issue a complete list of these articles, which can now be considered as not having existed."[17]

The manufactured Pike quote in *La Femme et L'Enfant dans la Franc-Maçonnerie Universelle* would have died in well-deserved obscurity except for

15 Abel Clarin de la Rive, *La Femme et L'Enfant dans la Franc-Maçonnerie Universelle* (Paris & Lyon: Delhomme & Briguet, Editeurs, 1894), 487–89; translated in Lady Queenborough, Edith Starr Miller, *Occult Theocrasy*, 2 vols. (1933; reprint, Hawthorne, CA: Christian Book Club of America, 1980), 233.

16 Bernheim, 137–68.

17 In Alec Mellor, *Strange Masonic Stories* (Richmond, VA: Macoy Publishing and Masonic Supply Co., 1982), 151.

Edith Starr Miller. The American wife of Lord Queenborough, she translated and published the quote in *Occult Theocrasy*, her 1933 magnum opus aimed at exposing all of the evil forces conspiring to destroy Christianity and western society. The fabricated quote was now available to English readers without the bothersome context of Taxil's hoax and subsequent confession. It has taken on a life of its own among conspiracists on the Internet. A quick Google search of the Internet using the search terms "Pike" and "say to the crowd" produces about 16,000 hits, most breathlessly warning readers about the evils of Freemasonry. This sadly confirms the observation of Mark Twain (Samuel Clemens), "A lie can get halfway around the world before the truth can even get its boots on."

In 1905, the final major anti-Masonic charge, that of being part of the "Jewish conspiracy," appeared in virulent full form with the publication of *The Protocols of the Learned Elders of Zion*. This forgery, originating in Russia, has been the justification for vicious anti-Semitism and anti-Masonry. Protocol 15 says, among other lies, "We will create and multiply free Masonic lodges in all countries of the world. ... We will put all these lodges under a central administration known only to us. ... Between the members of these lodges will be almost all the international and national police agents."[18] The charge of a Jewish–Masonic plot resonated with anti-Semites and conspiracists, and many books with similar charges followed. Adolf Hitler wrote in his 1925 *Mein Kampf*, "In Freemasonry, which has succumbed to [the Jew] completely, he has an excellent instrument with which to fight for his aims and put them across." Léon de Poncins continued this idea in 1929 with his book's explicit title: *Freemasonry and Judaism: The Secret Powers behind Revolution*.

Hamas, the Islamic Resistance Movement, sadly has accepted uncritically the idea of a Jewish–Masonic conspiracy. Their 1988 Covenant explicitly mentions Freemasonry three times.

> That is why you find [enemies] giving these attempts constant attention through information campaigns, films, and the school curriculum, using for that purpose their lackeys who are infiltrated through Zionist organizations under various names and shapes, such as Freemasons, Rotary Clubs, espionage groups and others, which are all nothing more than cells of subversion and saboteurs. (Article 17)

---

18 Leon Zeldis, "The Protocols of the Elders of Zion," *Heredom* 7 (1998): 103.

With their money [the enemies] formed secret societies, such as Freemasons, Rotary Clubs, the Lions and others in different parts of the world for the purpose of sabotaging societies and achieving Zionist interests. (Article 22)

[The Zionist invasion] relies greatly in its infiltration and espionage operations on the secret organizations it gave rise to, such as the Freemasons, The Rotary and Lions clubs, and other sabotage groups. (Article 28)[19]

One of the first original anti-Masonic charges in decades came from Stephen Knight who brought out *Jack the Ripper: The Final Solution* in 1976. He claimed that Freemasons acted as agents of the British crown to ritualistically murder several prostitutes who were aware that Prince Albert Victor, Duke of Clarence, had an illegitimate child with a Catholic commoner. It was these murders that were attributed to Jack the Ripper. While his theory caused a momentary stir and was the basis for the 1979 movie, *Murder by Decree*, "Ripperologists" have soundly debunked his ideas, and the charge seems to be languishing.

It took about 200 years to create the major elements of most anti-Masonic charges that are seen in the twenty-first century:

• Meeting in secret;

• Swearing oaths;

• Plotting to subvert governments and religions;

• Worshipping Lucifer;

• Working for/with the Jews.

Conspiracists, anti-Masons, and anti-Semites do not need solid evidence to advance their claims. In fact, the absence of evidence is often used as evidence of the conspiracy. They all seem to be looking for some "other" or perhaps for stars on which to blame the condition of the world (or their church or their lives). How else to explain their circumstances? They cannot imagine an internal blame, and must look endlessly for some way to

---

19 accessed March 7, 2009. http://avalon.law.yale.edu/20th_century/hamas.asp

explain the chaos they see. Perhaps as Cassius said, "The fault, dear Brutus, is not in our stars, but in ourselves. ..."

———————————————————————

First Published: *In this collection*

The Letter "G"

This past week, I went to a bookstore in a nearby shopping center to pick up a copy of the *New Oxford Annotated Bible* I had ordered for a Bible class. The shop was a "Christian bookstore," and I browsed a bit to see what books they might have on our gentle craft. I didn't expect much positive, but I was dismayed at the viciously deceitful material that was being purveyed in the name of Truth.

I have no problem with someone who honestly disagrees with me. There is a wide diversity of opinion among Christians on many topics, including divorce, baptism, gambling, and the nature of the sacraments, to name just a few. The debates on these subjects have been heated and may never be settled on this earth. If someone says his understanding of Christian duty prevents him from encouraging his neighbor to worship God, unless it is as a Christian, then I can understand why he would not want to be a Mason. When someone states, however, that he cannot be a Mason because we are phallic worshipers and the letter *G* stands for "generative force," I become angry. Such an allegation is a lie and a deliberate distortion of Masonic symbols.

The symbolism of the letter *G* is as simple as it is straightforward—it is an elementary play on words and has the dual meanings of *geometry* and *God*. Prichard's 1730 *Masonry Dissected*, one of the exposures of early Masonic ritual, captures the symbolism perfectly in two questions from the Fellow Craft Degree. **Q.** What doth G denote? **A.** One that's greater than you. **Q.** Who is greater than I, that am a Free and Accepted Mason, the Master of a Lodge? **A.** The Grand Architect and Contriver of the Universe, or He that was taken up to the top of the Pinnacle of the Holy Temple. Prichard certainly had no intent of helping the fraternity with his book, but even he didn't stoop to the disgusting perversions spread by our modern detractors.

The record shows that otherwise respected Masonic scholars of the middle to late 1800s, such as Albert Mackey, Albert Pike, and their followers, had ideas about the origins of Freemasonry that are discredited today. No one, in fact, knows where our gentle craft began, but Pike and Mackey were strong proponents of the theory Freemasonry was descended from the Ancient Mysteries and various forms of pagan worship. While their ideas were quite fashionable a century ago, no serious Masonic student takes seriously these parts of their writings.

Henry W. Coil, 33°, is often quoted by anti-Masons as an expert—but only when they think his ideas support their preconceived notions about Freemasonry. They conveniently overlook *Coil's Masonic Encyclopedia* when it contradicts their twisted fancies, as it does in the case of the Ancient Mysteries:

> From about 1779, [the Ancient Mysteries] came more and more into prominence. It was a fertile field and there was scarcely the possibility of disputing anything at all that was said within its limits. ... [T]he theme spread like wildfire. ... Mackey and Pike embraced it avidly, and the latter's *Morals and Dogma* is largely given over to Ancient Paganism. Mackey, in *Masonic Ritualist* (1867) and *Symbolism of Freemasonry* (1869) carried it not only to an absurd degree, but to an extent which can hardly be less than revolting to a Christian. ...
>
> In order properly to interpret Mackey and Pike on Paganism, one must understand that both of them entered the Fraternity in the 1840s, when the fabulous type of Masonic literature was at its height and both walked unsuspectingly into the circle of magism, paganism, and occultism before they were properly seasoned in the history or doctrine of the Craft. Those things that were indisputably Masonic, such as the *Gothic Constitutions*, the minutes of lodges in the pre-Grand Lodge era, and the Constitutions of the premier Grand Lodge, they ignored, but followed irresponsible writers who were teaching doctrines neither then nor since approved or adopted by any Grand Lodge of symbolic Freemasonry. (460–61)

Albert Mackey, quoted so religiously by our foes, repudiated the idea of Masonic descent from the Ancient Mysteries in his *History of Freemasonry* (1906). His last writings can hardly be called support for his earlier theories, and hence are ignored by those looking for lurid accusations.

> It has been a favorite theory with several German, French, and British scholars to trace the origin of Freemasonry to the Myster-

ies of Pagans, while others, repudiating the idea that the modern association should have spring from them, still find analogies so remarkable between the two systems as to lead them to suppose that the Mysteries were an offshoot from the pure Freemasonry of the Patriarchs.

In my opinion there is not the slightest foundation in historical evidence to support either theory, although I admit the existence of many analogies between the two systems, which can, however, be easily explained without admitting any connection in the way of origin and descent between them. (185)

Is modern Freemasonry a lineal and uninterrupted successor of the ancient Mysteries, the succession being transmitted through the Mithraic initiation which existed in the 5th and 6th centuries; or is the fact of the analogies between the two systems to be attributed to the coincidence of a natural process of human thought, common to all minds and showing its development in symbolic forms?

For myself, I can only arrive at what I think is a logical conclusion; that if both the Mysteries and Freemasonry have taught the same lessons by the same method of instruction, this has arisen not from a succession of organizations, each one a link of a long chain of historical sequences leading directly to another, until Hiram is simply substituted for Osiris, but rather from those usual and natural coincidences of human thought which are to be found in every age and among all peoples. (197)

The real test of Masonic acceptance of the Ancient Mystery theories of Mackey and Pike is to study the writings of serious Masonic historians from the authentic school, not those from the romantic period. The publications of Quatuor Coronati Lodge No. 2076, the American Lodge of Research, the Texas Lodge of Research, the Ohio Chapter of Research, and others show that these absurd theories have been politely ignored. They have died the quiet death they deserved. The pathetic irony is that only one group today believes the tall tales of Mackey and Pike—not the Grand Lodges, not the Scottish Rite, but the anti-Masons. Our enemies are so anxious to believe the worst about us, they rush to embrace hypotheses long since abandoned, if ever widely accepted. Whether they are incompetent as historians or simply facile liars is for others to decide.

First published: *The Plumbline*, vol. 1, no. 3 (September 1992)

The Eye in the Pyramid

H istorians must be cautious about many well-known "facts." George Washington chopped down a cherry tree when a boy and confessed the deed to his father. Abner Doubleday invented the game of baseball. Freemasons inserted some of their emblems (chief among them the eye in the pyramid) into the reverse of the Great Seal of the United States. These historical "facts" are widely popular, commonly accepted, and equally false.

The eye in the pyramid (emblazoned on the dollar bill, no less) is often cited as "evidence" that sinister conspiracies abound which will impose a "New World Order" on an unsuspecting populace. Depending on whom you hear it from, the Masons are planning the takeover themselves, or are working in concert with European bankers, or are leading (or perhaps being led by) the Illuminati (whoever they are). The notion of a world-wide Masonic conspiracy would be laughable, if it weren't being repeated with such earnest gullibility by conspiracists like Pat Robertson.

Sadly, Masons are sometimes counted among the gullible who repeat the tall tale of the eye in the pyramid, often with a touch of pride. They may be guilty of nothing worse than innocently puffing the importance of their fraternity (as well as themselves), but they're guilty nonetheless. The time has come state the truth plainly and simply.

The Great Seal of the United States Is Not a Masonic Emblem, Nor Does It Contain Hidden Masonic Symbols.

The details are there for anyone to check, who's willing to rely on historical fact rather than hysterical fiction.

- Benjamin Franklin was the only Mason on the first design committee, and his suggestions had no Masonic content.
- None of the final designers of the seal were Masons.
- The interpretation of the eye on the seal is subtly different from the interpretation used by Masons.
- The eye in the pyramid is not nor has been a Masonic symbol.

The First Committee

On Independence Day, 1776, a committee was created to design a seal for the new American nation. The committee's members were Benjamin Franklin, Thomas Jefferson, and John Adams, with Pierre Du Simitière as artist and consultant.[1] Of the four men involved, only Benjamin Franklin was a Mason, and he contributed nothing of a Masonic nature to the committee's proposed design for a seal.

Du Simitière, the committee's consultant and a non-Mason, contributed several major design features that made their way into the ultimate design of the seal: "the shield, E Pluribus Unum, MDCCLXXVI, and the eye of providence in a triangle."[2] The eye of providence on the seal thus can be traced not to the Masons, but to a non-Mason consultant to the committee.

"The single eye was a well-established artistic convention for an 'omniscient Ubiquitous Deity' in the medallic art of the Renaisance. Du Simitière, who suggested using the symbol, collected art books and was familiar with the artistic and ornamental devices used in Renaissance art."[3] This was the same cultural iconography that eventually led Masons to add the all-seeing eye to their symbols.

The Second and Third Committees

Congress declined the first committee's suggestions as well as those of its 1780 committee. Francis Hopkinson, consultant to the second committee, had several lasting ideas that eventually made it into the seal: "white and red stripes within a blue background for the shield, a radiant constellation of thirteen stars, and an olive branch."[4] Hopkinson's greatest contribution to the current seal came from his layout of a 1778 50-dollar colonial note in which he used an unfinished pyramid in the design.

The third and last seal committee of 1782 produced a design that finally satisfied Congress. Charles Thomson, Secretary of Congress, and William Barton, artist and consultant, borrowed from earlier designs and sketched what at length became the United States seal.

---

1   Robert Hieronimus, *America's Secret Destiny* (Rochester, VT: Destiny Books, 1989), 48.
2   Patterson and Dougall, in Hieronimus, 48.
3   Hieronimus, 81.
4   Hieronimus, 51.

The misinterpretation of the seal as a Masonic emblem may have been first introduced a century later in 1884. Harvard Professor Eliot Norton wrote that the reverse was "practically incapable of effective treatment; it can hardly, (however artistically treated by the designer,) look otherwise than as a dull emblem of a Masonic fraternity."[5]

Interpreting the Symbol

The "Remarks and Explanations" of Thomson and Barton are the only explanation of the symbols' meaning. Despite what anti-Masons may believe, there's no reason to doubt the interpretation accepted by the Congress.

The Pyramid signified Strength and Duration: The Eye over it & the Motto allude to the many signal interpositions of providence in favor of the American cause.[6]

The committees and consultants who designed the Great Seal of the United States contained only one Mason, Benjamin Franklin. The only possibly Masonic design element among the very many on the seal is the eye of providence, and the interpretation of it by the designers is different from that used by Masons. The eye on the seal represents an active intervention of God in the affairs of men, while the Masonic symbol stands for a passive awareness by God of the activities of men.

The first "official" use and definition of the all-seeing eye as a Masonic symbol seems to have come in 1797 with *The Freemason's Monitor* of Thomas Smith Webb—14 years after Congress adopted the design for the seal. Here's how Webb explains the symbol.

[A]nd although our thoughts, words and actions, may be hidden from the eyes of man, yet that *All-Seeing Eye,* whom the *Sun, Moon* and *Stars* obey, and under whose watchful care even comets perform their stupendous revolutions, pervades the inmost recesses of the human heart, and will reward us according to our merits.[7]

---

5   Hieronimus, 57.
6   C. Thomas and W. Barton, in Hieronimus, 54.
7   Thomas Smith Webb, *The Freemasons Monitor or Illustrations of Masonry* (Salem, MA: Cushing and Appleton, 1821), 66.

The Eye in the Pyramid

Besides the subtly different interpretations of the symbol, it is notable that Webb did not describe the eye as being in a triangle. Jeremy Ladd Cross published *The True Masonic Chart or Hieroglyphic Monitor* in 1819, essentially an illustrated version of Webb's *Monitor*. In this first "official" depiction of Webb's symbol, Cross had illustrator Amos Doolittle depict the eye surrounded by a semi-circular glory.[8]

The all-seeing eye thus appears to be a rather recent addition to Masonic symbolism. It is not found in any of the gothic constitutions, written from about 1390 to 1730. The eye—sometimes in a triangle, sometimes in clouds, but nearly always surrounded by a glory—was a popular Masonic decorative device in the latter half of the eighteenth century. Its use as a design element seems to have been an artistic representation of the omniscience of God, rather than some generally accepted Masonic symbol.

Its meaning in all cases, however, was that commonly given it by society at large—a reminder of the constant presence of God. For example, in 1614, the frontispiece of *The History of the World* by Walter Raleigh showed an eye in a cloud labeled "Providentia" overlooking a globe. It has not been suggested that Raleigh's *History* is a Masonic document, despite the use of the all-seeing eye.

The eye of Providence was part of the common cultural iconography of the seventeenth and eighteenth centuries. When placed in a triangle, the eye went beyond a general representation of God to a strongly Trinitarian statement. It was during this period that Masonic ritual and symbolism evolved, and it is not surprising that many symbols common to and understood by the general society made their way into Masonic ceremonies. Masons may have preferred the triangle because of the frequent use of the number 3 in their ceremonies: three degrees, three original grand masters, three principal officers, and so on. Eventually, the all-seeing eye came to be used officially by Masons as a symbol for God, but this happened toward the end of the eighteenth century, after congress had adopted the seal.

A pyramid, whether incomplete or finished, however, has never been a Masonic symbol. It has no generally accepted symbolic meaning, except

---

8   Jeremy Ladd Cross, *The True Masonic Chart or Hieroglyphic Monitor*, 3rd ed. (New Haven, CT: By the Author, 1824), plate 22.

perhaps permanence or mystery. The combining of the eye of providence overlooking an unfinished pyramid is a uniquely American, not Masonic, icon, and must be interpreted as its designers intended. It has no Masonic context.

Conclusion

It's hard to know what leads some to see Masonic conspiracies behind world events, but once that hypothesis is accepted, any jot and tittle can be misinterpreted as "evidence." The Great Seal of the United States is a classic example of such a misinterpretation, and some Masons are as guilty of the exaggeration as many anti-Masons.

The Great Seal and Masonic symbolism grew out of the same cultural milieu. While the all-seeing eye had been popularized in Masonic designs of the late eighteenth century, it did not achieve any sort of official recognition until Webb's 1797 *Monitor*. Whatever status the symbol may have had during the design of the Great Seal, it was not adopted or approved or endorsed by any Grand Lodge. The seal's Eye of Providence and the Mason's All-Seeing Eye each express Divine Omnipotence, but they are parallel uses of a shared icon, not a single symbol.

REFERENCES

Cross, Jeremy Ladd. *The True Masonic Chart or Hieroglyphic Monitor*, 3rd ed. New Haven, CT: By the Author, 1824.

Hieronimus, Robert. *America's Secret Destiny*. Rochester, VT: Destiny Books, 1989.

Webb, Thomas Smith. *The Freemasons Monitor or Illustrations of Masonry*. Salem, MA: Cushing and Appleton, 1821.

First published: *Short Talk Bulletin,* September 1995, Masonic Service Association

Pike, Mackey, and
The Ancient Mysteries

When I served as book review editor of the *Scottish Rite Journal* from 1989 to 1996, I didn't receive much correspondence from readers. One thing, however, was guaranteed always to produce a few letters: criticize Albert Pike or Albert Mackey. It didn't matter how much factual evidence may have been stacked against them, many Masons have all but deified them and refuse to believe they could have made any mistake. Neither Pike nor Mackey would be comfortable with this apotheosis; they held strong opinions, but they didn't think they were infallible. Many today feel that only a heretic could challenge anything they wrote. My comments in "The Letter G" (*The Scottish Rite Journal*, Aug. 1997) have produced a similar response.[1]

Let me begin with a disclaimer: Albert Pike and Albert Mackey were geniuses. They researched and wrote about Freemasonry at a time when there was virtually no reliable historical material available. They did the best they could with what they had, and they did very well indeed. Their administrative skills alone, especially those of Pike, expanded the Scottish Rite Southern Jurisdiction and created the organization that has grown so successfully into our modern fraternity today. We owe each of them a great debt of gratitude.

I also owe them apologies in referring to their theories as "tall tales," which was hyperbole on my part. Their historical theories were put forth sincerely, based on the best available data (and quite a bit of speculation to fill in the gaps). Pike and Mackey had little access to European Masonic records, many of which weren't discovered until after their deaths. What confirms Pike and Mackey as serious students of history was their willingness to change their ideas, as will be shown later.

Let me also say that not everything they wrote was right nor have all their historical theories held up to contemporary research. For example, Mackey's list of twenty-five "Landmarks" is a reasonable attempt to deduce the

---

1   S. Brent Morris, "The Letter 'G.'" *The Scottish Rite Journal* 105, no. 8 (August 1997):20–23.

fundamental principles governing the Craft. Albert Pike, among many others for over a century, denounced the list in the strongest possible terms from its first appearance.[2] Nonetheless, Mackey's presentation was so persuasive that dozens of Grand Lodges have adopted his list as the foundation of their jurisprudence. These adoptions don't mean Mackey's "Landmarks" are the all-inclusive, historically supported list, just that he made a persuasive case.

Similarly, both Pike and Mackey early in their literary careers fell under the sway of the historical theory that Freemasonry was descended from the ancient mysteries of Egypt, Greece, and the Middle East. As a theory, this is plausible. As a teaching tool in ritual, it is excellent. As a historical fact, it fails utterly.

Albert Pike clearly believed Freemasonry was not much older than the 1717 formation of the premier Grand Lodge in London, but many of its symbols adopted to teach our lessons were of far greater age. Here is Pike's straightforward declaration, written shortly before his death but after *Morals and Dogma,* his revisions of the rituals, and most of his voluminous works.

> [Freemasonry] has no secret knowledge of any kind. There was, in the ancient initiations, something like the modem spiritualism; but there is nothing of this or of magic in Freemasonry....
>
> It is of greater antiquity than other orders or associations; but it is not so old as to give it the superiority once supposed; for it is now certain that there were no Degrees in Masonry two hundred years ago; and that the Master's Degree is not more than one hundred and sixty years of age.
>
> But those who framed its Degrees adopted the most sacred and significant symbols of a very remote antiquity used, many centuries before the Temple of King Solomon was built, to express to those who understood them, while concealing from the profane, the most recondite and mysterious doctrines in regard to God, the universe and man....
>
> I have, at least, arrived at this conviction after patient study and reflection during many years.[3]

---

2   S. Brent Morris, "Landmarks and Liabilities." *The Philalethes* 44, no. 3 (June 1991): 8.

3   Albert Pike, *Lecture on Masonic Symbolism* (New York?: Long, Little & Co.?, ca. 1890),

Pike also spelled out his thoughts on historical versus symbolic truth in his degrees. In the ritual of the Knight Kadosh, Pike has the Orator tell the candidate:

> We do not delude ourselves that the many legends we recite are necessarily true. But we speak in the language of symbols, and the discerning mind will understand. Those who do not understand our symbols were too easily allowed into our sanctuary.

Like Pike, Mackey came to and published new conclusions about the origins of Freemasonry after the main corpus of his works were in print. The establishment of Quatuor Coronati Lodge No. 2076 in 1886 in and the publication of Robert Freke Gould's *History of Freemasonry* in 1885 ushered in the "authentic school" of Masonic research. Both Pike and Mackey appear to have been influenced by the new insistence on concrete historical evidence as the *sine qua non* of theories about Freemasonry. Mackey's thoughts on Masonic origins, in his posthumously published 1906 *History of Freemasonry,* reflect his new understanding of the ancient mysteries.

> It has been a favorite theory with several German, French, and British scholars to trace the origin of Freemasonry to the Mysteries of Pagans, while others, repudiating the idea that the modem association should have sprung from them, still find analogies so remarkable between the two systems as to lead them to suppose that the Mysteries were an offshoot from the pure Freemasonry of the Patriarchs.

> In my opinion there is not the slightest foundation in historical evidence to support either theory, although I admit the existence of many analogies between the two systems, which can, however, be easily explained without admitting any connection in the way of origin and descent between them.

> Is modern Freemasonry a lineal and uninterrupted successor of the ancient Mysteries, the succession being transmitted through the Mithraic initiation which existed in the 5th and 6th centuries; or is the fact of the analogies between the two systems to be attributed to the coincidence of a natural process of human

---

13–15. Some of the earliest evidence of a separate third degree comes from Samuel Pritchard's 1730 exposé *Masonry Dissected.*

thought, common to all minds and showing its development in symbolic form?

For myself, I can only arrive at what I think is a logical conclusion; that if both the Mysteries and Freemasonry have taught the same lessons by the same method of instruction, this has arisen not from a succession of organizations, each one a link of a long chain of historical sequences leading directly to another, until Hiram is simply substituted for Osiris, but rather from those usual and natural coincidences of human thought which are to be found in every age and among all peoples.[4]

Pike and Mackey are to be admired for their early efforts to find the historical origins of the Craft, and they are to be admired even more for changing (and rejecting) their original theories as better data became available. Only fools and dead men never change their minds, and neither Pike nor Mackey were fools. If there is fault to be found, it is with contemporary readers who have not studied in detail the history and records of Freemasonry, some of them admittedly obscure and difficult to access, and who insist on deifying our illustrious predecessors.

Pike, Mackey, and others did not have a monopoly on historical truth, and their opinions—historical, symbolic, allegorical, and ritual—are not binding on any Freemason. It is not "political correctness" to differ with them or to insist that their conclusions be reexamined in light of the best historical evidence. Pike and Mackey reached their conclusions—early and late—in this way, and they would insist that their successors today apply standards no less rigorous.

———————————————

First published: *The Plumbline,* vol. 6: 3, Winter 1998

---

4   Albert G. Mackey and William R. Singleton, *History of Freemasonry,* 6 vols. (New York and London: Masonic History Co., 1906), vol. 1, 185.

Albert Pike and the Ku Klux Klan

The "original sin" of American society is racism, and it lingers today. We have "black" and "white" churches, "black" and "white" universities, and "black" and "white" Masonic lodges. There is a persistent legend connecting the Ku Klux Klan and Albert Pike, Confederate general, author of *Morals and Dogma*, and grand commander of the Southern Jurisdiction. A Google search for "Albert Pike" and KKK yields 63,500 results. However, it's hard to find solid evidence, just lots and lots of claims.

It is sadly too easy to find ugly, racist comments by Albert Pike indicating, at least in 1875, his unwillingness to accept African-Americans as social equals. His repugnant opinions are on the spectrum with those of Abraham Lincoln who favored colonizing African-Americans to Africa.[1]

Albert Pike's repellant comment, "When I have to accept Negroes as brothers or leave Masonry, I shall leave it," is usually taken out of context. Pike was responding to an 1875 query from the Grand Lodge of Ohio about the legitimacy of Prince Hall Freemasonry. Unlike other white Masons, he was intellectually honest enough to accept the legitimacy of Prince Hall Freemasonry and not to hide his intolerance behind legalisms. His "on the one hand" response highlights the irrationality of racial prejudice.

> The chairman of this Committee having written to Bro. Alfred [*sic*] Pike, who had been acknowledged by the Grand Lodge of Arkansas some years ago as Grand Representative of the Grand Orient of the Dominican Republic, acquainting him that Hamburg and Peru had appointed representatives of colored men near the Colored Grand Lodge of Ohio, and that this body might be recognized by the Grand Lodge of Ohio, the following answer was received before the subject was brought before the Grand Lodge:

---

1 "I can not make it better known than it already is that I strongly favor colonization…." Abraham Lincoln: "Second Annual Message," December 1, 1862. Online by Gerhard Peters and John T. Woolley, The American Presidency Project. http://www.presidency. ucsb.edu/ws/?pid=29503.

Alexandria, Va., 13th September, 1875.

My Dear Friend and Brother,—

...

Prince Hall Lodge was as regular a lodge as any lodge created by competent authority, and had a perfect right (as other lodges in Europe did) to establish other lodges, making itself a mother Lodge.

...

I took my obligations to white men, not to negroes. When I have to accept negroes as brothers or leave Masonry, I shall leave it.

...

Truly, yours,
Albert Pike[2]

The fitting "on the other hand" epilogue is Pike's gift of manuscript rituals of the Scottish Rite degrees ca. 1887–91 to Thornton Jackson, Grand Commander of the United Supreme Council, 33°, SJ, PHA.[3] Pike says in short: Prince Hall is legitimate; I won't accept them as brothers; but I'm happy to help them with their rituals. Go figure!

The question of Pike's membership in the Ku Klux Klan is more complex as KKK archives are not available. However, the U.S. Congress conducted an inquiry into "The Ku-Klux Conspiracy" in 1871 and published thirteen volumes of testimony.[4] This is secondary material, but it is some of the best available. I can only find one mention of an "Albert Pike" (probably the Freemason); he is mentioned in the context of the U.S. flag being displayed in Alabama after the Civil War.

> *Question.* I mean have you seen it [the United States flag] displayed by that portion of your people who went into the war?

---

2   *Proceedings of the Grand Lodge ... of Free and Accepted Masons of the State of Ohio; Sixty-sixth Annual Grand Communication* (Cincinnati: John D. Caldwell, 1875), appendix: 49–50. The *Proceedings* can be read online at the George Washington Masonic National Memorial Masonic Digital Archives: http://173.254.20.132/archives/

3   Art de Hoyos, "On the Origins of the Prince Hall Scottish Rite Rituals." *Heredom* 5 (1997): 51–67.

4   *Testimony Taken by the Joint Select Committee to Inquire into the Condition of Affairs in the Late Insurrectionary States,* 13 vols. (Washington: Government Printing Office, 1872).

Answer. I saw in this court-house yard, in the presidential campaign of 1868, a platform beautifully decorated with the United States flag; it was a large democratic meeting.

Question. Any other occasion that you remember?

Answer. It occurs to me that in a large meeting in Colbert County, at which the Hon. Albert Pike was the principal democratic speaker, the United States flag was displayed; I think that it was—about that I am not positive.[5]

Joseph Walkes, founder of the Phylaxis Society, was usually a meticulous researcher, but he had passionate feelings about Albert Pike. Walkes claimed that Pike was the Chief Justice of the Klan and Grand Dragon of Arkansas, but these can be traced back to two secondary sources.

1. "General Albert Pike, who stood high in the Masonic order, was the chief judicial officer of the Klan." (Fleming 1905)[6]

2. "General Pike organized the Ku Klux Klan in Arkansas. ... He was also appointed at that time Chief Judicial Officer of The Invisible Empire." (Davis 1924)[7]

As far I know, these are the *only* sources of the Pike–KKK claim. I have found nothing published earlier, and everything else can be ultimately traced back to them. They are at best secondary and published 14–33 years after Pike's death in 1891, when he had no opportunity to refute them. The 1905 reference is due to Walter L. Fleming, who wrote the introduction to the reprint of Lester and Wilson's *Ku Klux Klan: Its Origin, Growth and Disbandment,* and Fleming only makes the "Chief Judicial Officer" claim. Nineteen years later in 1924, Susan L. Davis adds the "Arkansas organizer" claim and from this, the frequent "Grand Dragon" claim must have been inferred. By the time of Davis's book, the "second Klan" was near its peak of prestige and popularity, and it was beneficial for it to be associated with

---

5 *Testimony Taken by the Joint Select Committee,* Alabama, 2 (1872): 825.

6 J. C. Lester and Daniel Love Wilson, *Ku Klux Klan: Its Origin, Growth and Disbandment,* W. L. Fleming intro. (New York and Washington: Neale Publishing, 1905), 27.

7 Susan Lawrence Davis, *Authentic History Ku Klux Klan, 1865–1877* (New York: S. L. Davis, 1924), 276.

Pike's memory. Even Dr. James Carter, Supreme Council Librarian, accepted Davis's claim as accurate and repeated it in a presentation he made in Wilmington, Delaware.[8]

It would be invaluable to historians to find another, better reference connecting Pike and the Klan—if such exists. Until such evidence is found, however, historians should be cautious repeating this claim that is potentially hurtful to Freemasonry and yet supported by such weak evidence. At the very least, those making the claim should acknowledge the source of their claims.

First published: *Journal of the Masonic Society,* no. 37 (Summer 2017)

------

8   James D. Carter, *Albert Pike, Pioneer: An Address Delivered at Wilmington, Delaware, November 18, 1966.*

The Tripos of 1688 at Trinity College, Dublin

Mr. John Jones, B.A., gave this commencement speech—the "Tripos"—at Trinity College Dublin on July 11, 1688. It is contained in a manuscript in the Trinity College Library, TCD MS 879/1, *The Whimsical Medley or a Miscellaneous Collection of severall Pieces in Prose & Verse some Latin, most English, being an Agreeable Variety of Satyr and Elogy, Epigram & Sonnet, Fable and Ballad, Lampoon and Pasquinade. ... Vollume the First.* It is important in understanding pre-1717 Freemasonry in Dublin and has received scant attention from Masonic historians.

> In medieval universities the role of the university funnyman ... corresponded to that of the official Court Fool. ... At Cambridge Commencements the jester was known as the *Prevaricator,* and his speech (as it was also later to be called at T.C.D.) was termed the *Tripos,* or Tripod, from the three-legged stool upon which he sat. ... For at Trinity College, Dublin, they called both the speaker and his speech "the Tripos."[1]

The speech appears to have been first published in Rev. John Barrett's *An Essay on the Earlier Part of the Life of Swift* (London: J. Johnson et al. 1808) and later reprinted in some collections of Swift's works. Barrett argued that Jonathan Swift was the author; subsequent scholars have disagreed with this conclusion. He also argued much more convincingly that *The Whimsical Medley* was written prior to 1723 by or for Theophilus, first Lord Newtown Butler.[2] The fact that the Tripos included important references to early Masonic practices in Dublin was immaterial to Barrett, but without his interest in proving Swift's authorship, the speech would likely still be resting on the library shelves of Trinity College, Dublin.

---

1 George Mayhew, "Swift and the Tripos Tradition." *Philological Quarterly* 45, no. 1 (January 1966): 86–87.

2 John Barrett, *An Essay on the Earlier Part of the Life of Swift* (London: J. Johnson, 1808), 23.

The Tripos seems to have first come to Masonic attention when W. J. Chetwode Crawley commented on it in the introduction of Henry Sadler's *Masonic Reprints and Revelations* (1898), and then Rev. George Oliver briefly referred to it in *The Revelations of a Square* (1855). It is mentioned in John H. Lepper and Philip Crossle's *History of the Grand Lodge of Free and Accepted Masons of Ireland*, vol. 1 (1925) and in a few articles in *AQC*, and then almost dropped out of sight. It was most recently alluded to by Robert Bashford in "Aspects of the History of Freemasonry in Ireland," *AQC* 129 (2016).

The Masonic portion of the 1688 Tripos begins on page 159 in "Act the 2d."

It was lately order'd, that, for the honour and Dignity of the University, there should be introduced a Society of Free Masons, consisting of Gentlemen, Mechanicks, Porters, Parsons, Ragmen, Hucksters, Bayliffs, Divines, Tinkers, Knights, Thatchers, Coblers, Poets, Justices, Drawers, Beggars, Aldermen, Pavors, Sculls, Freshmen, Batcherlors, Scavingers, Masers, Sow-gelders, Doctors, Ditchers, Pimps, Lds., Butchers, and Taylors, who shall Bind themselves by an Oath, never to discover their Mighty no secret. ...

George W. Speth, Secretary of Quatuor Coronati Lodge, made the most important deduction about the passage: "And then we are introduced to the most startling discovery of all: viz., that in 1688, Freemasonry was so well known in Dublin, its leading features were so easily recognizable by all, that it was actually made the text and theme of a satirical discourse ..."[3] Next is the wildly dissimilar list of occupations of lodge members, possibly indicative of the broad spectrum of men attracted to Freemasonry. Of course, since the Tripos is a satirical speech, the list of varied occupations could be poking fun at an organization known for its homogeneity. Finally, in the opening sentence is a reference to the Mason's oath and secrets. References, especially in Scotland, to the Mason word, a "secret" that enabled Masons to identify and summon each other, increased during the seventeenth century, from the accusation in 1637 that John Earl of Rothes "had the Masone word," to the 1649 mention in John Lamont's diary "anent the Meason Word," to the 1652 objection to the Presbytery of Kelso that Rev. James Ainslie had the Mason Word, to the 1653 description of the power of the Masson word in the book, *Logopandecteision*, to Robert Plot's 1686

---

3   G. W. Speth, "Sadler's *Reprints and Revelations*" in "Reviews." *Ars Quatuor Coronatorum* 11 (1898): 191.

mention of the "secret signes" "whereby they [Masons] are known to one another all over the *Nation*.[4] Surely, this growing awareness of Mason's secrets must have reached the learned circles of Trinity College by 1688.

Immediately following this brief introduction to the Society of Freemasons, Mr. Jones alludes to Masonic charity by referring to "a Collection ... lately made for, and the Purse of Charity well stuft for, a Reduced Brother." There follows a list of charitable donations from the list of Benefactors, which must have been hilarious to those who knew the idiosyncrasies of the donors. We can only guess with amusement why Sawny Richardson is said to have given a bottle of ale and Mr. Hasset a pair of old shoes. Of greatest Masonic important is the entry "From Sr. Warren, for being freemasonis'd the new way, five shillings." The immediate implication is if there was a "new way," there must have been an "old way" of being made a Mason.

Indeed, Speth said,

> Therefore we may safely assert that in 1668 there were two ways of being made a Mason recognised in Dublin, an old way, and Jones' "new way." This points to some recent change, reformation, innovation, or what-not, and it must probably ever remain a puzzle what this change consisted of. But it is curious that we have assertions elsewhere of important changes taking place in or about 1663, new "Articles" said to date from that time, and so on. Are we justified in connecting these two statements?[5]

The Grand Lodge of Ireland website goes even further and suggests "that the phrase '... *freemasonis'd the new way'* is the most telling remark in the speech and indicative of a change from Operative Freemasonry to Speculative Freemasonry during the latter part of the 17th century."[6] At the risk of

4   John Earl of Rothes, *A Relation of Proceedings Concerning the Affairs of the Kirk of Scotland* (Edinburgh: Bannatyne Club, 1830), 30; *The Diary of John Lamont of Newton, 1649–1671* (Edinburgh: James Clarke, 1830), 7; Hew Scott, *Fasti Ecclesiæ Scoticanæ: The Succession of Ministers in the Church of Scotland from the Reformation* (new ed., Edinburgh: Oliver and Boyd, 1917), 2:132; Thomas Urquhart, *Logopandecteision, or an Introduction to the Vniversal Language* (London: Giles Calvert, 1653), 9; Robert Plot, *The Natural History of Stafford-Shire* (Oxford: 1686), 316.

5   Speth, "Sadler's *Reprints*," 191–92.

6   Anon. "The Trinity Tripos 1688," *Irish Masonic History and the Jewels of Irish Freemasonry*, accessed February 18, 2017, http://www.irishmasonichistory.com/the-trinity-tripos-1688.html.

being a spoilsport, a counter explanation is possible. Warren may have been involved with some change at Trinity College perhaps involving a five-shilling fee and the phrase "freemasonis'd the new way" refers not to the Dublin Masons but to some event at Trinity College, lost on modern readers.

Next is a Latin passage on pages 160–61 beginning "Tam Liberâ potitus Contributione. ..." The Grand Lodge of Ireland website includes an appendix with a translation.

> Our Brother, the scoundrel, having become master of so generous a col lection gets his wallets together with a view of making off, and crossed the square with a more cheerful countenance than usual. And while, through his excess of joy, he advances with head erect and talks with prancing pace, who of all men came to meet him but the most brother of brothers, Cooper! As soon as he recognises this faithful fellow, he runs to him with all speed, cordially grasps his hand, and, as their wont is, beslobbers him with a most glutinous kiss. Thereafter they walk towards the Library, with the object of viewing Ridley among the other wonders of the place. While the visitor is examining him with the prying eyes of a lynx, and is ransacking, with particular care, whatever the judges, the executioner, and the surgeons have left of the poor fellow's carcase, alas! and alas! he descried—whether on the nobler or the hinder parts, I know not for certain—the *Signum* (in plain English, the Freemasons' Mark). As soon as he saw this, good Heavens! with what a yell he filled the building. Over and over again he thumped his breast, lacerated his pallid cheeks, and tore to rags his garments, already, alas! too ragged. After a while, when his paroxysm had cooled down a bit, he poured forth his ludicrous grief in verses after this fashion.[7]

Then follows on pages 161–62 of the manuscript "Eulogium Ridlæanum. An Elegy upon Ridley." The poem is apropos because "there existed in the Library of the College the stuffed skin of a wretched police informer called Ridley" who is made to be a Mason.[8] It is said in the preceding Latin passage that the "The Freemason's Mark" is found on his body, perhaps a sly

---

7   http://www.irishmasonichistory.com/the-trinity-tripos-1688.html, accessed February 19, 2017.
8   Speth, "Sadler's *Reprints*," 191.

allusion to a later general belief that Masonic initiation included branding on the buttocks.[9]

The elegy is followed on pages 162–63 by another Latin passage beginning, "Hoc munere elaborato, non diutius Lacrymis indulgent. ..."

> Having carefully attended to this duty, they give way to tears no longer, but wiping their eyes on their knuckles [*lit.,* their grief being stifled with the thumb], make off in silence. They summon a Lodge forthwith, and inform all the brethren of the load of disgrace in store for themselves, and of suffering for their most unhappy little brother. The Fraternity and aforesaid lit- tle brother take it greatly to heart, and, amid signs heaved from the inmost breast, arrangements are made on the spot, that hereafter no one deserving of the extreme penalty of the law, or sure to be hanged, shall be admitted to the Society of Freemasons. As soon as this has been formally ruled and the Register of the Lodge produced, each of them, gentlemen and scoundrels alike, bids farewell to the other with most solid kisses indiscriminately bestowed.[10]

On page 168, there is a brief mention of "Free Masons that Built Babell," but it doesn't seem to refer to the Masonic lodge mentioned earlier. Mr. Jones then concludes by wondering where he can now go, having offended so many. In particular on page 177, he laments that he cannot go to the library because "Ridley's Ghost will haunt me for scandallizing him with the name of Free Mason." And that concludes the Masonic references in the Tripos. For his efforts, Mr. Jones "on July 3, 1688, two days after delivering the *Tripos* at Commencement, was first sentenced by the Board of Senior Fellows to be deprived of his degree. Six days later, however, because of the powerful intercession of someone, the Board remitted his degradation and, only suspended Jones from his Scholar's and his 'Native's' place and from his chamber in the College. ..."[11]

---

9   Yasha Beresiner, "Masonic Caricatures: For Fun or Malice—300 years of English Satirical Prints." in *Reflections on 300 Years of Freemasonry*, ed. John S. Wade, ed., (London: Lewis Masonic, 2017), 39–75.

10 http://www.irishmasonichistory.com/the-trinity-tripos-1688.html, accessed February 19, 2017.

11 Mayhew, "Swift and the Tripos Tradition," 98.

142 *A Tripos or Speech*
Deliver'd in the University of
Dublin att a Comēncement held there
The 11ᵗʰ of July 1688 by Mr John Jones
then Batchelr of Arts aferwards. D:D. ⁓

Act: 1ˢᵗ

Occidit Miseros Crambe Repetita Magistros.
Your Probabo, probabo, is as dull as a ⁓
Trinity Sunday Sermon.
Dii boni quas novas aves hic video! Tot habemus
Barbaros Ignoramos et Foppos Tot Doctores Indoctos,
Rummos Academicos, Cives Aldermanicos, Rusticos
Personas, and so Many Pritty, Pritty Little Rogues,
That, should I speak Lattin, I should Banter Ten parts
of the Company. Wherefore, for the sake of the Ladys,
Bullies, The Rums, and Fellow Comoners, I'll Order it,
(as I know You all would have it,) that the English ⁓
be Ten to One against the Roman.
Lenite Clamorem, till I shew these Gentlemen
the Civilitys of the House.
Non Temere decet Quidem ut salutemus libenter;
Salvete igitur Quotquot Reverenda Vel Ridicula,
Docta Vel Rummosa Capita sed imprimis salvus
sit Doctr Acton, (ut inquit Erasmus) Athleticè; su=
perannuati Omnes salvi sint Pancraticè; et, si
Qui adsint Cornuti (quod Verisimile est) Valeant
Tauricè; deinde si Quis adsit Medicus Immedicabilis,

Qui ſkulkat ſubter id Manticæ, quod in Tergo eſt — 143
docto in cujus Capite Æſculapius Viget, ſed in oſsibus
dominatus aſtronomia et effæto Corpore totus in=
hæret Galenus et Hypocrates, ſi poſsibile ſit? inquam
Valeat ille: ſed præ ceteris Clelericum iſtuin Clerico=
rum ſalvere Jubeo who preaches in an Oven, and is
of the ſame Name and Heraldry With an Eminent
Blind Cobler; Who, when the Kingdom was all out of
the ſtitches, Vampt Himſelf a Collonell; if his Gra=
vity be here I ſalute him for 7 ſeveral Reaſons:
Firſt, becauſe he drinks and goes to the Bogg-houſe
for fourteen Reaſons, but cannot give one for
ſelling his Organs to a Maſs-houſe.

Secondly, becauſe (according to his own Phraſe)
he Preaches by the London ſtandard, which never
hapen'd, as I know of, but Thrice, and then Stilling=
fleet and Tillotson themſelves were not one jot
better or Worſe, unleſs we ſay with the Poet —
Sed Male dum rècitas, incipit eſse tuus.

Thirdly, becauſe When he came from England
He wore as much ſilk for a Doublet as made his ~
Siſter (joy be with her, as he ſaid) a Manteo and
Petticoat. Quare, whether then Mr Parson wore
the Breaſt Plate of Righteouſneſs? it is plain he
did, and that his Intentions Were honourable, for
the Next Sunday fol lowing he Preached Give Cesar
his due. It is ill Nature then in Bunbury's
Wife's husband to Revile him for this; and, to ſpeak
in the Phraſe of a pritty Little Senior Fellow, There's
no Jew but would be more gentle.

144 *Fourthly, Becaufe He Consecrates as much Water*
att once, as makes Chriftians for a Month.
   Fifthly, Becaufe he invited to his Sifter's Funerall
none but (as he was pleas'd to Call them) The Cream of
the Parifh. Viz: Thofe that kept Coaches. now himfelf ~
upon himfelf; his Conclufion in fuch a Cafe will be ~
thus, That all the Curds and Cream in the Parifh Tour it
in Coaches, while the Poor fkim-Milk and Bonny-Clabber
trudge a Foot. I Wonder, Mr Leefon, with his Cream of
Theology, is not his Parifhioner. There is a Mefs for the
Frefhmen. but
   Sixthly, Because He lives by the Canon, and Yett ~
corrects the Rubrick.
   Seeventhly and laftly, Because He made Himfelf
a Large and ponderous Night-Cap, after the Exact ~
Modell of his Church, and This he did for two Reafons.
   Firft, to fhow that no Noddle in the Diocese could bear
such a Weight as his. Secondly, to Cure a Diftemper,
which, to the Grief of his Congregation, has Troubl'd
his Brains these Many Years. Sed ad Rem.
   Salvus sit ille inter focios Juniores cum ~
pede brevi et Naso Rhinocerotis Who by his one
fermon of Angles and Triangles has thrice fhewn
his fmattering in the Mathematicks.
   Valeat etiam Doctor ille Civilis, fed Polygamifta,
Edentulus fed Polyglottus; Qui adeo plenus eft Uteris,
ut in ipsâ Facie Omnes Linguarum Characteres
graphicè Scribuntur; fruftra igitur, Reverende
Doctor, fufurrant invidi, Tejam Senio Confectum Ori=
entales Linguas non calere, cum revera Index tui animi fit
                                        vultus.

Sed etiam atq$_{ue}$ etiam salvus sit Purpuratus noster 145
grandiloquus—Cui dedit Ore Rotundo
  Musa Loqui—
Quen Quoad Faciem et Linguam Vocamus Ulyssem:
  Non Famosus erat, sed erat Facundus Ulysses.
No Tartar is more fair, no Athenian better hung,
Sol Varnisht Ore his Face, and Mercury his Tongue.
Quoad Altitudinem salutemus Ajacem, Quoad Gra=
cilitatem Tithonum, Quoad Caput Versatile Pria=
mum Paralyticum, Quoad pedes Achillem, quoad
Crura deniq$_{ue}$ Colossum.
  Sponte sua properant. Labor est inhibere Volentes.
    Anglicè,
  With Awkward Gown tuck'd up He scow'rs along,
  And at each stride Measures a Parasang.
Inter cæteros, peculiari dignus est salutatione bellus
quidam homunculus, I do not mean M.ʳ Brady's pritty
Little Man, but the Neat spruce, dapper, finicall ~
Nice, spark, Who'd rather sing and dance in his cham=
ber, than Bowl without an Umbrella: Who Con=
stantly carrys as many Patch Boxes in his Pocket
as would Beautify Our Beadle; as many severall
sorts of snuff, as would furnish Major Gen.ʳˡ Mac=
Carty, and Co.ˡ Dempsy for a Year and as Much
Essence as would perfume S.ʳ Stampe's Chamber,
as Many Comfitts as would sweeten M.ʳ Travers's
Hocksters: together with as Many Jewels as would
Make S.ʳ Jephson a Gentleman, or Buy M.ʳ De=
launy a Coat of Arms; Besides he has such a Veneration

146 *for the Fair fex, that he wou'd not presume to
visit a Lady in a fhirt he had Worn a day, but by
Way of Apology fent her this Billet-deux:*

I gad Madam I Begg Your Pardon ten Thousand
times for not paying my devoir to Your Ladyship
to day; of Which Transcendent Happineſs nothing
under the Planetts cou'd have depriv'd me, but the ~
damn'd diſapointment of My Sempſtreſs, by whose
Neglect I have att preſent but seven day ſhirts by
which means I am unprovided with Linen, and ſo
render'd utterly incapable of Attending Your Ladyſ^{hip}
now; but as ſoon as My Dress is agreeable I flye with
the Wings of Duty and Obedience to implore Your
Ladyſ^{p's} Mercy for My unfortunate Absence and ~
will ever ſnatch att all Opportunitys of Manifeſting
My ſelf,

    Madam

        Your Ladyſ^{p's}

           Moſt Hum^{ble} and devoted

         Slave to the ſtarrs or Center

          Tommy Weaver.

    O curas hominum, ô quantum eſt in rebus inané.
Ipsiſsimum hunc homuncionem hoc in Epigram=
mate Notat Martialis. ————————

    Cottile Bellus homo es, &c. ————

         Anglicè,

    There's ſcarce a well-dreſt Coxcomb, but will own
Tommy's the prittieſt ſpark about the Town,

This all the Tribe of Fringe and Feather say, 147
Because he Nicely moves by Algebra:
And does with Method Tye his Cravat string,
Takes snuff with Art, and shews his sparkling Ring.
Can sett his Fore Top, Manage well his Wigg;
Can Act a Proverb, and can dance a Jigg.
Does sing French songs can Rhime & furnish thatt,
To Inquisitive Miss, from Letter or Gazette:
Knows the Affair of Cock-Pitt, and the Race
And who were Conquerors att either Place:
If Crop or Trotter took the Prize away;
And who a fortune gain'd the other day.
He swings Fringe Gloves, sees Plays, writes Billedeux,
Fill'd up with Beauty, Love, Oaths, Lyes, and Vows.
Does scent his Eybrows, perfum'd Comfitts eat,
And smells like Phœnix' Nest, or like Civet Cat:
Does shave with Pumice stone, compose his Face,
And Rowls his stockings by a Looking Glass;
Accomplish'd thus, Tommy, you'll grant, I hope,
A pretty spark att least, if not a Fop.

Finita salutatione, (more Erasmiano) paucis vobiscum
confabulandum est. Sed uti solet Graculus ille Mad=
dison, mihi cordi est Totum occupare sermonem. I'll
take all the Chat to my self.

In Familiaritatem me nuper Exceperunt Vir=
tuosi, (hominum genus in Minimis non Minimum La=
borans) et Mihi quædam naturæ non Vulgaria nota
fecere, quæ humanitatis Ergo, et Publicæ salutis gratia

148 in *Lucem jam profero.*
First, M.ᵣ Allen's Infallible Cure
for the Maw Worms.

℞. *Poti fortis ab Hatcho Quartum unum, Row=*
lorum, five Brownorum, five Alborum, ad Mini=
mum Tres; his addatur Butyri Culinaris quantum
valet Duos Denarios, cum Bunfho Radifhorum ~
vel Watergrafsi, deinde ftomachi Equini Quan=
tum fufficit hæc omnia Forâ Octavâ Anteme=
ridiana quotidie Devorentur, et certe vix ad ~
prandium usque Latrabit ftomachus.

Secondly, Doc.ᵗᵣ Mollineux his rare
Discovery of part of the Meat's fudden
digeftion and Corruption in the Mouth, Thus

℞. *Pinquis Caponis Leggum unum et Wingum,*
Tofti fhouldromotontis, et Carnis Boevinæ Una
flizum unum vel alterum; Anseris Juvenilis
cum faufo Gofberiano Modicum qᵈ. Panis Do=
meftici Lunfheum moderatum, Vini Rubri,
et Poti minoris Ana Pocula bina Vel tria, et
quod inftar Omnium eft fœtidifsimi fpiritus
quantum fufficit: Comprefsu Oris fiat Bolus;
et procul dubio interr hiatus dentium, et fuper
Gingivas tam ftatim fœtida fiat Concoctio,
Quod primus Omnium Mortalium, fi modo Credibile
fit ingenuus Notavit ille Medicus. ~

Thirdly, The Colledge Butler's admirable 149
Invention of selling a Mixture of
Ale and Mum for Nine pence p^er Quart,
And his Water Bewitched: viz. small Beer
and water for a Penny a Bottle. ========
Likewise his Elixir Bonse famee
or Cure for his first fault.

The Experiment of the Liquids is wrought by the
help of a Trap-door att Midnight.
　　　　The Elixir is made thus
　　　　========

R/: Vini Rubri Flaskum Duplex, Canarii, sive
Vini Hispanici Amphoram unam, Vel Alteram;
academici et Grubbinorum Tolemanni quantum
sufficit: Deferantur ad Camœram Junioris Decani
Quo participante ingurgitente Omnia post Noc=
turnum Catalogum. ==========
　　If this will not work the Effect alone, I referr
You to his Wonderfull sympathetick Prescription
which is thus. ==========
　　R/: the Tongue of Mother Jenkinson, alias Madam
University W will sooth the Affections of the
Head of the society, This being done Let the —
Patient Dine thrice a Week on a National Dish
and if this faile 'tis an Odd Thing, nam probatum est.
　　　　Moreover I Recommend to you,
Dean Manby's and Arch Deacon Baynard's Oint=
ment for a Warping Conscience.
　　　　==========

150 M.ʳ Oliver Talent's Prefcription for the Worms
in the noddle.
Sʳ Conolly's new Treatife of Armory, Entitled —
Ex Quovis Ligno non fit Mercurius.
Madam Dicky Barry's ingenious Machine for
putting on Finicall Bands.
M.ʳ Scroggs's Composition of Puns.
M.ʳ Griffiths's approv'd of Opium Matutinum for
foaking.
M.ʳ Downes his Excellent Potic Coffiana, for Ex=
pelling foporiferous humours.
Prifcianus Vulneratus, alias Methodus Credendi
Articulos, by the Revᵈ Doc.ᵗʳ King.
Doctor Nappier's Elegy on a Broken Bellarmine
of Ale, Intitled
              Amphora non Meruit tam prætiofa mori.
An Excellent Engine for Working Embroidery –
by my Very Good Lord Charlemount.
Likewise his Lordship's Praxis Arithmetica –
fhewing that 24 and 24 make 48: this, as fimple
as it feems to be, coft the Honourable Lord some pains
and his Lady fome blufhes.
    An infallible unguent for the fpleen in the
toe, by the Revᵈ Doc.ᵗʳ Foy.
And laftly, M.ʳ Smith's Art of Compliance, proveing
humility to be the Practice of the Age, and
fhewing how the Colledge Butler may be the
Dear Companion of the Junior Dean.
For all which I Refer You to the Refpective authors

except the last which Mr Smith proves   151
syllogistically thus.

    Moris est Humilitas, Ergo
    Junior Decanus et Promus Senior
    possint esse Magni.
        Probo AntecedEns.
    Si Generosus marmorizat cum puero
    anglicè, plays Marbles with his boy,
    Tunc moris est Humilitas.
    Sed Generosus Marmorizat cum puero. Ergo.
        Probo Minorem Instantiâ-
    Magister Sayers marmorizat cum Puero,
    Sed Magister Sayers est Generosus. Ergo.
        Probo aliter.
    Si doctissimus, altissimus, nec non
    longe notissmus Doctor in Universitate
    scrubbat suas Tabulas et Brushat suas
    Cathedras Tunc Moris est Humilitas.
    Sed Talis Doc.^{tr} scrubbat suas Tabulas, &c. Ergo
        Hoc etiam Probari potest instantiâ
  But the Tall Gentleman in the Robes would not have
it known. Cum itaq_{ue} Magister, (te Decanum alloquor)
argumentis hisce Validis Vindicetur tua humilitas
quid obstat quo minus inter Te et Danielum mutua
foveatur Familiaritas?
    Ede, Bibe, Dormi, post Mortem nulla Voluptas
    Namque inter Tanaim nihil est socerumque Viselli.
    Coach it away then and Empty His Pitchers.
Ditchers.

152 *Heu, heu, quanti hic desiderantur focci et hand —*
Handkerchiefi, tantum est inter Vos Clamoris,
Sudoris; tantum est Hogorum ut piget usq$_{ue}$ Morari.
pergat igitur (ut inquit Doc^{tr} Acton) suo modo
Dominus Barry. Sed heus tu, Magist^r Will-be, sive
Graduate Medioxime, Serenissimæ Elizabethæ
dormiant Cineres
            Not a Word of Protestant Befs.

ACT the 2^d

Oppon: Dom: Barry.
            In Tempore Veni quod omnium Rerum est
primum nam Vereor, Domine you are brought as
low as Withrington in Chivy Chafe, or Mr Lloyd in the
Chappell. Ridicula Capita! inepto Rifu res ineptior
nulla est.
            Absint Joci (as Sr Jephson said when he had none)
res feria jam, imo de funeribus, agitur; Muliercu=
la enim Misella humanifsima, Nobis vicina, et ~
Magistri Hewetson foror Unica non ita pridem
Moriebatur; nec Amicorum immemor ingrata
difcefsit: sed Quicquid Vel Corpufculi sui Vel Rei
humano foret usui, hoc fupremo Testamento
amicis fuis in formam fubsequentem Benigna
Legavit.
            The Last Will and Testament
            of Mrs Mary Hewetson.

            She Bequeathed her Brains to a Learned
grave Gentleman who has fhaked his own out of
his Noddle, Whose Name I was forbid to tell you,

*But I'll do as good as Well; I'll find somebody here y*ᵗ — 153
Amoveate quæso, amoveate paulisper; oh! salve —
*Mag*ᵗʳ *Burridge. I Remember Tommy Cox told me*
Your's Were Addle, and therefore I present them to you,
if her Brother Lays no claim to them.

Her Tongue (which even after Death is the Cause of
*Controversy) some affirm she left to M*ʳˢ *Horncastle,*
*but the true opinion is, she Bequeathed it to M*ʳˢ
Jenkinson, Whose speaking Organ (as I told you before)
*is employ'd in M*ʳˢ *Donnell's Elixir Bonæ Famæ.*

*Her Teeth she left to M*ʳˢ *Horncastle, Who has such*
an unruly Member of her own, that it needs at least
a Double Guard.

*She Bequeathed her Hair to M*ʳ *Leeson, to make*
him a Wigg. her Colour'd silk Petticoat, to furnish
*M*ʳ *Delauny with a pair of Breeches; and her*
Looking Glass and Nightrail to My Lady Neddy Hall.
*Her Tooth pick to D*ʳ *Loftus, and patch Box to M*ʳˢ
Lucy Coghill, which so disguised her at the Confir=
*mation in S*ᵗ *Warbrós Church that the Zealous Arch=*
*deacon did not know S*ᵗ *John's Daughter. Sed Zelo vere*
Fitz-geraldino Exclamavit, My Lord, My Lord, her —
Face is against the Canon; I know not who she is,
and I won't Present her.

*Sed, Rev*ᵈ·ᵉ *Vi, monstrat tibi Poeta, quo pacto*
agnosceres Virginem,

    Cui numerosa Linunt Stellantem Splenia Frontem,
    Ignoras Quæ sit? splenia tolle, Leges.
But to Return she left her Couragious Heart to —
*pritty M*ʳ *Weaver.*

154 *Her Beauty (now You all Expect I'll say to ~*
S.ʳ Bayly, and Fitzſimons) no truly, but to as Wor=
thy a Gentleman, the Reverend the Provoſt and her
Conscience to the Clerk of the kitchen, of Whom
(by way of Digreſsion) take this Character:
A Colledge Stewart is

An Animal mixtum, a Medly or Hodge–Podge
of Butcher, and Cook; of ſkullion and Scholar:
he Lives negatively by the Privation of Others
and Mortifyes more fleſh than all the Divines
in the kingdom; did He Live Among the Ancients
he would be taken for a Wreſtling Master, with
his skin Oyl'd for the Palæstra; hence it comes
to paſs, that his greaſy ſhirt pays his Laundreſs,
and finds her in ſoap and candles. You may
follow him (like the Old Pye Woman) by his
Smell; Strangers paſsing by his Door take it for
the Colledge Chandler's: an Ignorant Woman ~
went thither directed by her noſe to ſell her
Kitchen ſtuff. The Butcher's Dogs fawn upon him
and follow him for his hogoes: without doubt They
fancy He carries a ſlaughter house about him.
He ſpends half his ſalary a Year in Wash-Balls,
Fuller's Earth, and ſocks. The ſcent of the Kitchen
has infected his Breath and poyson'd his Whole
Maſs of Blood; What the Hyperbolicall Poet
ſaid of the Cappodocian is verify'd in him
without a Trope ~

Vipera Capadocem malè sana momordit, at ipsa 155
Gustato periit sanguine Cappadocis.
Anglicè

A Famisht Ratt progging one night for food,
Bit M.ʳ Hogoe's Toe, and suck'd the Blood:
Then dull and Drooping, the pensive Vermin sat
Gorg'd with infectious Gore, and poysoning Fate.
If he goes to Market fasting, he Taints all the Meat
he Cheapens, therefore the Butchers, in their own De=
fence treat him to a Breakfast. Ev'ry Sunday—
Morning he so stuffs himself that if You come nigh
him, you'll know what's for dinner. Every Belch is
a Bill of Fare. his Bedfellow dreams of Grubbins
all night. One that Lay with him by Accident fan=
cy'd himself at the Mouth of an Oven, full of tainted
Mutton Pyes. M.ʳ Butler Junior who to stifle his
hogoes, Lyes in his socks, would Match him for a Bed=
fellow, provided that They Lay heads and Points. The
Pestilence of the head wou'd be requited by the Plague
of the Heels. Were He in Orders, 'twou'd be dangerous
in him to Baptize, he would make more Ghosts than
Christians, and with Good Words send the sucklings
packing to the other World. Were he Doct.ʳ in the
Civil Law, his Bretheren wou'd rather not Comence
than kiss him; he wou'd be as Terrible as the Old Gentle=
man with the Rainbow about his Eyes. He never
sayes Grace before Meat, and very good Reason—
his Victuals like the Scotchman's snuf, will not bide
a Blessing

156 The Holy words wou'd Tranſubſtantiate them into Maggots. The greateſt ſin he has to ſtruggle with is — the fleſh. and (which is wonderful) the oftener He~ gains the Victory the Wickeder he becomes. he thwarts the Rubrick, and Makes more Good Frydays than Sundays in the Year: When We keep Lent, he keeps Carnival; and well he may, when other men faſt for his Sins: he takes upon him to be Deputy Burser, and is call'd Mr Stewart, but by the ſame Figure that the Hang= man is ſtil'd the King's Officer. In the kitchen he Rules the Roaſt, is abſolute Lord over the Cleave-Men half Maſter of the ſkullions, and partly Tutor, partly Companion, to the Cooks; but always ſworn brother in iniquity to the Clerks of the Buttery, Which brings me to Consider them together in One Word, and ſo have done. When theſe Two meet, (like Malevolent Planetts in Conjunction) 'tis Ominous, and denotes a Dearth in Commons and Sizings. nay, ſometimes it foretells a generall Puniſhment. The Maeking of either of Theſe is the ſpoiling of a Schollar, as a Gentleman, bound Apprentice forfeits His~ Heraldry; or the Knighthood of an Alderman ſpoils a Cit. They Live Plentifully with Traffick Between themselves, and Yet ev'ry day eat and Drink their~ Bargains: to Conclude, they Caſt up their ſins once a Month but don't Repent, becauſe their Iniquitys are Confirm'd by Theſe honeſt Men: (the Senr fellows.)

But to Return to the Will. 157
She Bequeath'd her Breasts to M.ʳˢ Mary C—ll,
of whom hear the Poett
  Mammas, atque Tatas habet Afra, sed ipsa Papila
    Mammarum dici et Maxima Mamma potest.
Her Paint she left to One of those Ladys; and Her
Nose she knew not whither to Leave to M.ʳ Loftus
or M.ʳ Loyd; but at last order'd it for the former;
and out of her great Charity gave permission to
the Latter (I mean M.ʳ Loyd) to furnish himself af=
ter the Hudibrasian Manner with a Supplemen=
tall snout out of her Posteriors.
Lastly, she Bequeath'd all her Money for the Foun=
ding and Endowment of a New Colledge, and there=
fore order'd that there be a fair Tract of Ground —
Purchas'd out of Jack Cusack's Estate, on a Conveni=
ent part whereof there be Erected a Stately Pile
of Building after the modell of M.ʳ Allen's Man=
sion house; that S.ʳ Butler's famous Library be
Bought for the Colledge use, together with Stil=
lingfleet's and Tillotson's Sermons for the Assis=
tance of the Young Divines. That M.ʳ Doyle, for his
Excellent Moralls, and profound Learning, be —
Provost; and M.ʳ Boreman for the same Reasons
be Vice Provost: That Nickumbottum be Univer=
sity Orator; S.ʳ Stampe Singing Master and Ma=
gician; and that ingenious Bachelor of Arts who
Read out all Gassendus's Astronomy in a Week—
but the A.s and B.ˢ if S.ʳ Moor pleases be Mathema=
tick Professor; and Doctor Mercer be Bursor.

158 *Several Officers are Yet wanting, as Divini=*
ty Professor; Preachers, Physitians, Lecturers,~
Surgeons, Historians, Chymists, Civilians, Register;
Linguist and Many others, all which are to be ~
supplied by that Colossus of Learning, Mr Foley.
Hic Vero dubium Oritur; num Doctr Mercer
cum sponsa sua (satis Eleganti) inhabitare possit
Academiam, si negatur tunc actum est de Bur=
sario, Qui adeo Integer Vitæ, scelerisque purus: si
Affirmatur; Dii boni, quam Clamosum nec non
Rixosum habituri sumus Collegium, nam fama
refert esse inter illos Conjugium Conjurgium,
quod Martiali parum Credibile Videtur; ut Ex
his Versiculis constat

> *Cum sitis similes, paresque Vita,*
> *Uxor pessima, pessimus Maritus,*
> *Miror; non bene convenire Vobis.*

It was first order'd that Mr Loyd should be the Uni=
versity Poet, ferunt autem, Magister Te quonda~
pesimum egisse Poetastrem, ideoque

> *Mutato nomine, de te*
> *Fabula narratur——*

> *Qui Bavium non Odit, amet tua Carmina, Mævi.—*
> *Nam tu Cosconi, Disticha Longa facis.*

Hanc igitur Provineiam habeat Dean Glandee
vel Mr Hewetson.
Order'd moreover; that all the Fellows dine and
sup constantly in the Hall uti apud nos Moris
est. Hortemur etiam, ut Præpositus parcius absit.

and to be strictly observ'd, that all the students   159
in the Hall especially att Meats speak Latin, as we do.
    It was lately order'd, that, for the honour and Dig=
nity of the University, there should be introduced a
Society of Free Masons, consisting of Gentlemen, ~
Mechanicks, Porters, Parsons, Ragmen, Hucksters,
Bayliffs, Divines, Tinkers, Knights, Thatchers, Coblers,
Poets, Justices, Drawers, Beggars, Aldermen, Pavors,
Sculls, Freshmen, Batcherlors, Scavingers, Masers,
Sowgelders, Doctors, Ditchers, Pimps, L^{ds}, Butchers,
and Taylors, who shall Bind themselves by an Oath,
never to discover their Mighty no secret; and to Re=
lieve whatsoever strolling distress'd Bretheren ~
they meet with, after the Example of the Fraternity
of Freemasons in and About Trinity Colledge; by whom
a Collection was lately made for, and the Purse of
Charity well stuft for, a Reduced Brother who Re=
ceiv'd their Charity as follows in this List of Benefactors.
From Sawny Richardson, a Bottle of Ale and Two Rowls.
From Mr Hasset, a Pair of old shoes.
From a kind hearted Butcher at Lazy hill, a Calve's Countenance.
From y.^e R.^t Honble Lord Charlemont a Cast hat.
From Long Laurence, an Inch of Tobacco.
From Mr Ryder, a Groat.
From Dr Gwithers, an old Glister-Pipe.
From Mr Marsh and Sr Tenison a Bundle of Godly Ballads.
From Mr Smith, an Old Pair of Quilted Stockings.
From a Tapster at ye sign of the hog in Armour, a Comfit.

160 *From S.ʳ Goodlet a Piece of an Old Smigletius*
for a Naturall use, cunningly procur'd by
the means of S.ʳ Goodlet.
From S.ʳ Warren, for being freemasonis'd
the new way, five shillings.
From M.ʳ Edward Hall, a pair of Caft Night Gloves.
Laftly from M.ʳ Hancock, a flice of Chefhire
chees which the Hungry Brother eat up with
fuch a Gufto, and lik'd fo well, that he ftole —
away the reft in his Breeches.
Tam Liberâ potitus Contributione, Frater Scoun=
drellus farcinnulas fuas difcefsurus colligit,
et vultu hilariori folito Quandrangulum Tranfit,
dumque præ nimio Gaudio porrectiore incedit Fronte,
altioresque tendit grefsus, Quisnam inter homines ~
Obviam dedit illi, nifi Frater fraterrimus Cooper, ~
Qui ut fidelem Novit hominem, feftinatius accurrit,
humaniter corripit Dextram, utque moris eft, et fpis=
fifsimo confpuit Bafio; deinde Bibliothecam verfus
comiter Ambulant, ut inter Cætera Admirabilia ~
Ridlæum vifitent, Quem dum Hofpes curiosis Lyn=
ceis Oculis perscrutatur, et diligentius Rimatur
Quantum homuncionis Judlces, Carnifex, et Medici
Reliquerunt; Proh dolor! inter Partes ᵃⁿNobiliores, an
Pofteriores nefcio, privatum Fraternitatis nota=
vit Signum (Anglicè, The Freemason's Mark). quo viso
Dii boni! quanto Clamore totam infecit Domum. Ter
et fæpius pulsavit pectus, Exfangues dilaniavit ~
genas, et Eheu nimium laceratas dilaceravit vefte,
tandem vero paulo Modeftius insaniens, hujusmodi versiculis

Ridiculum effudit Dolorem. ============ **161**

Eulogium Ridlæanum.
An Elegy upon Ridley.

Unhappy brother, what can be
In Wretchedness compar'd to Thee,
Thou Grief and Shame of our Society?
Had We in due time understood
That Thou Wer't of the Brotherhood,
By Fraud or Force Thou hadst got Loose.
From shameful Tree and Dismal noose;
And now perhaps with Life bein blest,
As comely a Brother as the best,
Not thus Expos'd a Monumentall Jest.
When Lady Longs for Colledge Beer,
Or Little Dame, or Country Squire,
Walk out an Afternoon to Look
On Thee, and Devil-Raiseing Book.
and kindly rather chose to dye
Than Blemish our Fraternity.
The First of us e'er hang'd for Modesty.
And now alack, and Welladay,
Thy Parchment Hide is stuff'd with Hay.
Nay worse the Æsculapians,
Thy mighty Mis'ry to Enhance,
Have cruelly Cut Thee out of Countenance.
And, to show witty Spight att once,
Preserv'd thy skin and Lost thy Bones.

Why Thirty-Three?

162 Thus here, in Wooden Hatch you stand,
With scornfull Musket at Your hand;
The Mice and Ratts mock Centinell
A poor Ridiculous Spectacle,
To Gibeing Joan, to Kate and Nan
Thou Worse than Skeleton of Man.
So does he measure out his Grief,
For Loss of Brother and of Thief.
    Nor Less concern'd does Cooper stand,
But sobing with his Clout in hand,
And destitute of Consolation,
Kept time with all his Tribulation.
Their grumbling Woe Runs thro' and thro' em,
If all were known, 'twould quite undo them.
The sighs which up and downward goe
Their unfeigned Sorrow show:
For the Devil's in't if They Pretend,
Who Vent their Grief att either End.

Hoc munere elaborato, non diutius Lachrymis in=
dulgent, sed dolore police suppresso, taciti discedunt.
protinus Lodgum convocant, fratresq$_{ue}$ omnes certi=
ores faciunt quantum sibi infamiæ, et quantum
Miseriæ infælicissimo accedit fraterculo; graviter
luget Fraterculus et Societas, et suspiriis ex imo ~
pectore petitis, statim provisum est in posterum,
Nominem Qui Crucem Meretur, Vel Qui Suspenden=
dus est, in Societatem Free Masonorum Admitti,
Quo Authoritate Statuto, et Albo Lodgi prolato, singuli,
tam Generosi quam scoundrelli, Olidissimis Basiis

ACT. 3ᵈ

Enter a Wadling Doctor, and his Man, James.

Dᵣ   James, have you read out the Chapter, and can you
        tell how many days' Work was the Creation?

Ja.   Marry here's so many hard Words, I can't Remember.

Dᵣ   Well, but this is not the Businefs now; You must
        get things in readinefs against to-morrow.

Ja.   Master, whats the matter with to-morrow, more
        than another day?

Dᵣ (afide.)   Oh, the ignorance of thofe People that are not ~
        Mathematicians. I tell you, a fupernaturall Thing
        will happen.

Ja. (afide)   Oh! oh! This is the Eclipse now, I warrant.
        Nay, Master an you fay it, it is as fure as a Gun;
        then what Mun I do fay You?

Dᵣ   Go to the Steward and provide double Commons.
        and be sure You call at the Chandlers, for to=
        morrow I dine by Candle Light.

Ja.   Oh! the Wonderfull Wonderfullnes of You Schol=
        lards!—And what Mun I bring Drink in?

Dᵣ   A materiall Question:—in the Tankard, and do
        that in the Morning

Ja.   Marry, but I had better Buy a Pitcher fo
        I had, and then I need not go fo often as I do.
        This Tankard, I wish it were e'en hang'd, fo I do.

164 D.ͬ *What ails You at it, why do you Grumble?*
~Ja.   *Grumble, Quoth- a? I'm ſure it wears me more*
     ſhoe Leather than I little, and I cannot ſay my
     Prayers in a Morning for it, ſo I can't.
D.ͬ   *If I thought it did You anny injury, or Con=*
     tributed to the doing You anny harm, or were
     an irregular Veſſell, I wou'd part with it; I~
     wou'd no more Entertain it than I did My Bed;
     Go, then, and bring a Pitcher.
                              Exeunt ſeverally.

          Enter Sainty Aſhe and
          Samuell Foley (Senior Fellows)

S.ͭʸ   *Where do you keep your Eclipſe tomorrow?*
Sam.   *In My Chamber; I do not care for Gropeing*
     my Way to My Dinner.
S.ͭʸ   *What, will it be Total? No Glimmering to*
     be allow'd, to Eat our Meat by?
Sam.—   *So it ſeems. I have taken a great deal*
     of Pains to Calculate it, and can now de=
     monſtrate it.
S.ͭʸ—   *If you pleaſe, I wou'd be Very glad to ſee*
     your Calculation.
Sam:—   *Thus then—Invenitur ex Tabulis Pleni=*
     Lunium Medium, addita Dimidia Lunatione
  et tunc, ex Poſtaphæreſi et Motu Lunæ Horario, in=
veniantur digiti Eclíptici, et. Parallaxis Altitudinis. ~

S.^{ty}— *Tis wonderfull Well, from Whence I con=* 165
        clude We are all like to be in the Dark.

Sam:— *I doubtless, or I'll Burn My Books. I woud*
        not want this little smattering in Astronomy
        for a great deal I protest.

S.^{ty}— *I confess there is some advantage in it.*

Sam:— *Advantage? I could not live without it,*
        I cut My hair by the stars, and will tell ~
        the Physiognomy and sex of My Child before
        my Wife's brought to Bed.

S.^{ty}— *But do the Planets never Wander, are*
        You not sometimes mistaken ?

Sam.— *Oh, never, att least in things of this kind:*
        it is as easy to Calculate an Eclipse, as to ~
        Curle, and if You Doubt in Any Point, I'll——

S.^{ty}— *No, No, I'm satisfy'd 'twill be as clear as the*
        Sun.

                Exeunt.

      The Scene, Drogheda.
    Enter Mr Doyl, and his Damsel, Nelly,
   after them, the Tapster, with a Porringer
   of Burnt Brandy and a Mutton Pye.

Doyl.– *Come, Nelly, sitt down, and give me a kiss.*

Nelly.– *Fough, S.^r stand of, I profess You smell so ~*
        strong of Brandy and Tobacco, a body can't
        endure You.

166 *Doyle.–* *Nay, leave this peevish humour, and sit –*
down, if you knew who I'm to be, you'd be as
kind to me, as to the Smith's Boy.

Nell:– *Prithee, let go My Apron, and don't pull me so.*

Doyl.– *But you won't hear me; I tell you, Woman–*
as simple as I stand here, I'm to be a Fellow
of Dublin Colledge.

Nell.– *You, a Fellow, never the sooner for an hasty*
word: pray, keep your Filthy hand away, or I'll
Cry out so I will. Come, come, S^r don't think You
are with Peggy what do you call her.

Doyl.– *But I'll tell you, Nelly—*

Nell:– *Tell me no tellings; keep down your Fingers*
and do not you tear my Pettycoats. I'm afraid
'twas for what you did in the Blanketts, the
Dean made You stand in the White=Sheet.—

Doyl.– *Here Drawer, t'other Porringer of*
brandy, and so to Pay. That, and This Quar=
ter Cob will put you into a Little better humour;
Come, Lett us—now Lett us—

Nell:– *In Verity, Mr Doyl You have the Cunning=*
est Way with You of pleasing a Woeman—
You see how loath I am to refuse a Gentle=
man that's just on the Prick of Preferment;
but hold—There's somebody coming.
Enter the Drawer.

Drawer–   This makes Two and Two Pence now,   167
be sides the Nineteen and Seven Pence before
and My Mistress bid me tell you, she can trust
no longer.

Doyl.–   Why so, You Scoundrel?

Drawr.–   Because You putt her of, with Mandraks
from the King.

Doyl.–   Bid Your Mistress go hang herself, and
look for her Money, You Whore's Kitling.

(Throws the Mutton)
(Pye att him.—)

Exit Drawer, Maundring. —

Nell:–   Why so sleepy, Mr Doyl?

Doyl.–   Oh this scowering and Lying most Plagues me
Here, Nelly, here's to you.— Aw, ', I am damn'd
sleepy, I gad, Damn'd sleepy. (Drops asleep.)

Nelly.–   Lye there for a Drunken Sot. The Colle=
gioners are like to have a sweet Tool of Thee
for a Fellow. But Let Me see what We have
got in his Pocketts. Out upon the Scoundrell
nothing but a pair of Beads, Two Inches of
Tobacco and one of Pipe. = The Scene closes.==

And here We Leave him, and as he sleeps, take
a View of his Breeches, which I would describe,
but They have so many ends, I know not where
to Begin, he that wou'd presume to Mend them
wou'd Run the Risque of a Tincker Botching
a kettle, for, Hydra like out of one Hole wou'd come
three or four.

168   *You may Compare them to Jason's ship They have not one jot of their primitive stuff left: Or to Doctor Mercer's Yearn Stockings, that were darned into Worsted. The Lineing had serv'd a long Apprentieship for it self and therefore away it crept to sett up for it self att the Paper Mill; They were most Worn at the Codpiece, and least at the Pockets. The Crow that Borrowed Fea= thers from her Neighbours, is the liveing Emblem of these. Shou'd every Tavlor's Boy take his own Cabbage, Mr. Doyl would be an Heathen Philosopher. Doll — Kitchen comeing into his Kennel before He rose, thought he had purloyn'd her Mopp. by their shread's of all Nations, You wou'd have thought They belong'd — to One of the Free Masons that Built Babell; but by the Multiplicity of White fleas, You wou'd swear they had been Campaigning with the Vacancy. 'tis allmost incredible so many Cattle shou'd Thrive on so Bare a Pasture. Every Night he dares Venture them off, he's in danger of Looseing them: Once when he Lay without them, They Crept from the Garret to the Street Door, and had bid him adieu for Ever, but his Landlady seiz'd them by an habeas Corpus and brought them to him with a paire of Tongues. I Believe the Ladys for once are Tired of the Breeches; and Therefore, as Dean Glandee sayes This one Word of Comfort, and so have done. — One — Morning Crawling their Progress, They were devour'd By a Monkey, & the next day poor Pug dy'd of Pym's Disease.*

Quid obstat (Dii boni) quo minus Doc.ͬ Bladen 169
fiat Episcopus? Why should not Nick: Knight be Dean
of S.ͭ Patrick's? En hominem, Qui Sodalitium Ambit!
(ut inquit M.ͬ Griffith) Qui licet socius sit, Nollem ta=
men ut socius esset Meus: et jam in Mentem venit
mini, unde est quod nondum Reddiit socius ille Er=
raticus; ni Fallor causam assignat Barclæus ～
Poeta hunc in Modum. ══════════════

   Urbs Spatiosa, potens Opibus, Tectisq.ᵤₑ superba,
     O et præsidium, Deliciæq.ᵤₑ Meæ.
   Quicquid Mortalis fingit solertia Curæ,
     Vel Natura Suo parturit alma Sinu;
   Hæc Tu Sola dabis, &c.
══════════════════════════

        Anglice.
        ══════

Let formall Priests Look Grave and dull at home, ⎫
To Whom the worth of a Licentious Town   ⎬
Nor the Gay Blessings of a Court are known;   ⎭
Thither my Wiser Inclinations tend,
Where I a Chirping Bottle with a friend,
May Drink without Controul, nor stand in fear
Of ev'ry Saucy ill-bred Censurer.
Where I may strut along yᵉ Mall, Look Bigg
In Point-Cravat, and Toss a Flaxen Wigg:
Dress in a Gaudy Waistcoat, and May weare   ⎫
A Sword, Cock'd Hatt, Gold Fringe, and Whatsoe'er ⎬
The Libertine Town affords to Charm the Fair.   ⎭

170   *Miror quod his de Causis Magiſtᵉʳ Patrickson
non hue usque commoratus eſt Londini; ſed
        Quantum Quisqᵤₑ ſuâ nummorum habet in Areâ,
        Tantum habet et Gaudii—
Salve Magiſter; gratulor tibi Reduci; ſunt qui
Affirmant te pedeſtri itinere Londinum Versus
Ambulaſse, quod mihi equidem vix credibile Vide=
tur, perfacetus etenim Miles ſe tibi Socium præ=
buit, et jucundus Comes pro Vehiculo eſt a Good
Companion is as Good as a Coach.*

―――――――――――――――――――――――――

        *Enter Sʳ Michaell Craige, and
        another Alderman.*

        ―――――――――――――――

*Ald:-   I have been Man and Boy in this Town, Let
        me see, ſome Six and Fifty Years, and never ~
        knew the little Penny so hard to be gott as Now.
Sʳ Mich:-   Never diſpair, old Boy. We have a brave
        young Prince and the World's our Own.
Ald:-   Nay, I have not Remembered Salt Butter
        ſo ſcarce a Comodity, I know not the day When.
Sʳ Mich:-   Hang Sorrow—Boy, fill me a Glass of
        Wine—more—more Yett, fill it higher ſtill—
        So here, Father Grey Beard, here is a health
        to the Family of the Creaghs.
Ald:-   I pledge you, if it be ſack—But, now I ~
        think on't, Sʳ Michael, who was Your Father?*

S.ͬ Mich:– My Father was a Worthy Gentleman, 171
Inferior to none of his Rank, upon My honour.
Aldm:– Ads-hartlikins, you may be mistaken in that
I assure you.
S.ͬ Mich:– Mistaken S.ͬ; no, he was a Travelling Mer=
chant, One that saw More Towns than You have done
Chimneys.
Aldm:– But, under Favour, S.ͬ Michael, I have heard
Schollards say, he was Losopher?
S.ͬ Mich:– Ay, that May be too: He allwayws took, delight
to Carry Books about with him.
Aldm:– But take me along with You, You Reprehend
me not, They say he carryd Books on his Back.
S.ͬ Mich:– I say, I say he was a North Country Merchand
as I told You before. Come Drink Your Wine and
lett us be gone.   Exeunt.

Now You'll ask, to what end I brought all these on yᵉ
stage; to which I answer, I Brought them in by head
and shoulders, and out by head and shoulders, for –
nothing att all, as M.ͬ Bays did his Beasts.
Plurimis denuo salutatis et tot hominum Ordi=
nibus comiter Exceptis, videor forsan reprehensi=
one dignus, Quod Machaonas Omnes (Anglicè The –
Simplers) negligenter prætermisi: Cur autem.
Tristia horum fata, et Lacrymabilis Nova Me=
tamorphosis non vos diutius latent, cum certiores

259

172 facti eritis, Ingenuos hoſce Æsculapii Filios
in Plantas Transmigraſse, Injuriâ tamen non ~
ſum Arguendus, quod ſchemate Mortuos non Exce=
pi, the ſad Cauſes of whoſe Death are att Large de=
ſcribed in this
Heroick Poem.

A worthy Sage dwelt att Allhallowes,
That did defye all Goals and Gallowes;
His punctuall honeſty was ſuch,
Some Authors Write, he had too much:
And Lo! Actonio was his Name,
Actonio Loudly ſung by Fame;
A weight Inferiour to None,
For Ponderosity of Bumm.
And That took more Pains to go,
Than Courſe Jepſonio wou'd to Plow:
A Mortall Enemy to Punning,
Nor mightily inclin'd to Running,
He ſtill with Care did Guard his hart,
From all the Wounds of Cupid's Dart;
And Yett was plump, and ſoft confeſt,
All but his Petrify'd Breaſt:
That ſtill, alaſs! did ſtubborn prove
To all the Charming powers of Love:
In Town or Court, no Beauteous Dame
E'er Fann'd his Paſsion to a Flame,
For tho' he enjoy'd Luxurious Peace,
Melting his hours in holy eaſe;

He ne'er was *Vex'd* by that unruly *Member,* 173
But *Liv'd* as *Chaste* as *Cold December:*
Tho *Cupids* in his *Eyes* did *Play,*
Yet in his heart *Diana Lay.*
Lively and *sanguine* was his *Face,*
Tho *Phlegmatick* the other *Place:*
Colour as good as ever *struck,*
But *Other Things Bly'd* his *Look.*
    When *Drowsy Aurora* rub'd her *Eyes,*
And came down *stealing* from the *skies;*
Whilst that *Sol's Naggs* att *Mangers Tarry,*
Before the *Clerks* say, *Ave Mary:*
Actonio with his *Learned Friends,*
From Soaking Downy Bed Descends;
And with the *Charioteer's Afsistance.*
Heaving himself with *All Puifsance,*
He *Waddles* into *Coach Marine,*
And joggs his *Way,* a *Simpleing.*
And now *They* reach the *Inchanted Shore,*
Where Circe, in the *Days* of *Yore,*
By powerfull *Herbs Dispos'd* of *Doom,*
And Magick Spells did *Charm* the *Moon;*
Whilst Tyred here with th *Toils* of *Day*
Our Hero picking *Scions Lay:*
Rowling Securely on the *Grafs,*
Too *Nigh* a *fatal Precipice,*
A Down, A Down, A Down he drops
'twixt *Cruell* unrelenting *Rocks.*

174 Three times he made Effort to Rise
But Thrice; and Thrice wou'd not suffice;
His Weighty Crupper kept him down,
To Seas and Rocks to Make his Moan.

Dumq$_{ue}$ hie Vicini Maris auget Murmura,
Dum Liquido Dolore tritissimum plorat Fatum,
et Philosophorum Adagiis se Miserum solari Cona=
tur; Æsculapius Filii sui Quærelis Mitem præbens
Aurem, et Paternâ comotus Misericordiâ, Heroem
Nostrum in Umbilicum Veneris transformavit;
Socii Nequicquam plorant Amissum.
        Non illos Cereris, non illos Cura Quietis
        Abstrahere inde potest.—
Sed iteratis clamoribus surdum feriunt Littus; ægra
terq$_{ue}$ Quaterque pulsant pectora; Altâ Voce Deorum
Proclamant Tyrannidem, nec diutius insano Luc=
tui indulgent, sed pedibus Telluri Affixis, Pelli=
busq$_{ue}$ in Cortices Mutatis
        Nulli Color qui fuit Ante Manet.
Singulis Nova subeunt forma; et Mira quadam ~
Metamorphosi in Plantas proinde, ut hie sequitur
Transmutautur
Magister Downs in Cupressum.
Magister Smith in Pinguidinem (Anglice) Fatt Wort.
Magister Scroggs, in Hyacinhum. M.r Loyd in Quercum

Magiſter Aſh, into a Red-headed Poppy. 175
Sᵣ Fitzsimons, who allwayes dropt after; (as Our
Town of Berwick upon Tweed) into a Thiſtle,
which ſtill retains its primitive Roughneſs.
Magiſter Sayers in Narciſsum, de Quo olim Buchan=
anus ſci.

    Nescio an inspexti Narciſsi, Poſthume, Fontem
    Hoc scio, Deliras Poſthume, amore tui.
    Attamen Hui Merito; nam quod Male ſanus amavit,
    Ante Quidem id Multis causa Furoris erat:
    At tua non paulo eſt Major Vesania, qui te
    Sed ſine Rivali, Poſthume, ſolus Amas.
Sed dicat mihi Quis, Quod in Totâ hac Coronâ, vel ~
potius Crowdo et Preſso, nondum Vidi Dominum
Terrill, ni fallor; if he be not here, he's att home with
his Wife Who to gain intirely his Affections ſent ~
him this Stratagemicall Epiſtle. ════════
    The Argument
    ══════

The Quondam Widow, Sᵣ Terrill's Miſtres
hearing he had laid Siege to the Book Binder's
Siſter, and therefore fearing he ſhould Give
her the Willow, partly to be Reveng'd of
her Rivall, partly to ſecure him to herſelf
writes to him This Epiſtle:
══════════════

"Sᵣ I am inform'd you design to Bind yourſelf
"to the Stationer's Siſter: if ſo, take it from a friend,

176   *"She's a Gentlewoeman in Folio, and will confe=*
"quently will be very tedious to a young ftudent. I ~
"was concern'd to hear the Crafty Citifsen inten=
"ded to put into your hands the Lumber of His
"Shop; and therefore intreat you, if you have any
"kindnefs for Your Self, to have nothing to do with
"that Mufty Piece, Whofe Worm-Eaten Cover may
"Inform you, fhe has been Cheapen'd above thefe
"Twenty Years, and the Reason fhe did not go off
"is, fhe was found fo Old and Thumb'd, that fhe was
"not fitt to be perus'd; and of fo little Value, that
"None thought her Worthy the Prefs. Besides, Sᵣ ~
"She has liv'd fome time in a Learn'd House, where
"it may be presum'd for good reasons, that fome
"of the Young Scholars for their Curiosity, might
"ruftle her Leaves. I what I have faid cannot
"difsuade you, do but Turn her over carefully
"and tis Very probable You'll find fhe has been
"abused att leaft in the fheets, if not att the fetting
"forth of a New Edition Blotted in the Imprefsion.
                    Sᵣ   Your Humᵇˡᵉ Servᵗ
                    Jane Banks.

And now belike I have made a fair ~
afternoon's f, on't, I have not left myfelf One
friend of the Mammon of Unrighteousnes; if I
go to the Kitchen, the Steward will be My Enemy
as long as he Breathes; if to the Cellar, the Butler
will dash My ale with Water, and the Clerk of the

Buttery will ſcore up My Offences five-fold; 177
If I betake My Self to the library, Ridley's Ghoſt
will haunt me, for ſcandallizing him with the
name of Free Maſon: if I flye to the Divines for
ſuccour; Lo! Dean Mandby and Arch-Deacon Bay=
nard will pervert me. Doctr King will Break
my head, becauſe I am a Priſcian; and Dr Foy's ~
ſo full of ſpleen He'll Worry Me. Mrs Horncaſtle
and Sr Madison will talk with Me. Mother Jen=
kinſon Won't furnish me with Cale and Bacon
on Chriſtmaſs day, and Doctor Loftus will Bite
me. The Virtuoſi will ſett their Brains a Work
for Gimcracks to pull My Eyes out; The Free Ma=
ſons will banish me their Lodge, and Barr Me
the happineſs of kiſsing long Law-
rence. And the

Aſtronomers won't allow me one

Good ſtar;

nor inform me when the ſun will be

Totally Eclips'd that I may provide

My ſelf with Candles. Mr Loftus and

Mr Loyd will Noſe me. Mr Allen will

eat me without ſalt, Dr Acton too

I fear will Fall on Me. Nay, ye very

Provoſt will ſhake his head att me

and ſcowre away from Me, but

that which makes my Calamity

moſt insupportable, and me

Weary of Your Company, is, that in all my Tribula-
tion
You do nothing but Laugh att Me; and Therefore, I take My
Leave.

First published: *Heredom*, 24 (2016)

The Post Boy Sham Exposure of 1723

Then let us laugh, since we've impos'd
On those who make a Pother,

And cry, the Secret is disclos'd
By some false-hearted Brother :

The mighty Secret gain'd, they boak,
From Pok-Boy, or from Flying-Post.

With a fal, &c.

"Song VI"
A Collection of the Songs of Masons, 1734

Every now and then "Lady Luck" smiles upon your research. Such was the case in November 1998 when I visited by good friend and brother, Yasha Beresiner, Past Mater of Quatuor Coronati Lodge. He is a dealer in rare paper items—maps, prints, etc., and his London shop is a delight to visit. He had recently acquired the December 26–28, 1723, edition of a London newspaper, *The Post Boy*, which had an "exposure" of Masonic ritual, a catechism of forty-two questions and answers.

When I first looked at the approximately 81/2"′14" single sheet, I said, "Oh, this is '*A Mason's Examination*' from *The Flying-Post*, the first published Masonic catechism." A few minutes study proved me wrong (an experience I'm all too familiar with). Yasha's paper was *The Post Boy*, not *The Flying Post*, and it referred to the earlier "*A Mason's Examination*" (so-named by R.F. Gould in his *History of Freemasonry*). Yasha and I then checked Douglas Knoop, G.P. Jones, and Douglas Hamer's *The Early Masonic Catechisms* and *Early Masonic Pamphlets*, two books which catalog every early major publication on freemasonry. What we found was a shock to us.

Background[1]

In November 1998, a Channel Island dealer in old newspapers sold Bro. Beresiner a copy of *The Post Boy*, no. 5373 dated "Thursday December 26

---

1   Much of the material from the next two sections is taken verbatim from Yasha Beres-

to Saturday December 28, 1723." Halfway through the second column and ending nearly at the end of the next on the reverse side of the sheet is a letter addressed "To the Author of the Post-Boy" and signed "Yours &c. A. B." The catechism that follows is intended clearly to look like an exposure of masonic ritual to readers who are not freemasons. The author of the letter makes reference to the earlier and first such disclosure which had appeared in *The Flying Post* in April of the same year.[2] A facsimile of the newspaper is published with this volume of *Heredom* and a transcription of the catechism follows this article. The newspaper itself is now owned by the library of the Supreme Council 33°, S.J., Washington, D.C.

Identification

The text of the catechism was unknown previously and the issue no. 5373 of the newspaper is exceedingly rare. Searches in the well-known Burney[3] and Nichols[4] collections, in the British Library and the Bodleian Library, respectively, in other major U.K. library collections, and in similar repositories in the United States resulted in a complete failure to trace a copy of this issue of *The Post Boy*. A search in the "Union List of Serials" held by the Smithsonian Institute in Washington, DC revealed that twelve American libraries have holdings of *The Post Boy*. None had a copy of issue no. 5373.[5]

The Post Boy

The Post Boy was first published in London on September 28, 1695, under the ownership of "A. Roper." Initially, it appeared three times a week.

---

iner, "The 'Sham Exposure' in *The Post Boy*, December 1723: A Discovery," *Ars Quatuor Coronatorum (AQC)* 111 (1998): 198–202, and is reprinted with the permission of the author and of the Quatuor Coronati Lodge No. 2076, London. Bro. Beresiner comments extensively on newspapers and other ephemeral publications dealing with Freemasonry in his inaugural address, "Aspects of Masonic Ephemera ... Before 1813," in the same volume, 1–23.

2   *The Flying Post, or Post-Master,* no. 4712, 11–23 April 1723, anonymous letter, untitled and commonly referred to as *A Mason's Examination.*

3   The Burney Collection of Newspapers. The Library of Rev. Dr. Charles Burney, D.D. (1757–1817) was purchased by the British Museum in 1818 for the sum of £13,500! It consisted of, among other things, 700 volumes of newspapers dating from 1603 to 1818. The collection is now kept in the British Library Newspapers Collection (Colindale).

4   The John Nichols Collection is in the Bodleian Library, Oxford.

5   Bro. David B. Board provided the search of the Smithsonian collection.

The first editor was L. Beardwell who was based at Black Friars. In 1705, the well-known and versatile Abel Boyer in Fleet Street took over as editor. From the start, inclusive of this issue in question, the printer was George James, based in Little Britain and the political inclinations of the newspaper were toward the Tory party.

The Post Boy figures prominently in the early published references to the fraternity, carrying the first such publication.

> But within a very few weeks of the latter advertisement appearing [for a "Society in Hampstead" which Bro. Robbins believed was a veiled allusion to Freemasonry], Freemasonry—seemingly of its own volition—came for the first time into the open; and the earliest newspaper record of any of its proceedings is the following paragraph, published in the *Post-Boy* of June 24ᵗʰ–27ᵗʰ, 1721, and copied into two of the weekly journals the following Saturday.

There was a Meeting on Saturday last [June 24ᵗʰ] at Stationers Hall of between two and three hundred of the ancient Fraternity of Free-Masons, who had a splendid Dinner, and Musick. Several Noblemen and Gentlemen were present at this Meeting, and his Grace the Duke of Montague was unanimously chosen Master for the ensuing Year, and Dr. Beale Sub-Master. The Reverend Dr. Desaguliers made a Speech suitable to the Occasion.[6]

Further references and advertisements quickly followed in *The Post Boy*.

> [A] further fillip was given to such talk [about Freemasonry] a very little later, by the publication in the Post-Boy of March 25ᵗʰ, 1722–3, of the announcement that
>> This evening [Tuesday, March 5ᵗʰ] the corpse of that worthy FREE MASON, Sir Christopher Wren, Knight, is to be interr'd under the dome of St. Paul's Cathedral. ...
>
> The brochure [*The Free-Masons: An Hudibrastick Poem*] was launched with an amount of enterprise unusual in those days, for its advertisement is to be found also in the *Post-Boy* of February 14ᵗʰ–16ᵗʰ, [1723]. ...

---

6   Alfred F. Robbins, "The Earliest years of English Organized Freemasonry," AQC 22 (1909), 68.

[A]n event of high importance in our history was thus advertized in the *Post-Boy* of February 26th–28th, 1722–3,
This day is publish'd
The CONSTITUTIONS of the FREE-MASONS.[7]

The advertisement for Anderson's *Constitutions* is headed "This day is published. ..." and thus gives an exact date for the publication of the *Constitutions*. The dual year "1722–3" is given because until 1752, the civil or legal year began on March 25 under the "Old Style" of calendar.

The Tax Stamp

In August 1712, a tax of one half-penny was imposed on all English newspapers and this appears on the top left-hand side of the second page of *The Post Boy*. The distinctive red stamped design, unique to English newspapers, consists of a Royal "Rose of England" below a crown device within a decorative border. It was designed by John Rollos, engraver to the King, and often incorporates a die number below the main design. This is "402" in the case of the issue in question. The publishers would have transported the blank sheets to the Stamp Office in Lincoln's Inn for the tax stamp to be applied on each sheet. After that the text of the newspaper would have been printed thereon.

There were a total of twenty-five tax dies on each copper plate sheet, indicating that this issue of *The Post Boy* would have been stamped from plate no. 17 which is on record as that plate used for a period of one year from June 1723. A record was kept at the Stamp Office matching the die number to the source for which it was used. These records can be inspected in the British Library.

The highest die number for the half-penny tax used on newspapers would have been "2350," reached in 1757 when the tax was increased to one penny (as was frequently the case when war broke out and additional revenues were need by the government for the war effort). Rollos died in 1743 and was replaced by John Pine whose new designs for the tax stamp were used, with minor alterations, mainly in the thickness of the die numbering and more "stoic" designs in general. Since each tax stamp was hand-engraved individually, in spite of the availability of templates, no two tax stamps are absolutely identical.

---

7   Robbins, 74, 75, 75–76.

Titles

The Post Boy continued intermittently until September 30, 1728. At its peak circulation in the first two decades of the eighteenth century, it was one of four major newspapers published in London in quantities of between 3,000 and 4,000 copies per issue. The publishers took pride in their special coverage of news from outside England and this factor was reflected in the changes in the title and the addition of subtitles at different periods:

- *The Post Boy, Foreign and Domestick*
- *Post Boy, With Foreign and Domestick News*
- *Post Boy and the Historic Account*
- *Post Boy, the Freshest Advices, Foreign and Domestick*
- *Daily Post Boy*

Contemporary References

In *The Free-Mason's Accusation and Defence* (1726),[8] a father, purportedly writing to his son, makes an extended reference to the "examination" of the Freemasons published in *The Post Boy*. The relevant statement begins as follows:

I remember, when I was last in Town, there was a Specimen of their Examinations published in the Post-Boy; but so industrious were the Masons to suppress it that in a Week's time not one of the Papers was to be found; where-ever they saw 'em they made away with them.

The author continues at length on the methods used by the freemasons to do away with all available copies of the newspaper. He states "I cannot change my Mind with the Date of the Paper," and urges his son to obtain a copy "by any Means." He continues, stating that the freemasons were angered by the publication, although they pretended not to give it any importance and that they "presently put out a sham Discovery to invalidate the other." He ends this part of his letter by stating that "a friend and Mason let me understand that this was a genuine Discovery."

---

8 An anonymous anti-masonic publication comprising six letters between father and son, three supposedly written by the former attacking the Craft and the other three are feeble responses by the latter.

"Song VI" of *A Collection of the Songs of Masons*, 1734, contains a stanza (reprinted at the beginning of this article) referring to "the mighty secret" gained "from *Post Boy* or from *Flying Post*."[9] This song with references to *The Post Boy* was slightly rewritten to become "The Swordbearer's Song" in Anderson's *Constitutions* of 1738.

Thus, we see that *The Post Boy* exposure was well known in its day, even if the masons were accused of "making away" with all copies of the newspaper. This accusation could be supported by the existence of only one known copy of No. 5373. The reference to only two exposures in "Song VI" and "The Swordbearer's Song" would indicate the publications were familiar to all (or perhaps that their titles fit the rhyme and meter of the song).

Explaning the Evidence

The Original Interpretation

Knoop, Jones, and Hamer in their introduction to *Early Masonic Pamphlets* stated that no issue of *The Post Boy* containing the "examination" had been traced by them and they proceeded with several suggestions to explain this.

- *The Briscoe Pamphlet* (1726)[10] contains the "sham discovery" alluded to in *The FreeMason's Accusation and Defence* detailed above.

- This "sham discovery" in the *Briscoe Pamphlet* was intended to invalidate the "examination" in *The Post Boy*.

- The author of *The Free-mason's Accusation and Defence* may have confused *The Post Boy* with *The Flying Post* of April 11–13, 1723, in which, as mentioned above, the well-known *A Mason's Examination* appeared first.

- The same "examination" may have appeared in both *The Post Boy* and *The Flying Post*.

- Two different "examinations" appeared, one in *The Post Boy* and the other in *The Flying Post*.

A preliminary examination of the text in *The Post Boy* led to be it being misidentified with *A Mason's Examination* (so named by Gould) from

---

9 Douglas Knoop, et al., *Early Masonic Pamphlets* (1944; reprint, London: Q.C. Correspondence Circle, 1978), 316–24.

10 *The Briscoe Pamphlet* is undated though the first issue is established to have been published in 1724. Knoop, *Early Masonic Pamphlets*, 111–30.

The Flying Post. After consulting *Early Masonic Pamphlets*, however, it was quickly realized just what a wonderful discovery this was because it presented an opportunity to analyze what is now the second oldest published exposure of Freemasonry: a catechetical examination of forty-two questions and answers.

With no copy of *The Post Boy* to hand, Knoop, Jones, and Hamer gave their five possible explanations for the comments in *The Free-Mason's Accusation and Defence*. While it is impossible to know what the author of the Accusation meant by "sham discovery," the phrase can be taken to mean "a misleading publication, appearing as a discovery, and intended to lead readers away from the real secrets of the Craft." On that basis, their first explanation is rejected.

Except for the "come-on" explanation of an accidental discovery of a secret history, the Briscoe Pamphlet is just another version of the Old Charges, surely well known and available in 1724. The second explanation is weak as *The Post Boy* examination is itself subtly flawed and needs no further invalidation.

The third explanation is quite possible as *The Post Boy* examination differs in essentials from almost all other catechisms, but *The Flying Post* is in agreement with the majority. Thus, if a freemason of the day described a 1723 newspaper examination as a genuine "discovery," he surely was referring to *The Flying Post*.

The fourth explanation is absolutely wrong and their fifth is entirely correct.

A Reinterpretation in Light of New Evidence

The Post Boy catechism is a well-written mixture of repetitions of neutral questions from other catechisms, logical extensions of those questions, and subtly different answers that disagree with other published exposures and manuscript catechisms. I have categorized the forty-two questions and answers as *Right and Consistent, Right but Inconsistent,* or *Wrong*.

A question and answer is *Right* if it "sounds right." That is, it's language and symbolism is in general agreement known masonic usages. It is *Consistent* if it agrees with at least one other manuscript or published catechism. It is *Inconsistent* if it is unlike any other manuscript or catechism. For example, question 1, "Q. Are you one of us? A. I'll stand Tryal," is in general agreement with several other catechisms from 1730 to 1762. It is classified as

Right and Consistent. Question 3, however, "Q. What's your Name? A. Base or Capital, according to my Degree," sounds right because it uses architectural terminology, but there is no other known usage of those terms. Thus, it is classified at *Right but Inconsistent.* Presumably, a brother seeking admission to a 1720 lodge would be accepted if he gave right but inconsistent answers to an examination, as long as he gives correct answers to the few essential questions.

A question is *Wrong* if it deals with an essential point of identification—a secret word, for example—and it disagrees with all other evidence. For example, question 34, "Q. What is the Apprentice's Word? A. Babel," disagrees with every other early revelation of masonic secrets, which give *Boaz* at the apprentice's word. Someone saying his name was "base or capital," would probably be admitted as a visitor, but if he gave *Babel* as the apprentice's word, he would be immediately rejected as an imposter.

For purposes of this analysis, I have relied on Knoop, Jones, and Hamer's *The Early Masonic Catechisms* and *Early Masonic Pamphlets* and compared their manuscripts, catechisms, and pamphlets from *The Edinburgh Register Register Ms.,* 1696, through *Jachin and Boaz,* 1762. My idea is that any knowledge of masonry published in this period would likely have been available to the author of *The Post Boy* in 1723.

By my analysis of the forty-two questions, twenty-three are right and consistent, fourteen are right but inconsistent, and five are wrong:

> *Right and Consistent:* 1, 2, 5, 6, 8*, 9*, 16, 17, 18, 20, 21, 24, 26, 27, 28, 29, 30, 31, 32, 33, 37, 40, 41
> *Right but Inconsistent:* 7, 10, 11, 12, 13, 14, 15, 19, 22, 23, 25⁺, 38, 39, 42
> *Wrong:* 3, 4, 34, 35, 36
> *positive, reflecting well on masonry; ⁺negative

The Post Boy catechism is a sham, "a misleading publication appearing as a discovery, intended to lead readers away from the real secrets of the Craft." A casual reader of this second exposure of masonic "secrets" would find questions and answers that mostly agree with the previously published examination in *The Flying Post* and with what we can conclude were generally held beliefs about masonry. The *Wrong* answers, however, are "fatally" wrong for anyone trying to pass themselves off as a true freemason, and would lead to their immediate exposure. The effect of *The Post Boy* catechism is at the least to confuse the reader about what are the secrets of masonry.

The questions that remain and which cannot be definitely answered are: Who prepared this catechism and why? It is possible that it was either

- a practical joke prepared by some wits who were relying on the published secrets of the freemasonry, or

- a disinformation campaign by freemasons designed to misdirect the general public from their workings of the period.

I conclude that it was a clever disinformation campaign by the freemasons. First, the tone of the questions is almost entirely positive, leaving the reader with a favorable image of the Craft. Second, the only really wrong answers are "fatally" wrong and would identify anyone relying on them as an impostor. Third, there are references of the period to "sham" or "mock" exposures which until now have not been identified. *The Free-Mason Accusation and Defence*, 1726, claims that the masons "put out a sham Discovery to invalidate the other," but it also claims "*the Post-Boy* is a genuine Discovery." I believe that the author of the *Accusation* confused *The Post Boy* with the *Flying Post* in making the latter claim. *A Letter from the Grand Mistress of Female Free-Masons*, 1724, refers to "a Sheet full of Mock-Masonry, purely to puzzel and banter the Town," though the examples of "false Signs and Words" it gives do not agree with those given in *The Post Boy*.

Finally, there is only one extant copy of *The Post Boy* No. 5373. This entirely agrees with the charge in the Accusation that

> so industrious were the Masons to suppress it, that in a Week's time not one of the Papers was to be found; where-ever they saw 'em they made away with them. They went from Coffee-house to Coffee-house, and tore them privately out of the Books. Those they could come at so easily they bought, even at the extravagant Price of 2s. 6d. and 5s. a Paper. By this means there is hardly one to be met with.

I imagine a group of freemasons carefully writing the catechism, "leaking" it to *The Post Boy*, and then asking their brothers to gather up some of the copies of the paper to give the impression the masons were concerned about it. The total absence of copies can be explained by over-zealous brothers gathering up too many issues.

Analysis of the Questions

In the analysis that follows I have relied on Knoop, Jones, and Hamer's *The Early Masonic Catechisms* (EMC) and *Early Masonic Pamphlets* (EMP), the Masonic Book Club's reprints of Anderson's *Constitutions* of 1723 and 1738, *Masonry Dissected, Three Distinct Knocks,* and *Jachin and Boaz,* and Wallace McLeod's *The Old Charges.* It is my hope that future researchers will be able to build on my preliminary analysis of this unique document.

[1] Q. Are you one of us ? A. I'll kand Tryal.

[2] Q. How will you be try'd ? A. By Quekion and Answer.

These questions agree in spirit with most of the catechisms from 1730 to 1760, where the questioner is invited to prove or disprove the examinee, presumably with further questions. Prior to that date, the response seems to have been a simple positive assertion.

Right and Consistent

> Quest. 1 Are you a mason. Answer yes
> *The Edinburgh Register House Ms.,* 1696 (EMC, 31)
>
> Quest. 1. Are yow a Mason? Ans^r, Yes indeed that I am.
> *Chetwode Crawley Ms.,* c. 1700 (EMC, 37)
>
> 1 Are you a Masone, Answer Yes endeed that I am
> *The Kevan Ms.,* c. 1714–20 (EMC, 42)
>
> (Quest^n.) are you a mason (Answ^{er}) yes I am a freemason
> *Sloane Ms.* 3329, c. 1700 (EMC, 47)
>
> Q. Are you a Master-Mason? A. I am; try me, prove, disprove me if you can.
> *Masonry Dissected,* 1730, 25
>
> Q. Are you a Mason? A. I am.
> *The Mystery of Free-Masonry,* 1730 (EMC, 154)
>
> Q. Are you a Mason. A. I am so taken to be Among Brothers & fellows.
> *Wilkinson Ms.,* 1724–30 (EMC, 121)

Mas. Brother, are you a Fellow-Craft? Ans. I am; try me, prove me.
Three Distinct Knocks, 1760, 39

Mas. Brother, are you a Fellow Craft? Ans. I am. Try me, prove me.
Jachin and Boaz, 1762, 30

[3] Q. What's your Name ? A. Base or Capital, according to my Degree.

The answer to this question uses architectural terminology, which "sounds" masonic. The answer seems right, but there is no comparable response in any other catechism. The most frequent name given by the catechisms is Jachin. This is an example of a test question that could be innocently asked in a public setting to determine if someone were a Mason. The answer of "Base or Capital" is in total disagreement with all other catechisms.

Wrong

... to you good fellow wᵗ is your name (A) J or B.
Sloane Ms. 3329, c. 1700 (EMC, 48)

Q. I greet you well Brother what is your Name. A. Jachin
The Whole Institutition of Masonry, 1724 (EMC, 81)

I greet you well Brother, God's Greeting be at our Meeting, what is your Name answer Jachin.
The Whole Institutions of Free-Masons Opened, 1725 (EMC, 87)

I greet you well brother craveing your name—answere J and the other is to say his is B.
Graham Ms., 1726 (EMC, 90)

Ex. What's a Master-Mason Nam'd?
R. Cassia is my name and from a Just and Perfect Lodge I came.
Masonry Dissected, 1730, 29.

[4] Q. From whence come you ? A. From Solomon's Temple.

The catechisms that have this question all agree that the answer is from a Lodge of St. John. This is another example of a test question in total disagreement with all other catechisms.

Wrong

Q. From whence came You. A. I came from a Right Worshipful Lodge of Masters and Fellows belonging to Holy St. John.

The Whole Institution of Masonry, 1724 (EMC, 81)

The Sallutation is as ffollows—ffrom whence came you—I came ffrom a right worshipfull Lodge of Masters and ffelows belonging to God and holy saint John....
Graham Ms., 1726 (EMC 90)

Q. Whence Come you A. from the Holy Lodge of S^t. Iohn
The *Wilkinson Ms.*, 1724–30 (EMC, 137)

Q. From whence came you? A. From the Holy Lodge of St. John's. ...
Ex. Of the Right Worshipful and Holy Lodge of St. John's. Resp. From whence I came.
Masonry Dissected, 1730, 9, 23

[5] Q. What did you see there ? A. A folded square Paper.

[6] Q. What was the Use of that Paper ? A. It was a Pasport to the Sancum Sancorum, and all the private Parts of the Temple.

These two questions seem to allude to an early secret or perceived secret of masons. No less than five catechisms indicate that a Mason must respond to the receipt of a paper square—either folded or cut like a mason's square. Wallace McLeod, commenting on *An Hudibrastick Poem*, says the idea the paper must be folded in a square of is "a misunderstanding of a genuine secret" (W. McLeod, *The Grand Design*, 73). Question 5 conforms to the idea that a paper square is important to masons, and question 6 gives a nice explanation of it.

 Right and Consistent

Another signe is by lending you a crooked pin or a bit of paper cut in the forme of a Square....
Sloane Ms. 3329, c. 1700, (EMC, 46)

A MASON, when he needs must drink,
Sends Letter, without Pen and Ink,
Unto some Brother, who's at hand,
And does the Message understand;
The Paper's of the Shape that's square,
Thrice-folded with the nicest Care; ...
An Hudibrastick Poem, 1722/23 (EMP, 89)

what other tenours did your oath Cary—my second was to obey God

and all true Squares made or sent from a brother....
Graham Ms., 1726 (EMC, 91)

As, if one were in a company, and to send for another mason, he does
it by sending a piece of paper, with a square point folded in at the
corner....
A Mason's Confession, (? 1727) 1756 (EMC, 104)

Sim. Sr. I have just now received inclosed in a letter a piece of Paper in
this form
Dialogue between Simon and Philip, c. 1740 (EMC, 176)

[7] Q. What office did you bear there ? A. I was Scali-ger, or Ladder-Bearer,
at the Makings.

There is no office of Scaliger or Ladder-Bearer mentioned in any catechism.
The word *Scaliger* seems to be derived from the Latin word for *ladder, sca-
lae*. (I am indebted to Wallace McLeod for this observation.) Anderson's
Constitutions of 1738 include "The Swordbearer's Song," so a Ladder Bearer
isn't out of place, even if it appears no where else. Hogarth's 1742 painting,
"The Mysteries of Masonry Brought to Light by the Gormogons," shows a
hapless candidate carrying a ladder with his head between two rungs.

Right but Inconsistent

[8] Q. How many Engagements have you ? A. Five.

[9] Q. Which are they ? A. Firk, to be true to the King and the Grand Maker. 2dly, Not to meddle with Politicks or Disputes about Religion in the
Lodge. 3dly, Not to abuse or lander one another. 4thly, To answer all Signs
and Tokens. 5thly, To keep the Secrets and be Merry and Wise.

The catechisms are consistent that masons have either five "points" or
"points of fellowship," though questions eight and nine rather seem to refer to five duties of a mason. These duties or engagements agree in general
with the "Old Charges" and other lists of duties of masons, and they are
admirable civic virtues.

Right, Consistent, and Positive

Q. How many proper Points [pertain to a Free-Mason]? A. Five; Foot
to Foot, Knee to Knee, Hand to Hand, Heart to Heart, and Ear to Ear.
The Grand Mystery of Free- Masons Discover'd, 1724 (EMC, 79)

… at the ffull and totall agreement thereof to ffollow with five points of ffree Masons fellowshipe which is ffoot to ffoot knee to knee breast to breast cheeck to cheeck and hand to Back which ffive points hath refferance to the ffive cheife signes which is head ffoot body hand and heart and allso to the ffive points off artitectur and allso to the ffive orders of Masonry yet takes thire strength ffrom five primitive one devine and ffour temporall which is as ffollows ffirst christ the chiefe and Cornerston secondly Peter called Cephas thirdly moses who cutte the commands ffourthly Bazalliell the best of Masons ffiffthly hiram who was ffilled with wisdom and understanding
Graham Ms., 1726 (EMC, 95–96)

Ex. What are they [the Five Points of Fellowship]? Hand to Hand, Foot to Foot, Cheek to Cheek, Knee to Knee, and Hand to Back.
Masonry Dissected, 1730, 28

[Chapter Nineteen. The Charges General]
1 The first charge is that ye shall be true men to God and the Holy Church; and that ye use no error not heresy, by your understanding or by discreet or wise men's teaching.
2 and also that ye shall be true liege men to the King without treason or falsehood; and that ye know no treason or treachery, but that ye amend it if ye may, or else warn the King or his council thereof.
3 And also ye shall be true each one to another; that is to say, to every Master and Fellow of the Craft of Masonry that be Masons allowed, ye shall do to them as ye would they should do to you.
4 and also that every Mason keep true counsel of lodge and of chamber, and all other counsel that ought to be kept by the way of Masonry.
…
7 And also you shall call Masons your Fellows or Brethren, and no other foul name.…
"A Tentative Reconstruction of the 'Standard Original' of the Old Charges [1520/83] in Modern Spelling," *The Old Charges,* 47–48.

THE FREE-MASON'S OATH. You must serve God according to the best of your Knowledge and Institution, and be a true Leige Man to the King, and help and assist any Brother as far as your Ability will allow.…
The Grand Mystery of Free-Masons Discover'd, 1724 (EMC, 79)

... Euclydes gave them these Admonitions following:

I. To be true to their King.

II. To be true to the Master they serve.

III To be true and love one another.

IV. Not to miscall one another, &c.

...

I will, by God's Grace, begin the Charge.

I. I am to admonish you to honour God in his holy Church. ...

II. To be true to our Sovereign Lodge the King, his Heirs and lawful Successors; committing no Treason, Misprision of Treason, or Felony; and if any Man shall commit Treason that you know of, you shall forthwith give Notice thereof to his Majesty, his Privy Counsellors, or some other Person that hath Commission to enquire thereof.

III. You shall be true to your Fellows and Brethren of the Science of Masonry, and do unto them as you would be done unto.

IV. You shall keep Secret the obscure and intricate Parts of the Science, not disclosing them to any but such as study and use the same.

...

XVII. You shall not slander any of your Fellows behind their Backs, to impair their Temporal Estate or good Name.

Roberts Constitutions, 1722 (EMP, 76, 79)

Here followeth the Worth and Godly OATH of MASONS.

...

1. YOU shall be a True Man to God, and to the Holy Church; and that you use no Error, nor Heresy by your Understanding, or by the teaching of Men.

2. YOU shall bear true Agement to the King, without Treason, or Falshood.

3. AND that you know no Treason, but may amend it, if you may; or else warn the King, or his lawful Successors, or their Council thereof.

4. YOU shall be True one to another.

The Briscoe Pamphlet, 1724 (EMP, 117–18)

[10] Q. How do you begin to make a Mason? A. By building the Temple.

[11] Q. Who are the Four Corner Stones ? A. Four Fellow-Craftsmen,

[12] Q. Who are the four Capitals ? A. Four 'Prentices.

[13] Q. Who is Cupola ? A. The new Brother.

[14] Q. How high do you raise him ? A. Above Ground.

[15] Q. Who turns the Ladder ? A. The Junior Warden.

These six questions "sound right" because they contain architectural terms and give a hint of hazing new candidates. However, they have no counterparts in any catechisms. It's odd that the Junior Warden would turn the ladder and not the Ladder-Bearer.

Right but Inconsistent

[16] Q. What's the Sword-Bearer's buiness ? A. To examine and see that none but Men enter the Lodge.

While Anderson's *Constitutions* of 1738 has a "Sword Bearer's Song," there is no office of Sword Bearer per se mentioned in the catechisms. This is probably an allusion to the Tyler who guards the Lodge with a sword and keeps out all who are not members. He would incidently see that none but men enter the Lodge.

Right and Consistent

[17] Q. What's the Reason Women are not admitted into your Society ? A. Because they can't keep a Secret.

Only two catechisms contain any reason for limiting masonic membership to men, and both seem designed to hurt the fraternity. One says women are "incapable of Fellowship" and the other that their "innate curiosity" secluded the mysteries of masonry from them.

Right and Consistent

> These mean Wretches … are egg'd on by some silly Women , who (because for good Reasons their Sex are by the Constitutions judged incapable of Fellowship) are therefore nettled and seek revenge.
> *A Mason's Examination*, 1723, EMC 71–2

> The women, in particular, have a strange Opinion of them [Freemasons]; by them they are concluded utter Enemies to the Fair Sex, who, for the generality, have them in the greatest Abhorence. …
> That the Ladies are a little jealous of the Fraternity is natural, from their Innate Curiosity, by reason the Mysteries of Masonry are secluded from that Sex. …
> *Free-Masons Accusation and Defence*, 1726 (EMP, 159, 161)

[18] Q. What's the Master's Buiness ? A. To give the Charges, receive the Fees, and teach the Lodge the Art of Masonry.

No catechism gives these explicit duties to the Master, but since he asks all of the catechism questions, he is giving the charges and teaching the Lodge. The receipt of fees would be handled today by the Treasurer or Secretary, but it is not inappropriate for the Master to have had this duty.

Right and Consistent

> Mas. Why should the Master represent the Pillar of Wisdom? Ans. Because he gives instructions to the Crafts to carry on their Work in a proper manner with good harmony.
> *Three Distinct Knocks*, 1760, 33

[19] Q. What is done before the demolihing? A. The ham Words are taught by the Senior Warden.

The word "demolish" is not used in any catechisms, but it presumably refers to closing the lodge, perhaps symbolically "demolishing" it? Neither are "sham words" referred to in any other catechism. *The Grand Mystery Laid Open* gives the words Laylah Illallah and Whosly Powe Tigwawtubby, which are clearly gibberish, sham words, but not identified as such. It's possible that the answer is a sly confession of what this catechism is offering its readers.

Right but Inconsistent

> What is God called? Laylah Illallah.... What is the Square Call'd? Whosly Powu Tigwawtubby....
> *The Grand Mystery Laid Open*, 1726 (EMC, 97–8)

[20] Q. What do you do when you ?rt come into the Lodge ? A. I crook my Arm and bend my Foot.

Where the description of a candidate's posture is given, it seems to involve odd posture and foot and arm positions.

Right and Consistent

> [H]e is to behold a thousand different Postures and Grimaces, all of which he must exactly imitate, or undergo the Discipline till he does.
> *A Mason's Examination*, 1723 (EMC, 72)

Q. How did he make you a Mason? A. With my bare-bended Knee and Body within the Square … my naked Right Hand on the Holy Bible.…
Masonry Dissected, 1730, 11

Mas. What was the Instructions he gave you? Ans. He taught me to take one Step upon the First Step of a right Angle oblong Square, with my left Knee bare bent, my Body upright, my Right foot forming a Square.…
Three Distinct Knocks, 1760, 19

Mas. What Instructions did he give you? Ans. He taught me … to take two Steps upon the second Step of a Right angled oblong Square, with my Right Knee bent bare, my Left Foot forming a square, my Body upright, my Right Hand on the Holy Bible, my Left Arm supported by the Point of the Compasses, forming a Square; where I took the Obligation of a Fellow Craft.
Jachin and Boaz, 1762, 31–32

[21] Q. Which way were you brought into the Lodge ? A. Between the Wardens blind-folded.

The catechisms agree that the candidate is blindfolded and conducted by the two Wardens.

Right and Consistent

Then he is blind-folded and the Ceremony of—is performed.
A Mason's Examination, 1723 (EMC, 72)

who Conducted you into the Lodge—the warden and oldest fellow craft—
Graham Ms., 1726 (EMC, 91)

Q. How was you admitted? A. … two Wardens took me under each Arm, and conducted me from Darkness into Light, passing thro' two Rows of the Brotherhood.…
The Mystery of Free-Masonry, 1730 (EMC, 155)

Mas. How was you prepared Brother? Ans. I was … hoodwinked.…
Three Distinct Knocks, 1760, 16

[22] Q. How did you look before you were admitted ? A. Like a Fool.

[23] Q. How did you look afterwards ? A. As wise as my Neighbours.

There are no comparable questions in any of the catechisms, and early masons seemed to take their ceremonies very seriously. However, a candidate, as described in the catechisms, would certainly look foolish, but the next question has him quickly restored to "wisdom."

Right but Inconsistent

[24] Q. How came you off? A. In a whole Skin, but empty Pockets.

The "whole Skin" refers to a leather apron made from a whole animal skin, and the "empty Pockets" refers to being deprived of all metal.

Right and Consistent

> When a Free-Mason is enter'd, after having given to all present of the Fraternity a Pair of Men and Women's Gloves and Leathern Apron....
> *A Mason's Examination*, 1723 (EMC, 72)

> Q. How did he bring you? A. ... deprived of all Metal....
> *Masonry Dissected*, 1730, 10

> Mas. How was you prepar'd Brother? Ans. I was ... depriv'd of all Metal....
> *Three Distinct Knocks*, 1760, 16

[25] Q. What is the Masons Craft? A. One fool makes many.

There is no similar question in the catechisms. This could be a negative comment on masonry or a subtle hint of what the author is doing to the readers.

Right but Inconsistent and Negative

[26] Q. How do Masons work? A. By Rule and by Measure.

This question not only has an obvious reference to architectural tools but also agrees with one catechism.

Right and Consistent

> Q. How is it [a Lodge] govern'd? A. Of Square and Rule.
> *The Grand Mystery of Free-Masons Discover'd*, 1724 (EMC, 78)

[27] Q. What were the Dimensions of the Lodge? A. Three times three.

No catechism gives the dimensions of the lodge, but "three times three" is consistent with masonic symbolism.

Right and Consistent

> … if the Master proposed the Health or Toast with three Times three Claps. …
> *Jachin and Boaz*, 1762, 53

[28] Q. How high was your Lodge ? A. Out of the Reach of any but a Free Albans.

The catechisms agree that the height of a lodge is unreachable. While the expression "Free Albans" appears no where else, St. Alban has figured in the Old Charges for centuries.

Right and Consistent

> [Chapter Fourteen. Saint Alban]
> 3 And Saint Alban was a worthy knight, and was chief steward with the king, and had the governance of the realm, and also of the making of the town walls; 4 And he loved well Masons and cherished them much.
> "A Tentative Reconstruction of the 'Standard Original' of the Old Charges [1520/83] in Modern Spelling," *The Old Charges* (Toronto: Privately Printed, 1986), 47–8.

> Q. How high is your lodge A. Inches & spans Innumerable
> *Dumfries No. 4 Ms.*, c. 1710 (EMC, 62)

> How high is y^r lodge? A. As high as ye stars inches, & feet innumerable.
> *Trinity College, Dublin, Ms.*, 1711 (EMC, 70)

> Q. How high is your Lodge. A. Feet & Inches Innumerable.
> The *Wilkinson Ms.*, 1724–30 (EMC, 130)

> Q. How high? A. Inches, Feet and Yards innumerable, as high as the Heavens.
> *Masonry Dissected*, 1730, 12

> Sim. How high was your Lodge. Phil. As high as the Heavens and as low as the Earth.
> *Dialogue between Simon and Philip*, c. 1740 (EMC, 178)

Mas. How high [is your Lodge] Brother? Ans. From the Earth to the Heavens.
Three Distinct Knocks, 1760, 32

[29] Q. What is the Maker's Name ? A. Solomon.

This question appears in no other catechism, but agrees with the symbolism of Solomon's Temple and of Solomon as Grand Master at Jerusalem.

Right and Consistent

> ... the wise King Solomon was Grand Master of the Lodge at Jerusalem....
> *The Briscoe Pamphlet*, 1724 (EMP, 123)

[30] Q. Where was the first Lodge kept ? A. In the City of Enoch.

[31] Q. Who was the Maker Mason ? A. Cain.

[32] Q. Who was his Wardens ? A. Seth

[33] Q. Why so ? A. Because he set up the Pillars.

No catechism has these specific questions, but they are agree in sentiment with the idea that the patriarchs were masons.

Right and Consistent

> But godly ENOCH, of Seth's Loins,
>   Two Columns rais'd with mighty Skill:
> and all his Family enjoins
>   True Colonading to fullfil.
> "The Master's Song"
> Anderson's *Constitutions*, 1723 (EMP, 92)

> Now this is what the Remarker of the Constitutions wanted to know when he mentions the Two Pillars of Stone, whereon were engraven the liberal Sciences, one supposed to be raised by Seth and the other by Enoch....
> *The Briscoe Pamphlet*, 1724 (EMP, 121)

> Wherever Buildings Masons found,
>   To praise their Art they pick'd occasion;
> Hence Cain was for the Craft renown'd,
>   And mighty Nimrod was a Mason.
> Cain founded not his City fair,

Till mark'd for murthering of Abel. . . .
Ode to the Grand Khaibar, 1726 (EMP, 186)

From what he has said, the great Antiquity of the Art of Building or Masonry may be easily deduc'd. For without running up to Seth's Pillars or the Tower of Babel for Proof. . . .
Francis Drake's Speech, 1726 (EMP, 203)

[34] Q. What is the Apprentice's Word ? A. Babel.

All early catechisms agree that the apprentices' word is Boaz. The word Babel is strongly associated with Masonry and is indeed a biblical "B" word, but it is not the apprentice's word. Anyone using it would be recognized as an impostor.

Wrong

IF Hist'ry be no ancient Fable,
Free Masons came from Tower of Babel. . . .
An Hudibrastick Poem, 1722/3 (EMP, 86)

And at the Tower of Babylon, Masonry was much made on; for the King of Babylon, who was Nemorth, was a Mason, and serv'd the Science. . . .
Roberts Constitutions, 1722 (EMP, 73)

THUS when from Babel they disperse
In Colonies to distant Climes,
All Masons true, who could rehearse
Their Works to those of after Times.
"The Master's Song," Anderson's *Constitutions*, 1723 (EMP, 94)

The Grand Design to rear,
Was ever Masons Care,
From Adam down before the Flood,
Whose Art old Noah understood,
And did impart to Japhet, Shem, and Ham,
Who taught their Race
To Build space
Proud Babel's Town and Tow'r, until it came
To be admir'd too much, and then
Dispersed were the Sons of Men.
"The Warden's Song," Anderson's *Constitutions*, 1723 (EMP, 101)

Q. How many particular Points pertain to a Free-Mason? A. Three; Fraternity, Fidelity, and Tacity. Q. What do they represent? A. Brotherly Love, Relief, and Truth, among all right Masons; for which all Masons were ordain'd at the building of the tower of Babel, and the Temple of Jerusalem.
The Grand Mystery of Freemasons Discover'd, 1724 (EMC, 79)

[35] Q. What is the Fellow Crafts Word ? A. Jerusalem.

All early catechisms agree that the fellow crafts' word is *Jachin*, though there are references to a "Jerusalem word." The word Jerusalem is strongly associated with Masonry and is indeed a biblical "J" word, but it is not the fellow crafts' word. Anyone trying to use it would be immediately recognized as an impostor.

Wrong

Q. Give me the Jerusalem Word. A. Giblin.
The Grand Mystery of Free-Masons Discover'd, 1724 (EMC, 79)

37 Give me the Ierusalem Words? G... G...
Institution of Free Masons, c. 1725 (EMC, 85)

[36] Q. What is the Master Word ? A. Hiram Abif.

This is the most frustrating and tantalizing question of *the Post Boy* catechism. The first definite appearance of the Master Mason Degree occurs in Samuel Prichard's 1730 *Masonry Dissected,* and it would be a great discovery to have firm evidence of the degree being worked at an earlier date. Such evidence could be separate words for three classes of Masons: apprentices, fellow crafts, and masters. However, question 34 refers to "the Apprentice's Word" and question 35 refers to "the Fello Crafts Word." The former uses a possessive to mean the "Word belonging to the Apprentice." The latter lacks an apostrophe, but is clearly possessive. The phrase "Master Word," however, means the "chief or principal" word—like a "master key." Lacking either an apostrophe or a final s, unlike the phrase in *Masonry Dissected,* we can make no definite conclusion about *the Post Boy* hinting at the Master Mason Degree.

The Name Hiram Abif does appear in Anderson's Constitutions of 1723, where Anderson tries to argue that Hiram, King of Tyre, and Hiram Abif are different men. *The Briscoe Pamphlet* of 1724 tries to rebut Anderson's argument. In any event, Hiram Abif is not used by any catechism. Anyone trying to use it would be immediately recognized as an impostor.

Wrong

> Help by the learned Hiram Tyrian Prince,
> By Craftsmen good,
> That understood
> Wise Hiram Abif's charming Influence
> "The Warden's Song," Anderson's *Constitutions*, 1723 (EMP, 102)

> E. What was that which was lost and is now found? R. The Master-Mason's Word. ... Ex. Give me the Master's Word.
> *Masonry Dissected*, 1730, 26, 29

[37] Q. What is the grand or general Mason Word ? A. Ask S. John.

No catechism gives a "grand or general Mason Word," but this is similar to a "Universal Word" or a "Primitive Word." In any event nothing is revealed.

Right and Consistent

> Q. Give me the Universal Word. A. Boaz.
> *The Grand Mystery of Free-Masons Discover'd*, 1724 (EMC, 79)

> 38 Give me the Universal Words? ...
> *Institution of Free Masons*, c. 1725 (EMC, 85)

> Yet for all this I want the primitive Word. I answer it was God in six Terminations. ...
> *The Whole Institutions of Free-Masons Opened*, 1725 (EMC, 88)

[38] Q. How many states of Masonry do you reckon? A. Three. The ?rk before the Flood; The second after the flood; And the third after the Dekrucion of the Temple.

[39] Q. How do you call them? A. Nature Masonry, Law Masonry, and Gospel Masonry.

These two questions have no counterparts in any catechism though they maintain the established usage of the Bible for Masonic symbolism.

Right but Inconsistent

[40] Q. How many Orders of Masons are there ? A. Seven Orders.

[41] Q. What is the highest Order that our present Masons can attain to ? A. Few exceed the Fourth Order

These two questions support the popular idea of many—some very exclusive—levels or orders of masonic membership. This is a natural extension of apprentices, fellow crafts, master masons, and is supported by one pamphlet. By 1760, in France, a seven degree system was described in the anonymously published book Les Plus Secrets Mystères des Hauts Grades de la Maçonnerie Dévoilés.

Right and Consistent

> He makes wonderful Brags of being of the fifth order: I presume (as he is a Mason) he means the fifth order of Architecture....
> *Letters of Verus Comodus*, 1725 (EMP, 138)

[42] Q. What qualifies a Man for the Seventh Order ? A. These ?ve Things. Firk, Conquek over Nature. Secondly, the Composition of the Grand Elixir. Thirdly, The Mastery of the great Work. Fourthly, The Chaining of the Golden Dragon. Fifthly, The Enjoyment of the Silver Lady, &c.

This question expands on the idea of an hierarchy of orders but brings in alchemical terminology which is not found in any other catechism or early masonic document, even though it has an appropriately esoteric "sound."

Right but Inconsistent

Acknowledgments. I am deeply indebted to Bro. Yasha Beresiner for his generously helpful advice and guidance as well as for being a true friend and brother.

REFERENCES

Anderson, James. *The Constitutions of the Free-Masons*. Philadelphia: [Benjamin Franklin], 1734. Reprint. Bloomington, IL: Masonic Book Club, 1975.

———— . *Anderson's Constitutions of 1738.* Reprint. Bloomington, IL: Masonic Book Club, 1978.

Beresiner, Yasha. "The 'Sham Exposure' in *The Post Boy,* December 1723: A Discovery." *Ars Quatuor Coronatorum* 111 (1998):198–202.

Cox, S. and Budeit, J. L. *Early English Newspapers—Bibliography and Guide to the Microfilm Collection,* British Library Newspaper Library (1983).

Carry, Harry, ed. *Samuel Prichard's Masonry Dissected.* 1730. Reprint, Bloomington, IL: Masonic Book Club, 1977.

———— . *Three Distinct Knocks and Jachin and Boaz.* 1760 and 1762. Reprint (2 vols. in 1), Bloomington, IL: Masonic Book Club, 1981.

Knoop, Douglas, G. P. Jones, and Douglas Hamer. *The Early Masonic Catechisms.* Harry Carr, ed. 2nd ed. London: Quatuor Coronati Lodge, 1975.

———— . *Early Masonic Pamphlets.* 1944. Reprint. London: Q. C. Correspondence Circle, 1978.

McLeod, Wallace. *The Old Charges.* Toronto: Privately Printed, 1986.

———— . *The Grand Design.* Highland Springs, VA: Anchor Communications for Iowa Research Lodge No. 2, 1991.

Robbins, Alfred F. "The Earliest Years of English Organized Freemasonry." *Ars Quatuor Coronatorum* 22 (1909): 67–89.

The Transcription
The Post—Boy
Number 5373
From Thursday December 26 to Saturday December 28, 1723

The only known copy of this newspaper is in the library of the Supreme Council, 33°, S.J., Washington, DC. It has been published in facsimile and included in this volume of Heredom *and as a poster and distributed to the Supreme Council's Friends of the Library.*

Numb. 5373 Kkkkkkkkkk

THE
Post—Boy.

From Thursday December 26. to Saturday December 28. 1723.

To the Author of the Pok-Boy.

SIR,

HAVING for some time pak been a curious Observer of what was inserted in the Flying-Pok, and other
Papers, in relation to the Society of FREE MASONS, which has
made so much Noise of late ; I can now ajure you, that those
Accounts were not agreeable to the Pracice of our Modern
MASONS ; but the following Quekions and Answers you may de-
pend upon as Authentick, because I took them myself in Short-
hand, having heard the whole Ceremony thro' a thin Wainscot, at
the Admijion of some new Brethren at a famous Lodge in Wek-
minker,

[1]   Q. Are you one of us ?
        A. I'll kand Tryal.

[2]   Q. How will you be try'd ?
        A. By Quekion and Answer.

293

[3]   Q. What's your Name ?

        A. Base or Capital, according to my Degree.

[4]   Q. From whence come you ?

        A. From Solomon's Temple.

[5]   Q. What did you see there ?

        A. A folded square Paper.

[6]   Q. What was the Use of that Paper ?

        A. It was a Pasport to the Sancum Sancorum, and all the private Parts of the Temple.

[7]   Q. What office did you bear there ?

        A. I was Scali-ger, or Ladder-Bearer, at the Makings.

[8]   Q. How many Engagements have you ?

        A. Five.

[9]   Q. Which are they ?

        A. Firk, to be true to the King and the Grand Maker.

          2dly, Not to meddle with Politicks or Disputes about Religion in the Lodge.

          3dly, Not to abuse or lander one another.

          4thly, To answer all Signs and Tokens.

          5thly, To keep the Secrets and be Merry and Wise.

[10]   Q. How do you begin to make a Mason ?

        A. By building the Temple.

[11]   Q. Who are the Four Corner Stones ?

        A. Four Fellow-Craftsmen,

[12]   Q. Who are the four Capitals ?

        A. Four 'Prentices.

[13]   Q. Who is Cupola ?

        A. The new Brother.

[14]   Q. How high do you raise him ?

        A. Above Ground.

[15]   Q. Who turns the Ladder ?

        A. The Junior Warden.

[16]   Q. What's the Sword-Bearer's buiness ?

        A. To examine and see that none but Men enter the Lodge.

[17] Q. What's the Reason Women are not admitted into your Society?
    A. Because they can't keep a Secret.

[18] Q. What's the Master's Business?
    A. To give the Charges, receive the Fees, and teach the Lodge the Art of Masonry.

[19] Q. What is done before the demolihing?
    A. The ham Words are taught by the Senior Warden.

[20] Q. What do you do when you firk come into the Lodge?
    A. I crook my Arm, and bend my Foot.

[21] Q. Which way were you brought into the Lodge?
    A. Between the Wardens blind-folded.

[22] Q. How did you look before you were admitted?
    A. Like a Fool.

[23] Q. How did you look afterwards?
    A. As wise as my Neighbours.

[24] Q. How came you off?
    A. In a whole Skin, but empty Pockets,

[25] Q. What is the Masons Craft?
    A. One Fool makes many.

[26] Q. How do Masons work?
    A. By Rule and by Measure.

[27] Q. What were the Dimenions of the Lodge?
    A. Three times three.

[28] Q. How high was your Lodge?
    A. Out of the Reach of any but a Free Albans,

[29] Q. What is the Maker's Name?
    A. Solomon.

[30] Q. Where was the firk Lodge kept?
    A. In the City of Enoch.

[31] Q. Who was the Maker Mason?
    A. Cain.

[32] Q. Who was his Warden?
    A. Seth,

[33] Q. Why so?

A. Because he set up the Pillars.

[34] Q. What is the Apprentice's Word ?
       A. Babel.

[35] Q. What is the Fellow Crafts Word ?
       A. Jerusalem.

[36] Q. What is the Maker Word ?
       A. Hiram abif.

[37] Q. What is the grand or general Mason Word ?
       A. Ask S. John.

[38] Q. How many States of Masonry do you reckon ?
       A. Three. The firk before the Flood : The second after the Flood: And the third after the Dekrucion of the Temple.

[39] Q. How do you call them ?
       A. Nature Masonry, Law Masonry, and Gospel Masonry.

[40] Q. How many Orders of Masons are there ?
       A. Seven Orders.

[41] Q. What is the highest Order that our present Masons can attain to ?
       A. Few exceed the Fourth Order

[42] Q. What qualifies a Man for the Seventh Order ?
       A. These five Things. Firk, Conquek over Nature. Secondly, the Compoition of the Grand Elixir. Thirdly, The Makery of the great Work. Fourthly, The Chaining of the Golden Dragon. Fifthly, The Enjoyment of the Silver Lady, &c.

PS. In my next you hall have the rek of their Quekions and Answers, and a full Account of their Ceremonies ; by the Knowledge of which, I have been several times admitted at their Lodges, and receiv'd as a Free-Mason.

Yours, &c. A. B.

_____

First published: *Heredom,* vol. 7(1998)

New Light on the Gormogons

The year 1723 was an "interesting" year for the newly formed Grand Lodge of England. Philip, Duke of Wharton, a notorious libertine and rake, had been elected Grand Master June 24, 1722, and thus presided during 1723 until June 24 when he "went away from the Hall without Ceremony."[1] Several significant publications about Masonry came out that year, starting on February 15, 1723, when *The Daily Post* advertised the second pamphlet or book about the recently organized fraternity, *The Free-Masons: An Hudibrastick Poem*.[2] This mock-heroic poem is both humorous and vulgar, held up Freemasonry to ridicule, and went through three editions that year and a fourth in early 1724.[3] It so offended the sensibilities of Knoop, Jones, and Hamer that they heavily censored it in their *Early Masonic Pamphlets* and failed to recognize it as the first exposé of Masonic secrets.[4] On February 28, 1723, two weeks after *The Free-Masons* was published, the first official Masonic publication came out, James Anderson's *The Constitutions of the Free-Masons*. Then in mid-April, only eight weeks later, *The Flying Post*, No. 4712, April 11–14, 1723, ran an exposé of Masonic ritual, named by Robert F. Gould "The Masons Examination." And finally, as 1723 wound down, a second exposé appeared in *The Post-Boy*, No. 5373, December 26–28, 1723. From little prior notice in print, the Freemasons burst onto the public stage in 1723 with four historic publications and several minor references.

Birth of the Gormogons

Things calmed down a little for Wharton's successor as Grand Master, Francis Scott, Duke of Buccleuch, but Charles Lennox, Duke of Richmond, was installed Grand Master on June 24, 1724, and faced a new crisis

---

1   Robert F. Gould, "Masonic Celebrities: No. VI—The Duke of Wharton, G.M., 1722–23; with Which Is Combined the True History of the Gormogons," *AQC* 8 (1895): 122.

2   Wallace McLeod, "The Hudibrastic Poem of 1723," *AQC* 107 (1994): 9–52.

3   Douglas Knoop, G. P. Jones, and Douglas Hamer, *Early Masonic Pamphlets* (1943; London: Q.C. Correspondence Circle, 1978), 84.

4   Wallace McLeod, "Victorian Obscenity Laws," 12.

less than three months after taking office. On September 3, 1724, *The Daily Post* No. 1541 announced the institution of a chapter of the Ancient and Noble Order of Gormogons[5] at the Castle Tavern in Fleet Street.

***The Daily Post*, No. 1541, September 3, 1724:**

Whereas the truly Antient and Noble Order

of the Gormagons, Inſtituted by Chinquaw Kypo, the firſt Emperor of China (according to their Account) many Thouſand Years before Adam, of which Order the great Philoſopher Confucius, was Oecumenical Volgee, has lately been brought into England by a Mandarin, and he having admitted ſeveral Gentlemen of Honour into the Myſtery of that moſt illustrious Order, they have determin'd to hold a Chapter at the Caſtle Tavern in Fleet-ſtreet, at the particular Reſquest of ſeveral Persons of Quality. This is to inform the Publick, that there will be no drawn Sword at the Door, nor Ladder in a Dark Room, nor will any Maſon be receiv'd as a Member, till he has renounced his Novel Order, and been properly degraded. N. B. The great Mogul, the Czar of Muſcovy, and Prince Tochmas, are enter'd into this Hon. Society, but it has been refuſ'd to the Rebel Meriweys, to his great Mortification. The Mandarin will ſhortly ſet out for Rome, having a particular Commiſſion to make a Preſent of this Antient Order to his Holineſs; and it is believ'd the whole Sacred College of Cardinals will commence Gormagons. Notice will be given in the Gazette the Day the Chapter will be held.

This was a shot across the bow of the fledgling grand lodge, challenging its antiquity and the quality of its members. Just eight months before, Anderson's *Constitutions* had claimed Adam as the first mason, having taught the skills of geometry to his sons, as well as every prominent man in history. The Gormogon's announcement was followed by a barrage of at least eleven newspaper mentions in twenty-five weeks about this exotic group,

---

5   In contemporary announcements, the name of the society is spelled both *Gormagon* and *Gormogon*. The latter is the more common spelling, which is used in this paper. Similarly, the head of the order is known as the Œcumenical Vol-Gi, Volgee, and *Volgi*, and the latter spelling is used in this paper.

including the publication of William Hogarth's satirical engraving, "The Mystery of Masonry Brought to Light by the Gormogons." The claim of a pre-Adamite foundation is a tipoff that assertions by the Gormogons should be taken with a grain of salt, though some, including Robert Freke Gould, seem to have accepted these claims at face value.[6] Bro. Georg Kloss thought, "I. That the Œumenical [*sic*] Volgi was no less than the Chevalier Ramsay, then at Rome in attendance upon the Young Pretender; II That the movement was a deeply laid scheme on the part of the Jesuits to attain certain ends; and III. That in the Gormogons we meet with the precursors of the Schismatic Masons or 'Ancients.'"[7] Others who may not have been in at the beginning of the joke took the opportunity to take a swipe at the pretensions of the Masons.

The Plain Dealer, No. 51, September 14, 1724: This is a lengthy article starting with a discussion of credulity and ending with information about the Gormogons, followed by letters from Hang Chi to the *Plain Dealer* and Shin Shaw to Hang Chi.

The Weekly Journal or Saturday's Post, No. 312, October 17, 1724:

We hear another ancient Society is ſtarted up, in Town, of GORMOGONS, of much greater Antiquity and Reputation than the FREE MASONS; for whereas the latter can deduce their Original but from the Building of Babel, the former derive their's ſome thouſand Years before Adam. The Order was lately brought over from China by a Mandarine, who is now departed for Rome, to eſtabliſh a Lodge in that City, as he has done in London. We are informed a great many eminent Free Maſons have degraded themſelves, and come over to this Society, and ſeveral others rejected, for want of Qualification.

The Daily Post, No. 1583, October 22, 1724: Just seven weeks after the Gormogons first appeared and ten and one-half months after being first published, the second edition of *The Grand Mystery of the Free-Masons*

---

6   Robert F. Gould, "Duke of Wharton," 122.

7   Georg Kloss, *Geschichte dei Freimaurerei, England, Irland, Schottland,* 90, quoted in Robert F. Gould, "The Duke of Wharton," 125.

Discover'd was announced with "an account of the most ancient Society of Gormogons." Like the best of opportunistic publishers, the author of *The Grand Mystery* apparently took advantage of public curiosity and free publicity surrounding this new society and included enticing information on the Gormogons in the second edition. If readers hadn't purchased the first edition because of interest in Masonry, then perhaps information about the Gormogons would spur sales of the second edition.

This Day is publiſh'd, the 2d Edit. of,

The Grand Myſtery of the Free-Maſons diſ-

cover'd.   Wherein are the ſeveral Queſtions put to them at their Meetings and Inſtallations.   As alſo their Oath, Health, Signs, and Points, to know each other by; as they were found in the Cuſtody of a Free-Maſon who died ſuddenly, and now publiſh'd for the Information of the Publick.   To which are annex'd, two letters to a Friend, the firſt, concerning the Society of Free-Maſons; the ſecond, giving an Account of the moſt ancient Society of Gormogons, in its Original Inſtitution, Excellency, and Deſign; its Rules and Orders, and the Manner of its Introduction into Great Britain.   With an intire Collection of all that has been made Publick on that Occaſion. Together with the ſuppos'd Reaſon of their excluding the Free-Masons, without they previouſly undergo the Form of Degradation, &c. now firſt ſet forth for the Satisfaction and Emolument of the Publick.

Ambubajaram collegia, Pharmacapola,

Mendici, Medici, balatrones, hoc genus omne.   Hor.

———*Mulus ſcabit Mulum.*———

Printed for A. Moore, near St. Pauls.   Price 1 s.

The Daily Journal, **No. 1175, October 26, 1724:** This is a repeat announcement about the publication of the second edition of *The Grand Mystery of the Free-Masons Discover'd.*

The Daily Journal, No. 1177, October 28, 1724: The Guzzletonians' first meeting at the Salutation Tavern in Fleet Street is announced. This notice was surely a joke, but we cannot tell if it was coordinated with the origina-tors of the Gormogons or if it was an independent attempt to add another jibe at the Freemasons. Knoop, Jones, and Hamer in their *Early Masonic Catechisms* doubt that the Guzzletonians existed but do not seem to doubt the Gormogons: "Whether there really was a Society of Guzzletonians is very doubtful. The advertisement points to the prevalence of gluttony and intemperance which characterized the period, and which, in the mind of the advertiser, was associated with the Freemasons and the Gormogons."[8]

There being newly eftablish'd a Society

call'd the Guzzletonians, this is to give Notice that their firft meeting will be on Monday next, at the Salutation Tavern in Fleet-ftreet, the Temple-bar, from whence they propofe to fend a Challenge to the Gentlemen of the Gormagon Society at the Caftle, defying them to Gormandize as they fhall Guzzle, and the Gentlemen of the An-cient Society of Free-Mafons will be appointed the Umpires between them.

The Daily Post, No. 1620, 4 December 1724: William Hogarth got the joke and published "The Mystery of Masonry Brought to Light by yᵉ Gor-mogons." The advertisement embellishes the details by announcing that the engraving is from an original painting in the possession of Hang-chi the Mandarin. The well-known image features a parade led by Chin Quan Kypo, the first Emperor of China, Confucius, In-Chin, Oecumenical Volgi, and the Mandarin Hang-Chi. Following these exotic dignities are a mon-key in a Masonic apron, a candidate with his pants down on a donkey, an-other candidate with a ladder on his neck possibly kissing the buttocks of the bare-bottomed figure, and figures satirizing Freemasonry.[9]

---

8   Douglas Knoop, G. P. Jones, and Douglas Hamer, *The Early Masonic Catechisms* (1945; London: Q.C. Correspondence Circle, 1978), 135.

9   Robert F. Gould, "The Duke of Wharton," 138–40; it was said that during initiation, Masons had their bare bottoms flogged, their right buttock branded, and kissed each other's bare bottoms for identification, *The Freemasons; an Hudibrastick Poem,* 3ʳᵈ ed. (London: A Moore, 1723), 10, 11, 13,

This Day is publifhed,

A very curious Print, entitul'd the Grand

Myftery of MASONRY brought to light by the GORMOGONS, a number of which were brought over by a Merchant from China. Tis finely engrav'd by HO–GE from the original Painting of Matachauter, principal Painter to CHIN[Q]UAW-KYPO, firft Emperor of CHINA, and now in the Poffeffion of Hang-chi the Mandarin, who was lately in England. Price [-] s. Sold by the Printfellers of London and Weftminster.

The Weekly Journal or Saturday's Post, **No. 319, December 5, 1724:** A general chapter of the Gormogons was held on Monday, December 4. This is the first public announcement of a meeting of the Gormogons, even though the establishment of the society was announced three months previously. The tongue-in-cheek announcement says that the London Chapter of the Gormogons was "instituted by some Body with a hard Name." This apparently refers to the Mandarin Hang Chi or perhaps the Emperor Chinquaw-Kypo.

On Monday a general Chapter of the Gormogons, infti-
tuted by fome Body with a hard Name, was held at the Ca-
ftle-Tavern in Fleet-Street, when feveral Charities were beftowed by that Society, particularly five Pounds to the Charity School of St. Brides, it being in that Parifh where Hang
chi first prefented the Order.

The British Journal, **December 12, 1724:** It is announced that "a peer of the first rank" joined the Gormogons and left the Freemasons. This is an intriguing piece of gossip that seems to show the Gormogons attracting Masons to their ranks. Gould thought this "points with the utmost directness to the Duke of Wharton"; he also thought that a Gormogon meeting notice signed "P. W. T." corresponded to Philip Wharton.[10] Bro. John Acaster suggests, "The word 'degraded' may also have significance as it literally means

10 Gould, "Duke of Wharton," 126, 135.

to be stripped of the Degrees which Freemasonry will have accorded to its members."[11]

> We hear, That a Peer of the firft Rank, a noted Member of the Society of *Free-Mafons*, hath fuffer'd himfelf to be degraded as a Member of that Society, and his Leather Apron and Gloves to be burnt, and thereupon enter'd himfelf a Member of the Society of *Gormogons*, at the *Caftle*-Tavern in *Fleet-Street*.

The Daily Post, No. 1692, February 26, 1725: This is an announcement of a general chapter of the Gormogons to be held on March 1, 1725, only the second such meeting, even though there had been many other articles about the society. Note the statement that this announcement is "By Order of the VOL-GI General" and is signed with three initials, "B. G. T." This is the first of at least 23 pre-meeting announcements, 21 of which are signed by three initials, always ending with a "T." We will return to this later.

> On Monday the 1ft Day of March next, at the Caftle Tavern in Fleet-ftreet, will be held a General Chapter of the moft Ancient and Honourable Order of the GORMOGONS, of which every Graduate is defir'd to take Notice, and attend to dine at one of the Clock.
>
> By Order of the VOL-GI General,   B. G. T.

The Daily Post, No. 1693, February 27, 1725: This is a repeat of the pre-meeting announcement of February 26.

Thus, from the announcement of their birth on September 3, 1724, to that of their general chapter on February 27, 1725, the Gormogons had at least eleven mentions in twenty-five weeks in five different newspapers plus central prominence in one of Hogarth's popular prints. Their public relations firm should have received a bonus! On top of these mentions, the 1725 pamphlet, *Seasonable Advice*, gives unintended publicity to the

---

11 E. John T. Acaster, "My favourite Manchester Masonic Museum piece, and why: the Gormogon medal," *Transactions of the Manchester Association of Masonic Research* 101 (2011): 67.

Gormogons and Free-Masons when talking about their conflicting claims of precedence, "What a Figure would those of the Gormogons, Hums, or Free Masons, have made, do ye think, if they had not had Authors with them to have publish'd their Proceedings ..."[12] The Hums, by the way, appear to be another gentlemen's club, the earliest two mentions of which are announcements of meetings on November 5, 1724 and 1725 at the Kings Head Tavern in St. John Street.[13]

Public Acceptance of the Gormogons

The original September 3, 1724, birth announcement of the Gormogons includes the notice that "the Mandarin will shortly set out for Rome," and the Duke of Wharton left England for the Roman court of the Pretender in 1725. Gould interprets this notice as "such a close analogy with that of Wharton himself, as to justify our believing in there being more than a casual resemblance between the real and the fictitious characters."[14] However, just eleven days after the birth announcement, the *Plain Dealer* of September 14, 1724, published a letter "written from Rome to the author of the first ... SHIN SHAW, *to* HANG CHI, *at* London ... Your Presence is earnestly expected at ROME. His HOLINESS is fond of our *Order* and the CARDINALS have an Emulation to be first distinguish'd." These two letters so close together seem better interpreted as part of an original plan to create the public perception of an organization that rivaled the Freemasons in antiquity, prestige, and exclusivity. The entreaty to Hang Chi to come to Rome to make the Cardinals Gormogons should be taken in the same spirit as the claim of a pre-Adamite formation of the Order.

Gould notes that following August 1728, there is a "resurrection on the part of the Gormogons—whose 'General Chapters' are again advertised until six months after the Duke of Wharton's death (October 28th, 1732), when they are heard of no more."[15] As for meetings between 1724 and 1728, Gould said "Whether, indeed any similar notifications were printed in 1725, 1726, 1727, and the first eight months of 1728, I am not in a posi-

12 *Seasonable Advice* (London: A. Moore, 1725), 13.
13 *The Daily Journal*, No. 1183, November 4, 1724; *The Daily Courant*, No. 7504, November 3, 1725.
14 Gould, "Duke of Wharton," 141.
15 Gould, "Duke of Wharton," 142.

tion either to positively affirm or to deny. I do not think they did …."[16] After analyzing the notice of October 28, 1731, Gould said, "There may be later advertisements of a like tenor, but my own search for them has been a fruitless one."[17] However, there were indeed steady notices of the Gormogons' semiannual meetings from 1724 to 1736, usually on or about May 1 and November 1 (see Appendix 1). In particular, spring and fall meetings were held in 1725 through1734 plus one meeting each in 1735 and 1736. This is not a reflection on the research skills of Bro. Gould, but on his access to a searchable digital archive of British periodicals.

In *The Daily Post*, No. 3185, December 4, 1729, we see the Gormogons come into their own in the public perception as a companion organization of the Freemasons, at least for purposes of comparison and contrast—two men's groups with extravagant claims of antiquity and prestige. A "curtain lecture," presumably by Orator John Henley, was announced at the Oratory at Lincoln's Inn Fields for the next day.

At the Requeſt of ſome Ladies, that never were at it before,

At the ORATORY,

THE Corner of *Lincoln's-Inn-Fields,* near Clare-market, To-morrow, at half an Hour after Six, will be

A CURTAIN LECTURE;

What is he? Who is ſhe? What is what? What is the Inſide and Outſide of Matrimony? Tamquam, quidnunc, & quid pro quo? Fundamentals, Schiſms and Hereſies, in Wedlock: Honey-Moon; Wedding Days; Charivari, Dances proper; Yokes and Couples; Match-hunting, and Match-making; the whole Scheme of Goſſiping: Viſits, Neighbours, the Good Man and Good Woman; Spouse, my Dear, and Papa; falling out; Rights and Pretenſions, Fire and Tow; Endorſements, and inlaid Mother of Pearl; Pin-

---

16 Gould, "Duke of Wharton," 132.
17 Gould, "Duke of Wharton," 136.

money, Houſewife and Huſſy; Flea in the Ear, and wearing the Breeches: Marriage a Save-all; Aſtrology, what Stars for Weddings; compriſing a ſure and compleat Guide from VIRGINIA to MARYLAND.

II. An Enquiry into GORMOGONS, and FREE-MASONS, the Correſpondence of them, and whether a Lady may, can, will, or ought to be a Free-Maſon, or a Gormogon.

N. B. Lately are re-publiſhed: 1. Oratory-tranſactions, No. 1, 2, 3, 4, 5, 6; the Progreſs and Riſe of the Oratory; an Anſwer to Objections; Orations on Nonſence, Grave Buffoons, Errors of Church-Work, Butchers Lecture; Lectures at opening it.

On Sunday Morning in the Sermon will be the Caſe of the Power of the Pulpit; the Evening Lecture will be on the Shape and Trinity of the Muggletonian Gods.

In April 1730, a curious event is reported in *The Weekly Journal: or the British-Gazette*, No. 265, April 18, 1730, and *The Grub-street Journal*, No. 15, April 16, 1730.

On Saturday Night laſt at the Prince William Tavern at Charing-Cross, Mr Dennis the famous Poet and Critick was admitted a Free and Accepted Maſon at a Lodge then held there, having renounced the Society of the Gormogons, of which he had been a member for many Years.

Gould identifies the gentleman as John Dennis (1657–1734), "a poet, political writer, and critic,"[18] and he is the only person identified by name as a Gormogon. Gould could find no record of Dennis in the Grand Lodge archives and believed the announcement was a "malicious hoax."[19] Bro. Trevor Stewart also could find no record of Dennis and speculates the notice was to call attention to a well-known London theatrical gentleman who had

18 Robert Freke Gould, *The History of Freemasonry* (London: Thomas C. Jack, 1887), 2:379.
19 Gould, "Duke of Wharton," 142.

been willing to foreswear his allegiance to the Freemasons to join the more ancient and prestigious Gormogons.[20]

The Gormogon announcements in 1724 began by implying that Freemasons were "degrading" themselves to join, but now six years later, we have a Gormogon allegedly renouncing his membership to become a Freemason. This seems to be in step with the original tongue-in-cheek announcements about the Gormogons, but who is being parodied here: Mr. Dennis? The Freemasons? The Gormogons? The answer may be obvious to an expert on early eighteenth-century London, but it escapes this author.

Following on the heels of the peculiar announcement about Mr. Dennis are announcements about the spring 1730 meeting of the Gormogons and another presentation by Orator Henley at his "Oratory" at Lincoln-Inn's Fields.

At the ORATORY,

The Corner of Lincoln's-Inn-Fields, near Clare Market,

To Morrow, at Eleven. 1. The Poſtill; on, THIS GENERATION in the New Teſtament. A Diſputation free. 2.The Sermon, on the ROE UPON THE MOUNTAINS, or the FUGITIVE HEART RECALL'D.

II. At Six. 1. The Poſtill; "Whether Judas received the "Sacrament with Chriſt." A Diſputation free. 2. The Lecture on the Eagle in a Storm, or, the CONSTANT MOTHER, AND SUFFERING SONS; with Controverſy, Hiſtory, Criticiſm, and Moral.

III. On Wedneſday, to entertain the Rt. W. the D. G. Maſter: in the Abſence of the G. Maſter: the G Wardens; and the moſt antient and honourable Society of Free and Accepted Maſons, will be an Elogium of MASONRY, and a Diſpute of GORMOGANISM, free.[21]

---

20 Trevor Stewart to S. Brent Morris, September 14, 2012, private communication. "However, using QCA vol. X (ed. Songhurst) I cannot find a JOHN Dennis anywhere in the lodge lists there. There is a "Joseph Dennis" listed in 1725 (38) as being the JW of a lodge meeting at the Sun Inn/Tavern in Chester. It is probably not the same Dennis since the Gormogons appear to have been London-based."

21 *The Country Journal: Or The Craftsman,* No. 206, June 13, 1730; also *Fog's Weekly Jour-*

Before the month was out, the Gormogons had another passing mention in the significant "Notice to all Masons who have been made after the Antideluvian [sic] Manner" in *The Daily Post,* No. 3357, June 23, 1730. The implications of this notice are worthy of a separate paper, but at the very end, is a small humorous mention of the Gormogons.

> N. B. The Wax-Chandler near Pall-Mall, will provide three great Lights and a Gormogon to keep off the Cowin and Eves-droppers.

And October 1730 saw what was becoming a staple in the Gormogon's calendar: the announcement a fall meeting on October 31 at the Castle Tavern in Fleet Street.

At this point, the evidence left by the Gormogons is that of a masterful practical joke played to perfection. The Duke of Wharton may have started the joke, as Gould suggests, but the steady persistence of news accounts of the Gormogons when Wharton was out of the country implies other hands were surely involved in the publicity campaign. The success of the practical joke can be measured by the apparent public acceptance of the Gormogons as disputing the antiquity and prestige of the Freemasons, as witnessed by the two Oratory announcements and the mention in *Seasonable Advice.* From this distance, it's hard to tell if the author of the second edition of *The Grand Mystery of the Free-Masons Discover'd,* which included a letter from "Verus Commodus" on Gormogons, was in on the original joke, or if he saw the commercial possibilities and ran with them.

Theatrical Presentations of the Gormogons

A dramatic plot twist in the Gormogons' tale occurred in December 1730, propelling the initial joke into something that would persist in general society until the end of the century. On December 4 at the Theatre Royal in Drury Lane was presented a dramatic masque, *Cephalus and Procris,* with a new pantomime interlude, *Harlequin Grand Vol-Gi.* The Grand Volgi, of course, was the head of the Gormogons, and others characters in the pantomime included Mandarin Gormogons and Chinese attendants. Apparently six years' of news stories, mentions in books, and an appearance in a Hogarth print had convinced the public (or at least the playwright) that

nal, No. 901, June 13, 1730.

Gormogons were an elite group in China and the Grand Volgi was their head.

The theatrical custom of the day was to present a major performance followed by an extravagant pantomime involving elaborate scenic special effects and slapstick comedy. *Cephalus and Procris* with *Harlequin Grand Vol-Gi* followed the common but not universal format of "alternating a 'serious' plot, often drawn from classical mythology, with a "comic" or "grotesque" plot focusing on the escapades of Harlequin."[22] *Cephalus and Procris* with *Harlequin Grand Vol-Gi* became a staple at the Theatre Royal in Drury Lane while the main production changed regularly. The plot of *Harlequin Grand Volgi* is silly and more about scenic effects and slapstick than plot.

The Daily Post, No. 3496, December 2, 1730

By His Majefty's Company of Comedians,
AT the Theatre Royal in Drury-Lane,
on Friday next, being the 4th Day of December,
will be
prefented the Second Part of
KING HENRY the Fourth.
To which will be added, a Dramatic Masque,
called,
CEPHALUS and PROCRIS:
With a new Pantomime Interlude, call'd,
HARLEQUIN GRAND-VOL-GI.

The Part of Neptune by Mr. Fielding; Cephalus, Mrs. Roberts; Aurora, Mrs. Heron; Procris, Mifs Raftor; the Deities of Pleafure by Mr. Essex and Mrs. Booth; the Followers of Pleafure, by Mrs. Walter, Mrs. Delorme, Miss Mears, and Miss Williams; Forefters, Mr. Excell, Mr. Tenoe, Mr. Wright, and Mr. Rain-

---

22 Lance Bertelsen, *Cambridge History of English Literature 1660–1780* (Cambridge: 2005), 80–81, quoted in Kate Novotny "Dramatic Entertainment of the Mixt Kind: The Unruly Structure of Early Eighteenth Century Pantomime," unpublished manuscript, 2012. Ms. Novotny's careful analysis of 53 scripts from 1722 to 1732 shows that the "alternating format" was the most popular (14/53) but far from universal.

ton, Sen. Amphitrite, Mrs. Booth; Sea-Gods, by Mr. Effex
and Mr. Lally; Tritons, by Mr. Thurmond, Mr. Rainton, Jun.
Mr. Houghton, and Mr. Evans; Syrens, by Mrs. Walter, Mrs.
Delorme, Miss Mears, and Miss Williams; a noble Venetian,
Mr. Cibber, Jun. Colombine (his Sifter) Mrs. Cibber; Pierot,
(his Servant) Monf. Roger; Harlequin, Mr. Rainton, Jun. an
Italian Bravoe, Mr. Harper; a Miller, Mr. Oates; Mandarin-
Gormogons, by Mr. Thurmond, Mr. Lally; Mr. Houghton,
and Mr. Effex; Chinefe Guards, by Mr. Wetherilt, Mr.
Wright, Mr. Grey, and Mr. Burne; Gardeners and their Wives,
by Mr. Tench, Mr. Lally, Jun. Mifs Robinfon, and Mifs Brett;
the Winds, Zephyrs, Huntfmen, Chinefe Attendants, and others,
by the Reft of the comedians. With new Scenes, Habits, Ma-
chines, and other Decorations.

Performances of *Cephalus and Procris* with *Harlequin Grand Volgi* were advertised for December 3, 7, and 10, 1730, at the Theatre Royal. The plays
achieved royal recognition on their third performance on December 10,
when the King and Queen, the Prince of Wales, the Princess Royal, Princess Emilia, and Princess Caroline were in attendance.[23] The royal family
also attended the fifth and sixth advertised performances on 16 and 17
December. All together, there was a royal presence at three of the first six
performances of *Cephalus and Procris* with *Harlequin Grand Volgi*.[24] Surely,
this is recognition that would satisfy any theatrical company! There appear
to have been eight plays in December 1730 at the Theatre Royal in Drury
Lane that were offered with *Cephalus and Procris* with *Harlequin Grand Volgi*. At least seven plays with the dramatic masque and pantomime interlude
were advertised through May 4, 1731.

Building on the growing public awareness of the Gormogons, *"The Whitehall Evening Post* of July 3, 1731, states that on the previous Mid-summer
Day, the Curé of St. Sulpice, Paris, gave a great entertainment to the workmen employed in the building of that magnificent fabric. At one table sat

23 *The Daily Post.* December 11, 1730, No. 3504; *Read's Weekly Journal; or, British-Gazet-
teer,* December 12, 1730, No. 299,

24 *The Grub-street Journal,* No. 50, December 17, 1730; *The Daily Post,* No. 3510, December 18, 1730

about 400 Gormogons and at another, the Curé and Masons, who were of the Ancient and Honourable Order of Free Masons."[25] It's easy to imagine that someone is continuing the joke here, or perhaps this is a sly advertising campaign by the Theatre Royal to generate interest in their continuing inter-act entertainment.

Yet, further expansion of the Gormogon saga occurred with the announcement of a "New Dramatick Opera, call'd *The Emperor of China, Grand-Volgi: or, The Constant Couple, and Virtue Rewarded.*"[26] The author of the play was William Chetwood, the author of *The Generous Mason,* and its first performance was on August 24, 1731, at Bartholomew Fair.[27] Chetwood's opera does not appear to have been very successful. It was produced again a few weeks later at the Southwark Fair, but it was never published, and no further performances seem to have been advertised. It is likely that Chetwood tried to gain free publicity for his new work by using a theme already in the public mind (which is no different than entertainments seen today).

The fall meeting of the Gormogons was announced for November 1, 1731, at the Castle Tavern in Fleet Street. Perhaps, this was another attempt by theatrical forces to keep the Gormogons in the public eye and to generate interest in future theatrical productions; the wording of the announcement follows the pattern from before *Harlequin Grand Volgi* and ends with the initials "F. N. T."

The only hint we have of the extent of the membership of the Gormogons comes from the 1731 dedication of J. Morgan's *Phœnix Brittanicus,* which ran for six issues 1731–1732. The dedication is obsequious to Charles, Duke of Richmond and Lenox and Past Grand Master of the Grand Lodge of England. In particular, Morgan excoriates the Gormogons and gives us a hint of whom they might be. The particularly vituperative tone may be due to excesses in the unscripted mock initiation in *Harlequin Grand Vol-Gi.*

Should fifty mercenary Wretches, for a mi-
ferable *Pittance,* nefarioufly, not to fay perju-

---

25 *Whitehall Evening Post,* July 3, 1731, in F. W. Levander, "The Collectanea of the Rev. Daniel Lysons, F.R.S., F.S.A., Part II," *AQC* 29 (1916): 7–100.

26 *The Daily Advertiser,* No. 176, August 26, 1731.

27 William J. Burling, *A Checklist of New Plays and Entertainments on the London Stage, 1700–1737* (Cranbury, NJ, London, Mississauga, ONT, 1993), 195; the authorship of the play is implied in a brief review in *The Grub-street Journal,* No. 86, August 26, 1731.

riouſly, attempt to *beſpatter* thoſe who would only anſwer them with the Scorn they deſerve, they would only *be-mire* themſelves with their own *Filth*. And what mighty *Feats* of *Chivalry* have they done, who thro' Exceſs of *Gormogonian* Smartneſs, *exquiſitely* inſinuate, in the *New-Papers*, *That* *they are glad at not finding any thing* greatly Indecent *in* MASONRY! Have they done more than *turn* the *Tables* upon their own *inconſiderable* Selves? Are not the MASONS, obviouſly in the Eye of the Sun, a very numerous, a reſpectable body of MEN?

If Morgan is correct, then some fifty men were paid to be Gormogons and to publicize "Gormogonian Smartness" in the newspapers. This could be easily explained by Wharton or one of cronies—especially one who shared Wharton's apparent grudge against the Masons—funding a "society" with an endowment. After the initial burst of very successful publicity, the Gormogons devolved into a semiannual dining and drinking society with the tab paid from the initial endowment. After some two dozen meetings, the money ran out and the initial joke died a natural death.

No further performances of *Harlequin Grand Vol-Gi* were advertised in 1731, and only one advertisement for a performance is found in 1732. At least six performances were advertised in 1733, from November 12 to December 11, all at the Theatre Royal at Drury Lane and accompanied by *Cephalus and Procris*. Sometime, in 1733, the script was published by J. Watts in London. The description of the initiation as a Gormogon is sketchy with plenty of room for broad humor, slapstick, and parodies of the main production or current events. In 1735, for at least three productions, the main performance was Ben Johnson's *The Alchemist*, which has its own mock initiation scene. It's fun to imagine the comic possibilities of mocking a mock initiation.[28]

Pierrot and a Servant enter; while he is
informing the Servant of his Misfortunes,

---

28 For a detailed discussion of Ben Johnson's *The Alchemist*, see E. John T. Acaster, "Early 17th-Century Ritual: Ben Johnson and his Circle," *AQC* 124 (2011): 57–93.

Harlequin and *Colombine* croſs the Stage
and go to a Tavern to make merry. *Pie-*
rot obſerving them, ſends off the Servant
to inform their Maſter; the *Venetian* enters,
and *Pierot* attends him to the Tavern, in
order to find our *Harlequin* and *Colom-*
bine.

The Scene changes to an Arbour, ſuppos'd to be in a Tavern Garden. *Har-*
lequin and *Colombine* go into the Arbour, in
order to regale themſelves: *Pierot* enters
and diſcovers them: While *Pierot* goes to
inform his Maſter, *Harlequin* and *Colom-*
bine go into the Arbour: Then Pierot enters with the *Venetian,* and not finding
them, they pull open the Doors of the
Arbour, which changes to a magnificent
Chineſe Palace: *Harlequin* diſcover'd, ſit-
ting as the Emperor of *China:* His Guards
oppoſe the Entrance of the *Venetian* and
Pierot, who retire, out of Fear, to each ſide
of the Stage. After ſeveral Dances in odd
Poſtures, in the *Chineſe* Manner, by the
Mandarins and the Emperor, *Harlequin,*
in the Character of the Emperor of *China,*
goes through the Ceremony of making the
Venetian and *Pierot,* Gormogons; which
ended, the *Venetian* gives *Colombine* to
Harlequin, and they are carry'd off in
Triumph.[29]

---

29 *Cephalus and Procris. A Dramatic Masque. With a Pantomime Interlude, call'd Harlequin
Grand Volgi* (London: J. Watts, 1733), 12–13.

After the three performances with *The Alchemist* in September 1735, two "by command," it was announced, "For the Entertainment of his Highness the Prince of Modena. To-morrow will be presented the Miser. With a Grotesque Pantomime, call'd Harlequin Grand-Volgi."[30] While not performed as often, *Harlequin Grand-Volgi* still seemed to be a popular entertainment with staying power that could be trotted out for VIP audiences. Another meeting of the Gormogons was announced at Castle Tavern for December 10, 1735, well after the more traditional fall meeting at the end of October.[31] We still must wonder if this is truly the meeting of an organization, or subtle publicity by the Theatre Royal, or perhaps it had become a gathering of actors appearing in Harlequin Grand-Volgi. The last Gormogon meeting announcement that I have found is for July 2, 1736, again at the Castle Tavern in Fleet Street, and this time signed "J. B. T."

I have found no advertising for *Harlequin-Grand-Volgi* in 1736 or 1737, but in 1738, the Theatre Royal in Drury Lane again advertises *Harlequin Grand-Volgi* as accompanying the main production, but there is now no mention of *Cephalus and Procris*. At least eight performances of *Harlequin Grand-Volgi* were advertised in 1738. The performances of May 24 and October 3 were "by Command of their Royal Highnesses the Prince and Princess of Wales" with January 24 "at the desire of several persons of quality" and January 25 "by command".

The story of Mandarin Gormogons was being kept in front of audiences of the highest social standing, and so one would not be surprised that the terminology was being integrated into the language. Indeed, sometime in 1738, a poem, "An Ode for the Grand Khaibar" was published which praised the brotherhood of Grand Khaibars and included this line, "So antient our order, no Gormogon can contend with us."[32] So we see the Gormogons continuing to be used as an example of a group that claims greater antiquity than another, and this without reference to meetings at the Castle Tavern or the grotesque pantomime.

There were at least five advertised performances of *Harlequin Grand Volgi* at Theatre Royal in Drury Lane in 1739 including command performances by

---

30 *The London Daily Post, and General Advertiser*, No. 321, November 12, 1735.

31 *The London Daily Post, and General Advertiser*, No. 344, December 9, 1735.

32 Charles Marsh, "An Ode for the Grand Khaibar," in *Amasis King of Egypt* (London: Charles Marsh, 1738), 99–100.

the Prince and Princess of Wales on November 22 and 26, 1739. In 1740, at least two performances were advertised at Drury Lane, one by command of the Prince and Princess of Wales, and then there is a notice that performances would be given at Yeate's Great Theatrical Booth at Tottenham Court Fair.[33]

Harlequin Grand Volgi was not performed in 1742, but Alexander Pope includes a mention of the society in *The Dunciad: Book the Fourth.*

> Next bidding all draw near on bended knees,
> The Queen confers her *Titles* and *Degrees.*
> Her children firſt of more diſtinguiſh'd ſort,
> 560 Who ſtudy Shakeſpeare at the Inns of Court
> impale a Glow-worm, or Vertù profeſs,
> Shine in the dignity of F. R. S.
> Some, deep Free-Maſons, join the ſilent race
> Worthy to fill Pythagoras's place:
> 565 Some Botaniſts, or Floriſts at the least,
> Or iſſue Members of an Annual feaſt.
> Nor paſt the meaneſt unregarded, one
> Roſe a Gregorian, one a Gormogon.
> The laſt, not leaſt of honor or applauſe,
> 570 Iſis and Cam made Doctors of her Laws.

> VERSE 563. *Some, deep Free-Maſons, join the ſilent race.*] The Poet all along expreſſes a very particular concern for this ſilent Race: He has here provided, that in caſe they will not waken or open (as was before propoſed) to a *Humming Bird* or *Cockle,* yet at worſt they may be made Free-Maſons; where *Taciturnity* is the only eſſential

---

33 *The London Daily Post, and General Advertiser,* No. 1620, January 4, 1739–40, No. 1626, January 12, 1739–40; *The London Daily Post, and General Advertiser,* No. 1602, August 2, 1740.

Qualification, as it was one of the chief of the diſciples of Pythagoras.

VERSE 568.— *a Gregorian, or a Gor-mogon.*] A ſort of Lay-brothers, *Slips* from the root of the Free Maſons. [34]

There were no performances in 1743, but *Ebrietatis Encomium: or the Praise of Drunkenness* was published. Its title page lists the types of people who get drunk, including "Freemasons, Gormogons, and other Tope-ing Societies." We see again the use of the society as either a companion group to Freemasons, in this case, or a group claiming great antiquity. The seeds sown by the original jokers continue to bear fruit.

The Theatre Royal at Drury Lane advertised *Harlequin Grand Volgi* in January 1744 as "not acted these four years." This sounds like a revival of an audience favorite. There are least five performances in January 1744, but momentum at the Theatre Royal seems to be diminishing. The next year sees no more performances, but rather another use of Gormogons as a companion society to the Freemasons. In *Rantum-Scantum; or, Town-Topics*, there is a comparison of Masons, Scald Miserables, Gormogons, and other societies, continuing the acceptance of *Gormogon* into the language.

And now I am in the Humour to aſk Queſtions, Where is the Loyalty of your Free-Maſons, and your Scald-Miſerables? What, no Aſſociation entered into by thoſe two formidable Bodies! Shall they be reproached with Diſaffection by the *Clerks* and *Book-keepers*, by the *Ubiquarians*, the *Gormogons*, the *Gregorians*, and even by the Players, whoſe Regimentals are now actually beſpoke. The Poets are not to be rank'd with theſe, for they have moſt loyally drawn up an Aſſo-ciation, which I have, by the Help of my

---

34 Alexander Pope, *The Dunciad: Book the Fourth*, 2nd ed. (London: T. Cooper, 1742), 40.

friend *Crambo,* obtained a Copy of, for the
Perufal of the gentle Reader, and is as follows.[35]

Twilight of the Gormogons

T homas Gray wrote to his friend Horace Walpole on March 1, 1747,
to congratulate him on being elected a Fellow of the Royal Society.
He said, "I reckon next week we shall hear you are a Freemason, or a Gormogon at least!"[36] By 1747, the Gormogons had been wildly successful as
a practical joke, lasting well beyond the death of Wharton in 1731. They
went from tweaking the pretensions of antiquity and prestige of the Freemasons to entering the language as a term for someone claiming greater
precedence, and along the way they became associated with slapstick antics
that amused all from the king on down.

If this were the end of the story, then the originators could take pride in a
job well done. However, there is more. In May 1749, *Harlequin Grand Volgi*
reappears on the program at Sadler's Wells, the site for summer theatre in
London.

At SADLER's WELLS, Iflington, This Evening Mr.
Dominique, Mr. Williams and Mr. Pedro will perform
feveral new Tricks in Tumbling; Variety of Dancing by
Mr. Harvey, Mr. Vanderfluys, Mrs. Hough, and others;
The whole to conclude with an Entertainment of Muſick,
call'd *Scipio Africanus*; interfpers'd with a Piece in Gro-
teſque Characters, call'd *Harlequin Grand Volgi.*—Each
Perſon to be admitted for a Pint of Wine or Punch.—
To begin at 5 o'Clock.[37]

At least fifteen performances of *Harlequin Grand Volgi* are advertised from
May to July 1749, and *Scipio Africanus* has now become the companion

---

35 *Rantum-Scantum; or, Town-Topics* (London: J. Oldcastle, 1745), 8–9.

36 W. S. Lewis, ed., *The Yale Edition of Horace Walpole's Correspondence,* 48 vols. (New Haven, CT: Yale University Press, 1948), 14:22.

37 *The General Advertiser,* No. 4541, May 12, 1749.

piece rather than *Cephalus and Procris. Scipio Africanus* is a tragedy by Charles Beckingham published in 1718 and, to modern tastes, seems an odd pairing with the slapstick ribaldry of *Harlequin Grand Volgi,* but no odder than the original pairing with the tragedy of *Cephalus and Procris.* The year 1750 seems to have seen the end to advertisements of *Harlequin Grand Volgi* with an ad in *The General Advertiser,* No. 4847, May 4, 1750, for a performance at Sadler's Wells. The final sentence of the ad hints at the fate of our venerable amusement, "As the Proprietors are determined to make their Entertainments as full of Variety and agreeable as in their Power, they propose every Monday during the Season to perform a different Entertainment." After some twenty years on the stage, the humor of *Harlequin Grand Volgi* must have been getting long in the tooth and no longer "full of variety and agreeable." There may have been other performances, but no advertisements can be found. Thus faded the grand jest, and the Gormogons were no more on stage before the public. They were relegated to occasional minor roles as an allusion to society of great antiquity.

In 1757, "The Goose" is published in *Tim Bobbin's Collected Poems,* with this in the introduction, "As I have the honor to be a member of the ancient and venerable order of the Gormogons, I am obliged by the laws of the great Chin-Quaiw-Ki-Po, emperor of China, to read, yearly, some part of the ancient records of that country." Most likely, the author had come across the "emperor's" name while perusing Hogarth's print. The poem itself has a brief allusion to the emperor.

No fooner faid, than done—both Parties willing,

The Juftice twirls aloft a fplendid Shilling;

While fhe (ah! Nature, Nature!) calls for Tail,

and pity 'tis, the poor Soul, that fhe fhou'd fail!

But Chance decrees—up turns great *Chin-Quaw-Ki Po,*

Whofe very Name my Belly fore doth gripe—oh.[38]

A very odd reference to the society is in *The Prophetic Numbers of Daniel and John Calculated* (Boston: Thomas and John Fleet, 1759), which says it

---

38 "The Goose," *Tim Bobbin's Toy-Shop open'd; or, Whimsical Amusements* (Manchester: Joseph Harrop, 1763), 106–9.

comes "from a folio manuscript in the archive of a certain aged Gormogon." Much like Tim Bobbins, this allusion is used to give a patina of prestige and antiquity to the author and probably comes from Hogarth's print or perhaps a general use in the language to indicate the same.

Samuel Prichard's *Tubal-Kain* of 1760 is another exposé with this brief mention of the society: "From the Accepted Masons sprang the Real Masons, from both sprang the *Gormogons*, whose Grand-Master the *Volgi* deduce his Original from the *Chinese*, whose Writings, if to be credited, maintained the *Hypothesis* of the *Pre-Adamites*, and consequently must be more antique than Masonry."[39] This continues the steady reminders that the Freemasons have a competitor for precedence and reputation.

Sixty-one years after their creation, the Gormogons were fading from public view. They couldn't claim a peer as their leader. They never held public meetings or processions. They hadn't been advertised on the stage for thirty-five years. And yet, they seem to have integrated into the language, though not in a very sophisticated way. But for a practical joker, any remembrance is a victory. In the 1785 *Classical Dictionary of the Vulgar Tongue*, we find this trace of the pre-Adamite society, a crude but lasting testimony to a grand joke.

> GORMAGON, a Monſter with ſix eyes, three mouths, four
>
> arms, eight legs, five on one ſide and three on the other,
>
> three arſes, two tarſes and a **** upon its back; a man
>
> on horſeback with a woman behind him.[40]

And lest anyone think this obscure definition marked the end of the "truly ancient and noble order," in 1792, the satirist Henry W. Bunbury, writing as Geoffrey Gambado in *The Annals of Horsemanship*, speaks of "the theory and practice of the art of riding before a lady on a double horse, vulgarly termed à la *gormagon*."[41] Such a transformation of a crude riddle into a satirical "French" term is only funny if most of the readers or perhaps the

---

39 Samuel Prichard, *Tubal-Kain: Being the Second Part of Solomon in all His Glory* (London: W. Nicoll, 1760), 7.

40 *Classical Dictionary of the Vulgar Tongue* (London: S. Hooper, 1785).

41 Geoffrey Gambado [Henry W. Bunbury], *The Annals of Horsemanship* (Dublin: William Jones, 1792), 25–26.

author and his friends are in on the joke, which is evidence that the Gormogons, or at least their name, persisted in the popular mind till the end of the eighteenth century.

Here's how I interpret the facts. In 1724, someone (most likely Philip, Duke of Wharton) created and promoted the Gormogons to tweak the pretensions of the Freemasons—a grand practical joke. The Gormogons existed originally in the press, with the likelihood that some group later used their name as an excuse to hold semi-annual dinners at the Castle Tavern for twelve years, 1724–1736. It is also possible that Wharton set up an endowment to pay for the dinners for some 50 of his friends. Writers and artists (most notably William Hogarth) quickly latched upon the Gormogons as a foil to the Freemasons and as a group of fabled antiquity and prestige. The success of this publicity campaign, especially the unexpected boost from Hogarth's print, caused the public to believe that *Gormogons* were truly Chinese dignitaries and that *Grand Volgi* was the title for an actual Chinese official. From this grew the very successful pantomime *Harlequin Grand Vol-Gi* and the less successful opera *Emperor of China, Grand-Volgi*. The effect of these performances was to keep Gormogons in the public eye for another twenty years. By now the dining club had stopped dining, the theatrical productions were retired, and the press releases appeared no more. The order received occasional mention as a synonym for antiquity and prestige, and finally, in the linguistic equivalent of an alchemical transmutation, *Gormogon* became the answer to a vulgar riddle. This was either the sad end of a noble order ... or the magnificent triumph of a grand practical joke.

Epilogue. The 2007–2008 season of the successful American TV series *Bones* introduced a cannibalistic serial killer named "Gormogon." This introductory episode is called, "The Widow's Son in the Windshield," and Gormogon is killed in the season finale.

Acknowledgments. Bro. Trevor Stewart provided helpful insights and suggestions, several of which have been incorporated into this version. Bro. John Acaster shared his wonderful paper from the Manchester Lodge of Research and showed that great minds do indeed run in the same channel. Prof. Róbert Péter of the University of Szeged, Hungary, generously shared his Gormogon references that will be included in volume 5 of *British Freemasonry,*

1717–1813 (London: Pickering & Chatto, 2015) which he is editing. Prof. David Brewer, Ohio State University, put me in touch with Ms. Kate Novotny whose paper on eighteenth-century pantomimes helped me understand where the *Harlequin Grand Volgi* fit into the London stage of the 1730s.

APPENDIX 1

24 Known Meetings of the Gormogons

23 meetings were held at the Castle Tavern, in Fleet-Street
1 meeting was held at the Swan Tavern in Cornhill (May 1, 1727)
1 meeting was announced after the fact and is not signed (December 4, 1724)
1 meeting announcement was not signed (November 1, 1725)
20 meeting announcements were signed with three initials, the last being "T."
1 meeting announcement was signed "W. B. G. T." (April 30, 1731)
1 meeting announcement was signed "I. C. K. I. S." (March 4, 1734)
The meeting of October 31, 1730, was advertised in *The Daily Journal* and signed "P. W. T." Gould interpreted the first two initials as standing for "Philip Wharton."[42]

1. December 4, 1724: Castle Tavern, in Fleet-Street
    The Weekly Journal, No. 316, December 5, 1724

2. March 1, 1725: Castle Tavern, in Fleet-Street
    The Daily Post, No. 1692, February 26, 1725   B. G. T.
    The Daily Post, No. 1693, February 27, 1725   B. G. T.

3. November 1, 1725: Castle Tavern, in Fleet-Street
    The Daily Post, No. 1903, October 30, 1725

4. April 30, 1726: Castle Tavern, in Fleet-Street
    The Daily Journal, No. 1648, April 27, 1726   H. B. T.
    The Daily Journal, No. 1650, April 29, 1726   H. B. T.

5. October 31, 1726: Castle Tavern, in Fleet-Street
    The Daily Journal, No. 1801, October 22, 1726   R. M. T.
    The Daily Journal, No. 1807, October 29, 1726   R. M. T.

6. May 1, 1727: Swan Tavern in Cornhill
    The Daily Journal, No. 1963, April 29, 1727   H. M. T.
    The Daily Journal, No. 1964, May 1, 1727   H. M. T.

---

42 Gould, "Duke of Wharton," 135.

7. October 31, 1727: Castle Tavern, in Fleet-Street
    The Daily Journal, No. 2118, October 27, 1727   J. T. T.

8. April 30, 1728: Castle Tavern, in Fleet-Street
    The Daily Journal, No. 2276, April 29, 1728   P. R. T.
    The Daily Journal, No. 2277, April 30, 1728   P. R. T.

9. October 31, 1728: Castle Tavern, in Fleet-Street
    The London Evening-Post, No. 138, October 24–26,   R. J. T.
    The Daily Journal, No. 2436, October 29, 1728   R. J. T.
    The Daily Journal, No. 2437, October 30, 1728   R. J. T.
    The Daily Journal, No. 2438, October 31, 1728   R. J. T.

10. April 30, 1729: Castle Tavern, in Fleet-Street
    The Daily Journal, No. 259, April 26, 1729   P. E. T.
    The London Evening-Post, No. 217, April 16–29, 1729   P. E. T.
    The Daily Journal, No. 2591, April 27, 1729   P. E. T.

11. October 31, 1729: Castle Tavern, in Fleet-Street
    The Country Journal, No. 171, October 11, 1729   B. S. T.
    The Daily Journal, No. 2740, October 18, 1729   B. S. T.
    The Daily Journal, No. 2751, October 31, 1729   B. S. T.
    The Daily Journal, No. 2753, November 3, 1729

12. April 30, 1730: Castle Tavern, in Fleet-Street
    The Country Journal, No. 199, April 25, 1730   J. C. T.
    The Daily Journal, No. 2904, April 28, 1730   J. C. T.
    The Daily Journal, No. 2905, April 29, 1730   J. C. T.

13. October 31, 1730: Castle Tavern, in Fleet-Street
    The Daily Journal, No. 3059, October 26, 1730   P. W. T.

14. 30 April 1731: Castle Tavern, in Fleet-Street
    The Daily Journal, No. 3217, April 28, 1731   W. G. B. T.
    The Daily Journal, No. 3219, April 30, 1731   W. G. B. T.

15. November 1, 1731: Castle Tavern, in Fleet-Street
    The Daily Journal, No. 3374, October 28, 1731   F. N.T.
    The Daily Journal, No. 3376, October 30, 1731   F. N.T.
    The Daily Post, No. 3782, November 1, 1731   F. N.T.

16. May 1, 1732: Castle Tavern, in Fleet-Street
The London Evening-Post, No. 688, April 25–27, 1732   K. A. T.
The Country Journal, No. 304, April 29, 1732   K. A. T.

17. October 31, 1732: Castle Tavern, in Fleet-Street
The Daily Journal, No. 368, October 27, 1732   T. S. T.
The Daily Journal, No. 3688, October 28, 1732   T. S. T.
The Country Journal, No. 330, October 28, 1732   T. S. T.

18. April 30, 1733: Castle Tavern, in Fleet-Street
The Country Journal, No. 356, April 18, 1733   J. S. T.
The London Evening-Post, No. 843, April 24–26, 1733   J. S. T.
The Daily Journal, No. 5849, April 30, 1733   J. S. T.

19. October 31, 1733: Castle Tavern, in Fleet-Street
The London Evening-Post, No. 925, October 23–25, 1733 J. P. T.
The Country Journal, No. 382, October 27, 1733   J. P. T.

20. March 4, 1734: Castle Tavern, in Fleet-Street
The Daily Journal, No. 4408, March 4, 1735   I. C. K. I. S.
The London Daily Post, No. 104, March 4, 1734   I. C. K. I. S.

21 May 31, 1734: Castle Tavern in Fleet Street
The Daily Journal, No. 4170, May 30, 1734   J. C. T.

22. December 10, 1735: Castle Tavern, in Fleet-Street
The London Daily Post, No. 345, December 4, 1735   P. B. T.
The Daily Journal, No. 5547, December 5, 1735   P. B. T.
The Daily Journal, No. 5549, December 8, 1735   P. B. T.
The London Daily Post, No. 344, December 9, 1735   P. B. T.
The Daily Journal, No. 5531, December 10, 1735   P. B. T.

23. July 2, 1736: Castle Tavern, in Fleet-Street
The London Daily Post, No. 520, July 1, 1736   J. B. T.

APPENDIX 2

99 Known Performances of *Harlequin Grand Vol-Gi*

Starting December 4, 1730, His Majesty's Company of Comedians presented *Harlequin Grand-Volgi* at the Theatre Royal in Drury-Lane with *Cephalus and Procris*. The plays were a supplement to the main performance of the evening and ran together for at least sixty performances through 1734. The December 2 advertisement in the Daily Post is typical of how the two plays were advertised.

To which will be added, a Dramatic Maſque, call'd

CEPHALUS and PROCRIS:

With a new Pantomime Interlude, call'd

HARLEQUIN GRAND-VOLGI.

By His Majesty's Company of Comedians at the Theatre Royal in Drury Lane

1. December 4, 1730, with *King Henry IV*
    The Daily Post, December 2, 1730
    The Daily Post, December 3, 1730

2. December 7, 1730, with *Amphitryon*
    The Daily Post, December 7, 1730

3. December 9, 1730, with *Oroonoko*
    The Daily Post, December 9, 1730

4. December 10, 1730, with *The Fatal Marriage*
    The Daily Post, December 10, 1730

5. December 18, 1730, with *Timon of Athens*
    The Daily Post, December 18, 1730

6. December 25, 1730, with *Love's Last Shift*
    The Daily Post, December 15, 1730

7. **December 28, 1730, with *Greenwich Park***
    The Daily Post, December 28, 1730

8. **December 29, 1730, with *Cato***
    The Daily Post, December 29 1730

9. **December 30, 1730, with *The Generous Free-Mason***
    The Daily Post, December 30, 1730

10. **December 31, 1730, with *King Henry IV***
    The Daily Post, December 31, 1730

11. **January 2, 1731, with *The Orphan***
    The Daily Post, January 2, 1731

12. **January 4, 1731, with *Rule a Wife, and Have a Wife***
    The Daily Post, January 4, 1731

13. **January 5, 1731, with *Theodosius***
    The Daily Post, January 4, 1731

14. **January 11, 1731, with *The Provok'd Wife***
    The Daily Post, January 11, 1731

15. **January 14, 1731, with *The Way of the World***
    The Daily Post, January 14, 1731

16. **January 16, 1731, with *Hamlet***
    The Daily Post, January 16, 1731

17. **January 29, 1731, with *The Lover***
    The Daily Post, January 29, 1731

18. **February 4, 1731, with *The Funeral***
    The Daily Post, February 4, 1731

19. **February 15, 1731, with *The Jovial Crew***
    The Daily Post, February 15, 1731

20. **February 19, 1731, with *The Double Gallant***
    The Daily Post, February 19, 1731

21. **March 6, 1731, with *Eurydice***
    The Daily Post, March 5, 1731
    The Daily Post, March 6, 1731

22. **March 9, 1731, with *Eurydice***
    The Daily Post, March 9, 1731

23. **March 1731 11 with *Eurydice***
    The Daily Post, March 10, 1731
    The Daily Post, March 11, 1731

24. **March 1731 30 with *The Relapse***
    The Daily Post, March 20, 1731
    The Daily Post, March 24, 1731
    The Country Journal, March 27, 1730–31
    The Daily Post, March 30, 1731, ("with *The Orphan*" [sic])

25. **April 3, 1731, with *All for Love***
    The Daily Post, April 2, 1731
    The Daily Post, April 3, 1731

26. **April 6, 1731, with *Macbeth***
    The Country Journal, April 3, 1731
    The Daily Post, April 3, 1731
    The Daily Post, April 5, 1731
    The Daily Post, April 6, 1731

27. **April 10, 1731, with *The Mourning Bride***
    The Daily Journal, April 7, 1731
    The Daily Post, April 8, 1731
    The Daily Post, April 9, 1731
    The Daily Post, April 10, 1731

28. **April 24, 1731, with *Rule a Wife and Have a Wife***
    The Daily Post, April 21, 1731
    The Daily Post, April 24, 1731

29. **May 4, 1731, with *King Henry VIII***
    The Daily Post, April 17, 1731
    The London Evening Post, April 27–29, 1731
    The Daily Post, April 29, 1731

The Daily Post, May 1, 1731
The Daily Post, May 4, 1731

30. October 23, 1731, with *The London Merchant*
    The Daily Post, October 22, 1731

31. November 17, 1731, with *The Relapse*
    The Daily Post, November 17, 1731

32. November 29, 1731, with *King Henry VIII*
    The Daily Post, November 29, 1731

33. December 27, 1731, with *The London Merchant*
    The Daily Post, December 24, 1731

34. May 12, 1732, with *The Tragedy of Tragedies*
    The Daily Post, May 12, 1732

35. December 22, 1732, with *The Busy Body*
    The Daily Post, December 22, 1732

36. December 26, 1732, with *The Tempest*
    The Daily Post, December 23, 1732

37. January 2, 1733, with *Rule a Wife and Have a Wife*
    The Daily Post, January 2, 1733

38. January 3, 1733, with *The Provok'd Wife*
    The Daily Post, January 3, 1733

39. January 4, 1733, with *The Way of the World*
    The Daily Post, January 4, 1733

40. January 9, 1733, with *The Double Gallant*
    The Daily Post, January 9, 1733

41. January 10, 1733, with *The Distrest Mother*
    The Daily Post, January 10, 1733

42. November 13, 1733, with *The Unhappy Favourite*
    The Daily Post, January 12, 1733

43. **November 14, 1733, with *King Henry VIII***
    The Daily Post, November 14, 1733

44. **November 15, 1733, with *King Henry VIII***
    The Daily Post, November 15, 1733

45. **November 19, 1733, with *The Distress'd Mother***
    The Daily Post, November 17, 1733
    The Daily Post, November 19, 1733

46. **November 21, 1733, with *The Busybody***
    The Daily Post, November 20, 1733
    The Daily Post, November 21, 1733

47. **November 23, 1733, with *Timon of Athens***
    The Daily Post, November 22, 1733

48. **November 24, 1733, with *King Henry VIII***
    The Daily Post, November 24, 1733

49. **December 11, 1733, with *Love Makes a Man***
    The Daily Post, December 10, 1733
    The Daily Post, December 11, 1733

50. **December 17, 1733, with *Theodosius***
    The Daily Post, December 15, 1733

51. **December 26, 1733, with *The Beggar's Opera***
    The Daily Post, December 24, 1733

52. **December 27, 1733, with *King Henry VIII***
    The Daily Post, December 27, 1733

53. **December 31, 1733, with *Love Makes a Man***
    The Daily Post, December 31, 1733

54. **January 8, 1734, with *The Cornish Squire***
    The Daily Post, January 5, 1734
    The Daily Post, January 8, 1734

55. January 25, 1734, with *The Committee*
The Daily Post, January 25, 1734

56. 26. January 1734 with *Theodosius*
The Daily Post, January 26, 1734

57. May 15, 1734, with *The Tempest*
The Daily Post, May 14, 1734

58. November 4, 1734, with *Tamerlane*
The London Daily Post and General Advertiser, November 4, 1734

59. November 12, 1734, with *Julius Caesar*
The London Daily Post and General Advertiser, November 12, 1734

60. November 20, 1734, with *Love Makes a Man*
The London Daily Post and General Advertiser, November 20, 1734

Starting with September 15, 1735, *Harlequin Grand-Volgi* was performed at the Theatre Royal in Drury Lane without *Cephalus and Procris*, though the latter was sometimes invoked in advertising. The advertisement below from the *London Daily Post and General Advertiser* of September 15, 1735, was typical.

To which (by Command,) will be added, a Grotefque Pantomime, call'd

HARLEQUIN GRAND-VOLGI:
Being The Comic Interlude of the Mafque of
CEPHALUS and PROCRIS.

61. September 15, 1735, with *The Alchymist* and with *Le Chasseur Royal*
The London Daily Post and General Advertiser, September 12, 1735
The London Daily Post and General Advertiser, September 13, 1735
The London Daily Post and General Advertiser, September 15, 1735

62. November 13, 1735, with *The Miser*
The London Daily Post and General Advertiser, November 12, 1735

63. **January 24, 1738, with *The Plain Dealer***
The London Daily Post and General Advertiser, January 24, 1737–1738

64. **January 25, 1738, with *The Beggar's Opera***
The London Daily Post and General Advertiser, January 25, 1737–1738

65. **January 28, 1738, with *The Siege of Damascus***
The London Daily Post and General Advertiser, January 28, 1737–1738
The Daily Post, January 28, 1738

66. **January 31, 1738, with *Macbeth***
The London Daily Post and General Advertiser, January 31, 1737–1738

67. **February 1, 1738, with *The Confederacy***
The Daily Post, February 1, 1738

68. **February 11, 1738, with *The Miser***
The London Daily Post and General Advertiser, February 11, 1737–1738

69. **February 13, 1738, with *King Richard III***
The London Daily Post and General Advertiser, February 13, 1737–1738
The Daily Post, February 13, 1738

70. **May 24, 1738, with *Volpone***
The London Daily Post and General Advertiser, May 23, 1738
The London Daily Post and General Advertiser, May 24, 1738

71. **October 3, 1738, with *The Drummer***
The London Daily Post and General Advertiser, October 2, 1738
The Daily Post, October 3, 1738
The London Daily Post and General Advertiser, October 3, 1738

72. **October 5, 1738, with *The Drummer***
The London Daily Post and General Advertiser, October 4, 1738
The Daily Post, October 5, 1738
The London Daily Post and General Advertiser, October 5, 1738

73. **October 7, 1738, with *The Drummer***
The London Daily Post and General Advertiser, October 6, 1738
The London Daily Post and General Advertiser, October 7, 1738

74. **April 28, 1739, with *The Mother-In-Law***
    The London Daily Post and General Advertiser, April 24, 1739
    The London Daily Post and General Advertiser, April 25, 1739
    The London Daily Post and General Advertiser, April 26, 1739

75. **November 22, 1739, with *Love for Love***
    The London Daily Post and General Advertiser, November 22, 1739

76. **November 23, 1739, with *The Chances***
    The Daily Post, November 23, 1739

77. **November 26, 1739, with *Hamlet***
    The London Daily Post and General Advertiser, November 26, 1739

78. **November 27, 1739, with *Sir Walter Raleigh***
    The London Daily Post and General Advertiser, November 27, 1739

79. **December 5, 1739, with *Comus***
    The London Daily Post and General Advertiser, December 5, 1739

80. **December 13, 1739, with *Othello***
    The London Daily Post and General Advertiser, December 13, 1739

81. **January 2, 1740, with *King Henry VIII***
    The Daily Post, January 2, 1740

82. **January 4, 1740, with *The Tempest***
    The London Daily Post and General Advertiser, January 4, 1739,–40

83. **January 12, 1740, with *Aesop***
    The London Daily Post and General Advertiser, January 12, 1739,–40

Tottenham Court Fair, Yeates's Great Theatrical Booth

84. **August 4, 1740,— with *All Alive and Merry***
    The Daily Post, August 2, 1740
    Theatre Royal in Drury-Lane

85. **January 17, 1744, (not acted these Four Years) with *The Recruiting Officer***

The London Daily Post and General Advertiser, January 17, 1743–1744
The Daily Advertiser, January 17, 1744

86. **January 18, 1744, (acted but once these Four Years) with** *Macbeth*
The London Daily Post and General Advertiser, January 18, 1743–1744

87. **January 21, 1744, with** *Macbeth*
The London Daily Post and General Advertiser, January 21, 1743–1744
The Daily Advertiser, January 21, 1744

88. **January 23, 1744, with** *The Provok'd Wife*
The London Daily Post and General Advertiser, January 23, 1743–1744

89. **January 25, 1744, with** *The Miser*
The London Daily Post and General Advertiser, January 25, 1743–1744

At Sadler's Wells, Islington

90. **May 12, 1749, with** *Scipio Africanus*
The General Advertiser, May 12, 1749

91. **May 13, 1749, with** *Scipio Africanus*
The General Advertiser, May 13, 1749

92. **May 15, 1749, with** *Scipio Africanus*
The General Advertiser, May 15, 1749

93. **May 17, 1749, with** *Scipio Africanus*
The Daily Advertiser, May 17, 1749

94. **May 18, 1749, with** *Scipio Africanus*
The General Advertiser, May 18, 1749

95. **May 20, 1749, with** *Scipio Africanus*
The General Advertiser, May 20, 1749

96. **May 25, 1749, with** *Scipio Africanus*
The General Advertiser, May 25, 1749

97. **June 3, 1749, with** *Scipio Africanus*
The General Advertiser, June 3, 1749

98. June 15, 1749, with *Scipio Africanus*
The General Advertiser, June 15, 1749

99. June 21, 1749, with *Scipio Africanus*
The General Advertiser, June 21, 1749

APPENDIX 3

Performances of *The Emperor of China, Grand Vol-gi: or,*
The Constant Couple and Virtue Rewarded
by William Chetwood

1. **Bartholomew Fair at Fielding's, Hippisley's and Hall's Great Theatrical Booth**
   The Daily Post, August16, 18, 19, 20, 21, 24, 25, 27, 28, 30, & 31, September 1, 2, 3, 4, 6, & 10, 1731
   The Grub-street Journal, August 26, 1731,, September 2, 1731
   The Daily Advertiser, August 27 & 31, 1731
   The London Evening Post, September 2–4, 1731

2. **Southwark Fair at Fielding's, Hippisley's and Hall's Great Theatrical Booth**
   The London Evening Post, September 2–4, 1731
   The Daily Post, September 9, 10, 11, 13, 14, 15, 16, 17, 18, 20, 21, 22, 23, & 27, 1731
   The Country Journal, September 11, 1731
   The Daily Advertiser, September ,13, 1731

First Published: *Ars Quatuor Coronatorum,* Vol. 126(2013)

Lodged in the Canon

The adventures of Mr. Sherlock Holmes as related by Dr. John H. Watson provide the reader not only with exciting tales of mystery and detection but also with a delightful glimpse into late-Victorian and early-Edwardian life in England. An important aspect of middle and upper-middle class male sociability of that era was the fraternity of Ancient Free and Accepted Masons. The Freemasons are mentioned briefly in four of the adventures, and their mention gives us some insight to the character of Holmes and Watson (and peripherally into the character of Dr. Watson's literary agent, Sir Arthur Conan Doyle).

The Masonic Fraternity

No one is quite sure of where or even when the Freemasons originated. Some have speculated they descended from the mystery religions of the Mediterranean or perhaps from the Roman College of Artificers or perhaps from the crusading Knights Templar. Most historians, however, agree that the modern social fraternity evolved during the seventeenth century from a trade organization of freemasons who met in local organizations called "lodges." The oldest Masonic document is the *Regius Poem* or *Halliwell Manuscript* of ca. 1399 in the British Museum. It is the operating rules for a trade union, with regulations for apprentices and masters, guidance for behavior, and exhortations to the members for charity and mutual support.

The oldest extant minutes of a Masonic lodge are from 1599 and belong to the Lodge of St. Mary's Chapel in Edinburgh. In those minutes, a member of the lodge is reprimanded for hiring a non-Mason, that is, someone who had not gone through an apprenticeship and had been elected a member. This is exactly the behavior you would expect from a trade union. A century later in London, the Freemasons are now a social fraternity, composed almost entirely of "speculative" or gentlemen Masons. In that year, four of the old lodges came together to form a central authority, a "Grand Lodge," to govern the fraternity and particularly to restore the custom of the annual "Assembly and Feast."

In 1717 and before, the Masons had two levels or degrees of membership: Apprentice and Fellow-Master. Apprentices were boys or young men who served a time (usually seven years) with a Master in return for learning the trade. Upon completing an apprenticeship and satisfying a lodge of his skill, a man could be elected as a Fellow-Master in the Freemasons. Within a lodge, all Fellows were equal. A "Master" was a Fellow who was in charge of a job, supervised the work, and hired Fellows and Apprentices. About 1725, the fraternity in London introduced three levels of membership: Apprentice, Fellowcraft, and Master. This system was eventually adopted by all lodges and is still in effect around the world today.

The Masons are famous (or possibly notorious) for their "secrets." There were, of course, the trade secrets learned by apprentices. For example, a union carpenter drives a nail with a grace and fluidity that I cannot approach, and there must have been similar trade secrets with the stonemasons. There is reason to think that some of the inner secrets of the operative masons were the geometric "secrets" of making a right angle. There were also "modes of recognition"—passwords and handshakes (called "grips") by which they can identify each other. The premier Grand Lodge was formed in 1717, and these secrets were first published in 1723 and have been in continuous print since then. They are secret only from those who do not know how to do a Google search!

These modes of recognition are thought to have originated at a time when working freemasons needed a means to identify themselves as a lodge member when they traveled from one job site to another. Unlike members of other trades—bakers, carpenters, or tailors, for example—freemasons might not always have work in one location. When a town's bridge or church was completed, there might not be more work for decades within that community. Thus, the necessity for masons to travel arose, and soon thereafter came the requirement of some way for a traveling mason to identify himself at a new job site, if the integrity of the trade organization and its training were to be maintained.

This system of symbolic "secret knowledge" has been maintained for centuries, and even today a visiting Mason before gaining admission to a lodge must prove himself knowledgeable in the "secrets of Masonry." Since the Masons' secrets have been long published, one may well ask the question, "What's the point?" Today the secrets are purely symbolic, a token of a Mason's integrity and his fidelity to his trust.

After Freemasonry emerged in early eighteenth-century Britain, it migrated around the globe and found fertile soil in most European countries and their colonies. Other countries grafted additional levels of membership or degrees onto the original and universal three from England. A Masonic degree is a brief morality play or ceremony that teaches a lesson such as fidelity, truth, benevolence, and so on. The Scottish Rite, which originated in France, has thirty-three degrees; the York Rite, which originated in America, has twelve degrees; the Rite of Memphis, which originated in Italy, has over ninety degrees; and the Swedish Rite, which originated in Sweden, has eleven degrees.

Freemasonry in Victorian England

When Queen Victoria ascended to the throne in 1837, Freemasonry had become part of the accepted social activities for a gentleman. A place to gather with friends where rank and station meant much less than on the outside. The Duke of Sussex was Grand Master of England in 1837, and his participation represented the general approbation, given the fraternity. Victoria's son, Albert Edward, later served as Grand Master when he was Prince of Wales, and when he ascended the throne as Edward VII, he was succeeded as Grand Master by his brother, the Duke of Connaught. As an indication of the widespread nature of English Freemasonry, the 2,076[th] English lodge, Quatuor Coronati, was chartered in 1884.

Sir Charles Warren, an explorer and archeologist, was the first Master of Quatuor Coronati, a lodge devoted to the history of Freemasonry and limited to no more than forty members at any time. Their annual transactions, *Ars Quatuor Coronatorum*, have been published since 1885 and could be called the *Baker Street Journal* of Freemasonry. Sir Charles served as Metropolitan Police Commissioner from March 1886 to November 1887 during the Jack the Ripper murders. Stephen Knight latched upon the Masonic membership of Warren and built it into a complex Masonic conspiracy to explain the Ripper murders that were published in *Jack the Ripper: The Final Solution*. Knight's fantasy in turn served as the basis of the 1980 pastiche movie, *Murder by Decree*, in which Sir Charles Warren "is confronted by Sherlock Holmes who claims special knowledge of The Royal Order of Freemasons giving him some strange and curious signs and identifying Sir Charles as a 33rd Degree Mason by the insignia on his ring (Sir Charles, in fact, only reached the 30th Degree....)."[1]

---

1 Yasha Beresiner, "Arthur Conan Doyle: Spiritualist and Freemason," *Pietre-Stones*

Other prominent Victorian-era Masons include Sir Arthur S. Sullivan, the composer, Sir William S. Gilbert, the librettist, Anthony Trollope, the author, Rudyard Kipling, the author, Frédéric August Bartholdi, the designer of the Statue of Liberty, Sir Richard Francis Burton, the explorer and translator of *The Arabian Nights*, Mark Twain, the author, Alphonse Mucha, the Czech artist, Harry Houdini, the magician and anti-spiritualist crusader, and Sir Arthur Conan Doyle, the author and spiritualist.

Freemasonry in the Canon

Freemasonry is mentioned briefly in only four adventures, but it is possible to make a few tentative deductions from them. Let us consider each in turn.

A Study in Scarlet. As Sherlock Holmes investigates the murder of Enoch Drebber, he asks Inspector Tobias Gregson, "What did you find in the pockets?" Among the items Gregson listed from Drebber was a "gold ring, with Masonic device." The device was probably the well-known square and compasses, and as Drebber was American, there was most likely a letter "G" in the center of the tools, standing for both *geometry* and *God*. British and European Masons usually don't use the "G."

Drebber was a member of the Church of Jesus Christ of Latter Day Saints, a Mormon. The Prophet Joseph Smith was a Mason and helped initiate over 1,000 Mormons in Nauvoo, Illinois, where he was eventually murdered while being held in the Nauvoo jail. His brother Hyrum and Brigham Young were also Masons, so it would not be surprising to find an early Mormon who was a Mason, even though later events soured relations between the LDS Church and Freemasonry for decades.

A Scandal in Bohemia. Sherlock Holmes watched the habits and the house of Miss Irene Adler while disguised as a horse groom. He says to Watson, "There is a wonderful sympathy and freemasonry among horsy men. Be one of them, and you will know all there is to know." We can deduce little special about Holmes use of the term, which emphasizes the well-known closeness and friendliness of the fraternity.

The Adventure of the Retired Colourman. Holmes sends Watson to gather information on Josiah Amberly, a retired manufacturer of artists' supplies. When Watson reports back, he says that he thinks he was followed by a

Review of Freemasonry, accessed March 8, 2006, http://www.freemasons-freemasonry.com/beresiner10.html

"tall, dark" man. Holmes adds, before Watson can say so, that the man was mustached, wore dark glasses, and a Masonic tie-pin. This turns out to be Mr. Barker, and nothing else is said about his Masonic jewelry.

The Red-Headed League. When Sherlock Holmes first meets Jabez Wilson, he says, "Beyond the obvious facts that he has at some time done manual labour, that he takes snuff, that he is a Freemason, that he has been in China, and that he has done a considerable amount of writing lately, I can deduce nothing more." When Wilson presses him on how he knew, he was a Freemason, Holmes says, "I won't insult your intelligence by telling you how I read that, especially as, rather against the strict rules of your order, you use an arc and compass breast pin." Because Jabez Wilson was a client and needed a demonstration of Holmes' techniques, he was identified as a Mason and then politely reprimanded. Mr. Barker, Holmes' "hated rival upon the Surrey shore," on the other hand, needed no such demonstration and did not receive a reprimand. In fact, it was Watson who observed the Masonic pin, and Holmes deduced its presence from previous experience with Barker.

Holmes' statement indicates remarkable knowledge about the customs of the fraternity. Since the late 1700s, British and American applicants for Masonic membership must declare in writing that "Unbiased by friends and uninfluenced by mercenary motives, I freely and voluntarily offer myself a candidate for the mysteries of masonry."[2] There is no formal rule against English Masons wearing Masonic jewelry, but it has been discouraged within their lodges since the late 1800s. "English Masons are exhorted not to misuse their membership [for personal gain] and the wearing of such jewelry may be misconstrued as a discreet advertisement thereof for improper purposes."[3] This is not secret or even private information, but it is certainly something that wouldn't be known from a casual study of the fraternity.

Wilson wore an "arc and compass breast pin," not the much more common square and compass. Since 1814 in England, the arc or protractor and compass has been the emblem of a Past Grand Master. The pin is rarely seen since English Grand Masters usually serve for 20–30 years, and they have been selected from the nobility for nearly 300 years. However, in the Unit-

---

2   William Preston, *Illustrations of Free-Masonry* (London: The Author, 1772), 210–11.
3   Robert T. Runciman, "Sir Arthur Conan Doyle, Sherlock Holmes, and Freemasonry," *Ars Quatuor Coronatorum* 104 (1991): 178–87.

ed States, the arc and compass pin is the most common emblem of a Past Master of a lodge. With thousands of lodges generating a new Past Master each year, such a pin is not uncommon.

The mystery then is not how Sherlock Holmes identified the pin, for surely a man who studied cigar ashes would be familiar with the identifying jewelry of all sorts of organizations. Rather, the mystery is how Jabez Wilson came to have such a pin. A quick check of a list of English Past Grand Masters reveals that Jabez Wilson's name is conspicuous for its absence. Perhaps in his travels, he resided long enough in America to affiliate with a lodge and become its Past Master. It is more likely that he came across the pin in a pawn shop for a good price. If Wilson were a casual Mason, one who joined to rub shoulders with those he considered to be above his station, then he might not have appreciated the subtle distinction between the arc and square in the pin, and snatched it up for his personal and incorrect use.

The Adventure of the Norwood Builder. The "unhappy John Hector McFarlane" presents himself to Holmes as a client and is told, "Beyond the obvious facts that you are a bachelor, a solicitor, a Freemason, and an asthmatic, I know nothing whatever about you." Watson was able to follow these deductions and in particular observed McFarlane's watch-charm. We are not told which of several Masonic emblems was on the charm, but it gave away his Masonic membership.

Our attention is drawn to the curious incident of the watch-charm on the client. Holmes said nothing to his client about wearing such jewelry as he did to Jabez Wilson. That is the curious incident.

Here, again, we see Holmes remarkable knowledge of the fraternity. McFarlane's name indicates Scots descent. Cecil A. Ryder observed in "A Study in Masonry," that McFarlane "would probably have received his Masonic degrees in Scotland. It is not unusual for Scots Masons, who are not forbidden to do so, to wear the insignia."[4]

The Source of Holmes' Masonic Knowledge

The superficial conclusion is that Sherlock Holmes was a Freemason, given his detailed knowledge of the fraternity. This deduction flies in the face of what we know about Holmes as a social creature. While not lacking in so-

---

4   Cecil A. Ryder, quoted in Runciman, 185.

cial graces, the great detective did not seek out human companionship or maintain close friendships, except perhaps with Dr. Watson. In contrast, a Masonic lodge is a celebration of sociability and friendship, a place where men gather for the purpose of enjoying each other's company. It would be fair to describe a Masonic lodge as an "Anti-Diogenes Club," and this does not seem the sort of organization that would be attractive to Sherlock Holmes. Further, recall that Holmes tells Jabez Wilson, that wearing an arc and compass breast pin is "rather against the strict rules of *your* order." Had Holmes been a Mason, he would have referred to "*our* order."

I believe that the source of Holmes' familiarity with Masonic customs came from his chronicler, John H. Watson, M.D. As a veteran, Watson would have enjoyed the male-bonding experiences of the army. His outgoing and sociable nature would have fit naturally into a Masonic lodge. In his many discussions with Holmes, it would have been natural and not at all improper to explain the subtleties of Masonic jewelry and the different customs between English and Scots and other Masons.

Now, we must ask, was Watson an active Mason. The absence of any other mention of the fraternity in the Canon would indicate that Watson was very discrete about his membership, perhaps not wanting to use it for personal gain by attracting readers who might not have otherwise been interested in his writing. Watson would have preferred his literary efforts to stand or fall on their own merits. Of course, the evidence could also support the contention that Watson was inactive, perhaps because of the pressures of his medical practice or because the fraternity did not meet his needs.

It is illustrative if we compare Watson's career to a contemporary medical and literary colleague, Sir Arthur Conan Doyle. Dr. Doyle joined Phoenix Lodge No. 257 in 1887 and withdrew his membership only two years later in 1889. He remained unaffiliated and inactive until 1901 when the Lodge of St. Mary's Chapel in Edinburgh invited him to a meeting to give a toast to the "Immortal Memory of Queen Victoria," and they afterwards made him an honorary member. Doyle rejoined Phoenix lodge in 1902, but withdrew again in 1911. There is no evidence that he every participated after that.

Some insight to Doyle's disaffection with Freemasonry can be found in one of his Professor Challenger stories, *The Land of Mist*. A character is described as "a pompous ass named Weatherby. He is one of those who wander about on the obscure edges of Masonry, talking with whispers and reverence on mysteries where no mystery is. Spiritualism, with its very real and awful mysteries, is, to him, a vulgar thing because it brought consolation to common folk."[5]

We can understand the Masonic references lodged in the Canon with the simple insight that John H. Watson was a Freemason. Like his fellow author of that period, Arthur Conan Doyle, Watson apparently found that the fraternity did not satisfy his needs as he had hoped, and so he became inactive. But even if he withdrew his membership from his lodge, I am confident that he never forgot the principal teachings of Brotherly Love, Relief, and Truth.

First published: *Hibiscus Masonic Review,* vol. 1 (2007)

---

5   Beresiner, "Arthur Conan Doyle."

Lestrade's Boss:
Sir Charles Warren, KCMG, KCB

Charles Warren was born in Bangor, Wales, and attended the Sandhurst and Woolwich military academies. He was commissioned a Second Lieutenant in 1857 in the Royal Engineers. As an agent of the Palestine Exploration Fund in 1867 (at age twenty-seven!), he surveyed Herod's Temple and conducted excavations in Jerusalem, recording his discoveries in two books: *The Temple or the Tomb* and *Under Jerusalem*. Today, the large tunnel under the Temple Mount is known as Warren's Shaft. It is believed to have been used to bring water within the city. He also discovered the "Moabite Stone" with an inscription of thirty-four lines, the most extensive inscription ever recovered from ancient Israel. It was set up by King Mesha of Moab as a record and memorial of his victories in his revolt against the Kingdom of Israel, which he undertook after the death of his overlord, Ahab.

Inspector G. Lestrade first appears in "A Study in Scarlet," which Les Klinger dates to 1881, and he is mentioned in fourteen of the adventures. Lestrade said to Holmes in "The Adventure of the Six Napoleons," "We're not jealous of you down at Scotland Yard. No, sir, we are damned proud of you." Watson notes in passing that this little comment is one of the few instances where Holmes is visibly moved. Holmes returns the compliment in his laconic style when he commented to Dr. Watson in *The Hound of the Baskervilles* that Lestrade "is the best of the professionals, I think."

The paths of Warren and Lestrade crossed soon after Lestrade first came to Holmes' attention. In 1885, now Major General Charles Warren lost a close election to Parliament. In March, he was appointed Metropolitan Police Commissioner. His tenure was rocky, and he received considerable criticism from the press. He wore an elaborate military uniform and insisted that his constables have fine and well-polished boots. This was dismissed as a military man's affection for fine "kit," but his men walked up to twenty miles a day, and good boots were essential to their well-being. Warren was Lestrade's ultimate boss, and no doubt occasionally heard of Holmes' adventures through Lestrade's reports.

Warren's greatest crisis during his tenure as Police Commissioner came during seventy-one days in 1888 when a series of grisly murders of prostitutes occurred in Whitechapel. Eventually, five of these murders, involving horrible mutilation of the victims, were attributed to a madman who identified himself as "Jack the Ripper."

The generally accepted Ripper victims from among the Whitechapel murders are:

> Mary Ann Nichols, August 31, 1888,
> Annie Chapman, September 8, 1888,
> Elizabeth Stride, September 30, 1888,
> Catherine Eddowes, September 30, 1888,
> Mary Jane Kelly, November 9, 1888.

Warren's most famous action during this crisis was to wash a wall. After the two murders on September 30, the following graffiti was found on a wall on Goulston Street:

> The Jewes are
> The men that
> Will not
> be Blamed
> for nothing

Here is Warren's report to the Home Secretary on November 6, 1888, explaining his actions some six weeks before.

4 Whitehall Place, S.W. 6th November 1888

Confidential
The Under Secretary of State
The Home Office

Sir,

In reply to your letter of the 5th instant, I enclose a report of the circumstances of the Mitre Square Murder so far as they have come under the notice of the Metropolitan Police....

On the 30th September on hearing of the Berner Street murder, after visiting Commercial Street Station I arrived at Leman Street Station shortly before 5 A.M. and ascertained from the Superintendant Arnold all that was known there relative to the two murders.

The most pressing question at that moment was some writing on the wall in Goulston Street evidently written with the intention of inflaming the public mind against the Jews, and which Mr. Arnold with a view to prevent serious disorder proposed to obliterate, and had sent down an Inspector with a sponge for that purpose, telling him to await his arrival.

I considered it desirable that I should decide the matter myself, as it was one involving so great a responsibility whether any action was taken or not.

I accordingly went down to Goulston Street at once before going to the scene of the murder....

There were several Police around the spot when I arrived, both Metropolitan and City.

The writing was on the jamb of the open archway or doorway visible *in the street* and could not be covered up without danger of the covering being torn off at once.

A discussion took place whether the writing could *be left covered up* or otherwise or whether any portion of it could be left for an hour until it could be photographed; but after taking into consideration the excited state of the population in London generally at the time, the strong feeling which had been excited against the Jews, and the fact that in a short time there would be a large concourse of the people in the streets, and having before me the Report that if it was left there the house was likely to be wrecked (in which from my own observation I entirely concurred) I considered it desirable to obliterate the writing at once, having taken a copy of which I enclose a duplicate....

I may mention that so great was the feeling with regard to the Jews that on the 13th ulto. the Acting Chief Rabbi wrote to me on the subject of the spelling of the word "Jewes" on account of a newspaper asserting that this was Jewish spelling in the Yiddish dialect. He added "in the present state of excitement it is dangerous to the safety of the poor Jews in the East [End] to allow such an assertion to remain uncontradicted. My community keenly appreciates your humane and vigilant action during this critical time.".…

I do not hesitate myself to say that if that writing had been left there would have have been an onslaught upon the Jews, property would have been wrecked, and lives would probably have been lost.…

I am, Sir,

Your most obediant Servant, (signed) C. Warren

Source: *Ars Quatuor Coronatorum* 40 (1927): 43–44; Lodge of St. George No. 1152 EC, Singapore, records; Also see London Metropolitan Police.

Warren resigned on November 8, 1888, two days after submitting this report, and one day before the murder of Mary Jane Kelley. He returned to military service and commanded the British defeat at Spion Kop in South Africa during the Boer War.

- English outnumbered the Boers 2-1, 13,200 to 6,000, with more and heavier artillery.

- They thought they had taken the hill of Spion Kop, but when the mist cleared, they realized they were only half way up, and exposed to Boer rifle fire.

- The English had 383 causalities to 58 for the Boers. There is a famous picture of dead British soldiers lying in a trench.

- The Boers were ready to surrender, when they realized they English had retreated first.

- Boer Commander was Louis Botha who went on to establish Apartheid.

- The Lieutenant carrying instructions from the front to Warren was Winston Churchill.

- Mohandas Ghandi was a stretcher bearer and was decorated for his courage, and this influenced his non-violence philosophy.

Warren went on to be promoted to Lieutenant General and became a Knight Commander of Michael and George and a Knight Commander of Bath. In his retirement, he actively supported Lord Baden-Powel in organizing and spreading Boy Scouts.

Warren was elected Founding Master of Quatuor Coronati Lodge No. 2076, in 1884. The lodge warrant was granted on November 28, 1884 but, due to Warren's departure to Buchuana, Africa, the lodge did not meet until after his return at the end of 1885. He was installed at the first regular meeting on January 12, 1886, when the lodge was consecrated.

First Published: *Irene's Cabinet,* vol. 7 (2009)

www.ingramcontent.com/pod-product-compliance
Lightning Source LLC
Chambersburg PA
CBHW031423270326
41930CB00007B/551